HISTORY
OF THE RISE, PROGRESS
AND TERMINATION OF THE
AMERICAN REVOLUTION

MERCY OTIS WARREN

HISTORY
OF THE RISE, PROGRESS
AND TERMINATION OF THE
AMERICAN REVOLUTION

interspersed with Biographical,
Political and Moral
Observations

IN TWO VOLUMES

by Mrs. Mercy Otis Warren

EDITED AND ANNOTATED
BY LESTER H. COHEN

VOLUME I

Liberty*Classics*
INDIANAPOLIS

Liberty*Classics* is a publishing imprint of Liberty Fund, Inc., a foundation established to encourage study of the ideal of a society of free and responsible individuals.

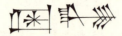

The cuneiform inscription that serves as the design motif for our end-papers is the earliest-known written appearance of the word "freedom" (*ama-gi*), or "liberty." It is taken from a clay document written about 2300 B.C. in the Sumerian city-state of Lagash.

Frontispiece portrait of Mercy Otis Warren by J. S. Copley. Courtesy of the Museum of Fine Arts, Boston, Massachusetts.

Facsimile title and index pages of the 1805 Manning and Loring edition courtesy of the Lilly Library, Indiana University, Bloomington, Indiana.

Cover art courtesy of the New York Public Library. Volume I, engraving by Paul Revere. Volume II, Painting by J. Trumbull.

Library of Congress Cataloging-in-Publication Data

Warren, Mercy Otis, 1728–1814.
    History of the rise, progress, and termination of the American Revolution.

    Reprint. Originally published: Boston : Printed by Manning and Loring. for E. Larkin, 1805.
    Bibliography: v. 1, p.
    Includes indexes.
    1. United States—History—Revolution, 1775–1783.
I. Cohen, Lester H., 1944–   .   II.   Title.
E208.W29   1988   973.3   87-26243

ISBN 0-86597-066-1 (set)
ISBN 0-86597-067-x (v. 1)
ISBN 0-86597-068-8 (v. 2)

ISBN 0-86597-069-6 (pbk.: set)
ISBN 0-86597-070-x (pbk.: v. 1)
ISBN 0-86597-071-8 (pbk.: v. 2)

10 9 8 7 6 5 4 3 2 1

Contents

VOLUME ONE

[VOLUME ONE OF THE 1805 EDITION]

VOLUME TWO

Foreword

MERCY OTIS WARREN (1728–1814) was the most formidable female intellectual in eighteenth-century America. In an era dominated by giants, she honorably may be numbered among the intellectuals of the second rank: those, for example, who served in colonial or state legislatures, the Continental Congress, and the Constitution-ratifying conventions and those who publicized the revolutionary cause through their writings.

Between 1772 and 1805, Warren published at least five plays[1]— three political satires and two verse tragedies—a collection of poems, a political pamphlet warning of the dangers of the proposed Constitution, and one of the two most important contemporary histories of the American Revolution. Beginning about 1770 she became a prolific letter writer, entering into a kind of literary apprenticeship in one of the century's more interesting genres—the "familiar letter"—and leaving to us a legacy of more than a thousand pages of correspondence devoted to a variety of political, cultural, economic, and social themes.

Warren's *History of the Rise, Progress and Termination of the American Revolution* was the culmination of her literary career. Through it she satisfied a powerful urge to fuse her personal and public convictions. It served as a means to unite her ethical, political, and philosophical concerns; it joined her personal religiosity with her ideological commitments; and it provided a vehicle for a female intellectual to be useful in a republican culture. For forty years Warren worked to develop the habits of mind and a style of writing that would satisfy these requirements. She thought it her principal responsibility as a

---

[1] She published "The Adulateur" in 1772, "The Defeat" in 1773, and "The Group" in 1775. "The Sack of Rome" and "The Ladies of Castille" appeared in her *Poems, Dramatic and Miscellaneous* in 1790. Her authorship of "The Blockheads: or, The Affrighted Officers" (1776) and "The Motley Assembly" (1779) is a matter of some controversy, though she very likely wrote neither. There is no reason to believe that she wrote "*Sans Souci*, alias Free and Easy; or, An Evening's Peep into a Polite Circle" (1785), which she referred to as a "little indigested farrago" in a letter to her son George. See Franklin, Introduction; Fritz, pp. 226–227.

poet, playwright, and historian "to form the minds, to fix the principles[,] to correct the errors, and to beckon by the soft allurements of love, as well as the stronger voice of reason, the young members of society (peculiarly my charge), to tread the path of true glory. . . ." Several years later she observed that "The Ladies of Castille," which would be published with her collected poems in 1790, was created by a writer "who wishes only to cultivate the sentiments of public and private virtue in whatsoever falls from her pen."[2] These letters reveal that she found in writing a way to integrate private and public roles: the traditional role of mother—the young were "peculiarly my charge"—and the less conventional ambition to be a woman who gave voice to the central principles and values of the political culture.

Warren's major literary and political aims—to form minds, fix principles, and cultivate virtue—characterized her writings from the beginning. Her satirical plays—"The Adulateur," "The Defeat," and "The Group"—are memorable chiefly as representative examples of early American political satire[3] and as well-timed propaganda.[4] Her

[2] MOW to Winslow Warren, November 20, 1780 and September 1785, MOWLB, pp. 254–257, 313–316.

[3] See Walter J. Meserve, *An Emerging Entertainment: The Drama of the American People to 1828* (Bloomington, Ind., 1977); Gerald Weales, " 'The Adulateur' and How It Grew," *Library Chronicles*, 43 (1979), pp. 103–133; Edmund M. Hayes, ed., "Mercy Otis Warren: 'The Defeat,' " NEQ, 49 (September 1976), pp. 440–458; Cheryl Z. Oreovicz, "Mercy Otis Warren and 'Freedom's Genius,' " *University of Mississippi Studies in English*, new series, 5 (August 1987).

[4] Warren published the three satires between 1772 and 1775, when popular agitation against the Crown, stimulated by the Boston Massacre (March 5, 1770), had deflated into sullen resentment by the failure of the nonimportation movement, then surged toward a crescendo with Parliament's passage of the Coercive Acts in May, 1774. In 1773 the long-suspected conspiracy between British administration and high Massachusetts officials—notably Governor Thomas Hutchinson and his brother-in-law, Lieutenant Governor Andrew Oliver—appeared to be exposed. The Hutchinsons and the Olivers had become fixtures in numerous lucrative political offices in Massachusetts, giving rise to James Otis, Jr.'s protests against plural office-holding. And letters that Hutchinson and Oliver had written to England were discovered and published in Boston. What exquisite personal satisfaction Warren must have felt in revealing the deceitful characters of "Rapatio" (Hutchinson) and "Limput" (Oliver), when it was they (it was commonly, if erroneously, believed) who had blocked James Otis, Sr.'s succession as chief justice of the Superior Court when Samuel Sewall died in 1760! See Waters, 118–125; Bernard Bailyn, *The Ordeal of Thomas Hutchinson* (Cambridge, Mass., 1974); Ellen E. Brennan, *Plural Office-Holding in Massachusetts, 1760–1780: Its Relation to the "Separation" of Departments of Government* (Chapel Hill, 1945).

poetry, long neglected, is now being taken seriously by scholars. That she was committed to poetry as an art and as a vehicle for political and didactic themes is evidenced by the dozens of poems that, until recently, remained unpublished and by her numerous, careful revisions of her work.[5] But the best of Warren is her prose, and the best of her prose is her *History*.

In historical narrative Warren found the medium which, better than poetry or satire, satisfied her urge to be both an artist and a political and moral force. In her *History* she sustained the republican persona that she had been developing in her letters since the 1770s.[6] And here she joined more successfully than ever the themes that lay at the center of her concern. These themes involved both her conception of history and her understanding of the proper role of the historian in a republican order.

Warren viewed history in terms of three fundamental conflicts: a political conflict between liberty and arbitrary power; an ethical conflict between virtue and avarice; and a philosophical conflict between reason and passion. The three were consistent with one another: History revealed a continual struggle between liberty, virtue, and reason against the blind pursuit of power, luxury, and passion. Beyond being mutually consistent, liberty, virtue, and reason were, for Warren as for many of her generation, necessary to sustain a republic. Liberty without virtue and reason to guide it led to licentiousness; virtue without reason and liberty to energize it led to passivity and quietism; and reason without liberty and virtue to focus it led to abstraction and cynicism. The need for all three animating principles demonstrated why republics had proven to be so fragile.

Warren sometimes characterized the three conflicts in the starkest terms, suggesting that she viewed history as a vast morality play— not unlike "The Sack of Rome," which she had based on Joseph Addison's "Cato" (1713)—in which simple, industrious, virtuous, liberty-loving republicans courageously resist the encroachments of

---

[5] See Emily Stipes Watts, *The Poetry of American Women from 1632 to 1945* (Austin, Tex., 1977). Watts argues that "In whatever literary form Warren wrote, she had but one theme: liberty. In her farces and history, it was national and political freedom. In her poems, it was intellectual freedom. In her anti-Federalist pamphlet, it was individual freedom" (p. 39). See also Patti Cowell, ed., *Women Poets in Pre-Revolutionary America, 1650–1775: An Anthology* (Troy, N.Y., 1981); Edmund M. Hayes, ed., "The Private Poems of Mercy Otis Warren," NEQ, 54 (June 1981), pp. 199–224; Oreovicz, "Mercy Warren and 'Freedom's Genius.'"

[6] See my "Mercy Otis Warren: The Politics of Language and the Aesthetics of Self," AQ, 35 (Winter 1983), pp. 481–498.

kings, despots, and mannered aristocrats who care only to gratify their baser passions. While, for Warren, history may have been easy enough to categorize into strict oppositions, its *outcomes* were neither obvious nor inevitable. If history revealed any consistent tendency, it was that arbitrary power, corruption, and irrationality tended to defeat enlightened principles. That was why most of the world remained enslaved. "Ambition and avarice," she wrote, "are the leading springs" of history, whereas "virtue in the sublimest sense, has an influence only on a chosen few," and "the guidance of reason . . . operates too little on the generality of mankind."[7] Faced with those who lusted for power and self-aggrandizement, most people in the history of the world submitted, too ignorant, cowardly, or despairing to resist.

There were, of course, exceptions to this grim scenario, the most conspicuous of which in the modern world was that of the American colonists who, according to Warren, manifested the kind of virtue and commitment to liberty only rarely witnessed in history. Warren "trembled for the events of the present commotion," she wrote in 1774; she believed that "there must be a noble struggle to recover the existing liberties of our injured country" and that no one could predict how the struggle would turn out. In retrospect, however, she was able to conclude: "Reduced nearly to a state of nature with regard to all civil or authoritative ties, it is almost incredible, that the principles of rectitude and common justice should have been so generally influential" among the people. From the Stamp Act to the introduction of a standing army in Massachusetts, from the nonimportation agreements to the Coercive Acts, and finally from these tensions to a state of war, "it must be ascribed to the virtue of the people . . . that they did not feel the effects of anarchy in the extreme."[8] The American Revolution was a signal victory over "an ungrateful, dissipated" Britain, a nation which had fallen into "barbarism" and internal corruption and whose "republican opinions and . . . freedom . . . had been on the wane" since the first Stuart.[9]

Yet despite the triumph of liberty, virtue, and reason on *this*

---

[7] *History*, I: 2 (p. 3 of this edition); MOW to John Adams, December 1786, in MOWLB, p. 197; *History*, I: 216 (p. 118 of this edition).

[8] MOW to Hannah Winthrop, 1774, in MOWLB, p. 70; *History*, I: 227, 147 (pp. 124, 81 of this edition).

[9] MOW to Janet Montgomery, November 25, 1777 and MOW to John Adams, August 2, 1775, in MOWLB, pp. 41–42, 153; *History*, III: 399 (p. 678 of this edition). See my "Explaining the Revolution: Ideology and Ethics in Mercy Otis Warren's Historical Theory," WMQ, third series, 37 (April 1980), pp. 200–218.

occasion, Warren was not confident and surely not complacent about the long-term prospects of the Revolution. On the contrary, when she drafted her *History* during the 1780s and '90s, she wrote in a mood of profound concern. The new nation seemed to be manifesting the same dreaded signs of decay that had characterized the decline of all earlier republics: political partisanship that would undermine revolutionary unity; financial insolvency that threatened the continued existence of government on all levels; social rivalries that could destroy stability; and, above all, moral and political degeneration that substituted private passion for enlightened self-interest and that eventually would make a mockery of a "republican" culture.

As early as 1780, she wrote to her friend John Adams, wishing for his speedy return from Amsterdam, where he was negotiating loans and a treaty. "We need the steady influence of all the old republicans," she wrote, "to keep the principles of the revolution in view." "The truth is," she added to her son Winslow, then in Europe, America has "deviated from the principles, manners, and spirit, that instigated to an opposition to Britain" and that were essential to the success of the republic. By 1786 she believed the revolutionary venture might fail entirely. Here were the new states, "emancipated from a foreign yoke," a long and bloody war finally ended, "with the liberty of forming our own governments, framing our own laws, choosing our own magistrates, and adopting manners the most favourable to freedom and happiness, yet sorry I am to say I fear we have not virtue sufficient to avail ourselves of these superior advantages." Instead, she wrote a year later to Catharine Macaulay, republicanism and independence "are nearly dwindled into theory." Republicanism was "defaced by a spirit of anarchy," while independence was "almost annihilated . . . by a kind of public gambling, instead of private industry."[10]

Events in Warren's personal life no doubt intensified her feelings of melancholy and heightened her sense of widespread public decline. Before her *History* went to press, three of the five Warren sons had died. Charles died of consumption at the age of twenty-four in 1786; the favored Winslow, seeking to avoid a lawsuit for moneys owed, joined General Arthur St. Clair's ill-fated expedition against the Miami Indians and died in battle in Ohio in 1791 at thirty-one; and the youngest, George, died in Maine at the age of twenty-four. Her oldest

---

[10] MOW to John Adams, December 28, 1780; to Winslow Warren, December 18, 1782; to John Adams, December 1786; to Catharine Macaulay, August 2, 1787, in MOWLB, pp. 183; 279–281; 195; 22.

son, James Jr., a naval lieutenant, returned from a mission to France in 1779, crippled for life with a shattered right knee that he suffered when the *Alliance* encountered two English sloops. Moreover, her husband James, distinguished for his service as speaker of the Massachusetts House of Representatives, president of the Provincial Congress, and commissary general in the Continental Army, had, incredibly, become politically suspect to the ruling Hancock forces in Massachusetts. James's sympathy for the Shaysites in 1786, his frequent laments about public corruption, and his moderate antifederalism placed him outside the growing federalist mainstream. Even John Adams, a long-time friend, found his views increasingly obnoxious. Though James was elected lieutenant governor in 1780 (to serve in a Hancock administration), he declined the post and sank into undeserved obscurity.

Although these private events added to Warren's gloom, they should not be allowed to overshadow her public vision or to depreciate her broader understanding of national affairs. In her fifties and sixties when her *History* was taking shape, Warren was seventy-seven when it was published, and her commitment to her role as a historian had long since developed into a public as well as a personal one. At the heart of that commitment was the complex of motives that she had mentioned in her letters to Winslow and implied in her letters to John Adams and Catharine Macaulay. Writing history was less a means of edification than a mode of exhortation. Narrative was a political and ethical performance, calculated to instill in a new generation a vigilance toward their liberties and to animate responsibility for their actions. History also provided an opportunity to define the terms—literally, the vocabulary—with which people could properly discuss politics and history.[11]

In short, history was "philosophy teaching by examples," as Lord Bolingbroke had written; it "inculcates images of virtue and vice," and its proper task was to train people, especially young people, in "public and private virtue."[12] This was the eighteenth-century version of the classical "exemplary theory of history," which swept the Revolutionary generation of historians and which accorded perfectly

[11] See my "Explaining the Revolution" and "Mercy Otis Warren: The Politics of Language and the Aesthetics of Self."

[12] Bolingbroke quoted in Isaac Kramnick, ed., *Lord Bolingbroke: Historical Writings* (Chicago, 1972), p. xvi. Warren evidently read Bolingbroke. See MOW to Winslow Warren, December 24, 1779, in MOWLB, pp. 242–243.

with Warren's understanding of her proper role.[13] If she frequently painted history in blacks and whites and with broad strokes, creating simple moral oppositions wherever possible, she did so in order to make utterly clear to the rising generation that the struggle never ended.[14] She stated the lesson plainly near the end of the *History*. Once corruption begins among individuals, it will, left unchecked, become systemic. If that should ever happen in America, she exhorted, "let some unborn historian, in a far distant day, detail the lapse, and hold up the contrast between a simple, virtuous, and free people, and a degenerate, servile race of beings. . . ."[15]

But, Warren lamented, that "far distant day" already had arrived, and something had to be done to reverse the decline. While a few "old republicans" sought political or constitutional remedies for the disease ailing the body politic, Warren turned to the word, for historical narrative had the power to redeem.

* * *

Warren's ambition to be useful was no accident. For four generations before her birth on September 14, 1728, the Otises had served in town and colony offices, reaching as high as the Massachusetts House of Representatives and the Governor's Council. Her father had been Speaker of the House. Mercy Otis entered the world, the third child and first daughter of James and Mary Allyne Otis, with all the family's privileges: wealth, social prestige, and political power; she added to these intellect and energy, and she made the most of her gifts.[16]

When Mercy Otis married James Warren in November 1754, two of the most prominent families in provincial Massachusetts were joined. The two families had taken similar routes to fortune and

---

[13] On the exemplary theory, see George H. Nadel, "Philosophy of History Before Historicism," *History and Theory*, III (1964), pp. 291–315; Lester H. Cohen, *The Revolutionary Histories: Contemporary Narratives of the American Revolution* (Ithaca, N.Y., 1980), pp. 188–192.

[14] See my "Creating a Useable Future: The Revolutionary Historians and the National Past," in Jack P. Greene, ed., *The American Revolution: The Unfinished Agenda* (forthcoming).

[15] *History*, III: 336–337 (pp. 645–646 of this edition).

[16] For Otis family history, I have relied on Waters, Fritz, and Mary Elizabeth Regan, "Pundit and Prophet of the Old Republic: The Life and Times of Mercy Otis Warren, 1728–1814" (unpublished Ph.D. dissertation, University of California, 1984); for Warren family history, I have used, among others, Mrs. Washington A. Roebling, *Richard Warren of the Mayflower and Some of His Descendants* (Boston, 1901), as well as such sources as Sibley's *Harvard Graduates*.

prestige; were the historical record less ample, both family histories would appear to be parodies of nineteenth-century success stories. John Otis I had emigrated to Bear Cove (later Hingham) in his fiftieth year in 1630. Richard Warren had arrived on the *Mayflower* ten years earlier. Both quickly acquired wealth and station, the result partly of being first in time and place, partly of their ability to recognize the economic and political possibilities of the new world. By the third generation, John Otis III (d. 1727) had become the most prominent citizen in Barnstable, having tripled the family assets (as his father had before him) and having served as judge of the Probate Court, chief justice of Barnstable County's Court of Common Pleas, captain of a militia company, and Barnstable's first representative to the Massachusetts General Assembly. In the same generation, Captain James Warren, also wealthy and respected, had had a similar career, serving as high sheriff of Plymouth County, captain of the militia, and Plymouth's representative to the General Assembly.

Mercy Otis and James Warren could thus look back upon distinguished ancestors and forward to lives of affluence and respectability befitting people of their station. Viewed from one perspective, they did lead the conventional lives of the provincial elite. They settled on the Warren family estate at Eel River (established by the founder, Richard Warren) and soon acquired the Winslow mansion in Plymouth town. James conducted the family commercial enterprise, engaging in coastal and overseas trade, and entered politics as his forebears had. He became sheriff of Plymouth County and justice of the peace in 1756, offices that suited a rising man of thirty; he later served as a colonel in the militia. Other positions of power and prestige would follow as a matter of course. The Warrens reared five sons with parental devotion and concern.

Viewed from another, more important, perspective, however, the events of the American Revolution made conventional life impossible. While James Warren helped found the Massachusetts Committee of Correspondence in 1772, Mercy was writing the plays that launched her political and literary career. When James went to Watertown to serve as president of the Massachusetts Provincial Congress (succeeding cousin Joseph Warren, who fell at the Battle of Bunker Hill), Mercy began firing the literary salvos that would lead to her collection of poetry, her pamphlet of 1788, and the *History*.

Warren may have had a history in mind as early as 1775, for Abigail Adams wrote to her in "hope the Historick page will increase to a volume." At the end of 1787, John Adams wrote from London thanking Warren for a copy of "The Sack of Rome" and cautioning her not to get her hopes up for an English edition of anything she might write. "Your Annals, or History, I hope you will continue, for there are few Persons possessed of more Facts, or who can record them in a more agreeable manner." But: "nothing American sells here"—not Ramsay's or Gordon's histories, or Barlow's poems.[17]

There is reason to believe that by 1791 Warren had completed the manuscript up to the Treaty of Paris and that she considered Chapter XXXI, which deals with the period from 1783 to the Constitution, as a "supplementary" chapter. "It is my purpose Sir," she wrote to Elbridge Gerry in a "Secret and Confidential" letter of 1791, "at the Conclusion of a certain Historical and biographical Work to make a few [strictures] on the origin[,] the nature & the pitiable consequences of the new government." She asked Gerry detailed questions about the numerous people he had known in the Continental Congress and the Constitutional Convention and concluded: "You may think sir the business I am upon is a bold undertaking; it was begun for the amusement of myself [,] continued with a view of conveying to my children the causes of a struggle & . . . information of the conduct & character of the principal actors at the beginning of the revolution[,] and I wish to finish it in a manner that may be useful to them & interesting to their friends. . . ." The design of the "supplement" was to carry the story forward through the turbulent formation of the new federal government: "to give a general view of the first fifteen years after the peace."[18]

The timing of the *History* is of some importance, for Warren may have delayed publication until 1805 because she thought it unlikely to gain approval as a result of its supposed antifederalist and Jeffersonian biases. It is clear from her letters to Gerry that she knew the *History* would raise political hackles. Moreover, La Rochefoucauld, who visited the Warrens in the late 1790s, said that Mercy and James had, "with great prudence, resolved not to send [the *History*] to the press while they live, but to leave for publication after their death;

---

[17] Abigail Adams to MOW, November 1775, WAL, I: 179; John Adams to MOW, December 25, 1787, WAL, II: 301.
[18] MOW to Elbridge Gerry, March 29, 1791, Elbridge Gerry Papers, I, Box 1 (1775–1805) and MOW to Elbridge Gerry, February 21, 1806, Knight-Gerry Papers, Box 3 (1798–1812).

the truth may then, they say, be safely declared."[19] And Judith Sargent Murray said as late as 1805 that "very many" people who otherwise admired Warren were not subscribing to the *History* because of its "political principles."[20]

Warren, however, had never balked before. While her political apprehensions probably played some role in delaying the *History*, they will not explain why the intrepid Warren, who had published "Observations on the New Constitution" in 1788, should have turned shy three years later. In addition to the likelihood of political opposition (which the *History* did not escape in any case), the delay in publication must be ascribed to Warren's aesthetic and moral concerns. The story she had set out to tell had not yet ended. She simply *could* not publish a history ending in 1783, when "the contrast" between the virtuous generation of the Revolution and the "degenerate, servile race of beings" which was succeeding it was so obvious to her. Such a history would not only be factually incomplete; it would also lack the moral unities of historical literature and represent a lost opportunity for Warren to drive home the political and ethical lessons of the American experience.[21]

Nor should the realities of daily life be overlooked. Warren was sixty-three years old in 1791 and isolated in Plymouth, far from Boston publishers. In the same year she lost her favorite son, Winslow, on whom she had lavished great affection (and apprehension) for years. Until Rev. James Freeman, who had experience in handling publications, began serving as her agent, she had little opportunity and less emotional incentive to see her work to publication.

Freeman's moral support and help with business transactions no doubt helped ease the mind of a distant author. In February 1803, Freeman encouraged Warren to publish the work as soon as possible

---

[19] Duc de la Rochefoucauld-Liancourt, *Travels Through the United States of North America, The Country of the Iroquois, and Upper Canada, in the Years 1795, 1796, and 1797* (4 vols., London, 1799), I: 485.

[20] Judith Sargent Murray to MOW, June 1, 1805, WAL, II: 346.

[21] David Ramsay also delayed the publication of his *History of the American Revolution*, which appeared in 1789, because "The revolution cannot be said to be compleated [sic] until [the Constitution] or something equivalent is established." Ramsay to Benjamin Rush, February 17, 1788, in Robert L. Brunhouse, ed., *David Ramsay, 1749–1815: Selections from his Writings*, American Philosophical Society, *Transactions*, new series, 55 (1965), p. 119.

and not to worry about possible political opposition to it.[22] In October he informed Warren of the terms on which Manning and Loring would publish the *History*.[23] As the work neared completion in press, Freeman offered to look for subscribers among the membership of the Massachusetts Historical Society.[24] He also suggested half a dozen possible mottoes for the book, drawn from Seneca, Lucretius, Terence, and Manilius, though he cautioned Warren: "The best passages of the ancient authors have been anticipated by former historians."[25] As usual, Warren followed her own inclinations and used the quotations from Saint Paul and Shakespeare that appear on her title page.

Although Freeman predicted that the *History* would be widely appreciated, it has been neglected since Warren's own day. In the decades following the Revolution, a large number of magazines, some devoted specifically to literature, appeared in virtually all of the major cities of America. While John Marshall's *Life of George Washington*, Abiel Holmes's *Annals of America*, and other historical works were announced, reviewed, and even excerpted in some of these periodicals, Warren's was announced twice and reviewed only once. The reviewer for *The Panoplist* criticized Warren's style, but it is difficult not to conclude that this criticism masked a less worthy agenda. He noted that, though authors should have a free hand in drawing characters, Warren sometimes exercised that freedom "in some instances which a *gentleman* would not, perhaps, have thought prudent." The reviewer also observed that all members of society "have our 'appropriate duties' . . . even 'aged women' have a sphere of usefulness. . . ."[26]

22 Freeman to MOW, February 22, 1803, MOWP, 1790–1806.

23 Freeman to MOW, October 13, 1803, MOWP, 1790–1806. Freeman wrote in some detail and offered a rare glimpse into the printing business. If the printer used small pica, labor would cost $16.50 per sheet; if he used large pica (which presumably Warren wanted) labor costs would be $13.50 per sheet. (A sheet would generate sixteen pages.) Freeman and the printers projected 400 pages per volume, or perhaps as many as 1,300 pages; hence the cost of eighty-two sheets would be $1,107. Fifteen hundred copies of each volume would require 265 reams of paper. Five dollars per ream for good-quality paper would run $1,325. Binding would cost ten cents per volume. Three times 1,500 volumes totalled 4,500 volumes and thus a cost of $450 for binding. The total cost of publication: $1,107 for printing; $1,325 for paper; $450 for binding—$2,882. To break even, the *History* would have to sell at sixty-four cents per volume, $1.92 the set. Freeman prudently suggested selling each set for $2.00.

24 Freeman to MOW, February 20, 1805, MOWP, 1790–1806.

25 Freeman to MOW, January 17, 1806, MOWP, 1790–1806.

26 *The Panoplist* (January–February 1807), pp. 380–384, 429–432. Emphasis added.

But if the *History* was long neglected because of Warren's politics or because she was a woman or because it prompted some powerful people (including her old friend John Adams) to personal outrage, it has properly become the subject of study in recent years.[27]

The *History* has attracted the attention of modern readers neither, principally, because it is the most complete account we have of the Revolution, nor because it satisfies a modern urge for narrative history. If anything, we know more about the Revolution than Warren could have hoped to know, and her style will seem quaint to some and florid to others. Instead, its appeal today lies in its simultaneous presentation of history and author, an appeal which is enhanced because the *History* is "interspersed with biographical, political and moral observations." Modern scholars have begun to take seriously Thoreau's notion that all literature, no matter how "documentary," is written in the first person—from some standpoint that is both here and now. As a result, we do not simply read *through* Warren's *History* to the historical world to which it points. We read Warren *in* her *History*, constantly aware of the narrative voice that presents the world beyond the words. In doing so, we gain a purchase on the political, ethical, and philosophical assumptions that lie behind the language. Historical narrative thus becomes less a window than a mirror—a mirror that reflects its author's values and expectations, and, if we read carefully, our own as well.

Lester H. Cohen

Lester H. Cohen is Associate Professor of History and American Studies at Purdue University, West Lafayette, Indiana.

[27] John Adams excoriated Warren in a virulent, if uncharacteristic, set of letters written after publication of the *History*. See Charles Francis Adams, ed., *Correspondence Between John Adams and Mercy Warren, Relating to her "History of the American Revolution,"* MHS, *Collections*, fifth series, IV (Boston, 1878).

Bibliography

The Writings of Mercy Otis Warren

MANUSCRIPTS AND COLLECTIONS

Mercy Warren Papers, MHS (Boston)
Otis Papers, MHS
Warren-Adams Manuscripts, MHS
Knight-Gerry Papers, MHS
Warren-Winthrop Letters, MHS
Elbridge Gerry Papers, MHS
Warren Family Letters and Papers, Pilgrim Museum (Plymouth)
Gay-Otis Papers, Butler Library (Columbia University)
Otis Family Manuscripts, Butler Library
Manuscript History, Houghton Library (Harvard University)

PUBLISHED COLLECTIONS

Charles Francis Adams, ed., *Correspondence Between John Adams and Mercy Warren, Relating to the "History of the American Revolution,"* MHS, *Collections,* fifth series, IV (Boston, 1878)
L.H. Butterfield, ed., *Adams Family Correspondence* (4 vols.; Cambridge: Harvard University Press, 1963–1973)
C. Harvey Gardiner, ed., *A Study in Dissent: The Warren-Gerry Correspondence, 1776–1792* (Carbondale: Southern Illinois University Press, 1968)
Warren-Adams Letters: Being Chiefly a Correspondence Among John Adams, Samuel Adams, and James Warren, MHS, *Collections,* vols. 72, 73 (1917, 1925)

WARREN'S PUBLICATIONS

"The Adulateur," *Massachusetts Spy,* March 26 and April 23, 1772
    Boston, 1773 (pamphlet)
    Magazine of History, 16 (1917–18), pp. 227–259
"The Defeat," *Boston Gazette,* May 24 and July 19, 1773
    Edmund M. Hayes, ed., NEQ, 49 (September 1976), pp. 440–458
"The Group," *Boston Gazette,* January 23, 1775
    Massachusetts Spy, January 26, 1775
    Boston: Edes and Gill, 1775
    New York: John Anderson, 1775 (*The Group, A Farce*)

Jamaica, printed; Philadelphia, reprint: James Humphreys, Jr., 1775. (*The Group, A Farce*) (No copy of the Jamaica edition is available.)

"Observations on the New Constitution and on the Federal and State Conventions. By A Columbian Patriot" (Boston, 1788)

> Reprinted in Paul Leicester Ford, ed., *Pamphlets on the Constitution of the United States, Published During Its Discussion by the People, 1787–1788* (Brooklyn, 1888): 1–23, where it is erroneously attributed to Elbridge Gerry.

> Reprinted in Herbert J. Storing, ed., *The Complete Anti-Federalist* (7 vols.; Chicago, 1981), 4: 270–287

Poems, Dramatic and Miscellaneous (Boston, 1790)

> (Includes two dramatic tragedies: "The Sack of Rome" and "The Ladies of Castille.")

Edmund M. Hayes, ed., "The Private Poems of Mercy Otis Warren," NEQ, 54 (June 1981), pp. 199–224

Plays and Poems of Mercy Otis Warren: Facsimile Reproductions Compiled and with an Introduction by Benjamin Franklin V (Delmar, N.Y.: Scholars' Facsimiles and Reprints, 1980)

> (Includes "The Adulateur," "The Defeat," and "The Group"; "The Blockheads" and "The Motley Assembly," the authorship of which is disputed; and the 1790 *Poems, Dramatic and Miscellaneous*.)

History of the Rise, Progress and Termination of the American Revolution. Interspersed with Biographical, Political and Moral Observations (Boston: Manning and Loring, 1805)

> Photo-facsimile, New York: A.M.S. Press, 1970

> Chapter XXXI reprinted in Herbert J. Storing, ed., *The Complete Anti-Federalist* (7 vols.; Chicago, 1981), 6: 195–249

Secondary Sources

The most comprehensive and complete biography of Warren is Mary Elizabeth Regan, "Pundit and Prophet of the Old Republic: The Life and Times of Mercy Otis Warren, 1728–1814" (unpublished Ph.D. dissertation, University of California, 1984). Jean Fritz, *Cast for a Revolution: Some American Friends and Enemies, 1728–1814* (Boston, 1972) is an admirable study of Warren's life in the context of Massachusetts politics. John J. Waters, Jr., *The Otis Family in Provincial and Revolutionary Massachusetts* (Chapel Hill, N.C., 1968) is a multigenerational family history which brilliantly illuminates local Massachusetts history as well as that of the Otises.

The best short introduction to Warren's thought and writings is Maud Macdonald Hutcheson, "Mercy Warren, 1728–1814," WMQ, third series, 10 (July 1953), pp. 378–402. Arthur H. Shaffer, *The Politics of History: Writing the History of the American Revolution, 1783–1815* (Chicago, 1975) discusses the historical writings of the Revolutionary era, with a focus on the development of a national historiography. William Raymond Smith, *History as Argument: Three Patriot Historians of the American Revolution* (The Hague, 1966) analyzes the historical theories and assumptions of David Ramsay, Mercy Warren, and John Marshall. I have discussed eighteenth-century historical thought generally in *The Revolutionary Histories: Contemporary Narratives of the American Revolution* (Ithaca, N.Y., 1980), and in "Creating a Useable Future: The Revolutionary Historians and the National Past," in Jack P. Greene, ed., *The American Revolution: The Unfinished Agenda* (New York: forthcoming, 1987). I have treated Warren's historical theory in its ideological context in "Explaining the Revolution: Ideology and Ethics in Mercy Otis Warren's Historical Theory," WMQ, third series, 37 (April 1980), pp. 200–218.

Warren's plays and poetry are usually discussed in passing—ordinarily in the context of eighteenth-century American satire or poetry generally. Moses Coit Tyler's *The Literary History of the American Revolution, 1763–1783* (2 vols.; New York, 1896) remains useful. Everett Emerson, ed., *American Literature, 1764–1789: The Revolutionary Years* is a good collection of essays, including Calhoun Winton's "The Theatre and Drama," pp. 87–104. Bruce Ingram Granger, *Political Satire in the American Revolution, 1763–1783* (Ithaca, N.Y., 1960) provides a good overview of an important topic. I learned much about American playwrights from Walter J. Meserve, *An Emerging Entertainment: The Drama of the American People to 1828* (Bloomington, Ind., 1977). Gerald Weales, " 'The Adulateur' and How It Grew," *Library Chronicles*, 43 (1979), pp. 103–133 is the most insightful essay on Warren's play specifically and on Warren as a playwright in general. Weales's "The Quality of Mercy, or, Mrs. Warren's Profession," *Georgia Review*, 33 (Winter 1979), pp. 881–894 is entertaining as well as instructive. Benjamin Franklin V provides an introduction to his compilation of Warren's poems and plays. Edmund M. Hayes has published an authoritative edition of Warren's "The Defeat," NEQ, 49 (September 1976), pp. 440–458, and hitherto unpublished poems, "The Private Poems of Mercy Otis Warren," NEQ, 54 (June 1981), pp. 199–224. Cheryl Z. Oreovicz treats the corpus of Warren's writings in "Mercy Warren and 'Freedom's Genius,' " *University of Mississippi Studies in English*, new series, 5 (August 1987). Emily Stipes Watts, *The Poetry of American Women from 1632 to 1945* (Austin, Tex., 1977) is the best discussion of its subject. Patti Cowell, ed., *Women Poets in Pre-Revolutionary America, 1650–1775: An Anthology* (Troy, N.Y., 1981) provides an introduction and well-chosen selections.

The two best books on eighteenth-century American women, both of which deal with Warren, are Linda K. Kerber, *Women of the Republic: Intellect and Ideology in Revolutionary America* (Chapel Hill, 1980) and Mary Beth Norton, *Liberty's Daughters: The Revolutionary Experience of American Women, 1750–1800* (Boston, 1980). Joan Hoff Wilson and Sharon Bollinger discuss

Warren's contributions to drama, poetry, and history in "Mercy Otis Warren: Playwright, Poet, and Historian of the American Revolution," in J.R. Brink, ed., *Female Scholars: A Tradition of Learned Women Before 1800* (Montreal, 1980). I have tried to show the relationship between Warren's roles as political thinker, artist, and woman in "Mercy Otis Warren: The Politics of Language and the Aesthetics of Self," AQ, 35 (Winter 1983), pp. 481–498.

Editor's Note

This edition of Mercy Otis Warren's *History of the Rise, Progress and Termination of the American Revolution. Interspersed with Biographical, Political and Moral Observations* reprints the first edition of the work published in Boston by Manning and Loring in 1805. To produce a new edition of the text, designed for general readers as well as scholars, we have made several concessions to modernity.

First, and most important, whereas the *History* originally appeared in three volumes, the present edition is in two. To help the reader make an easy correspondence between this edition and the first, we have used three devices: we have noted the original volume number in the running head; we have (following Manning and Loring's original) numbered the chapters consecutively through the volumes and (again like Manning and Loring) placed the chapter number in the margin of each page; and we have inserted the original page numbers in brackets in the text to mark page breaks. By noting the volume, chapter, and page numbers of the original edition on each page of this one, the reader can tell at a glance exactly how the two correspond. Dates in the margins, intended to remind the reader which year is being discussed, are also preserved from the original.

Second, Manning and Loring's typography has been modernized. The long "s" has been replaced by the less elegant but more readable standard "s." Also, where Manning and Loring placed quotation marks down the left margin as well as at the end of lengthy quotations, we have opted to place quotation marks only immediately before and after all quoted passages, except when they were best displayed as extracts, according to standard modern practice, without the marks. We have, in addition, silently corrected obvious misprints. We thought it unnecessary to announce such corrections—inserting a missing "i" in "reconciliation," for example—when reproducing the original typographical error would bear no significance to a modern reader.

We have not, however, altered Warren's orthography. We have preserved, for example, such spellings as "manoeuvre" and "connexion," and such abbreviations as the military title "gen." or the clerical title "rev." More important, Warren herself abandoned the "u" in "all words of Latin origin, such as honor, error &c. and [chose] to retain it only in words of Saxon origin, such as endeavour."[1] She rejected the extraneous "u" deliberately to repudiate a symbol of English cultural dominance and to announce that her work was *American*. Noah Webster, lexicographer, historian, and commentator on culture, called for precisely such a change in orthography in a ringing plea for an American national culture based upon a national language.[2]

Third, Warren's "Notes," contained in appendices at the end of each of her three volumes, have been divided for the sake of convenience. This division affects only the notes appearing in the original volume II, over half of which now appear at the end of the present first volume, the remainder falling at the end of the present second volume. The notes are keyed to the pages in both the original and the present edition.

Warren's original index, corresponding to the pagination of the 1805 edition, is reprinted here in facsimile. A new index, designed to support modern inquiries, is also provided.

Warren's References

Warren read widely all her life. Rev. Jonathan Russell introduced her to Sir Walter Raleigh's *The History of the World* (1614) when she was a youth, and she continued to read history avidly. She knew her native New England through the works of Cotton Mather and Thomas Prince as well as those of later writers, and she was knowledgeable about the history of the other colonies as well. Though she was

---

[1] James Freeman to MOW, January 17, 1806, MOWP, 1790–1807.

[2] Webster asked rhetorically: "[O]ught the Americans to retain these faults in [English orthography] which produce innumerable inconveniencies in the acquisition and use of the language, or ought they at once to reform these abuses, and introduce order and regularity into the orthography of the AMERICAN TONGUE?" Webster's project clearly went beyond the mere spelling of words. He characterized his aim as the quest for an American national language, for "a *national language* is a band of *national union*. Every engine should be employed to render the people of this country *national*; to call their attachments home to their own country; and to inspire them with the pride of national character." Webster, *Massachusetts Magazine*, 1 (August 1789), p. 476; *Dissertations on the English Language. . . .* (Boston, 1789), p. 397. The appendix to Webster's *Dissertations* was published in *Massachusetts Magazine*, 1 (October, November, December, 1789), pp. 605–608, 658–661, 743–746.

perfectly placed, as an Otis and a Warren, to have firsthand information about the most recent events, she also scoured the newspapers and magazines. She was familiar with the Massachusetts Historical Society and its recent *Collections*.

Nor did she confine her readings to America and its affairs. Her footnotes evidence her familiarity with such general works as William Belsham's *Memoirs of the Reign of George III* and the *Modern Universal History*, as well as Gibbon's *The History of the Decline and Fall of the Roman Empire*. She kept abreast of English periodicals such as *The Annual Register* and *The Remembrancer*, and she maintained a lively interest in Parliamentary debates. She was also remarkably up-to-date on new publications, particularly those concerned with politics and contemporary history and those that contained documents relating to recent events. Her interest in the French Revolution, about which she read in Edmund Burke, Catharine Macaulay, and James Mackintosh, among others, is a case in point.

Citations in the *History* and references in her letters show a strong familiarity not only with books and writers she admired—the Bible, of course, numerous classical authors, William Shakespeare, Jonathan Swift, Joseph Addison (especially his play "Cato"), William Paley, John Locke, Adam Smith, Mackintosh, Macaulay, and Burke (except on the French Revolution)—but also with those whom she deplored—David Hume (because he was a skeptic), Edward Gibbon (whom she admired, but thought suspect for his skepticism and Tory stance), Lord Bolingbroke (a great moralist, but a Tory), and Lord Chesterfield (who was, as Warren saw it, more concerned with style, taste, and wit than with substantive values).[3]

Many of the quotations in the *History* represent acts of virtuosity on her part, identifying her as a widely read and well-informed person. She was highly opinionated politically and morally, and she found support for her most cherished views in a great variety of sources. One consequence of her wide-ranging reading habits is that many of her quotations and citations have been difficult, and a few have been impossible, to track down.

[3] Warren wrote a long letter to her son Winslow (December 24, 1779, MOWLB, pp. 240–243) warning him about the "honey'd poison" contained in Chesterfield's letters. Warren's missive was published in the Boston *Independent Chronicle*, January 18, 1781, under the title "A Letter from an American Lady to her Son," and later reprinted in the *Boston Magazine* (June 1784) and the *Massachusetts Magazine* (January 1790). Edmund M. Hayes has republished the letter, with commentary, in WMQ, third series, 40 (October 1983), pp. 616–621.

To the modern reader, eighteenth-century footnotes are idiosyncratic, to say the least. They are frequently vague, oblique, and insufficient. The reader of Warren's text will find quotations from and references to "Gibbon on the decline and fall of the Roman empire," which originally appeared in six volumes; or what appears to be a lengthy quotation from "Mackintosh," which is accurate enough, but which turns out to be two quotations that are separated by a hundred pages; or citations to the same work under three different titles and an author of a different name; or a quotation from "Montesquieu," the sense of which is readily found in *The Spirit of the Laws*, though the quotation is not.

The point is not that Warren was unusually careless, or that she invented language to suit her needs. On the contrary, her relatively extensive use of footnotes evidences that she was uncommonly scrupulous in revealing her sources.[4] Like most historians prior to the twentieth century, Warren often wrote from memory. She did not always have at hand the book, pamphlet, or letter that she intended to quote. Occasionally, she worked from notes; even passages from her own letters, where she had turned a phrase particularly well, appear in the *History*. Until recently, moreover, precise quotation was not a scholarly ideal. (Warren would be amused, perhaps amazed, at the idea that one who professes to be a historian would, two hundred years later, attempt to find her sources.)

My point is that because Warren sometimes misquoted and sometimes provided inaccurate citations, I cannot be completely confident in all cases that I have found the sources that she used. I have, in preparing this annotated edition of the *History*, attempted to track down all of Warren's footnotes. While a few quotations that she did not footnote are scattered through the text, I confined myself to those for which she did provide references. She presupposed that she wrote for a broadly literate audience and that the members of that audience would either know the quotations or, more likely, take them for granted as common fare. It turns out, moreover, that many of her

---

[4] For example, whereas Warren frequently cited *The Annual Register* and other works that contained valuable information or documents, David Ramsay and William Gordon were, earlier in this century, excoriated for plagiarizing from *The Annual Register* to the point that Orin Grant Libby found both of their histories to be essentially useless. See Libby, "A Critical Examination of William Gordon's History of the American Revolution," AHA Annual Report (1899), I: 367–388, and "Ramsay as Plagiarist," AHR, 7 (October 1901–July 1902), pp. 697–703. Libby's criticism was unnecessary and wrong-headed, but that is beside the present point.

fugitive quotations are tied to a footnote a page or two later. All of Warren's original footnotes remain in place, indicated, as in the first edition, by asterisks, daggers, and double daggers. In most cases I have supplied a more complete reference, set off by brackets, immediately after her footnote.

Naturally, in providing expanded footnotes I have tried, wherever possible, to cite the specific source that Warren actually used. Failing that, I have cited a source—for instance, a collection such as Force's *American Archives*—which contains her specific source. In some cases, particularly when I cannot be sure that I have uncovered the correct document, I suggest a source that reads very much like the one Warren cites. In all such cases, I indicate my lack of surety by introducing the source with "See" or "Probably."

Acknowledgments

During the preparation of this edition, several friends and colleagues have proved to me, once again, how generous scholars are. Linda Levy Peck took valuable time from her own researches to wade through Nathanael Greene's letters at The Henry E. Huntington Library. Daniel J. McInerney found G.F.A. Wendeborn when I persisted in looking for Dr. F.A. Wenderburne and all the Wedderburnes in the British Museum Catalogue. Eugene F. Miller helped me narrow the field on Warren's fugitive quotation of "a celebrated writer." Mary Elizabeth Regan graciously provided me with a copy of her Ph.D. dissertation on Warren. Leonora Woodman, Dan McInerney, and Mark U. Edwards read versions of the introductory materials and made suggestions that improved them. Working with the staff at Liberty Fund, Inc. has been, yet again, a joy.

A number of librarians and archivists saved me much time and expense by responding to queries on some of Warren's references. Joel Silver helped make Indiana University's Lilly Library, where I did the bulk of my source work, accessible and enjoyable. Dennis M. Conrad, associate editor of the Nathanael Greene Papers, searched through as yet unorganized Greene letters to find specific ones for me. James Fox of the New-York Historical Society located Gates, Cadwallader, and Reed letters. Anne-Marie Schaaf helped me with references to holdings in the Historical Society of Pennsylvania. The staffs of the University of Michigan's Graduate Library and the William L. Clements Library were gracious and helpful.

I owe a special debt to my friend and colleague Cheryl Z. Oreovicz, who is preparing a biography of Warren. For most of the last dozen years we have taught together, shared materials, and fought over interpretations of Warren's religious thought, politics, intellectual influences, and style. She has generously allowed me to use Warren materials that she has collected, and she has read the introduction to this volume. I have received the lion's share of the benefit of these exchanges.

If these volumes were mine, rather than Warren's, to dedicate, I would dedicate them to my mother—like Warren a bright, talented woman who was years ahead of her time.

Lester H. Cohen

List of Abbreviations

Adams, *Works*	*The Works of John Adams*, edited by Charles Francis Adams (10 vols.; Boston, 1850–1856)
AHA	American Historical Association
AHR	American Historical Review
AQ	American Quarterly
Annual Register	*The Annual Register, or a View of the History, Politics, and Literature for the Year. . . .* (London: J. Dodsley, 1758–). Each issue of the *Annual Register* contains several sections, including a "History of Europe," an "Appendix to the Chronicle," and a collection of "State Papers." Since pagination is inconsistent, I have indicated the section to which each reference pertains.
Burgoyne, *Expedition*	[John Burgoyne], *A State of the Expedition from Canada, As Laid Before the House of Commons . . . With A Collection of Authentic Documents* (London, 1780). This pamphlet consists of six main sections: a prefatory speech; a narrative of events in Northern New York; evidence and testimony used by the committee of inquiry; Burgoyne's review of the evidence; Burgoyne's conclusion; an appendix containing Burgoyne's letters (most of which were written to George Germain). I refer to both the work and a specific subsection.
Cobbett	[William Cobbett], *Cobbett's Parliamentary History of England, from the Norman Conquest, in 1066 to the Year, 1803* (36 vols.; London: R. Bagshaw, 1806–1820). Warren never cited Cobbett specifically. Two other sources of Parliamentary debates were available in Warren's day: *The Debates and Proceedings of the British House of Commons* and *The Parliamentary Register; or, The History of the Proceedings and Debates of the House of Commons.* Cobbett is by far the most extensive and detailed; it includes debates in the House of Lords.

Force, *Archives*	Peter Force, compiler, *American Archives; Fourth and Fifth Series. Containing a Documentary History of the English Colonies in North America, From the King's Message to Parliament, of March 7, 1770, to the Declaration of Independence by the United States* (9 vols.; Washington, D.C., 1839–1853). The fourth series includes volumes 1–6; the fifth, 7–9.
Franklin	*Plays and Poems of Mercy Otis Warren: Facsimile Reproductions Compiled and with an Introduction By Benjamin Franklin V* (Delmar, N.Y., 1980)
Fritz	Jean Fritz, *Cast for a Revolution: Some American Friends and Enemies, 1728–1814* (Boston, 1970)
Howe, *Narrative*	[Sir William Howe], *The Narrative of Lieut. Gen. Sir William Howe, in a Committee of the House of Commons, on the 19th of April, 1779; Relative to His Conduct, During His Late Command of the King's Troops in North America, To Which Are Added, Some Observations Upon a Pamphlet, Entitled, Letters to A Nobleman* (London, 1780)
Hutchinson, *Letters*	*The Representations of Governor Hutchinson and Others, Contained in Certain Letters Transmitted to England, And Afterwards Returned From Thence, and Laid Before the General-Assembly of the Massachusetts-Bay* (Boston, 1773). The same letters were reprinted in England in 1774. See below, [Mauduit], *Letters*. Additional materials in the two volumes differ.
JCC	*Journals of the Continental Congress, 1774–1789*, edited by Worthington C. Ford, et al. (34 vols.; Washington, D.C., 1904–1937)
JHRM	*Journals of the House of Representatives of Massachusetts, 1715–1776* (52 vols.; Boston, 1919–)
LDC	*Letters of Delegates to Congress, 1774–1789*, edited by Paul H. Smith, et al. (12 vols.; Washington, D.C., 1976–)
Lee Papers	*The Lee Papers*, New-York Historical Society, *Collections*, (4 vols.; 1871–1874)
[Mauduit], *Letters*	[Israel Mauduit], *The Letters of Governor Hutchinson, and Lieut. Governor Oliver &c. Printed at Boston* (London, 1774). See above, Hutchinson, *Letters*.
MHS	Massachusetts Historical Society, Boston
MOWLB	Mercy Otis Warren, "Letter Book," Massachusetts Historical Society

MOWP   Mercy Otis Warren Papers, Massachusetts Historical Society

Modern   *An Universal History, from the Earliest Accounts to the Present*
Universal   *Time. Compiled from Original Authors.* (60 vols.; London,
History   1775–1784). Volumes 1–18 contain "The Antient Part" of
                    the *Universal History.* Volumes 19–60, renumbered 1–42,
                    constitute *The Modern Part of the Universal History. . . . By*
                    the Authors of the Antient Part.

NEQ   New England Quarterly

Remembrancer   *The Remembrancer, or Impartial Repository of Public Events,*
                    1775–1784 (17 vols.; London, 1775–1784)

Sparks,   Jared Sparks, editor, *Correspondence of the American Revolution;*
Correspondence   *Being Letters of Eminent Men to George Washington, From the*
                    Time of His Taking Command of the Army, to the End of His
                    Presidency (4 vols.; Boston, 1853)

Stevens,   B.F. Stevens, compiler, *The Campaign in Virginia, 1781. An*
Campaign   *Exact Reprint of Six Rare Pamphlets on the Clinton-Cornwallis*
                    Controversy (2 vols.; London, 1888)

Stevens,   B.F. Stevens, compiler, *Facsimiles of Manuscripts In European*
Facsimiles   *Archives, Relating to America, 1773–1783* (25 vols.; London,
                    1889–95)

WAL, I, II   *Warren-Adams Letters. Being Chiefly a Correspondence between*
                    John Adams, Samuel Adams and James Warren, Massachusetts
                    Historical Society, *Collections,* vols. 72, 73 (1917, 1925)

Waters   John J. Waters, Jr., *The Otis Family in Provincial and*
                    Revolutionary Massachusetts (Chapel Hill, 1968)

WMQ   *William and Mary Quarterly*

AN ADDRESS TO THE INHABITANTS OF THE UNITED STATES

[iii] At a period when every manly arm was occupied, and every trait of talent or activity engaged, either in the cabinet or the field, apprehensive, that amidst the sudden convulsions, crowded scenes, and rapid changes, that flowed in quick succession, many circumstances might escape the more busy and active members of society, I have been induced to improve the leisure Providence had lent, to record as they passed, in the following pages, the new and unexperienced events exhibited in a land previously blessed with peace, liberty, simplicity, and virtue.

As circumstances were collected, facts related, and characters drawn, many years antecedent to any history since published, relative to the dismemberment of the colonies, and to American independence, there are few allusions to any later writers.

Connected by nature, friendship, and every social tie, with many of the first patriots, and most influential characters on the continent; in the habits of confidential and epistolary intercourse with several gentlemen employed abroad in the most distinguished stations, and with others since elevated to the highest grades of rank [iv] and distinction, I had the best means of information, through a long period that the colonies were in suspense, waiting the operation of foreign courts, and the success of their own enterprising spirit.

The solemnity that covered every countenance, when contemplating the sword uplifted, and the horrors of civil war rushing to habitations not inured to scenes of rapine and misery; even to the quiet cottage, where only concord and affection had reigned; stimulated to observation a mind that had not yielded to the assertion, that all political attentions lay out of the road of female life.

It is true there are certain appropriate duties assigned to each sex; and doubtless it is the more peculiar province of masculine strength, not only to repel the bold invader of the rights of his country and of mankind, but in the nervous style of manly eloquence, to describe the blood-stained field, and relate the story of slaughtered armies.

Sensible of this, the trembling heart has recoiled at the magnitude of the undertaking, and the hand often shrunk back from the task; yet, recollecting that every domestic enjoyment depends on the unimpaired possession of civil and religious liberty, that a concern for the welfare of society ought equally to glow in every human breast, the work was not relinquished. The most interesting circumstances were collected, active characters portrayed, the principles of the times developed, and the changes marked; nor need it cause a blush to acknowledge, a detail was preserved with a view of transmitting it to the rising youth of my country, some of them in infancy, others in the European world, while the most interesting events lowered over their native land.

[v] Conscious that truth has been the guide of my pen, and candor, as well as justice, the accompaniment of my wishes through every page, I can say, with an ingenious writer, "I have used my pen with the liberty of one, who neither hopes nor fears, nor has any interest in the success or failure of any party, and who speaks to posterity— perhaps very far remote."

The sympathizing heart has looked abroad and wept the many victims of affliction, inevitably such in consequence of civil feuds and the concomitant miseries of war, either foreign or domestic. The reverses of life, and the instability of the world, have been viewed on the point of both extremes. Their delusory nature and character, have been contemplated as becomes the philosopher and the christian: the one teaches us from the analogies of nature, the necessity of changes, decay, and death; the other strengthens the mind to meet them with the rational hope of revival and renovation.

Several years have elapsed since the historical tracts, now with diffidence submitted to the public, have been arranged in their present order. Local circumstances, the decline of health, temporary deprivations of sight, the death of the most amiable of children, "the shaft flew thrice, and thrice my peace was slain," have sometimes prompted to throw by the pen in despair. I draw a veil over the woe-fraught scenes that have pierced my own heart. "While the soul was melting inwardly, it has endeavoured to support outwardly, with decency and dignity, those accidents which admit of no redress, and to exert that spirit that enables to get the better of those that do."

Not indifferent to the opinion of the world, nor servilely courting its smiles, no further apology is offered [vi] for the attempt, though many may be necessary, for the incomplete execution of a design, that had rectitude for its basis, and a beneficent regard for the civil and religious rights of mankind, for its motive.

The liberal-minded will peruse with candor, rather than criticise with severity; nor will they think it necessary, that any apology should be offered, for sometimes introducing characters nearly connected with the author of the following annals; as they were early and zealously attached to the public cause, uniform in their principles, and constantly active in the great scenes that produced the revolution, and obtained independence for their country, truth precludes that reserve which might have been proper on less important occasions, and forbids to pass over in silence the names of such as expired before the conflict was finished, or have since retired from public scenes. The historian has never laid aside the tenderness of the sex or the friend; at the same time, she has endeavoured, on all occasions, that the strictest veracity should govern her heart, and the most exact impartiality be the guide of her pen.

If the work should be so far useful or entertaining, as to obtain the sanction of the generous and virtuous part of the community, I cannot but be highly gratified and amply rewarded for the effort, soothed at the same time with the idea, that the motives were justifiable in the eye of Omniscience. Then, if it should not escape the remarks of the critic, or the censure of party, I shall feel no wound to my sensibility, but repose on my pillow as quietly as ever,—

> While all the distant din the world can keep,
> Rolls o'er my grotto, and but soothes my sleep.

Before this address to my countrymen is closed, I beg leave to observe, that as a new century has dawned [vii] upon us, the mind is naturally led to contemplate the great events that have run parallel with, and have just closed the last. From the revolutionary spirit of the times, the vast improvements in science, arts, and agriculture, the boldness of genius that marks the age, the investigation of new theories, and the changes in the political, civil, and religious characters of men, succeeding generations have reason to expect still more astonishing exhibitions in the next. In the mean time, Providence has clearly pointed out the duties of the present generation, particularly the paths which Americans ought to tread. The United States form a young republic, a confederacy which ought ever to be cemented by a union of interest and affection, under the influence of those principles which obtained their independence. These have indeed, at certain periods, appeared to be in the wane; but let them never be eradicated, by the jarring interests of parties, jealousies of the sister states, or the ambition of individuals! It has been observed, by a writer of celebrity,* that "that people, government, and constitution is the freest, which makes the best provision for the enacting of expedient and salutary laws." May this truth be evinced to all ages, by the wise and salutary laws that shall be enacted in the federal legislature of America!

May the hands of the executive of their own choice, be strengthened more by the unanimity and affection of the people, than by the dread of penal inflictions, or any restraints that might repress free inquiry, relative to the principles of their own government, and the conduct of its administrators! The world is now viewing America, as experimenting a new system of government, a FEDERAL REPUBLIC, including a territory to which the Kingdoms of Great Britain and Ireland [viii] bear little proportion. The practicability of supporting such a system, has been doubted by some; if she succeeds, it will refute the assertion, that none but small states are adapted to republican government; if she does not, and the union should be dissolved, some ambitious son of Columbia, or some foreign adventurer, allured by the prize, may wade to empire through seas of blood, or the friends of monarchy may see a number of petty despots, stretching their sceptres over the disjointed parts of the continent. Thus by the mandate of a single sovereign, the degraded subjects of one state, under the bannerets of royalty, may be dragged to sheathe their swords in the bosoms of the inhabitants of another.

The state of the public mind, appears at present to be prepared to weigh these reflections with solemnity, and to receive with pleasure an effort to trace the origin of the American revolution, to review the characters that effected it, and to justify the principles of the defection and final separation from the parent state. With an expanded heart, beating with high hopes of the continued freedom and prosperity of America, the writer indulges a modest expectation, that the following pages will be perused with kindness and candor: this she claims, both in consideration of her sex, the uprightness of her intentions, and the fervency of her wishes for the happiness of all the human race.

Plymouth, Mass., March, 1805   Mercy Warren

---

* Paley's Moral Philosophy. [William Paley, *The Principles of Moral and Political Philosophy* (London, 1785), p. 448 (Book VI, Ch. V).]

HISTORY
OF THE RISE, PROGRESS
AND TERMINATION OF THE
AMERICAN REVOLUTION

HISTORY

OF THE

RISE, PROGRESS AND TERMINATION

OF THE

AMERICAN REVOLUTION.

INTERSPERSED WITH

Biographical, Political and Moral Obfervations.

IN THREE VOLUMES.

BY MRS. MERCY WARREN,

OF PLYMOUTH, (MASS.)

..........Troubled on every fide.............
perplexed, but not in despair ; persecuted, but not forsaken ;
cast down, but not destroyed.   *ST. PAUL.*

    O God ! thy arm was here.........
    And not to us, but to thy arm alone,
    Ascribe we all.   *SHAKESPEARE.*

VOL. I.

BOSTON :

PRINTED BY MANNING AND LORING,

For E. LARKIN, No. 47, CORNHILL.

....
1805.

CHAPTER I

INTRODUCTORY OBSERVATIONS

[1] History, the deposite of crimes, and the record of every thing disgraceful or honorary to mankind, requires a just knowledge of character, to investigate the sources of action; a clear comprehension, to review the combination of causes; and precision of language, to detail the events that have produced the most remarkable revolutions.

To analyze the secret springs that have effected the progressive changes in society; to trace the origin of the various modes of government, the consequent improvements in science, in morality, or the national tincture that [2] marks the manners of the people under despotic or more liberal forms, is a bold and adventurous work.

The study of the human character opens at once a beautiful and a deformed picture of the soul. We there find a noble principle implanted in the nature of man, that pants for distinction. This principle operates in every bosom, and when kept under the control of reason, and the influence of humanity, it produces the most benevolent effects. But when the checks of conscience are thrown aside, or the moral sense weakened by the sudden acquisition of wealth or power, humanity is obscured, and if a favorable coincidence of circumstances permits, this love of distinction often exhibits the most mortifying instances of profligacy, tyranny, and the wanton exercise of arbitrary sway. Thus when we look over the theatre of human action, scrutinize the windings of the heart, and survey the transactions of man from the earliest to the present period, it must be acknowledged that ambition and avarice are the leading springs which generally actuate the restless mind. From these primary sources of corruption have arisen all the rapine and confusion, the depredation and ruin, that have spread distress over the face of the earth from the days of Nimrod to Cesar, and from Cesar to an arbitrary prince of the house of Brunswick.

[3] The indulgence of these turbulent passions has depopulated cities, laid waste the finest territories, and turned the beauty and harmony of the lower creation into an aceldama. Yet candor must bear honorable testimony to many signal instances of disinterested merit among the children of men; thus it is not possible to pronounce decidedly on the character of the politician or the statesman till the winding up of the drama. To evince the truth of this remark, it is needless to adduce innumerable instances of deception both in ancient and modern story. It is enough to observe, that the specious Augustus established himself in empire by the appearance of justice, clemency, and moderation, while the savage Nero shamelessly weltered in the blood of the citizens; but the sole object of each was to become the sovereign of life and property, and to govern the Roman world with a despotic hand.

Time may unlock the cabinets of princes, unfold the secret negociations of statesmen, and hand down the immortal characters of dignified worth, or the blackened traits of finished villany in exaggerated colours. But truth is most likely to be exhibited by the general sense of contemporaries, when the feelings of the heart can be expressed without suffering itself to be disguised by the prejudices of the man. Yet it is not easy to convey to posterity a just idea of the embarrassed situation of the western world, [4] previous to the rupture with Britain; the dismemberment of the empire, and the loss of the most industrious, flourishing, and perhaps virtuous colonies, ever planted by the hand of man.

The progress of the American Revolution has been so rapid, and such the alteration of manners, the blending of characters, and the new train of ideas that almost universally prevail, that the principles which animated to the noblest exertions have been nearly annihilated. Many who first stepped forth in vindication of the rights of human nature are forgotten, and the causes which involved the thirteen colonies in confusion and blood are scarcely known, amidst the rage of accumulation and the taste for expensive pleasures that have since prevailed; a taste that has abolished that mediocrity which once satisfied, and that contentment which long smiled in every countenance. Luxury, the companion of young acquired wealth, is usually the consequence of opposition to, or close connexion with, opulent commercial states. Thus the hurry of spirits, that ever attends the eager pursuit of fortune and a passion for splendid enjoyment, leads to forgetfulness; and thus the inhabitants of America cease to look

back with due gratitude and respect on the fortitude and virtue of CHAP. I
their ancestors, who, through difficulties almost insurmountable,
planted them in a happy soil. But the historian and the philosopher
will ever venerate the memory of those [5] pious and independent
gentlemen, who, after suffering innumerable impositions, restrictions,
and penalties, less for political, than theological opinions, left England,
not as adventurers for wealth or fame, but for the quiet enjoyment of
religion and liberty.

The love of domination and an uncontrolled lust of arbitrary power
have prevailed among all nations, and perhaps in proportion to the
degrees of civilization. They have been equally conspicuous in the
decline of Roman virtue, and in the dark pages of British story. It
was these principles that overturned that ancient republic. It was
these principles that frequently involved England in civil feuds. It
was the resistance to them that brought one of their monarchs to the
block, and struck another from his throne. It was the prevalence of
them that drove the first settlers of America from elegant habitations
and affluent circumstances, to seek an asylum in the cold and
uncultivated regions of the western world. Oppressed in Britain by
despotic kings, and persecuted by prelatic fury, they fled to a distant
country, where the desires of men were bounded by the wants of
nature; where civilization had not created those artificial cravings
which too frequently break over every moral and religious tie for their
gratification.

The tyranny of the Stuart race has long been proverbial in English
story: their efforts [6] to establish an arbitrary system of government
began with the weak and bigoted reign of James the first, and were
continued until the excision of his son Charles. The contests between
the British parliament and this unfortunate monarch arose to such an
height, as to augur an alarming defection of many of the best subjects
in England. Great was their uneasiness at the state of public affairs,
the arbitrary stretch of power, and the obstinacy of king Charles, who
pursued his own despotic measures in spite of the opposition of a
number of gentlemen in parliament attached to the liberties and
privileges of Englishmen. Thus a spirit of emigration adopted in the
preceding reign began to spread with great rapidity through the nation.
Some gentlemen endowed with talents to defend their rights by the
most cogent and resistless arguments were among the number who
had taken the alarming resolution of seeking an asylum far from their
natal soil, where they might enjoy the rights and privileges they

CHAP. I claimed, and which they considered on the eve of annihilation at home. Among these were Oliver Cromwell, afterwards protector, and a number of other gentlemen of distinguished name, who had actually engaged to embark for New-England. This was a circumstance so alarming to the court, that they were stopped by an order of government, and by royal edict all further emigration was forbidden. The spirit of colonization was not however much [7] impeded, nor the growth of the young plantations prevented, by the arbitrary resolutions of the court. It was but a short time after this effort to check them, before numerous English emigrants were spread along the borders of the Atlantic from Plymouth to Virginia.

The independency with which these colonists acted; the high promise of future advantage from the beauty and fertility of the country; and, as was observed soon after, "the prosperous state of their settlements, made it to be considered by the heads of the puritan party in England, many of whom were men of the first rank, fortune and abilities, as the sanctuary of liberty."* The order above alluded to, indeed prevented the embarkation of the Lords Say and Brook, the Earl of Warwick, of Hampden, Pym, and many others, who despairing of recovering their civil and religious liberty on their native shore, had determined to secure it by a retreat to the New World, as it was then called. Patents were purchased by others, within a short period after the present, who planted the thirteen American colonies with a successful hand. Many circumstances concurred to awaken the spirit of adventure, and to draw out men, inured to softer habits, to encounter the difficulties and dangers of planting themselves and families in the wilderness.

[8] The spirit of party had thrown accumulated advantages into the hands of Charles the second, after his restoration. The divisions and animosities at court rendered it more easy for him to pursue the same system which his father had adopted. Amidst the rage for pleasure, and the licentious manners that prevailed in his court, the complaisance of one party, the fears of another, and the weariness of all, of the dissensions and difficulties that had arisen under the protectorship of Cromwell, facilitated the measures of the high monarchists, who continually improved their advantages to enhance the prerogatives of the crown. The weak and bigoted conduct of his brother James increased the general uneasiness of the nation, until his abdication.

---

* Universal History. [*Modern Universal History*, 39: 281–282.]

Thus, through every successive reign of this line of the Stuarts, the CHAP. I colonies gained additional strength, by continual emigrations to the young American settlements.

The first colony of Europeans, permanently planted in North America, was by an handful of roving strangers, sickly, and necessitated to debark on the first land, where there was any promise of a quiet subsistence. Amidst the despotism of the first branch of the house of Stuart, on the throne of Britain, and the ecclesiastical persecutions in England, which sent many eminent characters abroad, a small company of dissenters from the national establishment left England, under the pastoral care of [9] the pious and learned Mr. Robinson, and resided a short time in Holland, which they left in the beginning of autumn, one thousand six hundred and twenty.

After a long and hazardous voyage, they landed on the borders of an inhospitable wilderness, in the dreary month of December, amidst the horrors of a North American winter.* They were at first received by the savage inhabitants of the country with a degree of simple humanity: They smoked with them the *calumet* of peace; purchased a tract of the uncultivated waste; hutted on the frozen shore, sheltered only by the lofty forest, that had been left for ages to thicken under the rude hand of time. From this small beginning was laid the stable foundations of those extensive settlements, that have since spread over the fairest quarter of the globe.

Virginia, indeed, had been earlier discovered by Sir Walter Raleigh, and a few men left there by him, to whom additions under various adventurers were afterwards made; but, by a series of misfortunes and misconduct, the plantation had fallen into such disorder and distress, that the enterprise was abandoned. The fate of those left there by this great and good man has never been known with certainty: It is [10] probable most of them were murdered by the savages; and the remnant, if any there were, became incorporated with the barbarous nations.

There was afterwards a more successful effort for the settlement of a colony in Virginia. In the beginning of the seventeenth century Lord Delaware was appointed Governor, and with him a considerable number of emigrants arrived from England. But his health was not equal to a residence in a rude and uncultivated wilderness; he soon returned to his native country, but left his son, with Sir Thomas

* Appendix, Note, No. I.

CHAP. I Gates and several other enterprising gentlemen, who pursued the project of an establishment in Virginia, and began to build a town on James-River, in the year one thousand six hundred and six. Thus was that state entitled to the prescriptive term of the Old Dominion, which it still retains. But their difficulties, misfortunes and disappointments, long prevented any permanent constitution or stable government, and they scarcely deserved the appellation of a regular colony, until a considerable time after the settlement in Plymouth, in one thousand six hundred and twenty.

The discovery of the New World had opened a wide field of enterprise, and several other previous attempts had been made by Europeans to obtain settlements therein; yet little of a permanent [11] nature was effected, until the patience and perseverance of the Leyden sufferers laid the foundation of social order.

This small company of settlers, after wandering some time on the frozen shore, fixed themselves at the bottom of the Massachusetts Bay. Though dispirited by innumerable discouraging circumstances, they immediately entered into engagements with each other to form themselves into a regular society, and drew up a covenant, by which they bound themselves to submit to order and subordination.

Their jurisprudence was marked with wisdom and dignity, and their simplicity and piety were displayed equally in the regulation of their police, the nature of their contracts, and the punctuality of observance. The old Plymouth colony remained for some time a distinct government. They chose their own magistrates, independent of all foreign control; but a few years involved them with the Massachusetts, of which, Boston, more recently settled than Plymouth, was the capital.

From the local situation of a country, separated by an ocean of a thousand leagues from the parent state, and surrounded by a world of savages, an immediate compact with the King of Great Britain was thought necessary. Thus, a charter was early granted, stipulating on the [12] part of the crown, that the Massachusetts should have a legislative body within itself, composed of three branches, and subject to no control, except his Majesty's negative, within a limited term, to any laws formed by their assembly that might be thought to militate with the general interest of the realm of England. The Governor was appointed by the crown, the representative body, annually chosen by the people, and the council elected by the representatives from the people at large.

Though more liberal charters were granted to some of the colonies, CHAP. I which, after the first settlement at Plymouth, rapidly spread over the face of this new discovered country, yet modes of government nearly similar to that of Massachusetts were established in most of them, except Maryland and Pennsylvania, which were under the direction of particular proprietors. But the corrupt principles which had been fashionable in the voluptuous and bigoted courts of the Stuarts, soon followed the emigrants in their distant retreat, and interrupted the establishments of their civil police; which, it may be observed, were a mixture of Jewish theocracy, monarchic government, and the growing principles of republicanism, which had taken root in Britain as early as the days of Elizabeth.

It soon appeared that there was a strong party in England, who wished to govern the colonists [13] with a rigorous hand. They discovered their inclinations by repeated attempts to procure a revision, an alteration, and a resumption of charters, on the most frivolous pretences.

It is true, an indiscreet zeal, with regard to several religious sectaries, which had early introduced themselves into the young settlements, gave a pretext to some severities from the parent state. But the conduct of the first planters of the American colonies has been held up by some ingenious writers in too ludicrous a light. Yet while we admire their persevering and self-denying virtues, we must acknowledge that the illiberality and weakness of some of their municipal regulations have cast a shade over the memory of men, whose errors arose more from the fashion of the times, and the dangers which threatened them from every side, than from any deficiency either in the head or the heart. But the treatment of the Quakers in the Massachusetts can never be justified either by the principles of policy or humanity.* The demeanor of these people was, indeed, in many instances, not only ridiculous, but disorderly and [14] atrocious; yet an indelible stain will be left on the names of those, who adjudged to imprisonment, confiscation and death, a sect made considerable only by opposition.

In the story of the sufferings of these enthusiasts, there has never

---

* However censurable the early settlers in New England were, in their severities towards the Quakers and other nonconformists, they might think their conduct in some degree sanctioned by the example of their parent state, and the rigours exercised in other parts of the European world at that time, against all denominations which differed from the religious establishments of government.

CHAP. I been a just discrimination between the sectaries denominated Quakers, who first visited the New England settlements, and the associates of the celebrated Penn, who, having received a patent from the crown of England, fixed his residence on the borders of the Delaware. He there reared, with astonishing rapidity, a flourishing, industrious colony, on the most benevolent principles. The equality of their condition, the mildness of their deportment, and the simplicity of their manners, encouraged the emigration of husbandmen, artizans and manufacturers from all parts of Europe. Thus was this colony soon raised to distinguished eminence, though under a proprietary government.* But the sectaries that infested the more eastern territory were generally loose, idle and refractory, aiming to introduce [15] confusion and licentiousness rather than the establishment of any regular society. Excluded from Boston, and banished the Massachusetts, they repaired to a neighboring colony, less tenacious in religious opinion, by which the growth of Rhode Island and Providence Plantations was greatly facilitated.

The spirit of intolerance in the early stages of their settlements was not confined to the New England *puritans,* as they have in derision been styled. In Virginia, Maryland, and some other colonies, where the votaries of the church of England were the stronger party, the dissenters of every description were persecuted, with little less rigour than had been experienced by the Quakers from the Presbyterians of the Massachusetts. An act passed in the assembly of Virginia, in the early days of her legislation, making it penal "for any master of a vessel to bring a Quaker into the province." "The inhabitants were inhibited from entertaining any person of that denomination. They were imprisoned, banished, and treated with every mark of severity short of death."†

---

* Mr. Penn published a system of government, on which it has been observed, "that the introductory piece is perhaps the most extraordinary compound that ever was published, of enthusiasm, sound policy, and good sense." The author tells us, "It was adapted to the great end of all government, viz. to support power in reverence with the people, and to secure the people from the abuse of power." Mod. Un. Hist. Vol. 41. p. 5. [*Modern Universal History,* 41: 5.]

† History of Virginia. [It is not possible to know which history of Virginia Warren had in mind. In any case, Thomas Jefferson (a favorite of Warren's in the 1790s) mentioned the same law in *Notes on the State of Virginia,* (London, John Stockdale, 1787; rpt. ed. by William Peden, University of North Carolina Press, 1954), Query XVII, "Religion": "Several acts of the Virginia assembly of 1659, 1662, and 1693 . . . had prohibited the unlawful assembling of Quakers; had made it penal for any

It is natural to suppose a society of men who had suffered so much CHAP. I from a spirit of religious bigotry, would have stretched a lenient hand towards any who might differ from themselves, either in mode or opinion, with regard to the [16] worship of the Deity. But from a strange propensity in human nature to reduce every thing within the vortex of their own ideas, the same intolerant and persecuting spirit, from which they had so recently fled, discovered itself in those bold adventurers, who had braved the dangers of the ocean and planted themselves in a wilderness, for the enjoyment of civil and religious liberty.

In the cool moments of reflection, both humanity and philosophy revolt at the diabolical disposition, that has prevailed in almost every country, to persecute such as either from education or principle, from caprice or custom, refuse to subscribe to the religious creed of those, who, by various adventitious circumstances, have acquired a degree of superiority or power.

It is rational to believe that the benevolent Author of nature designed universal happiness as the basis of his works. Nor is it unphilosophical to suppose the difference in human sentiment, and the variety of opinions among mankind, may conduce to this end. They may be permitted, in order to improve the faculty of thinking, to draw out the powers of the mind, to exercise the principles of candor, and learn us to wait, in a becoming manner, the full disclosure of the system of divine government. Thus, probably, the variety in the formation of the human soul may appear to be [17] such, as to have rendered it impossible for mankind to think exactly in the same channel. The contemplative and liberal minded man must, therefore, blush for the weakness of his own species, when he sees any of them endeavouring to circumscribe the limits of virtue and happiness within his own contracted sphere, too often darkened by superstition and bigotry.

The modern improvements in society, and the cultivation of reason, which has spread its benign influence over both the European and the American world, have nearly eradicated this persecuting spirit;

---

master of a vessel to bring a Quaker into the state; had ordered those already here, and such as should come thereafter, to be imprisoned til they should abjure the country; provided a milder punishment for their first and second return, but death for their third; had inhibited all persons from suffering their meetings in or near their houses, entertaining them individually, or disposing of books which supported their tenets." (Peden, p. 157.)]

CHAP. I and we look back, in both countries, mortified and ashamed of the illiberality of our ancestors. Yet such is the elasticity of the human mind, that when it has been long bent beyond a certain line of propriety, it frequently flies off to the opposite extreme. Thus there may be danger, that in the enthusiasm for *toleration*, indifference to all religion may take place.* Perhaps few will deny that religion, viewed merely in a political light, is after all the best cement of society, the great barrier of just government, and the only certain [18] restraint of the passions, those dangerous inlets to licentiousness and anarchy.

It has been observed by an ingenious writer, that there are proselytes from atheism, but none from superstition. Would it not be more just to reverse the observation? The narrowness of superstition frequently wears off, by an intercourse with the world, and the subjects become useful members of society. But the hardiness of atheism sets at defiance both human and divine laws, until the man is lost to himself and to the world.

A cursory survey of the religious state of America, in the early stages of colonization, requires no apology. It is necessary to observe, the animosities which arose among themselves on external forms of worship, and different modes of thinking, were most unfortunate circumstances for the infant settlements; more especially while kept in continual alarm by the natives of the vast uncultivated wilds, who soon grew jealous of their new inmates. It is true, that Massasoit, the principal chief of the north, had received the strangers with the same mildness and hospitality that marked the conduct of Montezuma at the south, on the arrival of the Spaniards in his territories. Perhaps the different demeanor of their sons, Philip and Guatimozin, was not the result of more hostile or heroic dispositions than their fathers possessed. It more probably arose from an apprehension of [19] the invasion of their rights, after time had given them a more perfect knowledge of the temper of their guests.

It may be a mistake, that *man*, in a state of nature, is more disposed to cruelty than courtesy. Many instances might be adduced to prove the contrary. But when once awakened to suspicion, that either his

* Since these annals were written this observation has been fully verified in the impious sentiments and conduct of several members of the national Convention of France, who, after the dissolution of monarchy, and the abolition of the privileged orders, were equally zealous for the destruction of the altars of God, and the annihilation of all religion.

life or his interest is in danger, all the black passions of the mind, CHAP. I
with revenge in their rear, rise up in array.* It is an undoubted truth,
that both the rude savage and the polished citizen are equally tenacious
of their pecuniary acquisitions. And however mankind may have trifled
away liberty, virtue, religion, or life, yet when the first rudiments of
society have been established, the right of private property has been
held sacred. For an attempt to invade the possessions each one
denominates *his own*, whether it is made by the rude hand of the
savage, or by the refinements of ancient or modern policy, little short
of the blood of the aggressor has been thought a sufficient atonement.
Thus, the purchase of their commodities, the furs of the forest, and
the alienation of their lands for trivial considerations; the assumed
superiority of the Europeans; their knowledge of arts and war, and
[20] perhaps their supercilious deportment towards the aborigines
might awaken in them just fears of extermination. Nor is it strange
that the natural principle of self-defence operated strongly in their
minds, and urged them to hostilities that often reduced the young
colonies to the utmost danger and distress.

But the innumerable swarms of the wilderness, who were not driven
back to the vast interior region, were soon swept off by the sword or
by sickness, which remarkably raged among them about the time of
the arrival of the English.† The few who remained were quieted by
treaty or by conquest: after which, the inhabitants of the American
colonies lived many years perhaps as near the point of felicity as the
condition of human nature will admit.

The religious bigotry of the first planters, and the temporary ferments
it had occasioned, subsided, and a spirit of candor and forbearance
every where took place. They seemed, previous to the rupture with

---

* A celebrated writer has observed, that "moral evil is foreign to man, as well as
physical evil; that both the one and the other spring up out of deviations from the
law of nature." [The statement could have been made by any one of a large number
of eighteenth-century philosophers or theologians—for example, Montesquieu,
Blackstone, St. Pierre, Locke, Hooker—depending upon the interpretation of the
"law of nature." The idea expressed in it is a common blend of natural law theory
and Stoicism, to which Warren was sympathetic. It echoes Marcus Aurelius's notion
in the *Meditations* that nothing is evil which is according to nature.]

† The Plymouth settlers landed the twenty-second of December, but saw not an
Indian until the thirty-first of January. This was afterwards accounted for by the
information of Samoset, an Indian chief who visited them, and told them the natives
on the borders had been all swept away by a pestilence that raged among them
three or four years before.

CHAP. I Britain, to have acquired that just and happy medium between the ferocity of [21] a state of nature, and those high stages of civilization and refinement, that at once corrupt the heart and sap the foundation of happiness. The sobriety of their manners and the purity of their morals were exemplary; their piety and hospitality engaging; and the equal and lenient administration of their government secured authority, subordination, justice, regularity and peace. A well-informed yeomanry and an enlightened peasantry evinced the early attention of the first settlers to domestic education. Public schools were established in every town, particularly in the eastern provinces, and as early as one thousand six hundred and thirty-eight, Harvard College was founded at Cambridge.*

In the southern colonies, it is true, there was not that general attention to early instruction; the children of the opulent planters only were educated in England, while the less affluent were neglected, and the common class of whites had little education above their slaves. Both knowledge and property were more equally divided in the colder regions of the north; consequently a spirit of more equal liberty was diffused. While the almost spontaneous harvests of the warmer latitudes, the great number of slaves thought necessary to secure their produce, [22] and the easy acquisition of fortune, nourished more aristocratic principles. Perhaps it may be true, that wherever slavery is encouraged, there are among the free inhabitants very high ideas of liberty; though not so much from a sense of the common rights of man, as from their own feelings of superiority.

Democratic principles are the results of equality of condition. A superfluity of wealth, and a train of domestic slaves, naturally banish a sense of general liberty, and nourish the seeds of that kind of independence that usually terminates in aristocracy. Yet all America, from the first emigrants to the present generation, felt an attachment to the inhabitants, a regard to the interest, and a reverence for the

* The elegant St. Pierre has observed, that there are three periods through which most nations pass; the first below nature, in the second they come up to her, and in the third, go beyond her. [Bernardin de St. Pierre, *Studies of Nature* (3 vols.; 3d. ed. London, 1807). *Etudes de la Nature* first appeared in four volumes (Paris, 1784). Most Americans who were acquainted with St. Pierre probably knew him through his novel, *Paul and Mary, an Indian Story*, which appeared as volume 4 of his collected works and went through numerous separate editions. The first of many English editions was published in 1789. *The Literary Tablet: or, A General Repository of Useful Entertainment* (Hanover, N.H.) carried "Extracts from St. Pierre's Studies of Nature," March 4, 1807 (pp. 33–34).]

laws and government of England. Those writers who have observed, CHAP. I
that "these principles had scarcely any existence in the colonies at
the commencement of the late war," have certainly mistaken the
character of their country.

But unhappily both for Great Britain and America, the encroachments of the crown had gathered strength by time; and after the
successes, the glory, and the demise of George the second, the sceptre
descended to a prince, bred under the auspices of a Scotch nobleman
of the house of Stuart. Nurtured in all the inflated ideas of kingly
prerogative, surrounded by flatterers and dependants, who always
swarm in [23] the purlieus of a palace, this misguided sovereign,
dazzled with the acquisition of empire, in the morning of youth, and
in the zenith of national prosperity; more obstinate than cruel, rather
weak than remarkably wicked, considered an opposition to the
mandates of his ministers, as a crime of too daring a nature to hope
for the pardon of royalty.

Lord Bute, who from the preceptor of the prince in the years of
pupilage, had become the director of the monarch on the throne of
Britain, found it not difficult, by that secret influence ever exercised
by a favorite minister, to bring over a majority of the house of commons
to co-operate with the designs of the crown. Thus the parliament of
England became the mere creature of administration, and appeared
ready to leap the boundaries of justice, and to undermine the pillars
of their own constitution, by adhering stedfastly for several years to
a complicated system of tyranny, that threatened the new world with
a yoke unknown to their fathers.

It had ever been deemed essential to the preservation of the boasted
liberties of Englishmen, that no grants of monies should be made, by
tolls, talliage, excise, or any other way, without the consent of the
people by their representative voice. Innovation in a point so interesting might well be expected to create a general ferment [24] through
the American provinces. Numberless restrictions had been laid on the
trade of the colonies previous to this period, and every method had
been taken to check their enterprising spirit, and to prevent the
growth of their manufactures. Nor is it surprising, that loud complaints
should be made when heavy exactions were laid on the subject, who
had not, and whose local situation rendered it impracticable that he
should have, an equal representation in parliament.

What still heightened the resentment of the Americans, in the
beginning of the great contest, was the reflection, that they had not

CHAP. I only always supported their own internal government with little expense to Great Britain; but while a friendly union existed, they had, on all occasions, exerted their utmost ability to comply with every constitutional requisition from the parent state. We need not here revert further back than the beginning of the reign of George the third, to prove this, though earlier instances might be adduced.

The extraordinary exertions of the colonies, in co-operation with British measures, against the French, in the late war, were acknowledged by the British parliament to be more than adequate to their ability. After the successful expedition to Louisburg, in one thousand seven hundred and forty-five, the sum of two hundred [25] thousand pounds sterling was voted by the commons, as a compensation to some of the colonies for their vigorous efforts, which were carried beyond their proportional strength, to aid the expedition.

Not contented with the voluntary aids they had from time to time received from the colonies, and grown giddy with the lustre of their own power, in the plenitude of human grandeur, to which the nation had arrived in the long and successful reign of George the second, such weak, impolitic and unjust measures were pursued, on the accession of his grandson, as soon threw the whole empire into the most violent convulsions.

A more particular narrative of the first settlement of America; their wars with the natives; their distresses at home; their perplexities abroad; and their disputes with the parent state, relative to grants, charters, privileges and limits, may be seen in the accounts of every historical writer on the state of the colonies.* As this is not comprehended in the design of the present work, the reader is referred to more voluminous, or more minute descriptions of the events preceding the transactions, which brought forward a revolution, that emancipated [26] the colonies from the domination of the sceptre of Britain. This is a story of so much interest to the minds of every son and daughter of America, endowed with the ability of reflecting, that they will not reluctantly hasten to the detail of transactions, that have awakened the attention and expectation of the millions among the nations beyond the Atlantic.

---

* These researches have been satisfactorily made by several literary gentlemen, whose talents were equal to the task.

CHAPTER II

The Stamp-Act • A Congress convened at New York, One thousand seven hundred and sixty-five • The Stamp-Act repealed • New Grievances • Suspension of the Legislature of New York

[27] The project of an American taxation might have been longer meditated, but the memorable era of the stamp-act, in one thousand seven hundred and sixty-four, was the first innovation that gave a general alarm throughout the continent. By this extraordinary act, a certain duty was to be levied on all bonds, bills of lading, public papers, and writings of every kind, for the express purpose of raising a revenue to the crown. As soon as this intelligence was transmitted to America, an universal murmur succeeded; and while the judicious and penetrating thought it time to make a resolute stand against the encroachments of power, the resentment of the lower classes broke out into such excesses of riot and tumult, as prevented the operation of the favorite project.

Multitudes assembled in the principal towns and cities, and the popular torrent bore down all before it. The houses of some, who were the avowed abettors of the measure, and of others, who were only suspected as inimical to the liberties of America, in Boston, in Newport, [28] Connecticut, and many other places, were rased to the ground. The commissioners of the stamp-office were every where compelled to renounce their employments, and to enter into the most solemn engagements to make no further attempts to act in this obnoxious business. At New York the act was printed, and cried about the streets, under the title *"The folly of England, and the ruin of America."* In Philadelphia the cannon were spiked up, and the bells of the city, muffled, tolled from morning to evening, and every testimony of sincere mourning was displayed, on the arrival of the stamp papers. Nor were any of the more southern colonies less opposed to the operation of this act; and the house of Burgesses, in

---

CHAP. II Virginia, was the first who formally resolved against the encroachments
1 7 6 4 of power, and the unwarrantable designs of the British parliament.

The novelty of their procedure, and the boldness of spirit that marked the resolutions of that assembly, at once astonished and disconcerted the officers of the crown, and the supporters of the measures of administration. These resolves* were ushered into the house, on the thirtieth of May, one thousand, seven hundred and sixty-five, by Patrick Henry, esq. a young gentleman of the law, till then unknown in political life. He was a man, possessed of strong powers, much professional knowledge, [29] and of such abilities as qualified him for the exigencies of the day. Fearless of the cry of *'treason,'* echoed against him from several quarters, he justified the measure, and supported the resolves, in a speech, that did honor both to his understanding, and his patriotism. The governor, to check the progress of such daring principles, immediately dissolved the assembly.

But the disposition of the people was discovered, when, on a new election, those gentlemen were every where re-chosen, who had shewn the most firmness and zeal, in opposition to the stamp-act. Indeed, from New Hampshire to the Carolinas, a general aversion appeared against this experiment of administration. Nor was the flame confined to the continent; it had spread to the insular regions, whose inhabitants, constitutionally more sanguine than those born in colder climates, discovered stronger marks of resentment, and prouder tokens of disobedience to ministerial authority. Thus several of the West India islands shewed equal violence, in the destruction of the stamp papers, disgust at the act, and indignation towards the officers who were bold enough to attempt its execution. Nor did they at this period appear less determined to resist the operation of all unconstitutional mandates, than the generous planters of the southern, or the independent spirits of the northern colonies.

[30] When the general assembly of the Massachusetts met this year, it appeared that most of the members of the house of representatives had instructions from their constituents to make every legal and spirited opposition to the distribution of the stamped papers, to the execution of the act in any form, and to every other parliamentary infringement on the rights of the people of the colonies. A specimen of the spirit of the times may be seen in a single instance of those instructions, which were given to the representative of the town of

* Appendix, Note, No. II.

Plymouth, the capital of the old colony.* Similar measures were CHAP. II
adopted in most of the other provinces. In consequence of which, 1 7 6 4
petitions from the respective assemblies, replete with the strongest
expressions of loyalty and affection of the king, and a regard to the
British nation, were presented to his majesty, through the hands of
the colonial agents.

The ferment was however too general, and the spirits of the people
too much agitated, to wait patiently the result of their own applications.
So universal was the resentment and discontent of the people, that
the more judicious and discreet characters were exceedingly apprehensive that the general clamor might terminate in the extremes of
anarchy. Heavy duties had been laid on all goods imported from such
of the West India islands as did not belong to Great Britain. [31]
These duties were to be paid into the exchequer, and all penalties
incurred, were to be recovered in the courts of vice-admiralty, by the
determination of a single judge, without trial by jury, and the judge's
salary was to be paid out of the fruits of the forfeiture.

All remonstrances against this innovating system had hitherto been
without effect; and in this period of suspense, apprehension and
anxiety, a general congress of delegates from the several provinces
was proposed by the honorable James Otis, of Barnstable, in the
Massachusetts. He was a gentleman of great probity, experience, and
parliamentary abilities, whose religious adherence to the rights of his
country had distinguished him through the long course of years, in
which he had sustained some of the first offices in government. This
proposal, from a man of his acknowledged judgment, discretion, and
firmness, was universally pleasing. The measure was communicated
to some of the principal members of the two houses of assembly, and
immediately adopted, not only by the Massachusetts, but very soon
after by most of the other colonies. Thus originated the first congress
ever convened in America by the united voice of the people, in order
to justify their claims to the rights of Englishmen, and the privileges
of the British constitution.

[32] It has been observed that Virginia and the Massachusetts made
the first opposition to parliamentary measures, on different grounds.
The Virginians, in their resolves, came forward, conscious of their
own independence, and at once asserted their rights as men. The
Massachusetts generally founded their claims on the rights of British

* See Appendix, Note, No. III.

CHAP. II

1 7 6 4

subjects, and the privileges of their English ancestors; but the era was not far distant, when the united colonies took the same ground, the claim of native independence, regardless of charters or foreign restrictions.

At a period when the taste and opinions of Americans were comparatively pure and simple, while they possessed that independence and dignity of mind, which is lost only by a multiplicity of wants and interests, new scenes were opening, beyond the reach of human calculation. At this important crisis, the delegates appointed from several of the colonies, to deliberate on the lowering aspect of political affairs, met at New York, on the first Tuesday of October, one thousand seven hundred and sixty-five.*

1 7 6 5

The moderate demands of this body, and the short period of its existence, discovered at once the affectionate attachment of its members.† [33] to the parent state and their dread of a general rupture, which at the time universally prevailed. They stated their claims as subjects to the crown of Great Britain, appointed agents to enforce them in the national councils, and agreed on petitions for the repeal of the stamp-act, which had sown the seeds of discord throughout the colonies. The prayer of their constituents was in a spirited, yet respectful manner, offered through them to the king, lords, and commons of Great Britain; they then separated, to wait the event.‡

A majority of the principal merchants of the city of London, the opulent West India proprietors, who resided in England, and most of the manufacturing towns, through the kingdom, accompanied with similar petitions, those offered by the congress, convened at New York. In consequence of the general aversion to the stamp-act, the British ministry were changed, in appearance, though the same men, who had fabricated the American system, still retained their influence

1 7 6 6

on the mind of the king, and in the councils of the nation. The parliamentary debates of the winter of one thousand seven hundred and sixty-six, evinced the important consequences expected from the

---

* Several of the colonies were prevented sending delegates to the congress at New York, by the royal governors, who would not permit the assemblies to meet.

† See Appendix, Note, No. IV.

‡ See their petition in the records of the congress at New York, in one thousand seven hundred and sixty-five. [*Proceedings of the Congress at New York* (Annapolis, 1766), pp. 17–19. Also reprinted in Edmund S. Morgan, ed., *Prologue to Revolution: Sources and Documents on the Stamp Act Crisis, 1764–1766* (Chapel Hill, 1959), pp. 63–65.]

decision of the question, relative to an American taxation. [34] Warm CHAP. II and spirited arguments in favor of the measure, energetic reasonings 1 7 6 6 against it, with many sarcastic strokes on administration, from some of the prime orators in parliament, interested the hearers, of every rank and description. Finally, in order to quiet the public mind, the execution of the *stamp-act* was pronounced *inexpedient* by a majority of the house of commons, and a bill passed for its repeal, on March the eighteenth, one thousand seven hundred and sixty-six. But a clause was inserted therein, holding up a parliamentary right to make laws binding on the colonies in all cases whatsoever; and a kind of condition was tacked to the repeal, that compensation should be made to all who had suffered, either in person or property, by the late riotous proceedings.

A short-lived joy was diffused throughout America, even by this delusive appearance of lenity; the people of every description manifested the strongest desire, that harmony might be re-established between Great Britain and the colonies. Bonfires, illuminations, and all the usual expressions of popular satisfaction, were displayed on the joyful occasion; yet, amidst the demonstrations of this lively gratitude, there were some who had sagacity enough to see, that the British ministry was not so much instigated by principles of equity, as impelled by necessity. These deemed any relaxation in parliament an act of justice, rather than favor, and [35] felt more resentment for the manner, than obligation for the design, of this partial repeal; their opinion was fully justified by the subsequent conduct of administration.

When the assembly of Massachusetts met, the succeeding winter, 1 7 6 7 there seemed to prevail a general disposition for peace; the sense of injury was checked, and such a spirit of affection and loyalty appeared, that the two houses agreed to a bill for compensation to all sufferers in the late times of confusion and riot; but they were careful not to recognize a *right* in parliament to make such a requisition. They ordered it to be entered on the journals of the house, that

for the sake of internal peace, they waved all debate and controversy, though persuaded, the delinquent sufferers had no just claim on the province: That, influenced by a loyal regard to his majesty's recommendation, (not considering it as a requisition,) and that, from a deference to the opinions of some illustrious patrons of America, in the house of commons, who had urged them to a compliance: They therefore acceded to the proposal, though, at the same time, they considered it a very reprehensible step in those who had suffered, to apply for relief to the parliament of Britain, instead of submitting to the justice and clemency of their own legislature.

They made several other just and severe observations on the high-toned speech of the governor, [36] who had said, "that the requisition of the ministry was founded on so much justice and humanity, that it could not be controverted." They inquired, if the authority with which he introduced the ministerial demand, precluded all disputation about complying with it, what freedom of choice they had left in the case? They said,

> With regard to the rest of your Excellency's speech, we are constrained to observe, that the general air and style of it favors much more of an act of free grace and pardon, than of a parliamentary address to the two houses of assembly; and we most sincerely with your excellency had been pleased to reserve it, if needful, for a proclamation.

In the bill for compensation by the assembly of Massachusetts, was added a very offensive clause. A general pardon and oblivion was granted to all offenders in the late confusion, tumults and riots. An exact detail of these proceedings was transmitted to England. The king and council disallowed the act, as comprising in it a bill of indemnity to the Boston rioters, and ordered compensation made to the late sufferers, without any supplementary conditions. No notice was taken of this order, nor any alteration made in the act. The money was drawn from the treasury of the province to satisfy the claimants for compensation, and no farther inquiries were made relative to the authors of the late tumultuary proceedings of the times, when [37] the minds of men had been wrought up to a ferment, beyond the reach of all legal restraint.

The year one thousand seven hundred and sixty-six had passed over without any other remarkable political events. All colonial measures agitated in England were regularly transmitted by the minister for the American department to the several plantation governors; who, on every communication endeavoured to enforce the operation of parliamentary authority, by the most sanguine injunctions of their own, and a magnificent display of royal resentment, on the smallest token of disobedience to ministerial requisitions. But it will appear, that through a long series of resolves and messages, letters and petitions, which passed between the parties, previous to the commencement of hostilities, the watchful guardians of American freedom never lost sight of the intrigues of their enemies, or the mischievous designs of such as were under the influence of the crown, on either side the Atlantic.

It may be observed, that the tranquillity of the provinces had for CHAP. II
some time been interrupted by the innovating spirit of the British 1 7 6 7
ministry, instigated by a few prostitutes of power, nurtured in the lap
of America, and bound by every tie of honor and gratitude, to be
faithful to the interests of their country. The social enjoyments of life
had long been disturbed, the mind fretted, and the people rendered
suspicious, [38] when they saw some of their fellow citizens, who did
not hesitate at a junction with the accumulated swarms of hirelings,
sent from Great Britain to ravish from the colonies the rights they
claimed both by nature and by compact. That the hard hearted judges
of admiralty, and the crowd of revenue officers, that hovered about
the custom houses, should seldom be actuated by the principles of
justice, is not strange. Peculation was generally the prime object of
this class, and the oaths they administered, and the habits they
encouraged, were favorable to every species of bribery and corruption.
The rapacity which instigated these descriptions of men had little
check, while they saw themselves upheld even by some governors of
provinces. In this grade, which ought ever to be the protectors of the
rights of the people, there were some, who were total strangers to all
ideas of equity, freedom, or urbanity. It was observed at this time,
in a speech before the house of commons, by colonel Barre, that, "to
his certain knowledge, some were promoted to the highest seats of
honor in America, who were glad to fly to a foreign country, to escape
being brought to the bar of justice in their own."*

However injudicious the appointments to American departments
might be, the darling [39] point of an American revenue was an object
too consequential to be relinquished, either by the court at St. James's,
the plantation governors, or their mercenary adherents dispersed
through the continent. Besides these, there were several classes in
America, who were at first exceedingly opposed to measures that
militated with the designs of administration;—some impressed by

* Parliamentary debates for 1766. [None of the three usual sources of Parliamentary
Debates (see Abbreviations under *Cobbett*) records any speech of Isaac Barre's in
1766. It is possible that Warren took some liberties with one of Barre's famous
speeches in the House of Commons in response to a comment of George Grenville's
during debates over the Stamp Act in 1765: "They [the Colonies] nourished by
your indulgence! They grew by your neglect of them: as soon as you began to care
about them, that care was exercised in sending persons to rule over them, who
were, perhaps, the deputies of some deputy, sent to spy out their liberty, to
misrepresent their actions, and to prey upon them; men whose behaviour, on many
occasions, has caused the blood of those sons of liberty to recoil within them."
Cobbett, XVI: 39 (March 6 [?], 1765).]

CHAP. II long connexion, were intimidated by her power, and attached by
1 7 6 7   affection to Britain. Others, the true disciples of passive obedience,
had real scruples of conscience with regard to any resistance to the
powers that be; these, whether actuated by affection or fear, by
principle or interest, formed a close combination with the colonial
governors, custom-house officers, and all in subordinate departments,
who hung on the court for subsistence. By the tenor of the writings
of some of these, and the insolent behaviour of others, they became
equally obnoxious in the eyes of the people, with the officers of the
crown, and the danglers for place; who, disappointed of their prey by
the repeal of the stamp-act, and restless for some new project that
might enable them to rise into importance, on the spoils of America,
were continually whispering malicious insinuations into the ears of
the financiers and ministers of colonial departments.

They represented the mercantile body in America as a set of
smugglers, forever breaking over the laws of trade and of society; the
[40] people in general as factious, turbulent, and aiming at independence; the legislatures in the several provinces, as marked with the
same spirit, and government every where in so lax a state, that the
civil authority was insufficient to prevent the fatal effects of popular
discontent.

It is indeed true, that resentment had in several instances arisen to
outrage, and that the most unwarrantable excesses had been committed
on some occasions, which gave grounds for unfavorable representations. Yet it must be acknowledged, that the voice of the people
seldom breathes universal murmur, but when the insolence or the
oppression of their rulers extorts the bitter complaint. On the contrary,
there is a certain supineness which generally overspreads the multitude, and disposes mankind to submit quietly to any form of
government, rather than to be at the expense and hazard of resistance.
They become attached to ancient modes by habits of obedience,
though the reins of authority are sometimes held by the most rigorous
hand. Thus we have seen in all ages the many become the slaves of
the few; preferring the wretched tranquillity of inglorious ease, they
patiently yield to despotic masters, until awakened by multiplied
wrongs to the feelings of human nature; which when once aroused to
a consciousness of the native freedom and equal rights of man, ever
revolts at the idea of servitude.

[41] Perhaps the story of political revolution never exhibited a more
general enthusiasm in the cause of liberty, than that which for several
years pervaded all ranks in America, and brought forward events little

expected by the most sanguine spirits in the beginning of the CHAP. II
controversy. A contest now pushed with so much vigour, that the 1 7 6 7
intelligent yeomanry of the country, as well as those educated in the
higher walks, became convinced that nothing less than a systematical
plan of slavery was designed against them. They viewed the chains
as already forged to manacle the unborn millions; and though every
one seemed to dread any new interruption of public tranquillity, the
impetuosity of some led them into excesses which could not be
restrained by those of more cool and discreet deportment. To the
most moderate and judicious it soon became apparent, that unless a
timely and bold resistance prevented, the colonists must in a few
years sink into the same wretched thraldom, that marks the miserable
Asiatic.

Few of the executive officers employed by the king of Great Britain,
and fewer of their adherents, were qualified either by education,
principle, or inclination, to allay the ferment of the times, or to
eradicate the suspicions of men, who, from an hereditary love of
freedom, were tenderly touched by the smallest attempt, to undermine
the invaluable possession. Yet, perhaps [42] few of the colonies, at
this period, suffered equal embarrassments with the Massachusetts.
The inhabitants of that province were considered as the prime leaders
of faction, the disturbers of public tranquillity, and Boston the seat
of sedition. Vengeance was continually denounced against that capital,
and indeed the whole province, through the letters, messages, and
speeches of their first magistrate.

Unhappily for both parties, governor Bernard was very illy calculated
to promote the interest of the people, or support the honor of his
master. He was a man of little genius, but some learning. He was by
education strongly impressed with high ideas of canon and feudal law,
and fond of a system of government that had been long obsolete in
England, and had never had an existence in America. His disposition
was choleric and sanguine, obstinate and designing, yet too open and
frank to disguise his intrigues, and too precipitant to bring them to
maturity. A revision of colony charters, a resumption of former
privileges, and an American revenue, were the constant topics of his
letters to administration.* To prove the necessity of these measures,

---

* See his pamphlet on law and polity, and his letters to the British ministry, while he
presided in the Massachusetts. [Francis Bernard, *Select Letters on the Trade and
Government of America; and the Principles of Law and Polity Applied to the American
Colonies.* . . . (London, 1774).]

CHAP. II the most trivial disturbance was magnified to a riot; and to give a
1 7 6 7 pretext to these wicked insinuations, it was [43] thought by many,
that tumults were frequently excited by the indiscretion or malignancy
of his own partizans.

The declaratory bill still hung suspended over the heads of the
Americans, nor was it suffered to remain long without trying its
operative effects. The clause holding up a right to tax America at
pleasure, and "to bind them in all cases whatsoever," was comprehensive and alarming. Yet it was not generally expected, that the
ministry would soon endeavour to avail themselves of the dangerous
experiment; but, in this, the public were mistaken.

It has already been observed, that the arbitrary disposition of George
the third; the absurd system of policy adopted in conformity to his
principles, and a parliamentary majority at the command of the
ministry, rendered it not difficult to enforce any measures that might
tend to an accession to the powers of the crown. It was a just sentiment
of an elegant writer, that

> almost all the vices of royalty have been principally occasioned by a slavish
> adulation in the language of their subjects; and to the shame of the English
> it must be said, that none of the enslaved nations in the world have
> addressed the throne in a more fulsome and hyperbolical style.*

[44] The dignity of the crown, the supremacy of parliament, and
the disloyalty of the colonies, were the theme of the court, the echo
of its creatures, and of the British nation in general; nor was it thought
good policy to let the high claims of government lie long in a dormant
state. Accordingly not many months after the repeal of the stamp-act,
the chancellor of the exchequer, Charles Townshend, Esq. came
forward and pawned his character on the success of a new attempt to
tax the American colonies. He was a gentleman of conspicuous abilities,
and much professional knowledge; endowed with more boldness than
discretion; he had "the talent of bringing together at once all that
was necessary to establish, to illustrate, and to decorate the side of
the question he was on."†

* Mrs. Macauley's letter to earl Stanhope. [Catharine Macaulay, "Observations on
the Reflections of the Right Hon. Edmund Burke, On the Revolution in France,
In a Letter to the Right Hon. the Earl of Stanhope," (London, 1790).]

† A writer has more recently observed that Charles Townshend was a man of rising
parliamentary reputation and brilliant talents; but capricious, insincere, intriguing,
and wholly destitute of discretion or solidity.

He introduced several bills in support of his sanguinary designs,
which without much difficulty obtained the sanction of parliament,
and the royal assent. The purport of the new project for revenue was
to levy certain duties on paper, glass, painters' colors, and several
other articles usually imported into America. It was also directed that
the duties on India teas, which [45] had been a productive source of
revenue in England, should be taken off there, and three pence per
pound levied on all kinds that should in future be purchased in the
colonies.

This inconsiderable duty on teas finally became an object of high
importance and altercation; it was not the sum, but the principle that
was contested; it manifestly appeared that this was only a financiering
expedient to raise a revenue from the colonies by imperceptible taxes.
The defenders of the privileges and the freedom of the colonies,
denied all parliamentary right to tax them in any way whatever. They
asserted that if the collection of this duty was permitted, it would
establish a precedent, and strengthen the claim parliament had
assumed, to tax them at pleasure. To do it by the secret modes of
imposts and excises would ruin their trade, corrupt the morals of the
people, and was more abhorrent in their eyes than a direct demand.
The most judicious and intelligent Americans at this time considered
all *imperceptible* taxes fraught with evils, that tended to enslave any
country plunged in the boundless chaos of fiscal demands that this
practice introduces.

In consequence of the new system, a board of customs was instituted
and commissioners appointed to set in Boston to collect the duties;
which were besides other purposes to supply a [46] fund for the
payment of the large salaries annexed to their office. A civil list was
soon after established, and the governors of the Massachusetts, judges
of the superior court, and such other officers as had heretofore
depended on the free grants of the representative body, were to be
paid out of the revenue chest.

Thus rendered wholly independent of the general assembly, there
was no check left on the wanton exercise of power in the crown
officers, however disposed they might be to abuse their trust. The

---

Belsham on the reign of George the third. [See, William Belsham, *Memoirs of the
Reign of George III. To the Session of Parliament ending A.D. 1793.* (4 vols.; London,
1795), I: 193–194, 201–202, 211, and, especially, 214–215.]

CHAP. II distance from the throne, it was said, must delay, if not wholly
1 7 6 7   prevent, all relief under any oppressions the people might suffer from
the servants of government; and to crown the long list of grievances,
specified by the patriots of the day, the extension of the courts of
vice-admiralty was none of the least. They were vested with certain
powers that dispensed with the mode of trial by jury, annihilated the
privileges of Englishmen, and placed the liberty of every man in the
hand of a petty officer of the customs. By warrant of a writ of assistance
from the governor or lieutenant governor, any officer of the revenue
was authorized to enter the dwelling of the most respectable inhabitant
on the smallest suspicion of a concealment of contraband goods, and
to insult, search, or seize, with impunity.

[47] An attorney* at law, of some professional abilities and ingenuity,
but without either property or principle, was, by the instigation of
Mr. Bernard, appointed sole judge of admiralty in the Massachusetts.
The dangerous aspect of this court, particularly when aided by writs
of assistance, was opposed with peculiar energy and strength of
argument, by James Otis, Esq. of Boston, who, by the exertion of
his talents and the sacrifice of interest, may justly claim the honor of
laying the foundation of a revolution, which has been productive of
the happiest effects to the civil and political interests of mankind.

He was the first champion of American freedom, who had the
courage to put his signature to the contest between Great Britain and
the colonies. He had in a clear, concise, and nervous manner, stated
and vindicated the rights of the American colonies, and published his
observations in Boston, while the stamp-act hung suspended. This
tract was written with such a spirit of liberality, loyalty, and impartiality,
that though at the time some were ready to pronounce it *treasonable*,
yet, when opposition run higher, many of the most judicious partizans
of the crown were willing to admit it as a [48] just criterion of political
truth.† But the author was abused and vilified by the scribblers of

* Jonathan Sewall, a native of the province, whose pen had been employed to vindicate
the measures of administration and the conduct of governor Bernard, under the
signature of Philalethes, Massachusettensis, &c. &c.

† See Mr. Otis's pamphlet, entitled, "The rights of the colonies stated and vindicated."
[Warren seems to have confused the titles of James Otis Jr.'s two earliest pamphlets:
"A Vindication of the Conduct of the House of Representatives of the Province of
the Massachusetts-Bay," (Boston, 1762) and "The Rights of the British Colonies
Asserted and Proved," (Boston, 1765). She almost certainly had the latter in mind.
The quotations that follow the asterisk in the text come from the transcript of Otis's
oral argument in the Writs of Assistance Case, Joseph Hawley Papers, II, New York
Public Library.]

the court, and threatened with an arrest from the crown, for the CHAP. II
boldness of his opinions. Yet he continued to advocate the rights of 1 7 6 7
the people, and in the course of his argument against the iniquitous
consequences of writs of assistance, he observed, that

> his engaging in this cause had raised the resentment of its abettors; but
> that he argued it from principle, and with peculiar pleasure, as it was in
> favor of *British liberty*, and in opposition to the exercise of a power, that in
> former periods of English history, had cost one king of England his head,
> and another his crown.

He added,

> I can sincerely declare, that I submit myself to every opprobrious name
> for conscience sake, and despise all those, whom guilt, folly or malice
> have made my foes.

It was on this occasion, that Mr. Otis resigned the office of judge
advocate, and renounced all employment under so corrupt an administration, boldly declaring in the face of the supreme court, at this
dangerous crisis, that "the only principle of public conduct, worthy a
gentleman or a man, was the sacrifice of health, ease, applause, estate,
or even life, to the sacred [49] calls of his country; that these manly
sentiments in private life made the good citizen, in public, the patriot
and the hero."—Thus was verified in his conduct the observation of
a writer* of merit and celebrity, that "it was as difficult for Great
Britain to frighten as to cheat Americans into servitude; that she ought
to leave them in the peacable possession of that liberty which they
received at their birth, and were resolved to retain to their death."

When the new parliamentary regulations reached America, all the
colonies in their several departments petitioned in the most strenuous
manner against any American taxation, and all other recent innovations
relative to the government of the British provinces. These petitions
were, when received by the ministry, treated by them with the utmost
contempt. But they were supported by a respectable party in the
parliament of Britain, who did not neglect to warn the administration
of the danger of precipitating measures, that might require before the

---

* Mr. Dickenson, author of the much admired *Farmer's Letters*, the first copy of which
  he inclosed to his friend, Mr. Otis, and observed to him, that "the examples of
  public spirit in the cold regions of the north, had roused the languid latitudes of
  the south, to a proper vindication of their rights." See Appendix, Note, No. V.
  [John Dickinson, *Letters from a Farmer in Pennsylvania, to the Inhabitants of the British
  Colonies* (Philadelphia, 1768). The *Letters* are available in Paul Leicester Ford, ed.,
  The Political Writings of John Dickinson (Philadelphia, 1895).]

termination of a contest thus hurried [50] on, "more virtue and abilities
than the ministry possessed."

By some steps taken by administration previous to the present
period, there was reason to suppose that they were themselves
apprehensive, that their system for governing the colonies in a more
arbitrary manner would give great offence, and create disturbances of
so alarming a nature, that perhaps the aid of military power might
become necessary to enforce the completion of their designs. Doubtless
it was with a view of facilitating the new projects, that an extraordinary
bill had been passed in parliament, making it lawful for the officers
of the British army to quarter their troops in private houses throughout
the colonies. Thus while mixed in every family, it might become
more easy to awe the people into submission, and compel them by
military terrors to the basest compliances. But the colony agents
residing in London, and the merchants concerned in the American
trade, remonstrated so warmly against the injustice and cruelty of
such a procedure, that a part of the bill was dropped. Yet it was too
important a point wholly to relinquish; of consequence a clause was
left, obliging the several legislative assemblies to provide quarters for
the king's marching regiments, and to furnish a number of specified
articles at the expense of the province, wherever they might be
stationed.

[51] This act continued in full force after the stamp-act was repealed,
though it equally militated with that part of the British constitution
which provides that no monies should be raised on the subject without
his consent. Yet rather than enter on a new dispute, the colonists in
general chose to evade it for the present, and without many observations thereon had occasionally made some voluntary provisions for
the support of the king's troops. It was hoped the act might be only
a temporary expedient to hold up the authority of parliament, and
that in a short time the claim might die of itself without any attempt
to revive such an unreasonable demand. But New York, more explicit
in her refusal to *obey*, was suspended from all powers of legislation
until the quartering act should be complied with in the fullest extent.
By this unprecedented treatment of one of the colonies, and the
innumerable exactions and restrictions on all, a general apprehension
prevailed, that nothing but a firm, vigorous and united resistance
could shield from the attacks that threatened the total extinction of
civil liberty through the continent.

CHAPTER III

Cursory Observations • Massachusetts Circular Letter • A new House of Representatives called • Governor Bernard impeached • A Riot on the Seizure of a Vessel • Troops applied for to protect the King's Officers • A Convention at Boston • Troops arrive • A Combination against all Commerce with Great Britain • A General Assembly convened at Boston—removed to Cambridge • Governor Bernard after his Impeachment repairs to England

[52] The British colonies at this period through the American continent contained, exclusive of Canada and Nova Scotia, the provinces of New Hampshire, and Massachusetts Bay, of Rhode Island, Connecticut, New York, New Jersey, Pennsylvania, the Delaware counties, Virginia, Maryland, the two Carolinas, and Georgia, besides the Floridas, and an unbounded tract of wilderness not yet explored. These several provinces had been always governed by their own distinct legislatures. It is true there was some variety in their religious opinions, but a striking similarity in their political institutions, except in the proprietary governments. At the same time the colonies, afterwards the thirteen states, were equally marked with that manly spirit of freedom, characteristic of Americans from New Hampshire to Georgia.

Aroused by the same injuries from the parent state, threatened in the same manner by the [53] common enemies to the rights of society among themselves, their petitions to the throne had been suppressed without even a reading, their remonstrances were ridiculed and their supplications rejected. They determined no longer to submit. All stood ready to unite in the same measures to obtain that redress of grievances they had so long requested, and that relief from burdens they had so long complained of, to so little purpose. Yet there was no bond of connexion by which a similarity of sentiment and concord in action might appear, whether they were again disposed to revert

CHAP. III to the hitherto fruitless mode of petition and remonstrance, or to leave that humiliating path for a line of conduct more cogent and influential in the contests of nations.

1 7 6 8   A circular letter dated February the eleventh, one thousand seven hundred sixty-eight, by the legislature of Massachusetts, directed to the representatives and burgesses of the people through the continent, was a measure well calculated for this salutary purpose.* This letter painted in the strongest colors the difficulties they apprehended, the embarrassments they felt, and the steps already taken to obtain relief. It contained the full opinion of that assembly relative to the late acts of parliament; while at the same time they expatiated [54] on their duty and attachment to the king, and detailed in terms of respect the representations that had been made to his ministers, they expressed the boldest determination to continue a free but a loyal people. Indeed there were few, if any, who indulged an idea of a final separation from Britain at so early a period; or that even wished for more than an equal participation of the privileges of the British constitution.

INDEPENDENCE was a plant of a later growth. Though the soil might be congenial, and the boundaries of nature pointed out the event, yet every one chose to view it at a distance, rather than wished to witness the convulsions that such a dismemberment of the empire must necessarily occasion.

After the circulation of this alarming letter,† wherever any of the governors had permitted the legislative bodies to meet, an answer was returned by the assemblies replete with encomiums on the exertion and the zeal of the Massachusetts. They observed that the spirit that dictated that letter was but a transcript of their own feelings; and that though equally impressed with every sentiment of respect to the prince on the throne of Britain, and feeling the strongest attachment to the house of Hanover, they could not but [55] reject with disdain the late measures, so repugnant to the dignity of the crown and the true interest of the realm; and that at every hazard they were determined to resist all acts of parliament for the injurious purpose of raising a revenue in America. They also added, that they had respectively offered the most humble supplications to the king; that they had remonstrated to both houses of parliament, and had

* See Appendix, Note, No. VI.
† See Appendix, Note, No. VII.

directed their agents at the British court to leave no effort untried to CHAP. III
obtain relief, without being compelled to what might be deemed by 1 7 6 8
royalty an illegal mode of opposition.

In consequence of the spirited proceedings of the house of representatives, the general assembly of Massachusetts was dissolved, nor
were they suffered to meet again until a new election. These
transactions were carefully transmitted to administration by several of
the plantation governors, and particularly Mr. Bernard, with inflammatory observations of his own, interlarded with the most illiberal
abuse of the principal leaders of the late measures in the assembly of
Massachusetts.

Their charter, which still provided for the election of the legislature,
obliged the governor to summon a new assembly to meet May the
twenty-fourth, one thousand seven hundred and sixty-eight. The first
communication laid before the house by the governor contained [56]
a haughty requisition from the British minister of state, directing in
his majesty's name that the present house should immediately *rescind*
the resolutions of a former one, which had produced the celebrated
circular letter. Governor Bernard also intimated, that it was his
majesty's pleasure, that on a non-compliance with this extraordinary
mandate, the present assembly should be dissolved without delay.

What heightened the resentment to the manner of this singular
order, signed by lord Hillsborough, secretary of state for the American
department, was, that he therein intimated to the governor that he
need not fear the most *unqualified obedience* on his part to the high
measures of administration, assuring him that it would not operate to
his disadvantage, as care would be taken in future to provide for his
interest, and to support the dignity of government, without the
interpositions or existence of a provincial legislature.

These messages were received by the representative body with a
steadiness and resolution becoming the defenders of the rights of a
free people. After appointing a committee to consider and prepare an
answer to them, they proceeded with great coolness to the usual
business of the session, without further notice of what had passed.

[57] Within a day or two, they received a second message from the
governor, purporting that he expected an immediate and an explicit
answer to the authoritative requisition; and that if they longer
postponed their resolutions, he should consider their delay as an
"oppugnation to his majesty's authority, and a negative to the command,
by an expiring faction." On this, the house desired time to consult

CHAP. III   their constituents on such an extraordinary question. This being
1 7 6 8   peremptorily and petulantly refused, the house ordered the board of
council to be informed, that they were entering on a debate of
importance, that they should give them notice when it was over, and
directed the door-keeper to call no member out, on any pretence
whatever.

The committee appointed to answer the governor's several messages, were gentlemen of known attachment to the cause of their
country, who on every occasion had rejected all servile compliances
with ministerial requisitions. They were not long on the business.
When they returned to the house, the galleries were immediately
cleared, and they reported an answer, bold and determined, yet
decent and loyal. In the course of their reply, they observed that it
was not an *"expiring faction,"* that the governor had charged with
"oppugnation to his majesty's authority," that it was the best blood of
the colony who opposed the ministerial measures, [58] men of
reputation, fortune and rank, equal to any who enjoyed the smiles of
government; that their exertions were from a conscious sense of duty
to their God, to their king, to their country, and to posterity.*

This committee at the same time reported a very spirited letter to
lord Hillsborough, which they had prepared to lay before the house.
In this they remonstrated on the injustice as well as absurdity of a
requisition, when a compliance was impracticable, even had they the
inclination to rescind the doings of a former house. This letter was
approved by the house, and on a division on the question of rescinding
the vote of a former assembly, it was negatived by a majority of
ninety-two to seventeen.

The same committee was immediately nominated to prepare a
petition to the king to remove Mr. Bernard from the government of
Massachusetts. They drew up a petition for this purpose without
leaving the house, and immediately reported it. They alleged a long
list of accusations against the governor, and requested his majesty
that one more worthy to represent so *great* and *good* a *king*, might be
sent to preside in the province. Thus impeached by the house, the
same [59] minority that had appeared ready to rescind the circular
letter, declared themselves against the impeachment of governor

---

* The principal members of this committee, were Major Joseph Hawley, of Northamp-
ton, James Otis, Esq. of Boston, Samuel Adams, James Warren, of Plymouth, John
Hancock, and Thomas Cushing, Esqrs.

Bernard.* Their servility was marked with peculiar odium: they were CHAP. III
stigmatized by the appellation of the *infamous seventeen*, until their 1 7 6 8
names were lost in a succession of great events and more important
characters.

When the doors of the house were opened, the secretary who had
been long in waiting for admission, informed the house that the
governor was in the chair, and desired their attendance in the council
chamber. They complied without hesitation, but were received in a
most ungracious manner. With much ill humor the governor reprimanded them in the language of an angry pedagogue, instead of the
manner becoming the first magistrate when addressing the representatives of a free people: he concluded his harangue by proroguing the
assembly, which within a few days he dissolved by proclamation.

In the mean time by warm and virulent letters from this indiscreet
governor; by others full of invective from the commissioners of the
customs, and by the *secret influence* of some, who yet concealed
themselves within the vizard of moderation, "who held the language
of patriotism, but trod in the footsteps of tyranny," [60] leave was
obtained from administration to apply to the commander in chief of
the king's troops, then at New York, to send several regiments to
Boston, as a necessary aid to civil government, which they represented
as too weak to suppress the disorders of the times. It was urged that
this step was absolutely necessary, to enable the officers of the crown
to carry into execution the laws of the supreme legislature.

A new pretext had been recently given to the malignant party, to
urge with a shew of plausibility, the immediate necessity of the
military arm, to quell the riotous proceedings of the town of Boston,
to strengthen the hands of government, and restore order and
tranquillity to the province. The seizure of a vessel belonging to a
popular gentleman,† under suspicion of a breach of the acts of trade,
raised a sudden resentment among the citizens of Boston. The conduct
of the owner was indeed reprehensible, in permitting a part of the
cargo to be unladen in a clandestine manner; but the mode of the
seizure appeared like a design to raise a sudden ferment, that might
be improved to corroborate the arguments for the necessity of standing
troops to be stationed within the town.

On a certain signal, a number of boats, manned and armed, rowed

* Journals of the house. [JHRM, 44; 45: 68–69, 89–94, 99–112.]
† John Hancock, Esq. afterwards governor of the Massachusetts.

CHAP. III   up to the wharf, cut the [61] fasts of the suspected vessel, carried her
1 7 6 8   off, and placed her under the stern of a ship of war, as if apprehensive
of a rescue. This was executed in the edge of the evening, when
apprentices and the younger classes were usually in the streets. It
had what was thought to be the desired effect; the inconsiderate
rabble, unapprehensive of the snare, and thoughtless of consequences,
pelted some of the custom-house officers with brick-bats, broke their
windows, drew one of their boats before the door of the gentleman
they thought injured, and set it on fire; after which they dispersed
without further mischief.

This trivial disturbance was exaggerated until it wore the complexion
of a riot of the first magnitude. By the insinuations of the party, and
their malignant conduct, it was not strange that in England it was
considered as a *London mob* collected in the streets of Boston, with
some formidable desperado at their head. After this *fracas*, the custom-
house officers repaired immediately to Castle William, as did the
board of commissioners. This fortress was about a league from the
town. From thence they expressed their apprehensions of personal
danger, in strong language. Fresh applications were made to general
Gage, to hasten on his forces from New York, assuring him that the
lives of the officers of the crown were insecure, unless placed beyond
the reach of popular resentment, [62] by an immediate military aid.
In consequence of these representations, several detachments from
Halifax, and two regiments lately from Ireland, were directed to repair
to Boston, with all possible dispatch.

The experience of all ages, and the observations both of the
historian and the philosopher agree, that a standing army is the most
ready engine in the hand of despotism, to debase the powers of the
human mind, and eradicate the manly spirit of freedom. The people
have certainly every thing to fear from a government, when the springs
of its authority are fortified only by a standing military force. Wherever
an army is established, it introduces a revolution in manners, corrupts
the morals, propagates every species of vice, and degrades the human
character. Threatened with the immediate introduction of this dread
calamity, deprived by the dissolution of their legislature of all power
to make any legal opposition; neglected by their sovereign, and
insulted by the governor he had set over them, much the largest part
of the community was convinced, that they had no resource but in
the strength of their virtues, the energy of their resolutions, and the
justice of their cause.

In this state of general apprehension, confusion, and suspense, the CHAP. III
inhabitants of Boston again requested governor Bernard to convoke 1 7 6 8
[63] an assembly, and suffer the representatives of the whole people
to consult and advise at this critical conjuncture. He rejected this
application with an air of insult, and no time was to be lost. Letters
were instantly forwarded from the capital, requesting a delegation of
suitable persons to meet in convention from every town in the province
before the arrival of the troops, and if possible to take some steps to
prevent the fatal effects of these dangerous and unprecedented
measures.

The whole country felt themselves interested, and readily complied
with the proposal. The most respectable persons from an hundred
and ninety-six towns were chosen delegates to assemble at Boston,
on the twenty-second of September. They accordingly met at that
time and place; as soon as they were convened, the governor sent
them an angry message, admonishing them immediately to disperse,
assuring them

> the king was determined to maintain his entire sovereignty over the
> province,—that their present meeting might be in consequence of their
> ignorance,—but that if after this admonition, they continued their *usur-*
> *pation*, they might repent their temerity, as he was determined to assert
> the authority of the crown in a more public manner, if they continued to
> disregard this authoritative warning.

[64] He however found he had not men to deal with, either ignorant
of law, regardless of its sanctions, or terrified by the frowns of power.
The convention made him a spirited but decent answer, containing
the reasons of their assembling, and the line of conduct they were
determined to pursue in spite of every menace. The governor refused
to receive their reply; he urged the illegality of the assembly, and
made use of every subterfuge to interrupt their proceedings.

Their situation was indeed truly delicate, as well as dangerous. The
convention was a body but known in the constitution of their
government, and in the strict sense of law it might be styled a
treasonable meeting. They still professed fealty to the crown of
Britain; and though the principle had been shaken by injuries, that
might have justified a more sudden renunciation of loyalty, yet their's
was cherished by a degree of religious scruple, amidst every species
of insult. Thus while they wished to support this temper, and to
cherish their former affection, they felt with poignancy the invasion

CHAP. III of their rights, and hourly expected the arrival of an armed force, to
1 7 6 8 back the threatenings of their first magistrate.

Great prudence and moderation however marked the transactions of an assembly of men [65] thus circumstanced; they could in their present situation only recapitulate their sufferings, felt and feared. This they did in a pointed and nervous style, in a letter addressed to Mr. De Berdt,* the agent of the province, residing in London. They stated the circumstances that occasioned their meeting, and a full detail of their proceedings. They inclosed him a petition to the king, and ordered their agent to deliver it with his own hand. The convention then separated, and returned to their respective towns, where they impressed on their constituents the same perseverance, forbearance and magnanimity that had marked their own resolutions.

Within a few days after their separation, the troops arrived from Halifax. This was indeed a painful era. The American war may be dated from the hostile parade of this day; a day which marks with infamy the councils of Britain. At this period, the inhabitants of the colonies almost universally breathed an unshaken loyalty to the king of England, and the strongest attachment to a country whence they derived their origin. Thus was the astonishment of the whole province excited, when to the grief and consternation of the town of Boston several regiments were landed, and marched sword in hand through the principal streets of their city, then in profound peace.

[66] The disembarkation of the king's troops, which took place on the first of October, one thousand seven hundred and sixty-eight, was viewed by a vast crowd of spectators, who beheld the solemn prelude to devastation and bloodshed with a kind of sullen silence, that denoted the deepest resentment. Yet whatever might be the feelings of the citizens, not one among the gazing multitude discovered any disposition to resist by arms the power and authority of the king of Great Britain. This appearance of decent submission and order was very unexpected to some, whose guilty fears had led them to expect a violent and tumultuous resistance to the landing of a large body of armed soldiers in the town. The peaceable demeanor of the people was construed, by the party who had brought this evil on the city, as a mark of abject submission.

As they supposed from the present acquiescent deportment, that

---

* See letter to Mr. De Berdt, in the journals of the house. [JHRM, 45: 64, 92, 149, 185, 195.]

the spirit of the inhabitants was totally subdued on the first appearance of military power, they consequently rose in their demands. General Gage arrived from New York soon after the king's troops reached Boston. With the aid of the governor, the chief justice of the province, and the sheriff of the county of Suffolk, he forced quarters for his soldiers in all the unoccupied houses in the town. The council convened on this occasion opposed the measure; but to such a height [67] was the insolence of power pushed, by their passionate, vindictive and wrong-headed governor, that in spite of the remonstrances of several magistrates, and the importunities of the people, he suffered the state house, where the archives of the province were deposited, to be improved as barracks for the king's troops. Thus the members of council, the magistrates of the town and the courts of justice were daily interrupted, and frequently challenged in their way to their several departments in business, by military centinels posted at the doors.

A standing army thus placed in their capital, their commerce fettered, their characters traduced, their representative body prevented meeting, the united petitions of all ranks that they might be convened at this critical conjuncture rejected by the governor; and still threatened with a further augmentation of troops to enforce measures in every view repugnant to the principles of the British constitution; little hope remained of a peaceful accommodation.

The most rational arguments had been urged by the legislative assemblies, by corporate bodies, associations, and individual characters of eminence, to shake the arbitrary system that augured evils to both countries. But their addresses were disdainfully rejected; the king and the court of Great Britain appeared equally deaf to the cry of millions, who only asked a restoration of their rights. At the same time [68] every worthless incendiary, who, taking advantage of these miserable times, crossed the Atlantic with a tale of accusation against his country, was listened to with attention, and rewarded with some token of royal favor.

In this situation, no remedy appeared to be left short of an appeal to the sword, unless an entire suspension of that commercial inter-course, which had contributed so much to the glory and grandeur of Britain, could be effected throughout the colonies. As all the American continent was involved in one common danger, it was not found difficult to obtain a general combination against all further importations from England, a few articles only excepted. The mercantile body

CHAP. III through all the provinces entered into solemn engagements, and
1 7 6 8 plighted their faith and honor to each other, and to their country, that
no orders should be forwarded by them for British or India goods
within a limited term, except for certain specified articles of necessary
use. These engagements originated in Boston, and were for a time
strictly adhered to through all the colonies. Great encouragement was
given to American manufactures, and if pride of apparel was at all
indulged, it was in wearing the stuffs fabricated in their own looms.
Harmony and union, prudence and economy, industry and virtue,
were inculcated in their publications, and enforced by the example
of the most respectable characters.

[69] In consequence of these determinations, the clamors of the
British manufacturers arose to tumult in many parts of the kingdom;
but no artifice was neglected to quiet the trading part of the nation.
There were some Americans, who by letters encouraged administration
to persevere in their measures relative to the colonies, assuring them
in the strongest terms, that the interruption of commerce was but a
temporary struggle, or rather an effort of despair. No one in the
country urged his opinion with more indiscreet zeal than Andrew
Oliver, Esq. then secretary in the Massachusetts. He suggested,

> that government should stipulate with the merchants in England to purchase
> large quantities of goods proper for the American market; agreeing
> beforehand to allow them a premium equal to the advance of their stock
> in trade, if the price of their goods was not sufficiently enhanced by a
> tenfold demand in future, even though the goods might lay on hand, till
> this temporary stagnation of business should cease.

He concluded his political rhapsody with this inhuman boast to his
correspondent;* *"By such a step the game will be up with my countrymen."*

The prediction on both sides the Atlantic, that this combination,
which depended wholly [70] on the commercial part of the community,
could not be of long duration, proved indeed too true. A regard to
private interest ever operates more forcibly on the bulk of mankind
than the ties of honor, or the principles of patriotism; and when the
latter are incompatible with the former, the balance seldom hangs
long in equilibrio. Thus it is not uncommon to see virtue, liberty,

---

* See the original letters of Mr. Oliver to Mr. Whately and others, which were
afterwards published in a pamphlet; also, in the British Remembrancer, 1773. [See
Hutchinson, *Letters;* (Mauduit), *Letters.*]

love of country, and regard to character, sacrificed at the shrine of
wealth.

The winter following this salutary combination, a partial repeal of
the act imposing duties on certain articles of British manufacture took
place. On this it immediately appeared that some in New York had
previously given conditional orders to their correspondents, that if the
measures of parliament should in any degree be relaxed, that without
farther application they should furnish them with large quantities of
goods. Several in the other colonies had discovered as much avidity
for an early importation as the Yorkers. They had given similar orders,
and both received larger supplies than usual, of British merchandize,
early in the spring one thousand seven hundred and sixty-nine. The
people of course considered the agreement nullified by the conduct
of the merchants, and the intercourse with England for a time went
on as usual, without any check. Thus, by breaking through the
agreement within the limited time of restriction, a measure was [71]
defeated, which, had it been religiously observed, might have prevented the tragical consequences which ensued.

After this event, a series of altercation and abuse, of recrimination
and suspense, was kept up on both sides the Atlantic, without much
appearance of lenity on the one side, or decision on the other. There
appeared little disposition in parliament to relax the reins of government, and less in the Americans to yield implicit obedience. But
whether from an opinion that they had taken the lead in opposition,
or whether from their having a greater proportion of British sycophants
among themselves, whose artful insinuations operated against their
country, or from other concurring circumstances, the Massachusetts
was still the principal butt of ministerial resentment. It is therefore
necessary yet to continue a more particular detail of the situation of
that province.

As their charter was not yet annihilated, governor Bernard found
himself under a necessity, as the period of annual election approached,
to issue writs to convene a general assembly. Accordingly a new house
of representatives met at Boston as usual on the thirty-first of May,
one thousand seven hundred and sixty-nine. They immediately
petitioned the governor to remove the military parade that surrounded
the state-house, urging, that such a hostile appearance [72] might
over-awe their proceedings, and prevent the freedom of election and
debate.

A unanimous resolve passed,

that it was the opinion of the house, that placing an armed force in the
metropolis while the general assembly is there convened, is a breach of
privilege, and totally inconsistent with the dignity and freedom with which
they ought to deliberate and determine;

adding

> that they meant ever to support their constitutional rights, that they should
> never voluntarily recede from their just claims, contained both in the letter
> and spirit of the constitution.

After several messages both from the council and house of representatives, the governor, ever obstinate in error, declared he had no
authority over the king's troops, nor should he use any influence to
have them removed.* Thus by express acknowledgement of the first
magistrate, it appeared that the military was set so far above the civil
authority, that the last was totally unable to check the wanton exercise
of this newly established power in the province. But the assembly
peremptorily determined to do no business while thus insulted by
the planting of cannon at the doors of the statehouse, and interrupted
in their solemn deliberations by the noisy evolutions of military
discipline.

[73] The royal charter required that they should proceed to the
choice of a speaker, and the election of a council, the first day of the
meeting of the assembly. They had conformed to this as usual, but
protested against its being considered as a precedent on any future
emergency. Thus amidst the warmest expressions of resentment from
all classes, for the indignity offered a free people by this haughty
treatment to their legislature, the governor suffered them to sit several
weeks without doing business; and at last compelled them to give
way to an armed force, by adjourning the general assembly to
Cambridge.

The internal state of the province required the attention of the
house at this critical exigence of affairs. They therefore, on their first
meeting at Cambridge, resolved,

> That it was their opinion that the British constitution admits no armed
> force within the realm, but for the purpose of offensive or defensive *war.*
> That placing troops in the colony in the midst of profound peace was a

---

* Journals of the house, one thousand seven hundred and sixty-nine. [JHRM, 45:
130–131, 135, 169–170 (the House's protest of a standing army); 132 (Bernard's
disavowal of authority to get rid of the troops).]

breach of privilege, an infraction on the natural rights of the people, and
manifestly subversive of that happy form of government they had hitherto
enjoyed. That the honor, dignity, and service of the sovereign should be
attended to by that assembly, so far as was consistent with the just rights
of the people, their own dignity, and the freedom of debate; but that
proceeding [74] to business while an armed force was quartered in the
province, was not a dereliction of the privileges legally claimed by the
colony, but from necessity, and that no undue advantage should be taken
from their compliance.

After this, they had not time to do any other business, before two
messages of a very extraordinary nature, in their opinion, were laid
before them.* The first was an order under the sign-manual of the
king, that Mr. Bernard should repair to England to lay the state of
the province before him. To this message was tacked a request from
the governor, that as he attended his majesty's pleasure as commander
in chief of the province, his salary might be continued, though absent.
The substance of the other message was an account of general Gage's
expenditures in quartering his troops in the town of Boston; accompanied by an unqualified demand for the establishment of funds for
the discharge thereof. The governor added, that he was requested by
general Gage to make requisition for future provision for quartering
his troops within the town.

The subsequent resolves of the house on these messages were
conformable to the usual spirit of that assembly. They warmly censured
[75] both governor Bernard and general Gage for wantonly acting
against the constitution; charged them with making false and injurious
representations against his majesty's faithful subjects, and discovering
on all occasions a most inimical disposition towards the colonies. They
observed that general Gage had rashly and impertinently intermeddled
with affairs altogether out of his line, and that he had betrayed a
degree of ignorance equal to his malice, when he presumed to touch
on the civil police of the province. They complained heavily of the
arbitrary designs of government, the introduction of a standing army,
and the encroachments on civil liberty; and concluded with a declaration replete with sentiments of men conscious of their own freedom
and integrity, and deeply affected with the injuries offered their
country. They observed, that to the utmost of their power they should
vindicate the rights of human nature and the privileges of Englishmen,

* Journals of the first session at Cambridge. [JHRM, 45: 132–133.]

and explicitly declared that duty to their constituents forbade a
compliance with either of these messages. This clear, decided answer
being delivered, the governor summoned the house to attend, and
after a short, angry, and threatening speech, he prorogued the assembly
to January, one thousand seven hundred and seventy.

Governor Bernard immediately embarked for Europe, from whence
he never more returned [76] to a country, he had, by his arbitrary
disposition and indiscreet conduct, inflamed to a degree, that required
both judgment and prudence to cool, perhaps beyond the abilities,
and certainly incompatible with the views, of the administration in
being.

The province had little reason to suppose, that considerations of
the interest of the people had any part in the recal or detention of
this mischievous emissary. His reception at court, the summary
proceedings with regard to his impeachment and trial, and the character
of the man appointed to succeed him, strongly counteracted such a
flattering opinion. Notwithstanding the high charges that had been
alleged against governor Bernard, he was acquitted by the king and
council, without allowing time to the assembly to support their
accusations, honored with a title, and rewarded with a pension of one
thousand pounds sterling per annum on the Irish establishment.

Governor Bernard had reason to be perfectly satisfied with the
success of his appointment to the government of Massachusetts, as it
related to his personal interest. His conduct there procured him the
smiles of the British court, an honorary title, and a pension for life.
Besides this, the legislature of that province had in the early part of
his administration, in a moment of complacency, or perhaps from
digested [77] policy, with a hope of bribing him to his duty and
stimulating him to defend their invaded rights, made him a grant of
a very large tract of land, the whole of the island of Mount Desert.
This was afterwards reclaimed by a Madame Gregoire, in right of her
ancestors, who had obtained a patent of some part of that country in
the early days of European emigration. But as governor Bernard's
property in America had never been confiscated, the general assembly
of Massachusetts afterwards granted to his son, Sir John Bernard, who
still possesses this territory, two townships of land near the river
Kennebeck, in lieu of the valuable isle recovered by Madame Gregoire.

CHAPTER IV

Character of Mr. Hutchinson • Appointed Governor of Massachu-setts • The attempted Assassination of Mr. Otis • Transactions on the fifth of March, one thousand seven hundred and seventy • Arrival of the East India Company's Tea-Ships • Establishment of Committees of Cor-respondence • The Right of Parliamentary Taxation without Represen-tation urged by Mr. Hutchinson • Articles of Impeachment resolved on in the House of Representatives against Governor Hutchinson and Lieutenant Governor Oliver • Chief Justice of the Province impeached • Boston Port-Bill • Governor Hutchinson leaves the Province

[78] It is ever painful to a candid mind to exhibit the deformed features of its own species; yet truth requires a just portrait of the public delinquent, though he may possess such a share of private virtue as would lead us to esteem the man in his domestic character, while we detest his political, and execrate his public transactions.

The barriers of the British constitution broken over, and the ministry encouraged by their sovereign, to pursue the iniquitous system against the colonies to the most alarming extremities, they probably judged it a prudent expedient, in order to curb the refractory spirit of the Massachusetts, perhaps bolder in sentiment and earlier in opposition than some of the other colonies, to appoint a man to preside [79] over them who had renounced the *quondam* ideas of public virtue, and sacrificed all principle of that nature on the altar of ambition.

Soon after the recal of Mr. Bernard, Thomas Hutchinson, Esq. a native of Boston, was appointed to the government of Massachusetts. All who yet remember his pernicious administration and the fatal consequences that ensued, agree, that few ages have produced a more fit instrument for the purposes of a corrupt court. He was dark, intriguing, insinuating, haughty and ambitious, while the extreme of avarice marked each feature of his character. His abilities were little

elevated above the line of mediocrity; yet by dint of industry, exact
temperance, and indefatigable labor, he became master of the accomplishments necessary to acquire popular fame. Though bred a merchant, he had looked into the origin and the principles of the British
constitution, and made himself acquainted with the several forms of
government established in the colonies; he had acquired some knowledge of the *common law* of England, diligently studied the intricacies
of *Machiavelian* policy, and never failed to recommend the Italian
master as a model to his adherents.

Raised and distinguished by every honor the people could bestow,
he supported for several years the reputation of integrity, and generally
[80] decided with equity in his judicial capacity;* and by the appearance
of a tenacious regard to the religious institutions of his country, he
courted the public *eclat* with the most profound dissimulation, while
he engaged the affections of the lower classes by an amiable civility
and condescension, without departing from a certain gravity of
deportment mistaken by the vulgar for *sanctity*.

The inhabitants of the Massachusetts were the lineal descendants
of the *puritans,* who had struggled in England for liberty as early as
the reign of Edward the sixth; and though obscured in the subsequent
bloody persecutions, even Mr. Hume has acknowledged that to them
England is indebted for the liberty she enjoys.† Attached to the
religious forms of their ancestors, equally disgusted with the hierarchy
of the church of England, and prejudiced by the severities their
fathers had experienced before their emigration, they had, both by
education and principle, been always led to consider the religious as
well as the political characters of those they deputed to the highest
trust. Thus a profession of their own religious mode of worship, and
sometimes a tincture of superstition, was with many a higher recommendation than brilliant talents. This [81] accounts in some measure
for the unlimited confidence long placed in the specious accomplishments of Mr. Hutchinson, whose character was not thoroughly
investigated until some time after governor Bernard left the province.

But it was known at St. James's, that in proportion as Mr. Hutchinson
gained the confidence of administration, he lost the esteem of the
best of his countrymen; for this reason, his advancement to the chair
of government was for a time postponed or concealed, lest the people
should consider themselves insulted by such an appointment, and

* Judge of probate for the county of Suffolk, and chief justice of the supreme court.
† Hume's History of England. [David Hume, *The History of England Under the House
of Tudor* (2 vols.; London, 1759), II: 505–509.]

become too suddenly irritated. Appearances had for several years been strong against him, though it was not then fully known that he had seized the opportunity to undermine the happiness of the people, while he had their fullest confidence, and to barter the liberties of his country by the most shameless duplicity. This was soon after displayed beyond all contradiction, by the recovery of sundry letters to administration under his signature.

Mr. Hutchinson was one of the first in America who felt the full weight of popular resentment. His furniture was destroyed, and his house levelled to the ground, in the tumults occasioned by the news of the stamp-act. Ample compensation was indeed afterwards made [82] him for the loss of property, but the strong prejudices against his political character were never eradicated.

All pretences to moderation on the part of the British government now laid aside, the full appointment of Mr. Hutchinson to the government of the Massachusetts was publickly announced at the close of the year one thousand seven hundred and sixty-nine. On his promotion the new governor uniformly observed a more high-handed and haughty tone than his predecessor. He immediately, by an explicit declaration, avowed his independence on the people, and informed the legislative that his majesty had made ample provision for his support without their aid or suffrages. The vigilant guardians of the rights of the people directly called upon him to relinquish the unconstitutional stipend, and to accept the free grants of the general assembly for his subsistence, as usually practised. He replied that an acceptance of this offer would be a breach of his instructions from the king. This was his constant apology for every arbitrary step.

Secure of the favor of his sovereign, and now regardless of the popularity he had formerly courted with such avidity, he decidedly rejected the idea of responsibility to, or dependence on, the people. With equal inflexibility he disregarded all arguments used for the removal of the troops from the capital, and permission to the [83] council and house of representatives to return to the usual seat of government. He silently heard their solicitations for this purpose, and as if with a design to pour contempt on their supplications and complaints, he within a few days after withdrew a garrison, in the pay of the province, from a strong fortress in the harbour of Boston; placed two regiments of the king's troops in their stead, and delivered the keys of the castle to colonel Dalrymple, who then commanded the king's troops through the province.

These steps, which seemed to bid defiance to complaint, created

CHAP. IV   new fears in the minds of the people. It required the utmost vigilance
1 7 7 0   to quiet the murmurs and prevent the fatal consequences apprehended
from the ebullitions of popular resentment. But cool, deliberate and
persevering, the two houses continued to resolve, remonstrate, and
protest, against the infractions on their charter, and every dangerous
innovation on their rights and privileges. Indeed the intrepid and
spirited conduct of those, who stood forth undaunted at this early
crisis of hazard, will dignify their names so long as the public records
shall remain to witness their patriotic firmness.

Many circumstances rendered it evident that the ministerial party
wished a spirit of opposition to the designs of the court might break
out into violence, even at the expense of blood. This they thought
would in some degree have [84] sanctioned a measure suggested by
one of the faction in America, devoted to the arbitrary system, "That
some method must be devised, to take off the original *incendiaries**
whose writings instilled the poison of sedition through the vehicle of
the Boston Gazette"†

Had this advice been followed, and a few gentlemen of integrity
and ability, who had spirit sufficient to make an effort in favor of
their country in each colony, have been seized at the same moment,
and immolated early in the contest on the bloody altar of power,
perhaps Great Britain might have held the continent in subjection a
few years longer.

That they had measures of this nature in contemplation there is
not a doubt. Several [85] instances of a less atrocious nature confirmed
this opinion, and the turpitude of design which at this period actuated

* See Andrew Oliver's letter to one of the ministry, dated February 13, 1769.
[Hutchinson, *Letters,* p. 28; (Mauduit), *Letters,* pp. 30–31. Also see, JHRM, 45: 130–
135.]

† This gazette was much celebrated for the freedom of its disquisitions in favor of
civil liberty. It has been observed that

> it will be a treasury of political intelligence for the historians of this country. Otis,
> Thacher, Dexter, Adams, Warren and Quincy, Doctors Samuel Cooper and
> Mayhew, stars of the first magnitude in our northern hemisphere, whose glory
> and brightness distant ages will admire; these gentlemen of character and influence
> offered their first essays to the public through the medium of the Boston Gazette,
> on which account the paper became odious to the friends of prerogative, but not
> more disgusting to the tories and high church than it was pleasing to the whigs.

See collection of the Massachusetts Historical Society. ["Continuation of the
Narrative of Newspapers Published in New-England, from the Year 1704 to the
Revolution. . . ." MHS, *Collections,* first series, VI (1799): 70.]

the court party was clearly evinced by the attempted assassination of
the celebrated Mr. Otis, justly deemed the first martyr to American
freedom; and truth will enroll his name among the most distinguished
patriots who have expired on the "blood-stained theatre of human
action."

This gentleman, whose birth and education was equal to any in
the province, possessed an easy fortune, independent principles, a
comprehensive genius, strong mind, retentive memory, and great
penetration. To these endowments may be added that extensive
professional knowledge, which at once forms the character of the
complete civilian and the able statesman.

In his public speeches, the sire of eloquence, the acumen of
argument, and the lively sallies of wit, at once warmed the bosom of
the stoic and commanded the admiration of his enemies. To his
probity and generosity in the public walks were added the charms of
affability and improving converse in private life. His humanity was
conspicuous, his sincerity acknowledged, his integrity unimpeached,
his honor unblemished, and his patriotism marked with the disinterestedness of the Spartan. Yet he was susceptible of quick feelings
and warm passions, which in the ebullitions of zeal for the interest of
his country sometimes betrayed him into [86] unguarded epithets that
gave his foes an advantage, without benefit to the cause that lay
nearest his heart.

He had been affronted by the partizans of the crown, vilified in
the public papers, and treated (after his resignation of office*) in a
manner too gross for a man of his spirit to pass over with impunity.
Fearless of consequences, he had always given the world his opinions
both in his writings and his conversation, and had recently published
some severe strictures on the conduct of the commissioners of the
customs and others of the ministerial party, and bidding defiance to
resentment, he supported his allegations by the signature of his name.

A few days after this publication appeared, Mr. Otis with only one
gentleman in company was suddenly assaulted in a public room, by
a band of ruffians armed with swords and bludgeons. They were
headed by John Robinson, one of the commissioners of the customs.
The lights were immediately extinguished, and Mr. Otis covered with
wounds was left for dead, while the assassins made their way through
the crowd which began to assemble; and before their crime was

* Office of judge advocate in governor Bernard's administration.

CHAP. IV   discovered, fortunately for themselves, they escaped soon enough to
1 7 7 0   take refuge on board one of the king's ships which then lay in the
harbor.

[87] In a state of nature, the savage may throw his poisoned arrow
at the man, whose soul exhibits a transcript of benevolence that
upbraids his own ferocity, and may boast his blood-thirsty deed among
the hordes of the forest without disgrace; but in a high stage of
civilization, where humanity is cherished, and politeness is become a
science, for the dark assassin then to level his blow at superior merit,
and screen himself in the arms of power, reflects an odium on the
government that permits it, and puts human nature to the blush.

The party had a complete triumph in this guilty deed; for though
the wounds did not prove mortal, the consequences were tenfold
worse than death. The future usefulness of this distinguished *friend*
of his country was destroyed, reason was shaken from its throne,
genius obscured, and the great man in ruins lived several years for
his friends to weep over, and his country to lament the deprivation
of talents admirably adapted to promote the highest interests of
society.

This catastrophe shocked the feelings of the virtuous not less than
it raised the indignation of the brave. Yet a remarkable spirit of
forbearance continued for a time, owing to the respect still paid to
the opinions of this unfortunate gentleman, whose voice though always
opposed to the strides of despotism was ever loud against all tumultuous
and illegal proceedings. [88] He was after a partial recovery sensible
himself of his incapacity for the exercise of talents that had shone
with peculiar lustre, and often invoked the messenger of death to
give him a sudden release from a life become burdensome in every
view but when the calm interval of a moment permitted him the
recollection of his own integrity. In one of those intervals of beclouded
reason he forgave the murderous band, after the principal ruffian had
asked pardon in a court of justice;* and at the intercession of the
gentleman whom he had so grossly abused, the people forebore
inflicting that summary vengeance which was generally thought due
to so black a crime.

Mr. Otis lived to see the independence of America, though in a
state of mind incapable of enjoying fully the glorious event which his

---

* On a civil process commenced against him, John Robinson was adjudged to pay five
thousand pounds sterling damages; but Mr. Otis despising all pecuniary compensation, relinquished it on the culprit's asking pardon and setting his signature on a
very humble acknowledgment.

own exertions had precipitated. After several years of mental derangement, as if in consequence of his own prayers, his great soul was
instantly set free by a flash of lightning, from the evils in which the
love of his country had involved him. His death took place in May,
one thousand seven hundred and eighty [89] three, the same year the
peace was concluded between Great Britain and America.*

Though the parliamentary system of colonial regulations was in
many instances similar, and equally aimed to curtail the privileges of
each province, yet no military force had been expressly called in aid
of civil authority in any of them, except the Massachusetts. From this
circumstance [90] some began to flatter themselves that more lenient
dispositions were operating in the mind of the king of Great Britain,
as well as in the parliament and the people towards America in
general.

They had grounded these hopes on the strong assurances of several
of the plantation governors, particularly lord Botetourt, who then
presided in Virginia. He had in a speech to the assembly of the
colony, in the winter of one thousand seven hundred and sixty-nine,
declared himself so confident that full satisfaction would be given to
the provinces in the future conduct of administration, that he pledged
his faith to support to the last hour of his life the interest of America.
He observed, that he grounded his own opinions and his assurances
to them, on the intimations of the confidential servants of the king

---

* A sister touched by the tenderest feelings, while she has thought it her duty to do
justice to a character neglected by some, and misrepresented by other historians,
can exculpate herself from all suspicion of partiality by the testimony of many of
his countrymen who witnessed his private merit and public exertions. But she will
however only subjoin a paragraph of a letter written to the author of these annals,
on the news of Mr. Otis's death, by John Adams, Esq. then minister plenipotentiary
from the United States to the court of France.

Paris, September 10th, 1783.

It was, Madam, with very afflicting sentiments I learned the death of Mr. Otis,
my worthy master. Extraordinary in death as in life, he has left a character that
will never die while the memory of the American revolution remains; whose
foundation he laid with an energy, and with those masterly abilities, which no
other man possessed. [WAL, II: 223–224.]

The reader also may not be displeased at an extemporary exclamation of a
gentleman of poetic talents, on hearing of the death of Mr. Otis.

> "When God in anger saw the spot,
>   On earth to Otis given,
>   In thunder as from Sinai's mount,
>   He snatch'd him back to heaven."

CHAP. IV which authorized him to promise redress. He added, that to his certain
1 7 7 0 knowledge his sovereign had rather part with his crown, than preserve
it by deception.

The credulity of this gentleman was undoubtedly imposed upon;
however, the Virginians, ever steady and systematic in opposition to
tyranny, were for a time highly gratified by those assurances from
their first magistrate. But their vigilance was soon called into exercise
by the mal-administration of a succeeding governor, though the
fortitude of this patriotic [91] colony was never shaken by the frown
of any despotic master or masters. Some of the other colonies had
listened to the soothing language of moderation used by their chief
executive officers, and were for a short time influenced by that, and
the flattering hopes held up by the governor of Virginia.

But before the period to which we have arrived in the narration of
events, these flattering appearances had evaporated with the breath
of the courtier. The subsequent conduct of administration baffled the
expectations of the credulous. The hand of government was more
heavily felt through the continent; and from South Carolina to Virginia,
and from Virginia to New Hampshire, the mandate of a minister was
the signal for the dissolution of their assemblies. The people were
compelled to resort to conventions and committees to transact all
public business, to unite in petitions for relief, or to take the necessary
preparatory steps if finally obliged to resist by arms.

In the mean time the inhabitants of the town of Boston had suffered
almost every species of insult from the British soldiery; who, countenanced by the royal party, had generally found means to screen
themselves from the hand of the civil officers. Thus all authority
rested on the point of the sword, and the partizans of the crown
triumphed for a time in the plenitude of [92] military power. Yet the
measure and the manner of posting troops in the capital of the
province, had roused such jealousy and disgust, as could not be
subdued by the scourge that hung over their heads. Continual
bickerings took place in the streets between the soldiers and the
citizens; the insolence of the first, which had been carried so far as
to excite the African slaves to murder their masters, with the promise
of impunity,* and the indiscretion of the last, was often productive

---

* Capt. Wilson of the 29th regiment was detected in the infamous practice; and it
  was proved beyond a doubt by the testimony of some respectable citizens, who
  declared on oath, that they had accidentally witnessed the offer of reward to the
  blacks, by some subaltern officers, if they would rob and murder their masters.

of tumults and disorder that led the most cool and temperate to be
apprehensive of consequences of the most serious nature.

No previous outrage had given such a general alarm, as the commotion on the fifth of March, one thousand seven hundred and seventy. Yet the accident that created a resentment which emboldened the timid, determined the wavering, and awakened an energy and decision that neither the artifices of the courtier, nor the terror of the sword could easily overcome, arose from a trivial circumstance; a circumstance which but from the consideration that these minute accidents frequently lead to [93] the most important events, would be beneath the dignity of history to record.

A centinel posted at the door of the custom house had seized and abused a boy, for casting some opprobrious reflections on an officer of rank; his cries collected a number of other lads, who took the childish revenge of pelting the soldier with snow-balls. The main-guard stationed in the neighborhood of the custom-house, was informed by some persons from thence, of the rising tumult. They immediately turned out under the command of a captain Preston, and beat to arms. Several *fracas* of little moment had taken place between the soldiery and some of the lower class of inhabitants, and probably both were in a temper to avenge their own private wrongs. The cry of fire was raised in all parts of the town, the mob collected, and the soldiery from all quarters ran through the streets sword in hand, threatening and wounding the people, and with every appearance of hostility, they rushed furiously to the centre of the town.

The soldiers thus ready for execution, and the populace grown outrageous, the whole town was justly terrified by the unusual alarm. This naturally drew out persons of higher condition, and more peaceably disposed, to inquire the cause. Their consternation can scarcely be described, when they found orders were given to [94] fire promiscuously among the unarmed multitude. Five or six persons fell at the first fire, and several more were dangerously wounded at their own doors.

These sudden popular commotions are seldom to be justified, and their consequences are ever to be dreaded. It is needless to make any observations on the assumed rights of royalty, in a time of peace to disperse by military murder the disorderly and riotous assemblage of a thoughtless multitude. The question has frequently been canvassed; and was on this occasion thoroughly discussed, by gentlemen of the first professional abilities.

The remains of loyalty to the sovereign of Britain were not yet extinguished in American bosoms, neither were the feelings of compassion, which shrunk at the idea of human carnage, obliterated. Yet this outrage enkindled a general resentment that could not be disguised; but every method that prudence could dictate, was used by a number of influential gentlemen to cool the sudden ferment, to prevent the populace from attempting immediate vengeance, and to prevail on the multitude to retire quietly to their own houses, and wait the decisions of law and equity. They effected their humane purposes; the people dispersed; and captain Preston and his party were taken into custody of the civil magistrate. A judicial inquiry was afterwards [95] made into their conduct; and so far from being actuated by any partial or undue bias, some of the first counsellors at law engaged in their defence; and after a fair and legal trial they were acquitted of premeditated or wilful murder, by a jury of the county of Suffolk.

The people, not dismayed by the blood of their neighbors thus wantonly shed, determined no longer to submit to the insolence of military power. Colonel Dalrymple, who commanded in Boston, was informed the day after the riot in King Street, "that he must withdraw his troops from the town within a limited term, or hazard the consequences."

The inhabitants of the town assembled in Faneuil Hall, where the subject was discussed with becoming spirit, and the people unanimously resolved, that no armed force should be suffered longer to reside in the capital; that if the king's troops were not immediately withdrawn by their own officers, the governor should be requested to give orders for their removal, and thereby prevent the necessity of more rigorous steps. A committee from the body was deputed to wait on the governor, and request him to exert that authority which the exigencies of the times required from the supreme magistrate. Mr. Samuel Adams, the chairman of the committee, with a pathos and address peculiar to [96] himself, exposed the illegality of quartering troops in the town in the midst of peace; he urged the apprehensions of the people, and the fatal consequences that might ensue if their removal was delayed.

But no arguments could prevail on Mr. Hutchinson; who either from timidity, or some more censurable cause, evaded acting at all in the business, and grounded his refusal on a pretended want of

authority.* After which, colonel Dalrymple, wishing to compromise
the matter, consented that the twenty-ninth regiment, more culpable
than any other in the late tumult, should be sent to Castle Island.
This concession was by no means satisfactory; the people, inflexible
in their demands, insisted that not one British soldier should be left
within the town; their requisition was reluctantly complied with, and
within four days the whole army decamped. It is not to be supposed,
that this compliance of British veterans originated in their fears of an
injured and incensed people, who were not yet prepared to resist by
arms. They were undoubtedly sensible they had exceeded their
orders, and anticipated the designs of their master; they had rashly
begun the slaughter of Americans, and enkindled the flames of civil
war in a country, where allegiance had not yet been renounced.

[97] After the hasty retreat of the king's troops, Boston enjoyed for
a time, a degree of tranquillity to which they had been strangers for
many months. The commissioners of the customs and several other
obnoxious characters retired with the army to Castle William, and
their governor affected much moderation and tenderness to his country;
at the same time he neglected no opportunity to ripen the present
measures of administration, or to secure his own interest, closely
interwoven therewith. The duplicity of Mr. Hutchinson was soon
after laid open by the discovery of a number of letters under his
signature, written to some individuals in the British cabinet. These
letters detected by the vigilance of some friends in England, were
procured and sent on to America.†

Previous to this event there were many persons in the province
who could not be fully convinced, that at the same period when he
had put on the guise of compassion to his country, when he had
promised all his influence to obtain some relaxation of the coercive

* See extracts of Mr. Hutchinson's letters, Appendix, No. VIII.

† The original letters which detected his treachery were procured by Doct. Franklin,
  and published in a pamphlet at Boston. They may also be seen in the British Annual
  Register, and in a large collection of historical papers printed in London, entitled
  the Remembrancer. The agitation into which many were thrown by the transmission
  of these letters, produced important consequences. Doct. Franklin was shamefully
  vilified and abused in an outrageous *philippic* pronounced by Mr. Wedderburne,
  afterwards lord Loughborough. Threats, challenges, and duels took place, but it
  was not discovered by what means these letters fell into the hands of Doct. Franklin,
  who soon after repaired to America, where he was eminently serviceable in aid of
  the public cause of his native country.

CHAP. IV system, that at that moment Mr. Hutchinson should be so soft to the
1 7 7 0 ideas of sincerity, as to be artfully plotting new embarrassments to
the colonies in general, and the most mischievous projects against the
province he was entrusted to govern. Thus convicted as the grand
incendiary [98] who had sown the seeds of discord, and cherished the
dispute between Great Britain and the colonies, his friends blushed
at the discovery, his enemies triumphed, and his partizans were
confounded. In these letters, he had expressed his doubt of the
propriety of suffering the colonies to enjoy all the privileges of the
parent state: he observed, that "there must be an *abridgment of English
liberties*, in colonial administration," and urged with malignant art the
necessity of the resumption of the charter of Massachusetts.

Through this and the succeeding year the British nation were much
divided in opinion relative to public measures, both at home and
abroad. Debates and animosities ran high in both houses of parliament.
Many of their best orators had come forward in defence of America,
with that eloquence and precision which [99] proved their ancestry,
and marked the spirit of a nation that had long boasted their own
freedom. But reason and argument are feeble barriers against the will
of a monarch, or the determinations of potent aristocratical bodies.
Thus the system was fixed, the measures were ripening, and a minister
had the boldness to declare publickly, that "America should be
brought to the footstool of parliament,"* and humbled beneath the
pedestal of majesty.

The inhabitants of the whole American continent, appeared even
at this period nearly ready for the last appeal, rather than longer to
submit to the mandates of an overbearing minister of state, or the
execution of his corrupt designs. The masterly writers of this enlightened age, had so clearly defined the nature and origin of government,
the equal claims and natural rights of man, the principles of the
British constitution, and the freedom the subject had a right to enjoy
thereby; that it had become a prevailing opinion, that government
and legislation were instituted for the benefit of society at large, and
not for the emolument of a few; and that whenever prerogative began
to stretch its rapacious arm beyond certain bounds, it was an indispensable duty to resist.

---

* Lord North's speech in the house of commons. [Cobbett records Lord North
speaking on numerous occasions in 1770. On only two occasions could his language
be construed as MOW does, though on neither did he use the term "footstool."
Cobbett, XVI: 714–720 (January, 1770) and 853–855 (March 5, 1770).]

Strongly attached to Great Britain, not only by the impression of CHAP. IV
ancient forms, and the habits [100] of submission to government, but 1 7 7 0
by religion, manners, language, and consanguinity, the colonies still
stood suspended in the pacific hope, that a change of ministry or a
new parliament, might operate in their favor, and restore tranquillity,
by the removal of the causes and the instruments of their sufferings.

Not yet conscious of her own strength, and scarcely ambitious of
taking an independent rank among the nations, America still cherished
the flattering ideas of reconciliation. But these expectations were
finally dissipated, by the repeated attempts to reduce the colonies to
unlimited submission to the supreme jurisdiction of parliament, and
the illegal exactions of the crown, until by degrees all parliamentary
decisions became as indifferent to an American ear, as the rescripts
of a Turkish divan.

The tame acquiescence of the colonies, would doubtless have given
great advantages to the corrupt party on one side of the Atlantic,
while their assiduous agents on the other, did not revolt at the meanest
and most wicked compliances to facilitate the designs of their
employers, or to gratify their own inordinate passion for power and
wealth. Thus for a considerable time, a struggle was kept up between
the power of one country, and the perseverance of the other, without
a possibility of calculating consequences.

[101] A particular detail of the altercations between the representatives, the burgesses, and the provincial governors, the remonstrances
of the people, the resolves of their legislative bodies, and the
dissolution of their assemblies by the *fiat* of a governor, the prayers
of corporate and occupational societies, or the petitions of more public
and respectable bodies; the provocations on the side of government,
and the riotous, and in some degree, unjustifiable proceedings of the
populace, in almost every town on the continent, would be rather
tedious than entertaining, in a compendious narrative of the times. It
may therefore, be well to pass over a year or two, that produced
nothing but a sameness of complaint, and a similarity of opposition,
on the one side; and on the other, a systematic effort, to push the
darling measure of an American taxation, while neither party had
much reason to promise themselves a speedy decision.

It has already been observed, that the revenue acts which had
occasioned a general murmur, had been repealed, except a small duty
on all India teas, by which a claim was kept up to tax the colonies at
pleasure, whenever it should be thought expedient. This was an

CHAP. IV article used by all ranks in America; a luxury of such universal
1 7 7 0 consumption, that administration was led to believe, that a monopoly
of the sales of tea, might be so managed, as to become a productive
source of revenue.

[102] It was generally believed that governor Hutchinson had
stipulated for the agency for his sons, as they were the first in
commission; and that he had solicited for them, and obtained this
odious employment, by a promise, that if they were appointed sole
agents to the East India company, the sales should be so executed as
to give perfect satisfaction, both to them and to administration. All
communities furnish examples of men sufficiently base, to share in
the spoils of their country; nor was it difficult to find such in every
colony, who were ready enough to execute this ministerial job. Thus
in consequence of the insinuations of those interested in the success
of the measure, a number of ships were employed by government,
to transport a large quantity of teas into each of the American colonies.
The people throughout the continent, apprized of the design, and
considering at that time, all teas a pernicious article of commerce,
summoned meetings in all the capital towns, and unanimously resolved
to resist the dangerous project by every legal opposition, before they
proceeded to any extremities.

The first step taken in Boston, was to request the consignees to
refuse the commission. The inhabitants warmly remonstrated against
the teas being landed in any of their ports, and urged the return of
the ships, without permitting them to break bulk. The commissioners
at [103] New York, Philadelphia, and in several other colonies, were
applied to with similar requests; most of them complied. In some
places the teas were stored on proper conditions, in others, sent back
without injury. But, in Massachusetts, their difficulties were accumulated by the restless ambition of some of her own degenerate sons.
Not the smallest impression was made on the feelings of their governor,
by the united supplications of the inhabitants of Boston and its
environs. Mr. Hutchinson, who very well knew that virtue is seldom
a sufficient restraint to the passions, but that, in spite of patriotism,
reason, or religion, the scale too frequently preponderates in favor of
interest or appetite, persisted in the execution of his favorite project.
As by force of habit, this drug had become almost a necessary article
of diet, the demand for teas in America was astonishingly great, and
the agents in Boston, sure of finding purchasers, if once the weed
was deposited in their stores, haughtily declined a resignation of

office, and determined when the ships arrived, to receive and dispose
of their cargoes at every hazard.

Before either time or discretion had cooled the general disgust, at
the interested and supercilious behaviour of these young pupils of
intrigue, the long expected ships arrived, which were to establish a
precedent, thought dangerously consequential. Resolved not to yield
to the smallest vestige of parliamentary taxation, [104] however
disguised, a numerous assembly of the most respectable people of
Boston and its neighborhood, repaired to the public hall, and drew
up a remonstrance to the governor, urging the necessity of his order,
to send back the ships without suffering any part of their cargoes to
be landed. His answer confirmed the opinion, that he was the instigator
of the measure; it irritated the spirits of the people, and tended more
to encrease, than allay the rising ferment.

A few days after this the factors had the precaution to apply to the
governor and council for protection, to enable them to receive and
dispose of their consignments. As the council refused to act in the
affair, the governor called on colonel Hancock, who commanded a
company of cadets, to hold himself in readiness to assist the civil
magistrate, if any tumult should arise in consequence of any attempt
to land the teas. This gentleman, though professedly in opposition
to the court, had oscillated between the parties until neither of them
at that time, had much confidence in his exertions. It did not however
appear, that he had any inclination to obey the summons; neither did
he explicitly refuse; but he soon after resigned his commission, and
continued in future, unequivocally opposed to the ministerial system.
On the appearance of this persevering spirit among the people,
governor Hutchinson again resorted to his usual arts of chicanery and
deception; he affected a mildness of deportment, [105] and by many
equivocal delays detained the ships, and endeavoured to disarm his
countrymen of that manly resolution which was their principal *fort*.

The storage or detention of a few cargoes of teas is not an object
in itself sufficient to justify a detail of several pages; but as the
subsequent severities towards the Massachusetts were grounded on
what the ministry termed their *refractory behaviour* on this occasion;
and as those measures were followed by consequences of the highest
magnitude both to Great Britain and the colonies, a particular narration
of the transactions of the town of Boston is indispensable. There the
sword of civil discord was first drawn, which was not re-sheathed until
the emancipation of the thirteen colonies from the yoke of foreign

CHAP. IV   domination was acknowledged by the diplomatic seals of the first
1 7 7 3   powers in Europe. This may apologize, if necessary, for the appearance
of locality in the preceding pages, and for its farther continuance in
regard to a colony, on which the bitterest cup of ministerial wrath
was poured for a time, and where the energies of the human mind
were earlier called forth, than in several of the sister states.

Not intimidated by the frowns of greatness, nor allured by the
smiles of intrigue, the vigilance of the people was equal to the
importance of the event. Though expectation was equally [106] awake
in both parties, yet three or four weeks elapsed in a kind of *inertia;*
the one side flattered themselves with hopes, that as the ships were
suffered to be so long unmolested, with their cargoes entire, the point
might yet be obtained; the other thought it possible, that some
impression might yet be made on the governor, by the strong voice
of the people.

Amidst this suspense a rumour was circulated, that admiral Montague
was about to seize the ships, and dispose of their cargoes at public
auction, within twenty-four hours. This step would as effectually have
secured the duties, as if sold at the shops of the consignees, and was
judged to be only a *finesse*, to place them there on their own terms.
On this report, convinced of the necessity of preventing so bold an
attempt, a vast body of people convened suddenly and repaired to
one of the largest and most commodious churches in Boston; where,
previous to any other steps, many fruitless messages were sent both
to the governor and the consignees, whose timidity had prompted
them to a seclusion from the public eye. Yet they continued to refuse
any satisfactory answer; and while the assembled multitude were in
quiet consultation on the safest mode to prevent the sale and
consumption of an herb, *noxious* at least to the political constitution,
the debates were interrupted by the entrance of the sheriff with an
order from the governor, styling them an illegal assembly, and directing
their immediate dispersion.

[107] This authoritative mandate was treated with great contempt,
and the sheriff instantly hissed out of the house. A confused murmur
ensued, both within and without the walls; but in a few moments all
was again quiet, and the leaders of the people returned calmly to the
point in question. Yet every expedient seemed fraught with insurmountable difficulties, and evening approaching without any decided
resolutions, the meeting was adjourned without day.

Within an hour after this was known abroad, there appeared a great

number of persons, clad like the aborigines of the wilderness, with CHAP. IV
tomahawks in their hands, and clubs on their shoulders, who without 1 7 7 3
the least molestation marched through the streets with silent solemnity,
and amidst innumerable spectators, proceeded to the wharves, boarded
the ships, demanded the keys, and with much deliberation knocked
open the chests, and emptied several thousand weight of the finest
teas into the ocean. No opposition was made, though surrounded by
the king's ships; all was silence and dismay.

This done, the procession returned through the town in the same
order and solemnity as observed in the outset of their attempt. No
other disorder took place, and it was observed, the stillest night
ensued that Boston had enjoyed for many months. This unexpected
event [108] struck the ministerial party with rage and astonishment;
while, as it seemed to be an attack upon private property, many who
wished well to the public cause could not fully approve of the measure.
Yet perhaps the laws of self-preservation might justify the deed, as
the exigencies of the times required extraordinary exertions, and every
other method had been tried in vain, to avoid this disagreeable
alternative. Besides it was alleged, and doubtless it was true, the
people were ready to make ample compensation for all damages
sustained, whenever the unconstitutional duty should be taken off,
and other grievances radically redressed. But there appeared little
prospect that any conciliatory advances would soon be made. The
officers of government discovered themselves more vindictive than
ever: animosities daily increased, and the spirits of the people were
irritated to a degree of alienation, even from their tenderest connexions,
when they happened to differ in political opinion.

By the frequent dissolution of the general assemblies, all public
debate had been precluded, and the usual regular intercourse between
the colonies cut off. The modes of legislative communication thus
obstructed, at a period when the necessity of harmony and concert
was obvious to every eye, no systematical opposition to gubernatorial
intrigues, supported by the king and parliament of Great Britain, was
to be expected [109] without the utmost concord, confidence, and
union of all the colonies. Perhaps no single step contributed so much
to cement the union of the colonies, and the final acquisition of
independence, as the establishment of committees of correspondence.
This supported a chain of communication from New Hampshire to
Georgia, that produced unanimity and energy throughout the continent.

CHAP. IV   As in these annals there has yet been no particular mention made
1 7 7 3 of this institution, it is but justice to name at once the author, the
origin, and the importance of the measure.

At an early period of the contest, when the public mind was agitated
by unexpected events, and remarkably pervaded with perplexity and
anxiety, James Warren, Esq. of Plymouth first proposed this institution
to a private friend, on a visit at his own house.* Mr. Warren had been
an active and influential member of the general assembly from the
beginning of the troubles in America, which commenced soon after
the demise of George the second. The principles and firmness of this
gentleman were well known, and the uprightness of his character had
sufficient weight to recommend the measure. As soon as the proposal
was communicated to a number of gentlemen in Boston, it was
adopted with zeal, and spread with the rapidity of [110] enthusiasm,
from town to town, and from province to province.† Thus an
intercourse was established, by which a similarity of opinion, a
connexion of interest, and a union of action appeared, that set
opposition at defiance, and defeated the machinations of their enemies
through all the colonies.

The plan suggested was clear and methodical; it proposed that a
public meeting should be called in every town; that a number of
persons should be selected by a plurality of voices; that they should
be men of respectable characters, whose attachment to the great cause
of America had been uniform; that they should be vested by a majority
of suffrages with power to take cognizance of the state of commerce,
of the intrigues of *toryism*, of litigious ruptures that might create
disturbances, and every thing else that might be thought to militate
with the rights of the people, and to promote every thing that tended
to general utility.

The business was not tardily executed. Committees were every
where chosen, who were directed to keep up a regular correspondence
with each other, and to give information of all intelligence received,
relative to the proceedings of [111] administration, so far as they
affected the interest of the British colonies throughout America. The
truth was faithfully and diligently discharged, and when afterwards
all legislative authority was suspended, the courts of justice shut up,

* Samuel Adams, Esq. of Boston.
† The general impulse at this time seemed to operate by sympathy, before consultation
  could be had; thus it appeared afterwards that the vigilant inhabitants of Virginia
  had concerted a similar plan about the same period.

and the last traits of British government annihilated in the colonies, CHAP. IV
this new institution became a kind of juridical tribunal. Its injunctions 1 7 7 3
were influential beyond the hopes of its most sanguine friends, and
the recommendations of committees of correspondence had the force
of law. Thus, as despotism frequently springs from anarchy, a regular
democracy sometimes arises from the severe encroachments of despotism.

This institution had given such a general alarm to the adherents of
administration, and had been replete with such important consequences through the union, that it was justly dreaded by those who
opposed it, and considered by them as the most important bulwark
of freedom. A representation of this establishment, and its effects,
had been transmitted to England, and laid before the king and
parliament, and Mr. Hutchinson had received his majesty's disapprobation of the measure. With the hope of impeding its farther operation,
by announcing the frown and the censure of royalty, and for the
discussion of some other important questions, the governor had thought
proper to convene the council and house of [112] representatives, to
meet in January one thousand seven hundred and seventy-three.

The assembly of the preceding year had passed a number of very
severe resolves, when the original letters mentioned above, written
by governor Hutchinson and lieutenant-governor Oliver were detected,
sent back to the Massachusetts, and laid before the house. They had
observed that "the letters contained wicked and injurious misrepresentations, designed to influence the ministry and the nation, and to
excite jealousies in the breast of the king, against his faithful
subjects."* They had proceeded to an impeachment, and unanimously
requested, that his majesty would be pleased to remove both Mr.
Thomas Hutchinson and Mr. Andrew Oliver from their public func-
tions in the province, forever.† But before they had time to complete
their spirited measures, the governor had as usual dissolved the
assembly. This was a stretch of power, and a manifestation of
resentment, that had been so frequently exercised both by Mr.
Hutchinson and his predecessor, that it was never unexpected, and
now totally disregarded. This mode of conduct was not confined to

---

* See 11th resolve in the sessions of one thousand seven hundred and seventy-two.
† Journals of the house. [JHRM, 50: 60 (June 16, 1773). See, "Proceedings on the
   Address of the Assembly of Massachusetts Bay, to Remove His Majesty's Governor
   and Lieutenant Governor," in (Mauduit), Letters, pp. 76–126; Hutchinson, Letters,
   pp. 59–94.]

CHAP. IV the Massachusetts; it was indeed the common signal of resentment
1 7 7 3 exhibited by most of the colonial governors: [113] they immediately
dissolved the legislative assemblies on the discovery of energy,
enterprise, or patriotism, among the members.

When the new house of assembly met at Boston the present year,
it appeared to be composed of the principal gentlemen and landholders
in the province; men of education and ability, of fortune and family,
of integrity and honor; jealous of the infringement of their rights, and
the faithful guardians of a free people.

Their independency of mind was soon put to the test. On the
opening of the new session, the first communication from the governor
was, that he had received his majesty's express disapprobation of all
committees of *correspondence;* and to enforce the displeasure of the
monarch, he very indiscreetly ventured himself to censure with much
warmth this institution, and every other stand that the colonies had
unitedly made to ministerial and parliamentary invasions. To complete
the climax of his own presumption, he in a long and labored speech
imprudently agitated the grand question of a parliamentary right of
taxation without representation;* he endeavoured to justify, both by
law and precedent, every arbitrary step that had been taken for ten
years past to reduce the colonies to a disgraceful subjugation.

[114] This gave a fair opening to the friends of their country which
they did not neglect, to discuss the illegality, injustice, and impolicy
of the late innovations. They entered on the debate with freedom of
inquiry, stated their claims with clearness and precision, and supported
them with such reasoning and perspicuity, that a man of less hardiness
than Mr. Hutchinson would not have made a second attempt to justify
so odious a cause, or to gain such an unpopular point by dint of
argument. But whether owing to his own intemperate zeal, or whether
instigated by his superiors on the other side of the Atlantic, to bring
on the dispute previous to the disclosure of some extraordinary
measures then in agitation, is uncertain. However this was, he
supported his opinions with industry and ingenuity, and not discouraged by strong opposition, he spun out the debate to a tedious and
ridiculous length. Far from terminating to the honor of the governor,
his officious defence of administration served only to indicate the
necessity of the most guarded watchfulness against the machinations
of powerful and designing men; and fanned, rather than checked the
amor patriae characteristic of the times.

---

* Appendix, No. IX. Extracts from governor Hutchinson's letters urging his designs.

Soon after this altercation ended, the representative body took CHAP. IV
cognizance of an affair that had given great disgust, and created much 1 7 7 3
uneasiness through the province. By the royal [115] charter granted
by William and Mary, the governor, lieutenant-governor and secretary
were appointed by the king; the council were chosen by the representatives of the people, the governor being allowed a negative voice;
the judges, justices, and all other officers, civil and military, were left
to his nomination, and appointed by him, with the advice and consent
of a board of counsellors. But as it is always necessary in a free
government, that the people should retain some means in their own
hands, to check any unwarrantable exercise of power in the executive,
the legislature of Massachusetts had always enjoyed the reasonable
privilege of paying their own officers according to their ability, and
the services rendered to the public.

It was at this time well known that Mr. Hutchinson had so far
ingratiated himself as to entitle him to peculiar favor from the crown;
and by a handsome salary from the king, he was rendered entirely
independent of the people. His brother-in-law also, the lieutenant-
governor, had obtained by misrepresentations, thought by some to
have been little short of perjury,* a pension which he had long
solicited; but chagrin at the detection of his letters, and the discovery
of his duplicity, soon put a period [116] to a life that might have been
useful and exemplary, had he confined his pursuits only to the
domestic walks of life.

A strong family as well as political connexion, had for some time
been forming among those who had been writing in favor of colonial
regulations, and urging the creation of a *patrician rank*, from which
all officers of government should in future be selected. Intermarriages
among their children in the near degree of consanguinity before the
parties were of age for maturity of choice, had strengthened the union
of interests among the candidates for preferment. Thus by a kind of
compact, almost every department of high trust as it became vacant
by resignation, suspension or death, was filled by some relation or
dependent of governor Hutchinson; and no other qualification was
required except a suppleness of opinion and principle that could
readily bend to the measures of the court.

But it was more recently discovered that the judges of the superior
court, the near relations or coadjutors of Mr. Hutchinson, and few of

* See lieutenant-governor Oliver's affidavit, on the council books. [Source of Oliver's
affidavit not identified. See Hutchinson, *Letters*, pp. 66, 86–88.]

CHAP. IV them more scrupulously delicate with regard to the violation of the
1 7 7 3 rights of their country than himself, had taken advantage of the times, and successfully insinuated that the dignity of their offices must be supported by an allowance from the crown sufficient to enable them to execute [117] the designs of government, exclusively of any dependence on the general assembly. In consequence of these representations, the judges were appointed to hold their places during the king's pleasure, and a yearly stipend was granted them to be paid out of the new revenue to be raised in America.

The general court had not been convened after the full disclosure of this system before the present period; of course no constitutional opposition could be made on the infraction of their charter, until a legal assembly had an opportunity to meet and deliberate. Uncertain how long the intriguing spirit of the governor would permit them to continue in existence, the sitting assembly judged it necessary early in the session to proceed to a parliamentary inquiry into the conduct of their judiciary officers. Accordingly the judges of the supreme court were called upon to receive the grants for their services as usual from the treasury of the province; to renounce all unconstitutional salaries, and to engage to receive no pay, pension or emolument in reward of services as justices of the court of judicature, but from the free grants of the legislative assembly.

Two of the judges, Trowbridge and Ropes, readily complied with the demand, and relinquished the offensive stipend. A third was William Cushing, Esq. a gentleman rendered [118] respectable in the eyes of all parties by his professional abilities and general integrity. He was a sensible, modest man, well acquainted with law, but remarkable for the secrecy of his opinions: this kept up his reputation through all the ebullitions of discordant parties. He readily resigned the royal stipend without any observations of his own; yet it was thought at the time that it was with a reluctance that his taciturnity could not conceal. By this silent address he retained the confidence of the court faction, nor was he less a favorite among the republicans. He was immediately placed on the bench of justice after the assumption of government in the Massachusetts.*

The next that was called forward was Foster Hutchinson, a brother

---

* The talents, the manners, the probity, and the urbanity of Mr. Cushing procured his advancement to the supreme bench under the new constitution afterwards adopted by the United States. In this station he was useful to his country, and respected by every class through all the changes of party and opinion which he lived to see.

of the governor's, a man of much less understanding, and as little CHAP. IV
public virtue; in short, remarkable for nothing but the malignancy of 1 7 7 3
his heart. He, after much altercation and abuse of the general assembly,
complied with a very ill grace with the requisitions of the house.

[119] But the chief seat of justice in this extraordinary administration
was occupied by a man* unacquainted with law, and ignorant of the
first principles of government. He possessed a certain credulity of
mind that easily seduced him into erroneous opinions; at the same
time a frigid obstinacy of temper that rendered him incapable of
conviction. His insinuating manners, his superficial abilities, and his
implicit devotion to the governor, rendered him a fit instrument to
give sanction by the forms of law to the most atrocious acts of arbitrary
power. Equally deaf to the dictates of patriotism and to the united
voice of the people, he peremptorily refused to listen to the demands
of their representatives; and boldly declared his resolution to receive
an annual grant from the crown of England in spite of the opinions
or resentment of his country: he urged as an excuse, the depreciation
of his private fortune by his judicial attentions. His station was
important and influential, and his temerity was considered as holding
a bribe to execute the corrupt measures of the British court.

The house of representatives not interrupted in their system, nor
intimidated by the presumption of the delinquent, proceeded directly
to exhibit articles of impeachment against Peter Oliver, Esq. accusing
him of high crimes and misdemeanors, and laid their complaints
before [120] the governor and council. On a division of the house
there appeared ninety-two members in favour of the measure, and
only eight against it. The governor, as was expected, both from
personal attachment and a full approbation of Mr. Oliver's conduct,
refused to act or sit on the business; of course all proceedings were
for a time suspended.

When a detail of these spirited measures reached England, exaggerated by the colorings of the officers of the crown, it threw the
nation, more especially the trading part, into a temporary fever. The
ministry rose in their resentment, and entered on the most severe
steps against the Massachusetts, and more particularly the town of
Boston. It was at this period that lord North ushered into the house
of commons the memorable bill for shutting up the port of Boston,
also the bill for better regulating the government of the Massachusetts.

The port-bill enacted that after the first of June one thousand seven

* Peter Oliver, Esq. a brother-in-law of the governor's.

hundred and seventy-four, "Every vessel within the points Alderton and Nahant, (the boundaries of the harbor of Boston,) should depart within six hours, unless laden with food or fuel." That no merchandize should be taken in or discharged at any of the stores, wharves, or quays, within those limits; and that any ship, barge or boat, attempting to convey from other parts of [121] America, either stores, goods or merchandize to Boston, (one of the largest maritime towns on the continent) should be deemed a legal forfeiture to the crown.

This act was opposed with becoming zeal by several in both houses of parliament, who still inherited the generous spirit of their ancestors, and dared to stand forth the defenders of English liberty, in the most perilous seasons. Though the cruelty and injustice of this step was warmly criminated, the minister and his party urged the necessity of strong measures; nor was it difficult to obtain a large majority to enforce them. An abstract of an act for the more impartial administration of justice in the province of Massachusetts, accompanied the port-bill. Thus by one of those severe and arbitrary acts, many thousands of the best and most loyal subjects of the house of Brunswick were at once cut off from the means of subsistence; poverty stared in the face of affluence, and a long train of evils threatened every rank. No discriminations were made; the innocent were equally involved with the real or imputed guilty, and reduced to such distresses afterwards, that, but from the charitable donations of the other colonies, multitudes must have inevitably perished.

The other bill directed, that on an indictment for riot, resistance of the magistrate, or [122] impeding the laws of revenue in the smallest degree, any person, at the option of the governor, or in his absence, the lieutenant-governor, might be transported to Great Britain for trial, and there be ordered to wait amidst his foes, the decisions of strangers unacquainted with the character of the prisoner, or the turpitude of a crime, that should subject him to be transported a thousand leagues from his own vicinity, for a final decision on the charges exhibited against him. Several of the southern colonies remonstrated warmly against those novel proceedings towards the Massachusetts, and considered it as a common cause. The house of burgesses in Virginia vigorously opposed this measure, and passed resolutions expressing

> their exclusive right to tax their constituents, and their right to petition
> their sovereign for redress of grievances, and the lawfulness of procuring
> the concurrence of the other colonies in praying for the royal interposition

in favour of the violated rights of America: and that all trials for treasons,
or for any crime whatsoever, committed in that colony, ought to be before
his majesty's courts within the said colony; and that the seizing any person
residing in the said colony, suspected of any crime whatsoever committed
therein, and sending such person to places beyond the sea to be tried,
was highly derogatory of the rights of British subjects.

[123] These acts were to continue in full force until satisfaction
should be made to the East India company for the loss of their teas;
nor were any assurances given, that in case of submission and
compliance, they should be repealed. The indignation which naturally
arose in the minds of the people on these unexpected and accumulated
grievances, was truly inexpressible. It was frequently observed, that
the only melioration of the present evils was, that the recal of Mr.
Hutchinson accompanied the bills, and his leaving the province at
the same period the port-bill was to be put in operation, seemed to
impress a dawn of hope from time, if not from his immediate successor.

Every historical record will doubtless witness that he was the
principal author of the sufferings of the unhappy Bostonians, previous
to the convulsions which produced the revolution. So deeply riveted
was this opinion among his enraged countrymen, that many apprehended the summary vengeance of an incensed populace would not
suffer so notorious a parricide to repair quietly to England. Yet such
were the generous and compassionate feelings of a people too virtuous
to punish without a legal process, that he escaped the blow he had
reason to fear would overtake him, when stripped of authority, and
no longer acting as the representative of *majesty*.

Chagrined by the loss of place, mortified by the neglect of some,
and apprehensive from the [124] resentment of others, he retired to
a small village in the neighborhood of Boston, and secluded himself
from observation until he embarked for London. This he did on the
same memorable day when, by act of parliament, the blockade of
Boston took place. Before his departure, the few partizans that still
adhered to the man and his principles, procured by much assiduity a
complimentary address, thanking him for past *services*, and held up to
him the idea, that by his *talents* he might obtain a redress of grievances,
which they well knew had been drawn on their country by the agency
of Mr. Hutchinson. Much derision fell on the character of this group
of flatterers, who were long distinguished only by the appellation of
Hutchinson's addressers.

Mr. Hutchinson furnished with these pitiful credentials, left his native country forever. On his arrival in England, he was justified and caressed by his employers; and notwithstanding the criminality of his political conduct had been so fully evinced by the detection and recovery of his original letters, his impeachment, which was laid before the lords of the privy-council, was considered by them in a very frivolous light. A professional character, by some thought to have been hired for the purpose, was permitted to abuse the petitioners and their agent in the grossest terms scurrility could invent; and the lords reported, that

> the petition [125] was groundless, vexatious, and scandalous, and calculated only for the seditious purposes of keeping up a spirit of discontent and clamour in the province; that nothing had been laid before them which did or could, in their opinion, in any manner or in any degree impeach the honour, integrity, or conduct of the governor or lieutenant-governor;

who had been at the same time impeached.

But the operation of his measures, while governor of the Massachusetts, was so productive of misfortune to Great Britain, as well as to the united colonies, that Mr. Hutchinson soon became the object of disgust to all parties. He did not live to see the independence of America established, but he lived long enough to repent in bitterness of soul, the part he had acted against a country once disposed to respect his character. After his mind had been involved many months in a state of chagrin, disappointment and despair, he died on the day the riots in London, excited by lord George Gordon, were at the height, in the year one thousand seven hundred and eighty. Those of the family who survived their unhappy father remained in obscurity in England.

It must however be acknowledged that governor Hutchinson was uniform in his political conduct. He was educated in reverential ideas [126] of monarchic government, and considered himself the servant of a king who had entrusted him with very high authority. As a true disciple of passive obedience, he might think himself bound to promote the designs of his master, and thus he might probably release his conscience from the obligation to aid his countrymen in their opposition to the encroachments of the crown. In the eye of candor, he may therefore be much more excusable, than any who may deviate from their principles and professions of republicanism, who have not been biassed by the patronage of kings, nor influenced in favor of monarchy by their early prejudices of education or employment.

CHAPTER V

General Gage appointed Governor of Massachusetts • General Assembly meet at Salem • A proposal for a Congress from all the Colonies, to be convened at Philadelphia • Mandamus Counsellors obliged to resign • Resolutions of the General Congress • Occasional observations • The Massachusetts attentive to the military Discipline of their Youth • Suffolk Resolves • A Provincial Congress chosen in the Massachusetts • Governor Gage summons a new House of Representatives

[127] The speculatist and the philosopher frequently observe a casual subordination of circumstances independent of political decision, which fixes the character and manners of nations. This thought may be piously improved till it leads the mind to view those casualties, directed by a secret hand which points the revolutions of time, and decides the fate of empires. The occasional instruments for the completion of the grand system of Providence, have seldom any other stimulus but the bubble of *fame*, the lust of *wealth*, or some contemptible passion that centres in *self*. Even the bosom of virtue warmed by higher principles, and the man actuated by nobler motives, walks in a narrow sphere of comprehension. The scale by which the ideas of mortals are circumscribed generally limits his wishes to a certain point without consideration, or a just calculation of extensive consequences.

[128] Thus while the king of Great Britain was contending with the colonies for a three-penny duty on *tea*, and the Americans with the bold spirit of patriotism resisting an encroachment on their rights, the one thought they only asked a moderate and reasonable indulgence from their sovereign, which they had a right to demand if withheld; on the other side, the most severe and strong measures were adopted and exercised towards the *colonies*, which parliament considered as only the proper and necessary chastisement of *rebellious subjects*. Thus on the eve of one of the most remarkable revolutions recorded in the page of history, a revolution which Great Britain precipitated by her

CHAP. V indiscretion, and which the hardiest sons of America viewed in the
1 7 7 4 beginning of opposition as a work reserved for the enterprising hand
of posterity, few on either side comprehended the magnitude of the
contest, and fewer still had the courage to name the independence
of the American colonies as the *ultimatum* of their *designs*.

After the spirits of men had been wrought up to a high tone of
resentment, by repeated injuries on the one hand, and an open
resistance on the other, there was little reason to expect a ready
compliance with regulations, repugnant to the feelings, the principles,
and the interest of Americans. The parliament of Britain therefore
thought it expedient to enforce obedience by the sword, and determined to send [129] out an armament sufficient for the purpose, early
in the spring one thousand seven hundred and seventy-four. The
subjugation of the colonies by arms, was yet considered in England
by some as a work of such facility, that four or five regiments, with a
few ships of the line, were equal to the business, provided they were
commanded by officers who had not sagacity enough to judge of the
impropriety of the measures of administration, nor humanity to feel
for the miseries of the people, or liberality to endeavour to mitigate
the rigors of government. In consequence of this opinion, admiral
Montague was recalled from Boston, and admiral Graves appointed
to succeed, whose character was known to be more avaricious, severe
and vigilant than his predecessor, and in all respects a more fit
instrument to execute the weak, indigested and irritating system.

General Gage, unhappily for himself, as will appear in the sequel,
was selected as a proper person to take the command of all his
majesty's forces in North America, and reduce the country to submission. He had married a lady of respectable connexions in New
York, and had held with considerable reputation for several years a
military employment in the colonies. He was at this time appointed
governor and commander in chief of the province of Massachusetts
Bay; directed to repair immediately there, and on his arrival to remove
the seat of [130] government from Boston, and to convene the general
assembly to meet at Salem, a smaller town, situated about twenty
miles from the capital. The governor, the lieutenant-governor, the
secretary, the board of commissioners, and all crown officers were
ordered by special mandate to leave Boston, and make the town of
Salem the place of their future residence.

A few days before the annual election for May, one thousand seven
hundred and seventy-four, the new governor of the Massachusetts

arrived. He was received by the inhabitants of Boston with the same CHAP. V
respect that had been usually shewn to those, who were dignified by 1 7 7 4
the title of the king's representative. An elegant entertainment was
provided at Faneuil Hall, to which he was escorted by a company of
cadets, and attended with great civility by the magistrates and principal
gentlemen of the town; and though jealousy, disgust and resentment
burnt in the bosom of one party, and the most unwarrantable designs
occupied the thoughts of the other, yet the appearance of politeness
and good humor was kept up through the *etiquette* of the day.

The week following was the anniversary of the general election,
agreeable to charter. The day was ushered in with the usual parade,
and the house of representatives proceeded to business in the common
form: but a specimen of [131] the measures to be expected from the
new administration appeared in the first act of authority recorded of
governor Gage. A list of counsellors was presented for his approbation,
from which he erased the names of thirteen gentlemen out of twenty-
eight, unanimously chosen by the free voice of the representatives of
the people, leaving only a quorum as established by charter, or it was
apprehended, in the exercise of his new prerogative he might have
annihilated the whole. Most of the gentlemen on the negatived list
had been distinguished for their attachment to the ancient constitution,
and their decided opposition to the present ministerial measures.
Among them was James Bowdoin, Esq. whose understanding, discernment, and conscientious deportment, rendered him a very unfit
instrument for the views of the court, at this extraordinary period.
John Winthrop, Hollisian professor of mathematics and natural philosophy at Cambridge; his public conduct was but the emanation of
superior genius, united with an excellent heart, as much distinguished
for every private virtue as for his attachment to the liberties of a
country that may glory in giving birth to a man of his exalted
character.* Colonel Otis of Barnstable, whose name has been already
mentioned; and John Adams, a [132] barrister at law of rising abilities;
his appearance on the theatre of politics commenced at this period;
we shall meet him again in still more dignified stations. These
gentlemen had been undoubtedly pointed out as obnoxious to administration by the predecessor of governor Gage, as he had not been
long enough in the province to discriminate characters.

* Dr. Winthrop was lineally descended from the first governor of the Massachusetts,
  and inherited the virtues and talents of his great ancestor, too well known to need
  any encomium.

CHAP. V   The house of representatives did not think proper to replace the
1 7 7 4 members of council by a new choice; they silently bore this indiscreet
exercise of authority, sensible it was but a prelude to the impending
storm. The assembly was the next day adjourned for a week; at the
expiration of that time, they were directed to meet at Salem. In the
interim the governor removed himself, and the whole band of revenue
and crown officers deserted the town of Boston at once, as a place
devoted to destruction.

Every external appearance of respect was still kept up towards the
new governor. The council, the house, the judiciary officers, the
mercantile and other bodies, prepared and offered congratulatory
addresses as usual, on the recent arrival of the commander in chief at
the seat of government. The incense was received both at Boston
and Salem with the usual satisfaction, except the address from the
remaining board of counsellors; this was checked with asperity, and
the reading it through forbidden, as the composition [133] contained
some strictures on administration, and censured rather too freely, for
the delicate ear of an infant magistrate, the conduct of some of his
predecessors. But this was the last compliment of the kind, ever
offered by either branch of the legislature of the Massachusetts to a
governor appointed by the king of Great Britain. No marks of
ministerial resentment had either humbled or intimidated the spirits,
nor shook the intrepidity of mind necessary for the times; and though
it was first called into action in the Massachusetts it breathed its
influence through all the colonies. They all seemed equally prepared
to suffer, and equally determined to resist in unison, if no mean but
that of absolute submission was to be the test of loyalty.

The first day of June, one thousand seven hundred and seventy-
four, the day when the Boston port-bill began to operate, was observed
in most of the colonies with uncommon solemnity as a day of fasting
and prayer. In all of them, sympathy and indignation, compassion
and resentment, alternately arose in every bosom. A zeal to relieve,
and an alacrity to support the distressed *Bostonians,* seemed to pervade
the whole continent, except the dependents on the crown, and their
partizans, allured by interest to adhere to the royal cause. There were
indeed a few others in every colony led to unite with, and to think
favorably of the measures of administration, from their attachment to
monarchy, [134] in which they had been educated; and some there
were who justified all things done by the hand of power, either from
fear, ignorance, or imbecility.

The session at Salem was of short duration, but it was a busy and CHAP. V an important period. The leading characters in the house of represen- 1 7 7 4 tatives contemplated the present moment, replete with consequences of the utmost magnitude; they judged it a crisis that required measures bold and decisive, though hazardous, and that the extrication of their country from the designs of their enemies, depended much on the conduct of the present assembly. Their charter was on the point of annihilation; a military governor had just arrived, with troops on the spot, to support the arbitrary systems of the court of St. James.

These appearances had a disagreeable effect on some who had before co-operated with the patriots; they began to tremble at the power and the severity of Britain, at a time when firmness was most required, zeal indispensable, and secrecy necessary. Yet those who possessed the energies of mind requisite for the completion or the defeat of great designs, had not their ardor or resolution shaken in the smallest degree, by either dangers, threats or caresses. It was a prime object to select a few members of the house, that might be trusted most confidentially [135] on any emergence. This task fell on Mr. Samuel Adams of Boston, and Mr. Warren of Plymouth. They drew off a few chosen spirits, who met at a place appointed for a secret conference;* several others were introduced the ensuing evening, when a discussion of circumstances took place. Immediate decision, and effectual modes of action were urged, and such caution, energy and dispatch were observed by this daring and dauntless secret *council,* that on the third evening of their conference their business was ripe for execution.

This committee had digested a plan for a general congress from all the colonies, to consult on the common safety of America;† named their own delegates; and as all present were convinced of the necessity and expediency of such a convention, they estimated the expense, [136] and provided funds for the liquidation, prepared letters to the

---

* Among these the names of Hancock, Cushing, and Hawley, of Sullivan, Robert Payne, and Benjamin Greenleaf of Newburyport, and many others, should not be forgotten, but ought always to be mentioned with respect, for their zeal at this critical moment.

† Such a remarkable coincidence of opinion, energy and zeal, existed between the provinces of Virginia and the Massachusetts, that their measures and resolutions were often similar, previous to the opportunity for conference. Thus the propriety of a general congress had been discussed and agreed upon by the Virginians, before they were informed of the resolutions of Massachusetts. Some of the other colonies had contemplated the same measure, without any previous consultation.

CHAP. V   other colonies, enforcing the reasons for their strong confederacy, and
1 7 7 4   disclosed their proceedings to the house, before the governmental
party had the least suspicion of their designs. Before the full disclosure
of the business they were upon, the doors of the house were locked,
and a vote passed, that no one should be suffered to enter or retire,
until a final determination took place on the important questions
before them. When these designs were opened, the partizans of
administration then in the house, were thunderstruck with measures
so replete with ability and vigour, and that wore such an aspect of
high and dangerous consequences.

These transactions might have been legally styled *treasonable*, but
loyalty had lost its influence, and power its terrors. Firm and disinterested, intrepid and united, they stood ready to submit to the
chances of war, and to sacrifice their devoted lives to preserve inviolate,
and to transmit to posterity, the inherent rights of men, conferred on
all by the God of nature, and the privileges of Englishmen, claimed
by Americans from the sacred sanctions of compact.

When the measures agitated in the secret conference were laid
before the house of representatives, one of the members a devotee
to all governors, pretended a sudden indisposition, and requested
[137] leave to withdraw; he pleaded the necessities of nature, was
released from his uneasy confinement, and ran immediately to governor
Gage with information of the bold and high-handed proceedings of
the lower house. The governor not less alarmed than the sycophant,
at these unexpected manœuvres, instantly directed the secretary to
dissolve the assembly by proclamation.

Finding the doors of the house closed, and no prospect of admittance
for him, the secretary desired the door-keeper to acquaint the house
he had a message from the governor, and requested leave to deliver
it. The speaker replied, that it was the order of the house, that no
one should be permitted to enter on any pretence whatever, before
the business they were upon was fully completed. Agitated and
embarrassed, the secretary then read on the stairs a proclamation for
the immediate dissolution of the general assembly.

The main point gained, the delegates for a congress chosen, supplies
for their support voted, and letters to the other colonies requesting
them to accord in these measures, signed by the speaker, the members
cheerfully dispersed, and returned to their constituents, satisfied, that
notwithstanding the precipitant dissolution of the assembly, they had
done all that the circumstances [138] of the times would admit, to
remedy the present, and guard against future evils.

This early step to promote the general interest of the colonies, and CHAP. V
lay the foundation of union and concord in all their subsequent 1 7 7 4
transactions, will ever reflect lustre on the characters of those who
conducted it with such firmness and decision. It was indeed a very
critical era: nor were those gentlemen insensible of the truth of the
observation, that "whoever has a standing army at command, has, or
may have the state." Nor were they less sensible, that in the present
circumstances, while they acknowledged themselves the subjects of
the king of England, their conduct must be styled *rebellion*, and that
death must be the inevitable consequence of defeat. Yet life was then
considered a trivial stake in competition with liberty.

All the old colonies except Georgia, readily acceded to the proposal
of calling a general congress; they made immediate exertions that
there might be no discord in the councils of the several provinces,
and that their opposition should be consistent, spirited and systematical. Most of them had previously laid aside many of their local
prejudices, and by public resolves and various other modes, had
expressed their disgust at the summary proceedings of parliament
against the Massachusetts. They reprobated the port-bill in terms of
detestation, raised liberal contributions for the suffering inhabitants
of [139] Boston, and continued their determinations to support that
province at every hazard, through the conflict in which they were
involved.

In conformity to the coercive system, the governors of all the
colonies frowned on the sympathetic part the several legislative bodies
had been disposed to take with the turbulent descendants, as they
were pleased to style the Massachusetts, of *puritans*, *republicans* and
regicides. Thus most of the colonial assemblies had been petulantly
dissolved, nor could any applications from the people prevail on the
supreme magistrate, to suffer the representatives and burgesses to
meet, and in a legal capacity deliberate on measures most consistent
with loyalty and freedom. But this persevering obstinacy of the
governors did not retard the resolutions of the people; they met in
parishes, and selected persons from almost every town, to meet in
provincial conventions, and there to make choice of suitable delegates
to meet in general congress.

The beginning of autumn, one thousand seven hundred and seventy-
four, was the time appointed, and the city of Philadelphia chosen, as
the most central and convenient place, for this body to meet and
deliberate, at so critical a conjuncture. Yet such was the attachment
to Britain, the strength of habit, and the influence of ancient forms;

CHAP. V such the reluctant dread [140] of spilling human blood, which at that
1 7 7 4 period was universally felt in America, that there were few, who did
not ardently wish some friendly intervention might yet prevent a
rupture, which probably might shake the empire of Britain, and waste
the inhabitants on both sides the Atlantic.

At this early period, there were some who viewed the step of their
summoning a general congress, under existing circumstances of
peculiar embarrassment, as a *prelude* to a *revolution* which appeared
pregnant with events, that might affect not only the political systems,
but the character and manners of a considerable part of the habitable
globe.*

America was then little known, her character, ability, and police,
less understood abroad; but she soon became the object of attention
among the potentates of Europe, the admiration of both the philosophic
and the brave, and her fields the theatre of fame throughout the
civilized world. Her principles were disseminated: the seed sown in
America ripened in the [141] more cultivated grounds of Europe, and
inspired ideas among the enslaved nations that have long trembled at
the name of the *bastile* and the *bastinado*. This may finally lead to the
completion of prophetic predictions, and spread universal liberty and
peace, as far at least as is compatible with the present state of human
nature.

The wild vagaries of the *perfectibility* of man, so long as the passions
to which the species are liable play about the hearts of all, may be
left to the dreaming *sciolist*, who wanders in search of impracticable
theories. He may remain entangled in his own web, while that rational
liberty, to which all have a right, may be exhibited and defended by
men of principle and heroism, who better understand the laws of
social order.

Through the summer previous to the meeting of congress, no
expressions of loyalty to the sovereign, or affection to the parent state,
were neglected in their public declarations. Yet the colonies seemed
to be animated as it were by one soul, to train their youth to arms,
to withhold all commercial connexion with Great Britain, and to
cultivate that unanimity necessary to bind society when ancient forms

---

* This observation has since been verified in the remarkable revolution in France;—
a struggle for freedom on one side, and the combinations of European monarchs on
the other, to depress and eradicate the spirit of liberty caught in America, was
displayed to the world; nor was any of the combination of princes at the treaty of
Pilnitz more persevering in the cause of despotism than the king of Great Britain.

are relaxed or broken, and the common safety required the assumption CHAP. V
of new modes of government. But while attentive to the regulations 1 7 7 4
of their internal [142] economy and police, each colony beheld with
a friendly and compassionate eye, the severe struggles of the Massachusetts, where the arm of power was principally levelled, and the
ebullitions of ministerial resentment poured forth, as if to terrify the
sister provinces into submission.

Not long after the dissolution of the last assembly ever convened
in that province on the principles of their former charter, admiral
Graves arrived in Boston, with several ships of the line and a number
of transports laden with troops, military stores, and all warlike
accoutrements. The troops landed peaceably, took possession of the
open grounds, and formed several encampments within the town.

At the same time arrived the bill for new modelling the government
of the Massachusetts. By this bill their former charter was entirely
vacated: a council of thirty-six members was appointed by *mandamus*,
to hold their places during the king's pleasure; all judges, justices,
sheriffs, &c. were to be appointed by the governor, without the advice
of council, and to be removed at his sole option. Jurors in future were
to be named by the sheriff, instead of the usual and more impartial
mode of drawing them by lot. All town-meetings without express
leave from the governor were forbidden, except those annually held
in the spring for the [143] choice of representatives and town-officers.
Several other violations of the former compact completed the system.

This new mode of government, though it had been for some time
expected, occasioned such loud complaints, such universal murmurs,
that several of the newly appointed counsellors had not the courage
to accept places which they were sensible would reflect disgrace on
their memory. Two of them* seemed really to decline from principle,
and publickly declared they would have no hand in the dereliction of
the rights of their country. Several others relinquished their seats for
fear of offending their countrymen; but most of them, selected by
Mr. Hutchinson as proper instruments for the purpose, were destitute
of all ideas of public virtue. They readily took the qualifying oaths,
and engaged to lend their hand to erase the last vestige of freedom
in that devoted province.

The people still firm and undaunted, assembled in multitudes and
repaired to the houses of the obnoxious counsellors. They demanded

* These were James Russell, Esq. of Charlestown, and William Vassal, Esq. of Boston.

an immediate resignation of their unconstitutional appointments, and
a solemn assurance that they would never accept any office incompatible with the former privileges enjoyed by their country. Some of them terrified by the [144] resolution of the people complied, and remained afterwards quiet and unmolested in their own houses. Others, who had prostrated all principle in the hope of preferment, and were hardy enough to go every length to secure it, conscious of the guilty part they had acted, made their escape into Boston where they were sure of the protection of the king's troops. Indeed that unhappy town soon became the receptacle of all the devotees to ministerial measures from every part of the province: they there consoled themselves with the barbarous hope, that parliament would take the severest measures to enforce their own acts; nor were these hopes unfounded.

It has been observed that by the late edict for the *better administration* of *justice* in the *Massachusetts*, any man was liable on the slightest *suspicion* of *treason*, or *misprision* of *treason*, to be dragged from his own family or vicinity, to any part of the king of England's dominions for trial. It was now reported that general Gage had orders to arrest the leading characters in opposition, and transport them beyond sea, and that a reinforcement of troops might be hourly expected sufficient to enable him to execute all the mad projects of a rash and unprincipled ministry.

Though the operation of this system in its utmost latitude was daily threatened and expected, [145] it made little impression on a people determined to withhold even a tacit consent to any infractions on their charter. They considered the present measures as a breach of a solemn covenant, which at the same time that it subjected them to the authority of the king of England, stipulated to them the equal enjoyment of all the rights and privileges of free and natural born subjects. They chose to hazard the consequences of returning back to a state of nature, rather than quietly submit to unjust and arbitrary measures continually accumulating. This was a dangerous experiment, though they were sensible that the necessities of man will soon restore order and subordination, even from confusion and anarchy: on the contrary, the yoke of despotism once rivetted, no human sagacity can justly calculate its termination.

While matters hung in this suspense, the people in all the shire towns collected in prodigious numbers to prevent the sitting of the courts of common law; forbidding the justices to meet, or the jurors

to empannel, and obliging all civil magistrates to bind themselves by CHAP. V
oath, not to conform to the late acts of parliament in any judiciary 1 7 7 4
proceedings; and all military officers were called upon to resign their
commissions. Thus were the bands of society relaxed, law set at
defiance, and government unhinged throughout the province. Perhaps
this may be [146] marked in the annals of time, as one of the most
extraordinary eras in the history of man: the exertions of spirit
awakened by the severe hand of power had led to that most alarming
experiment of levelling all ranks, and destroying all subordination.

It cannot be denied that nothing is more difficult than to restrain
the provoked multitude, when once aroused by a sense of wrong,
from that supineness which generally overspreads the common class
of mankind. Ignorant and fierce, they know not in the first ebullitions
of resentment, how to repel with safety the arm of the oppressor. It
is a work of time to establish a regular opposition to long established
tyranny. A celebrated writer has observed, that "men bear with the
defects in their police, as they do with their inconveniences and
hardships in living:" and perhaps the facility of the human mind in
adapting itself to its circumstances, was never more remarkably
exemplified, than it was at this time in America.

Trade had long been embarrassed throughout the colonies by the
restraints of parliament and the rapacity of revenue officers; the
shutting up the port of Boston was felt in every villa of the New
England colonies; the bill for altering the constitution of Massachusetts, prevented all [147] legislative proceedings; the executive officers
were rendered incapable of acting in their several departments, and
the courts of justice shut up. It must be ascribed to the virtue of the
people, however reluctant some may be to acknowledge this truth,
that they did not feel the effects of anarchy in the extreme.

But a general forbearance and complacency seemed for a time
almost to preclude the necessity of legal restraint; and except in a
few instances, when the indiscretion of individuals provoked abuse,
there was less violence and personal insult than perhaps ever was
known in the same period of time, when all political union was broken
down, and private affection weakened, by the virulence of party
prejudice, which generally cuts in sunder the bands of social and
friendly connexion. The people irritated in the highest degree, the
sword seemed to be half drawn from the scabbard, while the trembling
hand appeared unwilling to display its whetted point; and all America,
as well as the Massachusetts, suspended all partial opposition, and

waited in anxious hope and expectation the decisions of a continental congress.

This respected assembly, the *Amphyctions* of the western world, convened by the free suffrages of twelve colonies, met at the time proposed, on the fourth of September, one thousand seven hundred and seventy-four. They [148] entered on business with hearts warmed with the love of their country, a sense of the common and equal rights of man, and the dignity of human nature. Peyton Randolph, Esq. a gentleman from Virginia, whose sobriety, integrity, and political abilities, qualified him for the important station, was unanimously chosen to preside in this grand council of American peers.

Though this body was sensibly affected by the many injuries received from the parent state, their first wish was a reconciliation on terms of reciprocity, justice and honor. In consequence of these sentiments they cautiously avoided, as far as was consistent with the duty due to their constituents, every thing that might tend to widen the breach between Great-Britain and the colonies. Yet they were determined, if parliament continued deaf to the calls of justice, not to submit to the yoke of tyranny, but to take the preparatory steps necessary for a vigorous resistance.

 After a thorough discussion of the civil, political, and commercial interests of both countries, the natural ties, and the mutual benefits resulting from the strictest amity, and the unhappy consequences that must ensue, if driven to the last appeal, they resolved on a dutiful and loyal petition to the king, recapitulating their grievances, and imploring redress: they [149] modestly remonstrated, and obliquely censured the authors of those mischiefs, which filled all America with complaint.

They drew up an affectionate, but spirited memorial to the people of England, reminding them that they held their own boasted liberties on a precarious tenure, if government, under the sanction of parliamentary authority, might enforce by the terrors of the sword their unconstitutional edicts. They informed them, that they determined, from a sense of justice to posterity, and for the honor of human nature, to resist all infringements on the natural rights of men; that, if neither the dictates of equity, nor the suggestions of humanity, were powerful enough to restrain a *wanton* administration from shedding blood in a cause so derogatory to the principles of *justice,* not all the exertions of superior strength should lead them to submit servilely to the impositions of a foreign power. They forwarded a

well-adapted address to the French inhabitants of Canada, to which CHAP. V
they subjoined a detail of their rights, with observations on the 1 7 7 4
alarming aspect of the late Quebec bill, and invited them to join in
the common cause of America.

Energy and precision, political ability, and the genuine *amor patriae*,
marked the measures of the short session of this congress. They
concluded their proceedings with an address to the [150] several
American colonies, exhorting them to union and perseverance in the
modes of opposition they had pointed out. Among the most important
of these was a strong recommendation to discontinue all commerce
with Great Britain, and encourage the improvement of arts and
manufactures among themselves. They exhorted all ranks and orders
of men to a strict adherence to industry, frugality, and sobriety of
manners; and to look primarily to the supreme Ruler of the universe,
who is able to defeat the crafty designs of the most potent enemy.
They agreed on a declaration of rights, and entered into an association,
to which the signature of every member of congress was affixed;* in
which they bound themselves to suspend all farther intercourse with
Great Britain, to import no merchandize from that hostile country, to
abstain from the use of all India teas; and that after a limited time,
if a radical redress of grievances was not obtained, no American
produce should be exported either to England or the West India
islands under the jurisdiction of Britain.

To these recommendations were added several sumptuary resolves;
after which they advised their constituents to a new choice of delegates,
to meet in congress on the tenth of May, one thousand seven hundred
and seventy-five: they [151] judged it probable that, by that time,
they should hear the success of their petitions to the throne. They
then prudently dissolved themselves, and returned to their private
occupations in their several provinces, there to wait the operation of
their resolutions and addresses.

It is scarcely possible to describe the influence of the transactions
and resolves of congress on the generality of the people throughout
the wide extended continent of America. History records no injunctions
of men, that were ever more religiously observed; or any human laws
more readily and universally obeyed, than were the recommendations
of this revered body. It is indeed a singular phenomenon in the story
of human conduct, that when all legal institutions were abolished,

* See Appendix, No. X.

CHAP. V and long established governments at once annihilated in so many

1 7 7 4 distinct states, that the recommendations of committees and conventions, not enforced by penal sanctions, should be equally influential and binding with the severest code of law, backed by royal authority, and strengthened by the murdering sword of despotism. Doubtless the fear of popular resentment operated on some, with a force equal to the rod of the magistrate: the singular punishments,* inflicted in some instances by an inflamed rabble, on a few who endeavored [152] to counteract the public measures, deterred others from openly violating the public resolves, and acting against the general consent of the people.

Not the bitterest foe to American freedom, whatever might be his wishes, presumed to counteract the general voice by an avowed importation of a single article of British merchandize, after the first day of February, one thousand seven hundred and seventy-five. The cargoes of all vessels that happened to arrive after this limited period were punctually delivered to the committees of correspondence, in the first port of their arrival, and sold at public auction. The prime cost and charges, and the half of one per cent. was paid to the owners, and the surplus of the profits was appropriated to the relief of the distressed inhabitants of Boston, agreeable to the seventh article in the association of the continental congress.

The voice of the multitude is as the rushing down of a torrent, nor is it strange that some outrages were committed against a few obstinate and imprudent partizans of the court, by persons of as little consideration as themselves. It is true that in the course of the arduous struggle, there were many irregularities that could not be justified, and some violences in consequence of the general discontent, that will [153] not stand the test, when examined at the bar of equity; yet perhaps fewer than ever took place in any country under similar circumstances. Witness the convulsions of Rome on the demolition of her first race of kings; the insurrections and commotions of her colonies before the downfal of the commonwealth; and to come nearer home, the confusions, the mobs, the cruelties in Britain in their civil convulsions, from William the conqueror to the days of the Stuarts, and from the arbitrary Stuarts to the riots of London and Liverpool, even in the reign of George the third.

Many other instances of the dread effects of popular commotion,

---

* Such as tarring and feathering &c.

when wrought up to resistance by the oppressive hand of power, CHAP. V
might be adduced from the history of nations,* and the [154] ferocity 1 7 7 4
of human nature, when not governed by interest or fear. Considering
the right of personal liberty, which every one justly claims, the
tenacious regard to property, and the pride of opinion, which sometimes operates to the dissolution of the tenderest ties of nature, it is
wonderful, when the mind was elevated by these powerful springs,
and the passions whetted by opposition or insult, that riot and
confusion, desolation and bloodshed, was not the fatal consequence
of the long interregnum of law and government throughout the
colonies. Yet not a life was lost till the trump of war summoned all
parties to the field.

Valor is an instinct that appears even among savages, as a dictate
of nature planted for self-defence; but patriotism on the diffusive
principles of general benevolence, is the child of society. This virtue
with the fair acomplishments of science, gradually grows and increases
with civilization, until refinement is wrought to a height that poisons
and corrupts the mind. This appears when the accumulation of wealth
is rapid, and the gratifications of luxurious appetite become easy; the
seeds of benevolence are then often destroyed, and the *man* reverts
[155] back to selfish barbarism, and feels no check to his rapacity and
boundless ambition, though his passions may be frequently veiled
under various alluring and deceptive appearances.

America was now a fair field for a transcript of all the virtues and
vices that have illumined or darkened, disgraced and reigned trium-
phant in their turn over all the other quarters of the habitable globe.
The progress of every thing had there been remarkably rapid, from
the first settlement of the country. Learning was cultivated, knowledge

---

* France might have been mentioned, as a remarkable instance of the truth of these
  observations, had they not been written several years before the extraordinary
  revolutions and cruel convulsions, that have since agitated that unhappy country.
  Every one will observe the astonishing difference in the conduct of the people of
  America and of France, in the two revolutions which took place within a few years
  of each other. In the one, all was horror, robbery, assassination, murder, devastation,
  and massacre; in the other, a general sense of rectitude checked the commission of
  those crimes, and the dread of spilling human blood withheld for a time the hand
  of party, even when the passions were irritated to the extreme. This must be
  attributed to the different religion, government, laws and manners of the two
  countries, previous to these great events; not to any difference in the nature of
  man; in similar circumstances, revenge, cruelty, confusion, and every evil work,
  operate equally on the ungoverned passions of men in all nations.

CHAP. V disseminated, politeness and morals improved, and valor and patriotism
1 7 7 4 cherished, in proportion to the rapidity of her population. This
extraordinary cultivation of arts and manners may be accounted for,
from the stage of society and improvement in which the first planters
of America were educated before they left their native clime. The
first emigrations to North America were not composed of a strolling
banditti of rude nations, like the first people of most other colonies
in the history of the world. The early settlers in the newly discovered
continent were as far advanced in civilization, policy, and manners;
in their ideas of government, the nature of compacts, and the bands
of civil union, as any of their neighbors at that period among the most
polished nations of Europe. Thus they soon grew to maturity, and
became able to vie with their European ancestors in arts, in arms, in
perspicuity [156] in the cabinet, courage in the field, and ability for
foreign negociations, in the same space of time that most other colonies
have required to pare off the ruggedness of their native ferocity,
establish the rudiments of civil society, and begin the fabric of
government and jurisprudence. Yet as they were not fully sensible of
their own strength and abilities, they wished still to hang upon the
arm, and look up for protection to their original parent.

The united voice of millions still acknowledged the sceptre of
Brunswick; firmly attached to the house of Hanover, educated in the
principles of monarchy, and fond of that mode of government under
certain limitations, they were still petitioning the king of England
only to be restored to the same footing of privilege claimed by his
other subjects, and wished ardently to keep the way open to a reunion,
consistent with their ideas of honor and freedom.

Thus the grand council of the union were disposed to wait the
operations of time, without hurrying to momentous decisions that
might in a degree have sanctioned severities in the parent state that
would have shut up every avenue to reconciliation. While the
representatives of all the provinces had thus been deliberating, the
individual colonies were far from being idle. Provincial congresses
and conventions [157] had in almost every province taken place of
the old forms of legislation and government, and they were all equally
industrious and united in the same modes to combat the intrigues of
the governmental faction, which equally infested the whole, though
the eastern borders of the continent more immediately suffered. But
their institutions in infancy, commerce suspended, and their property
seized; threatened by the national orators, by the proud chieftains of

military departments, and by the British fleet and army daily augmenting, hostilities of the most serious nature lowered on all sides;
the artillery of war and the fire of rhetoric seemed to combine for the
destruction of America.

The minds of the people at this period, though not dismayed, were
generally solemnized, in expectation of events, decisive both to
political and private happiness, and every brow appeared expressive
of sober anxiety. The people trembled for their liberties, the merchant
for his interest, the tories for their places, the whigs for their country,
and the virtuous for the manners of society.

It must be allowed that the genius of America was bold, resolute
and enterprising; tenacious of the rights their fathers had endured
such hardships to purchase, they determined to defend to the last
breath the invaluable possession. To check this ardent characteristic
it [158] had, previous to the time we are upon, been considered, as
if by common consent among the plantation governors, a stroke of
policy to depress the militia of the country. All military discipline had
for several years been totally neglected; thus untrained to arms,
whenever there had been an occasional call in aid of British operations
in America, the militia were considered as a rustic set of auxiliaries,
and employed not only in the least honorable, but the most menial
services. Though this indignity was felt, it was never properly resented;
they had borne the burthen of fatigue and subordination without
much complaint: but the martial spirit of the country now became
conspicuous, and the inclination of the youth of every class was
universally cherished, and military evolutions were the interludes that
most delighted even children in the intermission of their sedentary
exercises at school.

Among the manœuvres of this period of expectation, a certain quota
of hardy youth were drawn from the train-bands in every town, who
were styled *minute men.* They voluntarily devoted a daily portion of
their time to improve themselves in the military art, under officers of
their own choice. Thus when hostilities commenced, every district
could furnish a number of soldiers, who wanted nothing but experience
in the operations of war, to make them a match for any troops the
sovereign of Britain could boast.

[159] This military ardor wore an unpleasant aspect in the eyes of
administration. By a letter from lord Dartmouth to general Gage, soon
after he was appointed governor of the Massachusetts, it appeared
that a project for disarming certain provinces was seriously contem-

CHAP. V   plated in the cabinet.* The parliament actually prohibited the expor-

1 7 7 4   tation of arms, ammunition and military stores to any part of America, except for their own fleets and armies employed in the colonies; and the king's troops were frequently sent out in small parties to dismantle the forts, and seize the powder magazines or other military stores wherever they could be found. The people throughout the colonies with better success, took similar measures to secure to themselves whatever warlike stores were already in the country. Thus a kind of predatory struggle almost universally took place; every appearance of hostilities was discoverable in the occasional rencontres, except the drawing of blood, which was for a time suspended; delayed on one side from an apprehension that they were not quite ripe for the conflict; on the other, from an expectation of reinforcements [160] that might ensure victory on the easiest terms; and perhaps by both, from the recollection of former connexion and attachment.

A disunion of the colonies had long been zealously wished for, and vainly attempted by administration; as that could not be effected, it was deemed a wise and politic measure, to make an example of one they judged the most refractory. Thus resentment seemed particularly levelled at the Massachusetts; consequently they obliged that colony first to measure the sword with the hardy veterans of Britain.

The spirited proceedings of the county of Suffolk, soon after the arrival of governor Gage, and his hasty dissolution of the general assembly, in some measure damped the expectation of the ministry, who had flattered themselves that the depression and ruin of the Massachusetts would strike terror through the other provinces, and render the work of conquest more easy. But the decision and energy of this convention, composed of members from the principal towns in the county, discovered that the spirit of Americans at that time was not to be coerced by dragoons; and that if one colony, under the immediate frowns of government, with an army in their capital, were thus bold and determined, new calculations must be made for the subjugation of all.

---

* General Gage in his reply to the minister upon the above suggestion, observes, "Your lordship's idea of disarming certain provinces, would doubtless be consistent with prudence and safety; but it neither is, nor has been practicable, without having recourse to *force:* we must first become masters of the country." [Gage to Lord Dartmouth, December 15, 1774, in Clarence Edwin Carter, ed., *The Correspondence of General Thomas Gage with the Secretaries of State, 1763–1775* (2 vols.; Archon Books, 1969), I: 386–388.]

[161] The convention met in Suffolk, at once unanimously renounced the authority of the new legislature, and engaged to bear
harmless all officers who should refuse to act under it. They pronounced
all those, who had accepted seats at the board of council by mandamus,
the incorrigible enemies of their country. They recommended to the
people to perfect themselves in the art of war, and to prepare to resist
by force of arms, every hostile invasion. They resolved, that if any
person should be apprehended for his exertions in the public cause,
reprisals should be made, by seizing and holding in custody the
principal officers of the crown, wherever they could be found, until
ample justice should be done. They advised the collectors and receivers
of all public monies, to hold it in their hands, till appropriations
should be directed by authority of a provincial congress. They earnestly
urged an immediate choice of delegates for that purpose, and recommended their convening at Salem.

These and several other resolves in the same style and manner,
were considered by government as the most overt acts of *treason* that
had yet taken place; but their doings were but a specimen of the
spirit which actuated the whole province. Every town, with the utmost
alacrity, chose one or more of the most respectable gentlemen, to
meet in provincial congress, [162] agreeable to the recommendation
on the fifteenth of October, one thousand seven hundred and seventy-
four. They were requested by their constituents, to take into consideration the distressed state of the country, and to devise the most
practicable measures to extricate the people from their present
perplexed situation.

In the mean time, to preclude the appearance of necessity for such
a convention, governor Gage issued precepts, summoning a new
general assembly to meet at Salem, the week preceding the time
appointed for the meeting of the convention. The people obeyed the
order of the governor, and every where chose their representatives;
but they all chose the same persons they had recently delegated to
meet in convention. Whether the governor was apprehensive that it
would not be safe for his mandamus council to venture out of the
capital, or whether conscious that it would not be a constitutional
assembly, or from the imbecility of his own mind, in a situation
altogether new to him, is uncertain; but from whatever cause it arose,
he discovered his embarrassment by a proclamation, dated the day
before he was to meet them at Salem, to dissolve the new house of
representatives. This extraordinary dissolution only precipitated the

CHAP. V   pre-determination of the delegates; they had taken their line of
1 7 7 4   conduct, and their determinations were not easily shaken.

[163] The council chosen by the house on the day of their last election had also, as requested, repaired to Salem. The design was, to proceed to business as usual, without any notice of the annihilation of their charter. Their determination was, if the governor refused to meet with or countenance them, to consider him as absent from the province. It had been usual under the old charter, when the governor's signature could not be obtained, by reason of death or absence, that by the names of fifteen counsellors affixed thereto, all the acts of assembly were equally valid, as when signed by the governor. But by the extraordinary conduct of the chief magistrate, the general assembly was left at liberty to complete measures in any mode or form that appeared most expedient; accordingly they adjourned to Concord, a town situated about thirty miles from Salem, and there prosecuted the business of their constituents.

As it was not yet thought prudent to assume all the powers of an organized government, they chose a president, and acted as a provincial congress, as previously proposed. They recommended to the militia to choose their own officers, and submit to regular discipline at least thrice a week, and that a fourth part of them should be draughted, and hold themselves in readiness to march at a moment's warning to any part of the province. They recommended [164] to the several counties to adhere to their own resolves, and to keep the courts of common law shut till some future period, when justice could be legally administered. They appointed a committee of supplies to provide ammunition, provisions, and warlike stores, and to deposite them in some place of safety, ready for use, if they should be obliged to take up arms in defence of their rights.

This business required talents and energy to make arrangements for exigencies, new and untried. Fortunately Elbridge Gerry, Esq. was placed at the head of this commission, who executed it with his usual punctuality and indefatigable industry. This gentleman entered from principle, early in the opposition to British encroachments, and continued one of the most uniform republicans to the end of the contest. He was the next year chosen a delegate to the continental congress. Firm, exact, perspicuous, and tenacious of public and private honor, he rendered essential service to the union for many years that he continued a member of that honorable body.*

* Mr. Gerry's services and exertions to promote the public interest through every

[165] The provincial congress appointed a committee of safety, CHAP. V consisting of nine members, and vested them with powers to act as 1 7 7 4 they should see fit for the public service, in the recess, and to call them together again, on any extraordinary emergence; and before they separated, they chose a new set of delegates, to meet in general congress the ensuing spring. After this they held a conference with the committees of donation and correspondence, and the selectment of the town of Boston, on the expediency of an effort to remove the inhabitants from a town blockaded on all sides. They then separated for a few weeks, to exert their influence in aid to the resolutions of the people; to strengthen their fortitude, and prepare them for the approaching storm, which they were sensible could be at no great distance.

Though the inhabitants of Boston were shut up in garrison, insulted by the troops, and in many respects felt the evils of a severe military government; yet the difficulty of removing thousands from their residence in the capital, to seek an asylum in the country on the eve of winter, appeared fraught with inconveniencies too great to be attempted; they were of consequence, the most of them obliged to continue [166] amidst the outrages of a licentious army, and wait patiently the events of the ensuing spring.

The principal inhabitants of the town, though more immediately 1 7 7 5 under the eye of their oppressors, lost no part of their determined spirit, but still acted in unison with their friends more at liberty without the city. A bold instance of this appeared, when Mr. Oliver, the chief justice, regardless of the impeachment that lay against him, attempted with his associates to open the superior court, and transact business according to the new regulations. Advertisements were posted in several public places, forbidding on their peril, the attornies and barristers at law, to carry any cause up to the bar. Both the grand and petit-jurors refused attendance, and finally the court was obliged to adjourn without day.

These circumstances greatly alarmed the party, more especially those natives of the country who had taken sanctuary under the

---

important station which he filled, from this period until he was appointed to negociate with the republic of France in the year one thousand seven hundred and ninety-eight, were uniform. There his indefatigable zeal, his penetration, and cool perseverance, when every thing appeared on the eve of a rupture between the two republics, laid the foundation and formed the outlines of an accommodation, which soon after terminated in an amicable treaty between France and the United States of America.

CHAP. V   banners of an officer, who had orders to enforce the acts of adminis-
1 7 7 5   tration, even at the point of the bayonet. Apprehensive they might
be dragged from their asylum within the gates, they were continually
urging general Gage to more vigorous measures without. They assured
him, that it would be easy for him to execute the designs of
government, provided he would by law-martial seize, try, or transport
[167] to England, such persons as were most particularly obnoxious;
and that if the people once saw him thus determined, they would
sacrifice their leaders and submit quietly.

They associated, and bound themselves by covenant, to go all
lengths in support of the projects of administration against their
country; but the general, assured of reinforcements in the spring,
sufficient to enable him to open a bloody campaign, and not remarkable
for resolution or activity, had not the courage, and perhaps not the
inclination, to try the dangerous experiment, till he felt himself
stronger. He was also sensible of the striking similarity of genius,
manners, and conduct of the colonies in union. It was observable to
every one, that local prejudices, either in religion or government,
taste or politics, were suspended, and that every distinction was sunk,
in the consideration of the necessity of connexion and vigor in one
general system of defence. He therefore proceeded no farther, during
the winter, than publishing proclamations against congresses, committees, and conventions, styling all associations of the kind unlawful
and treasonable combinations, and forbidding all persons to pay the
smallest regard to their recommendations, on penalty of his majesty's
severest displeasure.

[168] These feeble exertions only confirmed the people in their
adherence to the modes pointed out by those, to whom they had
intrusted the safety of the commonwealth. The only active movement
of the season was that of a party commanded by colonel Leslie, who
departed from Castle William on the evening of Saturday, February
twenty-seventh, one thousand seven hundred and seventy-five, on a
secret expedition to Salem. The design was principally to seize a few
cannon on the ensuing morning. The people apprized of his approach,
drew up a bridge over which his troops were to pass. Leslie, finding
his passage would be disputed, and having no orders to proceed to
blows, after much expostulation engaged, that if he might be permitted
to go on the ground, he would molest neither public nor private
property. The bridge was immediately let down, and through a line
of armed inhabitants, ready to take vengeance on a forfeiture of his

word, he only marched to the extreme part of the town, and then
returned to Boston, to the mortification of himself and of his friends,
that an officer of colonel Leslie's acknowledged bravery should be
sent out on so frivolous an errand.

This incident discovered the determination of the Americans,
carefully to avoid every thing that had the appearance of beginning
hostilities on their part; an imputation that [169] might have been
attended with great inconvenience; nor indeed were they prepared to
precipitate a conflict, the consequences and the termination of which
no human calculation could reach. This manœuvre also discovered
that the people of the country were not deficient in point of courage,
but that they stood charged for a resistance, that might smite the
sceptred hand, whenever it should be stretched forth to arrest by
force the inheritance purchased by the blood of ancestors, whose self-
denying virtues had rivalled the admired heroes of antiquity.

C H A P T E R   V I

Parliamentary Divisions on American Affairs—cursory Observations and Events • Measures for raising an Army of Observation by the four New England Governments of New Hampshire, Massachusetts, Rhode Island, and Connecticut • Battle of Lexington • Sketches of the Conduct and Characters of the Governors of the southern Provinces • Ticonderoga taken • Arrival of Reinforcements from England • Proscription and Characters of Samuel Adams and John Hancock, Esquires • Battle of Bunker-Hill • Death and Character of General Joseph Warren • Massachusetts adopt a stable Form of Government

CHAP. VI [170] We have seen several years pass off in doubtful anxiety, in 1 7 7 5 repression and repulsion, while many yet indulged the pleasing hope, that some able genius might arise, that would devise measures to heal the breach, to revive the languishing commerce of both countries, and restore the blessings of peace, by removing the causes of complaint. But these hopes evanished, and all expectations of that kind were soon cut off, by the determined system of coercion in Britain, and the actual commencement of *war* in *America*.

The earliest accounts from England, after the beginning of the year one thousand seven hundred and seventy-five, announced the ferments of the British nation, principally on account of American measures, the perseverance of the [171] ministry, and the obstinacy of the king, in support of the system;—the sudden dissolution of one parliament, and the immediate election of another, composed of the same members, or men of the same principles as the former.

Administration had triumphed through the late parliament over reason, justice, the humanity of individuals, and the interest of the nation. Notwithstanding the noble and spirited opposition of several distinguished characters in both houses, it soon appeared that the influence of the ministry over the old parliament was not depreciated,

or that more lenient principles pervaded the councils of the new one.
Nor did more judicious and favorable decisions lead to the prospect
of an equitable adjustment of a dispute that had interested the feelings
of the whole empire, and excited the attention of neighboring nations,
not as an object of curiosity, but with views and expectations that
might give a new face to the political and commercial systems of a
considerable part of the European world.

The petition of the continental congress to the king, their address
to the people of England, with general Gage's letters, and all papers
relative to America, were introduced early in the session of the new
parliament. Warm debates ensued, and the cause of the colonies was
advocated with ability and energy by the [172] most admired orators
among the commons, and by several very illustrious names in the
house of lords. They descanted largely on the injustice and impolicy
of the present system, and the impracticability of its execution. They
urged that the immediate repeal of the revenue acts, the recal of the
troops, and the opening the port of Boston, were necessary, preliminary
steps to any hope of reconciliation; and that these measures only
would preserve the empire from consequences that would be fatal to
her interests, as well as disgraceful to her councils. But, pre-determined
in the cabinet, a large majority in parliament appeared in favor of
strong measures. The ministerial party insisted that coercion only
could ensure obedience, restore tranquillity to the colonies, repair the
insulted dignity, and re-establish the supremacy of parliament.

An act was immediately passed, prohibiting New Hampshire,
Massachusetts, Rhode Island, and Connecticut from carrying on the
fishing business on the banks of Newfoundland. By this arbitrary step,
thousands of miserable families were suddenly cut off from all means
of subsistence. But, as if determined the rigors of power should know
no bounds, before parliament had time to cool, after the animosities
occasioned by the bill just mentioned, another* was introduced by
the [173] minister, whereby the trade of the southern colonies was
restrained, and in future confined entirely to Great Britain. The
minority still persevered in the most decided opposition both against
the former and the present modes of severity towards the colonies.
Very sensible and spirited protests were entered against the new bills,
signed by some of the first nobility. A young nobleman of high rank

* Parliamentary proceedings in one thousand seven hundred and seventy-five. [*Cobbett*,
   XVIII: 298–305 (February 10, 1775); 379–399 (February 24, 1775: New England);
   and 411–412 (March 9, 1775: southern colonies).]

CHAP. VI and reputation predicted, that "measures commenced in iniquity, and
1 7 7 5 pursued in resentment, must end in blood, and involve the nation in
immediate civil war."* It was replied, that the colonies were already
in a state of rebellion; that the supremacy of parliament must not
even be questioned; and that compulsory measures must be pursued
from absolute necessity. Neither reason nor argument, humanity or
policy, made the smallest impression on those determined to support
all despotic proceedings. Thus after much altercation, a majority of
two hundred and eighty-two appeared in favor of augmenting the
forces in America, both by sea and land, against only seventy in the
house of commons, who opposed the measure.

All ideas of courage or ability in the colonists to face the dragoons
and resist the power of Britain, were treated with the greatest derision,
[174] and particularly ridiculed by a general officer,† then in the
house, who soon after delivered his standards, and saw the surrender
of a capital army under his command, to those undisciplined Americans
he had affected to hold in so much contempt. The first lord of the
admiralty also declared, "the Americans were neither disciplined, nor
capable of discipline."

Several ships of the line and a number of frigates were immediately
ordered to join the squadron at Boston. Ten thousand men were
ordered for the land service, in addition to those already there. A
regiment of light-horse, and a body of troops from Ireland, to complete
the number, were directed to embark with all possible dispatch to
reinforce general Gage.

The speech from the throne, approving the sanguinary conduct of
the minister and the parliament, blasted all the hopes of the more
moderate and humane part of the nation. Several gallant officers of
the first rank, disgusted with the policy, and revolting at the idea of
butchering their American brethren, resigned their commissions. The
earl of Effingham was among the first, who, with a frankness that his
enemies styled a degree of insanity, assured his majesty,

> that though he loved the profession of a soldier, and would with the utmost
> [175] cheerfulness sacrifice his fortune and his life for the safety of his

* Debates in parliament, one thousand seven hundred and seventy-five. [None of the
Parliamentary sources reveals the quotation or the identity of the speaker. But see
the speeches of Charles James Fox and Edmund Burke, *Cobbett*, XVIII: 385–386,
389–392 (March 6, 1775). Also see *Annual Register* (1775), "History of Europe," pp.
78–93.]

† General Burgoyne, afterwards captured at Saratoga.

majesty's person, and the dignity of his crown; yet the same principles CHAP. VI
which inspired him with those unalterable sentiments of duty and affection, 1 7 7 5
would not suffer him to be instrumental in depriving any part of the people
of their liberties, which to him appeared the best security of their fidelity
and obedience; therefore without the severest reproaches of conscience
he could not consent to bear arms against the Americans.

But there is no age which bears a testimony so honorable to human
nature; as shews mankind at so sublime a pitch of virtue, that there
are not always enough to be found ready to aid the arm of the
oppressor, provided they may share in the spoils of the oppressed.
Thus many officers of ability and experience courted the American
service as the readiest road to preferment.

Administration not satisfied with their own severe restrictions, set
on foot a treaty with the Dutch and several other nations, to prevent
their aiding the colonies by supplying them with any kind of warlike
stores. Every thing within and without wore the most hostile appearance, even while the commercial interest of Great Britain was closely
interwoven with that of America; and the treasures of the colonies,
[176] which had been continually pouring into the lap of the mother
country, in exchange for her manufactures, were still held ready for
her use, in any advance to harmony.

The boundaries of the king of England's continental domains were
almost immeasurable, and the inhabitants were governed by a strong
predilection in favor of the nation from whom they derived their
origin: hence it is difficult to account on any principles of human
policy, for the infatuation that instigated to the absurd project of
conquering a country, already their's on the most advantageous terms.
But the seeds of separation were sown, and the *ball* of empire rolled
westward with such astonishing rapidity, that the pious mind is
naturally excited to acknowledge a superintending Providence, that
led to the period of independence, even before America was conscious
of her maturity. Precipitated into a war, dreadful even in contemplation, humanity recoiled at the idea of civil feuds, and their concomitant
evils.

When the news arrived in the colonies that the British army in
Boston was to be reinforced, that the coercive system was at all hazards
to be prosecuted, though astonished at the persevering severity of a
nation still beloved and revered by Americans, deeply affected with
the calamities that threatened the whole empire, and shocked at the
prospect of the convulsions and [177] the cruelties ever attendant on

civil war, yet few balanced on the part they were to act. The alternative held up was a bold and vigorous resistance, or an abject submission to the ignoble terms demanded by administration. Armed with resolution and magnanimity, united by affection, and a remarkable conformity of opinion, the whole people through the wide extended continent seemed determined to resist in blood, rather than become the slaves of arbitrary power.

Happily for America, the inhabitants in general possessed not only the virtues of native courage and a spirit of enterprise, but minds generally devoted to the best affections. Many of them retained this character to the end of the conflict by the dereliction of interest, and the costly sacrifices of health, fortune and life. Perhaps the truth of the observation, that "a national force is best formed where numbers of men are used to equality, and where the meanest citizen may consider himself destined to command as well as to obey," was never more conspicuous, than in the brave resistance of Americans to the potent and conquering arm of Great Britain, who, in conjunction with her colonies, had long taught the nations to tremble at her strength.

But the painful period hastened on, when the connexion which nature and interest had long [178] maintained between Great Britain and the colonies, must be broken off; the sword drawn, and the scabbard thrown down the gulf of time. We must now pursue the progress of a war enkindled by avarice, whetted by ambition, and blown up into a thirst for revenge by repeated disappointment. Not the splendor of a diadem, the purple of princes, or the pride of power, can ever sanction the deeds of cruelty perpetrated on the western side of the Atlantic, and not unfrequently by men, whose crimes emblazoned by title, will enhance the infamy of their injustice and barbarism, when the tragic tale is faithfully related.

We have already observed on the supplicatory addresses every where offered to the old government, the rebuffs attending them, the obstruction to legal debate, and the best possible regulations made by the colonies in their circumstances, under the new modes established by themselves.

The authority of congresses and committees of correspondence, and the spirit which pervaded the united colonies in their preparations for war, during the last six months previous to the commencement of hostilities, bore such a resemblance, that the detail of the transactions of one province is an epitome of the story of all.

[179] The particular resentment of Great Britain levelled at the

Massachusetts, made it necessary for that province to act a more CHAP. VI
decided part, that they might be in some readiness to repel the storm 1 7 7 5
which it appeared probable would first burst upon them. Their
provincial congress was sitting when the news first arrived, that all
hope of reconciliation was precluded by the hostile resolutions of
parliament. This rather quickened than retarded the important step,
which was then the subject of their deliberations. Persuaded that the
unhappy contest could not terminate without bloodshed, they were
consulting on the expediency of raising an army of observation, from
the four New England governments, that they might be prepared for
defence in case of an attack, before the continental congress could
again meet, and make proper arrangements for farther operations.
They proceeded to name their own commanding officers, and appointed delegates to confer with New Hampshire, Connecticut, and
Rhode Island, on the proportion of men they would furnish, and their
quota of expense for the equipment of such an armament.

Connecticut and New Hampshire readily acceded to the proposal,
but in Rhode Island several embarrassments were thrown in the way,
though the people in that colony were in general as ready to enter
warmly into measures for the common safety as any of the others;
[180] nor had they less reason. They had long been exasperated by
the insolence and rapacity of the officers of a part of the navy stationed
there to watch their trade. These had, without color of right, frequently
robbed Newport, and plundered the adjacent islands. They had seized
the little skiffs, in which a number of poor people had gained a scanty
subsistence; and insulted, embarrassed and abused the inhabitants in
various ways through the preceding year.

It is the nature of man, when he despairs of legal reparation for
injuries received, to seek satisfaction by avenging his own wrongs.
Thus, some time before this period,* a number of men in disguise,
had riotously assembled, and set fire to a sloop of war in the harbour.
When they had thus discovered their resentment by this illegal
proceeding, they dispersed without farther violence. For this imputed
crime the whole colony had been deemed guilty, and interdicted as
accessary. A court of inquiry was appointed by his majesty, vested
with the power of seizing any person on suspicion, confining him on
board a king's ship, and sending him to England for trial. But some
of the gentlemen named for this inquisitorial business, had not the

* See Appendix, Note No. XI, governor Hutchinson's representation of this affair.

CHAP. VI temerity to execute it in the [181] latitude designed; and after sitting
1 7 7 5 a few days, examining a few persons, and threatening many, they
adjourned to a distant day.

The extraordinary precedent of erecting such a court* among them
was not forgotten; but there was a considerable party in Newport,
strongly attached to the royal cause. These, headed by their governor,
Mr. Wanton, a man of weak capacity, and little political knowledge,
endeavoured to impede all measures of opposition, and to prevent
even a discussion on the propriety of raising a defensive army.

The news of an action at Lexington on the nineteenth of April,
between a party of the king's troops and some Americans hastily
collected, reached Providence on the same evening, a few hours after
the gentlemen entrusted with the mission for conference with the
colony had arrived there; they had not entered on business, having
been in town but an hour or two before this intelligence was received
by a special messenger.

On this important information, James Warren, Esq. the head of the
delegation, was of [182] opinion, that this event not only opened new
prospects and expectations, but that it entirely changed the object of
negociation, and that new ground must be taken. Their mission was
by the Massachusetts designed merely as a defensive movement, but
he observed to the principal inhabitants collected to consult on the
alarming aspect of present affairs, that there now appeared a necessity,
not only for defensive but for offensive operations; he urged his
reasons with such ability and address, that an immediate convention
of the assembly was obtained. They met at Providence the ensuing
day, where, by the trifling of the governor and the indiscretion of his
partizans, the business labored in the upper house for several days.
But the representative branch, impatient of delay, determined to act
without any consideration of their governor, if he continued thus to
impede their designs, and to unite, by authority of their own body,
in vigorous measures with their sister colonies. A majority of the
council however, at last impelled the governor to agree to the
determinations of the lower house, who had voted a number of men
to be raised with the utmost dispatch; accordingly a large detachment
was sent forward to the Massachusetts within three days.

When the gentlemen left congress for the purpose of combining

* The gentlemen who composed this court, were Wanton, governor of Rhode Island,
Horsemanden, chief justice of New York, Smith, chief justice of New Jersey, Oliver,
chief justice of Massachusetts, and Auchmuty, judge of admiralty.

and organizing an army in the eastern states, a short adjournment was CHAP. VI
[183] made. Before they separated they selected a standing committee 1 7 7 5
to reside at Concord, where a provincial magazine was kept, and
vested them with power to summon congress to meet again at a
moment's warning, if any extraordinary emergence should arise.

In the course of the preceding winter, a single regiment at a time
had frequently made excursions from the army at Boston, and
reconnoitred the environs of the town without committing any hostilities in the country, except picking up cannon, powder, and warlike
stores, wherever they could find and seize them with impunity. In
the spring, as they daily expected fresh auxiliaries, they grew more
insolent; from their deportment, there was the highest reason to
expect they would extend their researches, and endeavour to seize
and secure, as they termed them, the *factious leaders of rebellion.* Yet
this was attempted rather sooner than was generally expected.

On the evening of the eighteenth of April, the grenadiers and light
infantry of the army stationed at Boston, embarked under the command
of lieutenant colonel Smith, and were ordered to land at Cambridge
before the dawn of the ensuing day. This order was executed with
such secrecy and dispatch, that the troops reached Lexington, a small
village nine miles beyond Cambridge, and began the tragedy of the
day just as the sun rose.

[184] An advanced guard of officers had been sent out by land, to
seize and secure all travellers who might be suspected as going forward
with intelligence of the hostile aspect of the king's troops. But
notwithstanding this vigilance to prevent notice, a report reached the
neighboring towns very early, that a large body of troops accompanied
by some of the most virulent individuals among the *tories,* who had
taken refuge in Boston, were moving with design to destroy the
provincial magazine at Concord, and take into custody the principal
persons belonging to the committee of safety. Few suspected there
was a real intention to attack the defenceless peasants of Lexington,
or to try the bravery of the surrounding villages. But it being reduced
to a certainty, that a number of persons had, the evening before, in
the environs of Cambridge, been insulted, abused, and stripped, by
officers in British uniform; and that a considerable armament might
be immediately expected in the vicinity, captain Parker, who commanded a company of militia, ordered them to appear at beat of drum
on the parade at Lexington, on the nineteenth. They accordingly
obeyed, and were embodied before sunrise.

CHAP. VI   Colonel Smith, who commanded about eight hundred men, came
1 7 7 5   suddenly upon them within a few minutes after, and, accosting them
in language very unbecoming an officer of his rank, he ordered them
to lay down their arms, [185] and disperse immediately. He illiberally
branded them with the epithets of *rebel* and *traitor;* and before the
little party had time, either to resist or to obey, he, with wanton
precipitation, ordered his troops to fire. Eight men were killed on the
spot; and, without any concern for his rashness, or little molestation
from the inhabitants, Smith proceeded on his rout.

By the time he reached Concord, and had destroyed a part of the
stores deposited there, the country contiguous appeared in arms, as
if determined not to be the tame spectators of the outrages committed
against the persons, property, and lives of their fellow-citizens. Two
or three hundred men assembled under the command of colonel
Barrett. He ordered them to begin no onset against the troops of their
sovereign, till farther provocation; this order was punctually obeyed.
Colonel Smith had ordered a bridge beyond the town to be taken up,
to prevent the people on the other side from coming to their assistance.
Barrett advanced to take possession before the party reached it, and
a smart skirmish ensued; several were killed, and a number wounded
on both sides. Not dismayed or daunted, this small body of yeomanry,
armed in the cause of justice, and struggling for every thing they held
dear, maintained their stand until the British troops, though far
superior in numbers, and in all the advantage [186] of military skill,
discipline, and equipment, gave ground and retreated, without half
executing the purpose designed, by this forced march to Concord.

The adjacent villagers collected, and prepared to cut off their
retreat; but a dispatch had been sent by colonel Smith to inform
general Gage, that the county was arming, and his troops in danger.
A battalion under the command of lord Percy was sent to succour
him, and arrived in time to save Smith's corps. A son of the duke of
Northumberland,* previous to this day's work, was viewed by Americans with a favorable eye; though more from a partiality to the father,
than from any remarkable personal qualities discoverable in the son.
Lord Percy came up with the routed corps near the fields of Menotomy;
where barbarities were committed by the king's army, which might
have been expected only from a tribe of savages. They entered, rifled,

---

* The duke of Northumberland, father of earl Percy, had been uniformly opposed to
the late measures of administration, in their American system.

plundered, and burnt several houses; and in some instances, the aged
and infirm fell under the sword of the ruffian; women, with their
new-born infants, were obliged to fly naked, to escape the fury of the
flames in which their houses were enwrapped.

[187] The footsteps of the most remorseless nations have seldom
been marked with more rancorous and ferocious rage, than may be
traced in the transactions of this day; a day never to be forgotten by
Americans. A scene like this had never before been exhibited on her
peaceful plains; and the manner in which it was executed, will leave
an indelible stain on a nation, long famed for their courage, humanity,
and honor. But they appeared at this period so lost to a sense of
dignity, as to be engaged in a cause that required perfidy and meanness
to support it. Yet the impression of justice is so strongly stamped on
the bosom of man, that when conscious the sword is lifted against
the rights of equity, it often disarms the firmest heart, and unnerves
the most valiant arm, when impelled to little subterfuges and private
cruelties to execute their guilty designs.

The affair of Lexington, and the precipitant retreat after the ravages
at Menotomy, are testimonies of the truth of this observation. For,
notwithstanding their superiority in every respect, several regiments
of the best troops in the royal army, were seen, to the surprise and
joy of every lover of his country, flying before the raw, inexperienced
peasantry, who had ran hastily together in defence of their lives and
liberties. Had the militia of Salem and Marblehead have come on, as
it was thought they might have done, they would undoubtedly have
[188] prevented this routed, disappointed army, from reaching the
advantageous post of Charlestown. But the tardiness of colonel
Pickering, who commanded the Salem regiment, gave them an
opportunity to make good their retreat. Whether Mr. Pickering's*
delay was owing to timidity, or to a predilection in favor of Britain,
remains uncertain; however it was, censure at the time fell very
heavily on his character.

Other parts of the country were in motion; but the retreat of the
British army was so rapid, that they got under cover of their own
ships, and many of them made their escape into Boston. Others, too
much exhausted by a quick march and unremitting exercise, without
time for refreshment from sunrise to sunset, were unable, both from

* Timothy Pickering, afterwards secretary of state under the presidency of Mr. Adams,
  by whom he was dismissed from public business.

wounds and fatigue, to cross the river. These were obliged to rest the night, nor were they mistaken in the confidence they placed in the hospitality of the inhabitants of Charlestown; this they reasonably enough expected, both from motives of compassion and fear.

Intimidated by the appearance of such a formidable body of troops within their town, and touched with humanity on seeing the famished condition of the king's officers and soldiers, several of whom, from their wounds and their sufferings, [189] expired before the next morning; the people every where opened their doors, received the distressed Britons, dressed their wounds, and contributed every relief: nothing was neglected that could assist, refresh, or comfort the defeated.

The victorious party, sensible they could gain little advantage by a farther pursuit, as the British were within reach of their own ships, and at the same time under the protection of the town of Charlestown; they therefore retreated a few miles to take care of their own wounded men, and to refresh themselves.

The action at Lexington, detached from its consequences, was but a trivial *manoeuvre* when compared with the records of war and slaughter, that have disgraced the page of history through all generations of men: but a circumstantial detail of lesser events, when antecedent to the convulsions of empire, and national revolution, are not only excusable, but necessary. The provincials lost in this memorable action, including those who fell, who were not in arms, upwards of fourscore persons. It was not easy to ascertain how many of their opponents were lost, as they endeavoured by all possible means to conceal the number, and the disgrace of the day. By the best information, it was judged, including those who died soon after of wounds and fatigue, that their loss was very much greater [190] than that of the Americans. Thus resentment stimulated by recent provocation, the colonies, under all the disadvantages of an infant country, without discipline, without allies, and without resources, except what they derived from their own valor and virtue, were compelled to resort to the last appeal, the precarious decision of the sword, against the mighty power of Britain.

The four New England governments now thought proper to make this last appeal, and resolved to stand or fall together. It was a bold and adventurous enterprise; but conscious of the equal privileges bestowed by Heaven, on all its intelligent creatures on this habitable ball, they did not hesitate on the part they had to act, to retain them.

They cheerfully engaged, sure of the support of the other colonies,
as soon as congress should have time to meet, deliberate, and resolve.
They were very sensible, the middle and southern colonies were
generally preparing themselves, with equal industry and ability, for a
decision by arms, whenever hostilities should seriously commence in
any part of the continent.

As soon as intelligence was spread that the first blow was struck,
and that the shrill clarion of war actually resounded in the capital of
the eastern states, the whole country rose in arms. Thousands collected
within twenty-four hours, [191] in the vicinity of Boston; and the
colonies of Connecticut, Rhode Island, and New Hampshire seemed
all to be in motion. Such was the resentment of the people, and the
ardor of enterprise, that it was with difficulty they were restrained
from rushing into Boston, and rashly involving their friends in common
with their enemies, in all the calamities of a town taken by storm.

The day after the battle of Lexington, the congress of Massachusetts
met at Watertown. They immediately determined on the number of
men necessary to be kept on the ground, appointed and made
establishments for the officers of each regiment, agreed on regulations
for all military movements, and struck off a currency of paper for the
payment of the soldiers, making the bills a tender for the payment
of debts, to prevent depreciation. They drew up a set of judicious
rules and orders for the army, to be observed by both officers and
soldiers, until they should be embodied on a larger scale, under the
general direction of the continental congress.

In the mean time, the consternation of general Gage was equalled
by nothing but the rage of his troops, and the dismay of the *refugees*
under his protection. He had known little of the country, and less of
the disposition and bravery of its inhabitants. He had formed his
opinions entirely on the misrepresentations of men, who, [192] judging
from their own feelings more than from the general conduct of
mankind, had themselves no idea that the valor of their countrymen
could be roused to hazard life and property for the sake of the common
weal. Struck with astonishment at the intrepidity of a people he had
been led to despise, and stung with vexation at the defeat of some
of his best troops, he ordered the gates of the town to be shut, and
every avenue guarded, to prevent the inhabitants, whom he now
considered as his best security, from making their escape into the
country. He had before caused entrenchments to be thrown up across
a narrow isthmus, then the only entrance by land: still apprehensive

of an attempt to storm the town, he now ordered the environs fortified; and soon made an entrance impracticable, but at too great an expense of blood.

The Bostonians thus unexpectedly made prisoners, and all intercourse with the country, from whence they usually received their daily supplies, cut off; famine stared them in the face on one side, and on the other they beheld the lawless rapine of an enraged enemy, with the sword of vengeance stretched over their heads. Yet, with a firmness worthy of more generous treatment, the principal citizens assembled, and after consultation, determined on a bold and free remonstrance to their military governor. They reminded him of his repeated [193] assurances of personal liberty, safety, and protection, if they would not evacuate the town, as they had long been solicited to do by their friends in the country. Had this been seasonably done, the Americans would have reduced the garrison by withholding provisions. The inhabitants of the town now earnestly requested, that the gates might be opened, that none who chose to retire with their wives, families, and property, might be impeded.

Whether moved by feelings of compassion, of which he did not seem to be wholly destitute, or whether it was a premeditated deception, yet remains uncertain; however, general Gage plighted his faith in the strongest terms, that if the inhabitants would deliver up their arms, and suffer them to be deposited in the city hall, they should depart at pleasure, and be assisted by the king's troops in removing their property. His shameful violation of faith in this instance, will leave a stain on the memory of the governor, so long as the obligations of truth are held sacred among mankind.

The insulted people of Boston, after performing the hard conditions of the contract, were not permitted to depart, until after several months of anxiety had elapsed, when the scarcity and badness of provisions had brought on a pestilential disorder, both among the inhabitants [194] and the soldiers. Thus, from a reluctance to dip their hands in human blood, and from the dread of insult to which their feebler connexions were exposed, this unfortunate town, which contained near twenty thousand inhabitants, was betrayed into a disgraceful resignation of their arms, which the natural love of liberty should have inspired them to have held for their own defence, while subjected to the caprice of an arbitrary master. After their arms were delivered up and secured, general Gage denied the contract, and forbade their retreat; though afterwards obliged to a partial compliance,

by the difficulty of obtaining food for the subsistence of his own army.
On certain stipulated gratuities to some of his officers, a permit was
granted them, to leave their elegant houses, their furniture, and
goods, and to depart naked from the capital, to seek an asylum and
support from the hospitality of their friends in the country.

The islands within the harbour of Boston were so plentifully stocked
with sheep, cattle, and poultry, that they would have afforded an
ample supply to the British army for a long time, had they been
suffered quietly to possess them. General Putnam, an officer of
courage and experience, defeated this expectation by taking off every
thing from one of the principal islands, under the fire of the British
ships; at the same time, he was so fortunate as to burn [195] several
of their tenders, without losing a man.* His example was followed;
and from Chelsea to Point Alderton, the islands were stripped of
wheat and other grain, of cattle and forage; and whatever they could
not carry off, the Americans destroyed by fire. They burnt the light-
house at the entrance of the harbour, and the buildings on all the
islands, to prevent the British availing themselves of such convenient
appendages for encampments so near the town.

While these transactions were passing in the eastern provinces, the
other colonies were equally animated by the spirit of resistance, and
equally busy in preparation. Their public bodies were undismayed;
their temper, their conduct, and their operations, both in the civil
and military line, were a fair and uniform transcript of the conduct of
the Massachusetts; and some of them equally experienced thus early,
the rigorous proceedings of their unrelenting governors.

New York was alarmed soon after the commencement of hostilities
near Boston, by a rumor, that a part of the armament expected from
Great Britain, was to be stationed there to awe the country, and for
the protection of the numerous loyalists in the city. In some instances,
[196] the province of New York had not yet fully acceded to the
doings of the general congress; but they now applied to them for
advice, and shewed themselves equally ready to renounce their
allegiance to the king of Great Britain, and to unite in the common
cause in all respects, as any of the other colonies. Agreeable to the
recommendation of congress, they sent off their women, children,

* General Putnam was an old American officer of distinguished bravery, plain manners,
  and sober habits; nourished in agricultural life, and those simple principles, that
  excite the virtuous to duty, in every department.

CHAP. VI and effects, and ordered a number of men to be embodied, and hold
1 7 7 5 themselves in readiness for immediate service.

Tryon was the last governor who presided at New York under the crown of England. This gentleman had formerly been governor of North Carolina, where his severities had rendered him very obnoxious. It is true, this disposition was principally exercised towards a set of disorderly, ignorant people, who had felt themselves oppressed, had embodied, and styling themselves *regulators*, opposed the authority of the laws. After they had been subdued, and several of the ringleaders executed, governor Tryon returned to England, but was again sent out as governor of the province of New York. He was received with cordiality, treated with great respect, and was for a time much esteemed, by many of the inhabitants of the city, and the neighboring country. Very soon after the contest became warm between Great Britain and the inhabitants of America, he, like all the [197] other governors in the American colonies, tenacious of supporting the prerogatives of the crown, laid aside that spirit of lenity he had previously affected to feel.

Governor Tryon entered with great zeal into all the measures of administration; and endeavoured with art, influence, and intrigue, of which he was perfectly master, to induce the city of New York, and the inhabitants under his government, to submit quietly, and to decline a union of opinion and action with the other colonies, in their opposition to the new regulations of the British parliament. But he soon found he could not avail himself sufficiently of the interest he possessed among some of the first characters in the city, to carry the point, and subdue the spirit of liberty, which was every day appreciating in that colony.

On the determination of the provincial congress to arrest the crown officers, and disarm the persons of those who were denominated *tories*, governor Tryon began to be apprehensive for his own safety. The congress of New York had resolved,

> that it be recommended to the several provincial assemblies, or conventions, and councils, or committees of safety, to arrest and secure every person in their respective colonies, whose going at large may, in their opinion, endanger the safety of the colony, or the liberties of America.

[198] Though governor Tryon was not particularly named, he apprehended himself a principal person pointed at in this resolve. This awakened his fears to such a degree, that he left the seat of

government, and went on board the Halifax packet; from whence he CHAP. VI
wrote the mayor of the city, that he was there ready to execute any 1 7 7 5
such business, as the circumstances of the times would permit. But
the indifference as to the residence, or even the conduct of a plantation
governor, was now become so general among the inhabitants of
America, that he soon found his command in New York was at an
end. After this he put himself at the head of a body of loyalists, and
annoyed the inhabitants of New York and New Jersey, and wherever
else he could penetrate, with the assistance of some British troops
that occasionally joined them.

The governors of the several colonies, as if hurried by a consciousness
of their own guilt, flying like fugitives to screen themselves from the
resentment of the people, on board the king's ships, appear as if they
had been composed of similar characters to those described by a writer
of the history of such as were appointed to office in the more early
settlement of the American colonies. He said,

> it unfortunately happened for our American provinces, that a government
> in any of our colonies in those parts, was scarcely looked upon in any other
> light than that of a hospital, where the favorites [199] of the ministry might
> lie, till they had recovered their broken fortunes, and oftentimes they
> served as an asylum from their creditors.*

The neighbouring government of New Jersey was for some time
equally embarrassed with that of New York. They felt the effects of
the impressions made by governor Franklin, in favor of the measures
of administration; but not so generally as to preclude many of the
inhabitants from uniting with the other colonies, in vigorous steps to
preserve their civil freedom. Governor Franklin had, among many
other expressions which discovered his opinions, observed in a letter
to Mr. secretary Conway,

> it gives me great pleasure, that I have been able through all the late
> disturbances, to preserve the tranquillity of this province, notwithstanding
> the endeavours of some to stimulate the populace to such acts as have
> disgraced the colonies.

He kept up this tone of reproach, until he also was deprived by the
people of his command; and New Jersey, by the authority of
committees, seized all the money in the public treasury, and appropriated it to the pay of the troops raising for the common defence.

* Modern Universal History, vol. xxxix, p. 357. [Citation correct.]

CHAP. VI They took every other prudent measure in their power, to place
1 7 7 5 themselves in readiness for the critical moment.

[200] Pennsylvania, though immediately under the eye of congress, had some peculiar difficulties to struggle with, from a proprietary government, from the partizans of the crown, and the great body of the quakers, most of them opposed to the American cause. But the people in general were guarded and vigilant, and far from neglecting the most necessary steps for general defence.

In Virginia, Maryland, and the Carolinas, where they had the greatest number of African slaves, their embarrassments were accumulated, and the dangers which hung over them, peculiarly aggravated. From their long habit of filling their country with foreign slaves, they were threatened with a host of domestic enemies, from which the other colonies had nothing to fear. The Virginians had been disposed in general to treat their governor, lord Dunmore, and his family, with every mark of respect; and had not his intemperate zeal in the service of his master given universal disgust, he might have remained longer among them, and finally have left them in a much less disgraceful manner.

However qualified this gentleman might have been to preside in any of the colonies, in more pacific seasons, he was little calculated for the times, when ability and moderation, energy and condescension, coolness in decision, and delicacy [201] in execution, were highly requisite to govern a people struggling with the poniard at their throat and the sword in their hand, against the potent invaders of their privileges and claims.

He had the inhumanity early to intimate his designs if opposition ran high, to declare freedom to the blacks, and on any appearance of hostile resistance to the king's authority, to arm them against their masters. Neither the house of burgesses, nor the people at large, were disposed to recede from their determinations in consequence of his threats, nor to submit to any authority that demanded implicit obedience, on pain of devastation and ruin. Irritated by opposition, too rash for consideration, too haughty for condescension, and fond of distinguishing himself in support of the parliamentary system, lord Dunmore dismantled the fort in Williamsburg, plundered the magazines, threatened to lay the city in ashes, and depopulate the country: As far as he was able, he executed his nefarious purposes.

When his lordship found the resolution of the house of burgesses, of committees and conventions, was no where to be shaken, he

immediately proclaimed emancipation to the blacks, and put arms
into their hands. He excited disturbances in the back settlements,
and encouraged the natives bordering on the southern colonies, [202]
to rush from the wilderness, and make inroads on the frontiers. For
this business, he employed as his agent one *Connolly*, a Scotch
renegado, who travelled from Virginia to the Ohio, and from the Ohio
to general Gage at Boston, with an account of his success, and a detail
of his negociations. From general Gage he received a colonel's
commission, and was by him ordered to return to the savages, and
encourage them, with the aid of some British settlers on the river
Ohio, to penetrate the back country, and distress the borders of
Virginia. But fortunately, Connolly was arrested in his career, and
with his accomplices taken and imprisoned on his advance through
Maryland; his papers were seized, and a full disclosure of the cruel
designs of his employers sent forward to congress.

By the indiscreet conduct of lord Dunmore, the ferments in Virginia
daily increased. All respect towards the governor was lost, and his
lady terrified by continual tumult left the palace, and took sanctuary
on board one of the king's ships. After much altercation and dispute,
with every thing irritating on the one side, and no marks of submission
on the other, his lordship left his seat, and with his family and a few
loyalists retired on board the Fowey man of war, where his lady in
great anxiety had resided many days.* There he found some [203] of
the most criminal of his partizans had resorted before he quitted the
government; with these and some banditti that had taken shelter in
a considerable number of vessels under his lordship's command, and
the assistance of a few run-away negroes, he carried on a kind of
predatory war on the colony for several months. The burning of
Norfolk, the best town in the territory of Virginia, completed his
disgraceful campaign.†

The administration of lord William Campbel, and Mr. Martin, the
governors of the two Carolinas, had no distinguished trait from that
of most of the other colonial governors. They held up the supreme
authority of parliament in the same high style of dignity, and announced
the resentment of affronted majesty, and the severe punishment that
would be inflicted on congresses, conventions and committees, and

* Lady Dunmore soon after took passage for England.
† See Appendix, Note, No. XII. relative to Virginia. It has been asserted by some
    that the inhabitants themselves assisted in the conflagration of Norfolk, to prevent
    lord Dunmore's retaining it as a place of arms.

CHAP. VI the miserable situation to which the people of America would be
1 7 7 5 reduced, if they continued to adhere to the *factious demagogues* of
party. With the same spirit and cruel policy that instigated lord
Dunmore, they carried on their negociations with the Indians, and
encouraged the insurrections of the negroes, until all harmony [204]
and confidence were totally destroyed between themselves and the
people, who supported their own measures for defence in the highest
tone of freedom and independence. Both the governors of North and
South Carolina soon began to be apprehensive of the effects of public
resentment, and about this time thought it necessary for their own
safety to repair on board the king's ships, though their language and
manners had not been equally rash and abusive with that of the
governor of Virginia.

Henry Laurens, Esq. was president of the provincial congress of
South Carolina at this period; whose uniform virtue and independence
of spirit, we shall see conspicuously displayed hereafter on many other
trying occasions. It was not long after the present period, when he
wrote to a friend and observed, that "he meant to finish his peregri-
nations in this world, by a journey through the United States; then
to retire and learn to die." But he had this important lesson to learn
in the ordeal of affliction and disappointment, that he severely
experienced in his public life and domestic sorrows, which he bore
with that firmness and equanimity, which ever dignifies great and
good characters.

Sir Robert Eden, governor of Maryland, a man of social manners,
jovial temper, and humane disposition, had been more disposed to
[205] lenity and forbearance, than any of the great officers in the
American department. But so high wrought was the opposition to
British authority, and the jealousies entertained of all magistrates
appointed by the crown, that it was not long after the departure of
the neighbouring governors, before he was ordered by congress to
quit his government, and repair to England. He was obliged to comply,
though with much reluctance. He had been in danger of very rough
usage before his departure, from general Lee, who had intercepted a
confidential letter from lord George Germaine to governor Eden. Lee
threatened to seize and confine him, but by the interference of the
committee of safety, and some military officers at Annapolis, the order
was not executed. They thought it wrong to consider him as responsible
for the sentiments contained in the letters of his correspondents; and
only desired Mr. Eden to give his word of honor, that he would not

leave the province before the meeting of a general congress of that
state; nor did they suffer him to be farther molested. He was permitted
quietly to take leave of his friends and his province, after he had
received the order of the continental congress for his departure; and
in hopes of returning in more tranquil times, he left his property
behind him, and sailed for England in the summer, one thousand
seven hundred and seventy-six. *

[206] The influence of sir James Wright the governor of Georgia,
prevented that state from acceding to the measure of a general
congress, in one thousand seven hundred and seventy-four. Yet the
people at large were equally disaffected, and soon after, in an address
to his excellency, acknowledged themselves the only link in the great
American chain, that had not publicly united with the other colonies
in their opposition to the claims of parliament. They called a provincial
congress, who resolved in the name of their constituents, that they
would receive no merchandize whatever from Great Britain or Ireland
after the seventh day of July, one thousand, seven hundred and
seventy-five; that they fully approved and adopted the American
declaration and bill of rights, published by the late continental
congress; that they should now join with the other colonies, choose
delegates to meet in general congress; and that they meant invariably
to adhere to the public cause, and that they would no longer lie under
the suspicion of being unconcerned for the rights and freedom of
America.

Indeed the torch of war seemed already to have reached the most
distant corner of the continent, [207] the flame had spread and
penetrated to the last province in America held by Great Britain, and
a way opened to the gates of Quebec, before administration had

* See the conduct relative to sir Robert Eden, and the transactions between the
southern governors and the people, this year, at large in the British Remembrancer,
which is here anticipated to prevent interrupting the narration by any further detail
of general Lee's transactions in Maryland relative to governor Eden. [See *Remembrancer* (1776), pp. 188, 261, 335. Also see Charles Lee to Samuel Purvience, April
6, 1776 (directing Purvience to "seize the person of Governour Eden"); President
of Congress (Hancock) to Maryland Council of Safety, April 16, 1776 (Eden carrying
on a "dangerous correspondence with the Ministry of Great Britain"); "In Congress,"
April 16, 1776 (Resolve to seize Eden and his papers); Maryland Council of Safety
to Congress, April 17, 1776; Eden to Charles Carroll, J. Hall, and William Paca
(Maryland Council of Safety), April 17, 1776; Council of Safety to Eden, April 18,
1776; Maryland Convention, May 14, 1776 (granting Eden parole), in Force, *Archives*,
4th. ser., 5: 800–801; 954; 960–961; 963–964; 1594.]

CHAP. VI dreamed of the smallest danger in that quarter. Soon after the action
1 7 7 5 at Lexington, a number of enterprising young men, principally from
Connecticut, proposed to each other a sudden march towards the
lakes, and a bold attempt to surprize Ticonderoga, garrisoned by the
king's troops. These young adventurers applied to governor Trumbull,
and obtained leave of the assembly of Connecticut to pursue their
project; and so secretly, judiciously, and rapidly was the expedition
conducted, that they entered the garrison, and saluted the principal
officer as their prisoner, before he had any reason to apprehend an
enemy was near.* This enterprise was conducted by the colonels
Easton, Arnold, and Allen; the invaders possessed themselves of a
considerable number of brass and iron cannon, and many warlike
stores, without suffering any loss of life.

It has been proved beyond a doubt that the British government
had spared no pains to encourage the inroads of the savages; of
consequence this *coup de main* was deemed a very meritorious [208]
and important step. Ticonderoga commanded all the passes between
Canada and the other provinces. The possession of this important
fortress on the lake Champlain, in a great measure secured the frontiers
from the incursions of the savages, who had been excited by the cruel
policy of Britain to war, which, by these ferocious nations, is ever
carried on by modes at which humanity shudders, and civilization
blushes to avow.†

Thus was the sword brandished through the land, and hung
suspended from cruel execution of all the evils attendant on a state
of civil convulsion, only by the faint hope, that the sovereign of
Britain might yet be softened to hold out the olive-branch in one
hand, and a redress of grievances in the other. But every pacific hope
was reversed, and all prospect of the restoration of harmony annihilated
early in the summer, by the arrival of a large reinforcement at Boston,
commanded by three general officers of high consideration.

All former delusive expectations now extinguished, both the statesman and the peasant, actuated by the feelings of the man and the
patriot, discovered a most unconquerable magnanimity [209] of spirit.

* On the surprise of Ticonderoga, the commanding officer there inquired by whose
  authority this was done? Colonel Allen replied, "I demand your surrender in the
  name of the great Jehovah and of the continental congress."
† A few months after this expedition, colonel Allen experienced a reverse of fortune,
  by falling into the hands of the British near Montreal, was loaded with irons, and
  immediately sent to England.

Undismayed by the necessity of an appeal to the sword, though CHAP. VI
unprovided with sufficient resources for so arduous a conflict, they 1 7 7 5
animated each other to sustain it, if necessary, until they should leave
their foes only a depopulated soil, if victory should declare in their
favor. Nature revolts at the idea, when the poniard is pushed by
despair; yet preferring death to thraldom, the Americans were every
where decisive in council, and determined in action. There appeared
that kind of enthusiasm, which sets danger at defiance, and impels
the manly arm to resist, till the warm current that plays round the
heart, is poured out as a libation at the shrine of freedom.

On the other hand, the fears of the dependents on the crowd were
dissipated by the augmentation of the British army, their hopes
invigorated, and every artifice used, to spread terror and dismay among
the people. The turpitude of *rebellion,* and the dread consequences
of defeat, were painted in the most gloomy colours; the merits and
the abilities of the principal officers extolled, their distinguished names
and characters enhanced, and every thing circulated that might tend
to weaken the resolution of the people.

It was said, general Burgoyne commanded a squadron of light-
horse, which was to scour the [210] country, and pick up the leading
insurgents in every quarter. The capacity, bravery, and virtues of
general Clinton were every where announced by the votaries of
administration; and the name of *Howe* was at that time, at once
revered, beloved, and dreaded in America. A monumental tribute of
applause had been reared in honor of one brother, who had fallen in
that country in the late war between Great Britain and France; and
the gratitude of the people had excited a predilection in favor of the
other, and indeed of every branch of that family. But this partiality
was soon succeeded by an universal disgust towards the two surviving
brothers, lord and general Howe, who undertook the conquest of
America; a project held reproachful, and which would have reflected
dishonor on the perpetrators, even had it been crowned with success.

In the beginning of June, one thousand seven hundred and seventy-
five, general Gage thought proper to act a more decided part than he
had hitherto done. He published a proclamation, denouncing *martial
law* in all its rigors against any one who should supply, conceal, or
correspond with any of those he was pleased to stigmatize by the
epithets of *traitors, rebels,* or *insurgents.* But as an act of grace, he
offered pardon in the king's name to all who should lay down their
arms and submit to mercy, only excluding by name, Samuel Adams

CHAP. VI and [211] John Hancock; he alleged that their crimes were of too
1 7 7 5 flagitious a nature to hope for pardon.

This proscription discovered the little knowledge which general
Gage then possessed of the temper of the times, the disposition of
the people at large, or the character of individuals. His discrimination,
rather accidental than judicious, set these two gentlemen in the most
conspicuous point of view, and drew the particular attention of the
whole continent to their names, distinguished from many of their
compeers, more by this single circumstance, than by superior ability
or exertion. By this they became at once the favorites of popularity,
and the objects of general applause, which at that time would have
been the fortune of any one, honored by such a mark of disapprobation
of the British commander in chief.

Mr. Adams was a gentleman of a good education, a decent family,
but no fortune. Early nurtured in the principles of civil and religious
liberty, he possessed a quick understanding, a cool head, stern
manners, a smooth address, and a Roman-like firmness, united with
that sagacity and penetration that would have made a figure in a
conclave. He was at the same time liberal in opinion, and uniformly
devout; social with men of all denominations, grave in deportment;
placid, yet severe; sober and [212] indefatigable; calm in seasons of
difficulty, tranquil and unruffled in the vortex of political altercation;
too firm to be intimidated, too haughty for condescension, his mind
was replete with resources that dissipated fear, and extricated in the
greatest emergencies. Thus qualified, he stood forth early, and
continued firm, through the great struggle, and may justly claim a
large share of honor, due to that spirit of energy which opposed the
measures of administration, and produced the independence of America. Through a long life he exhibited on all occasions, an example of
patriotism, religion, and virtue honorary to the human character.

Mr. Hancock was a young gentleman of fortune, of more external
accomplishments than real abilities. He was polite in manners, easy
in address, affable, civil, and liberal. With these accomplishments,
he was capricious, sanguine, and implacable: naturally generous, he
was profuse in expense; he scattered largesses without discretion, and
purchased favors by the waste of wealth, until he reached the ultimatum
of his wishes, which centered in the focus of popular applause. He
enlisted early in the cause of his country, at the instigation of some
gentlemen of penetration, who thought his ample fortune might give
consideration, while his fickleness could not injure, so long as he was
under the influence of men of superior judgment. They complimented

him by nominations to committees [213] of importance, till he plunged
too far to recede; and flattered by ideas of his own consequence, he
had taken a decided part before the battle of Lexington, and was
president of the provincial congress, when that event took place.

By the appearance of zeal, added to a certain alacrity of engaging
in any public department, Mr. Hancock was influential in keeping
up the tide of opposition; and by a concurrence of fortuitous circumstances, among which this proscription was the most capital, he
reached the summit of popularity, which raised him afterwards to the
most elevated stations, and very fortunately he had the honor of
affixing his signature as president, to many of the subsequent proceedings of the continental congress, which will ever hold an illustrious
rank in the page of history.

Mr. Hancock had repaired to Philadelphia, to take his seat in
congress, immediately after he made his escape from Lexington. Part
of the object of the excursion of the eighteenth of April, was the
capture of him and Mr. Adams; they were both particularly inquired
for, and the house in which they lodged surrounded by the king's
troops, the moment after these gentlemen had retreated half-naked.
Had they been found, they would undoubtedly have been shut up
in Boston, if nothing more fatal had [214] been inflicted, instead of
being left at liberty to pursue a political career that will transmit their
names with applause to posterity.

The absence of the late worthy president of congress, Mr. Randolph,
and the arrival of Mr. Hancock at Philadelphia, at the fortunate
moment when the enthusiasm inspired by Gage's proclamation was
at the height, both concurred to promote his elevation. He was chosen
to preside in the respectable assembly of delegates, avowedly on the
sole principle of his having been proscribed by general Gage. It was
uncouthly said, by a member of congress, that "they would shew
mother Britain how little they cared for her, by choosing a Massachusetts
man for their president, who had been recently excluded from pardon
by public proclamation." The choice was suddenly made, and with
rather too much levity for the times, or for the dignity of the office.
Mr. Hancock's modesty prompted him for a moment to hesitate on
the unexpected event, as if diffident of his own qualifications; when
one of the members,* of a more robust constitution, and less delicacy

* A Mr. Harrison, from Virginia, the same who made the above speech. These
circumstances were verbally detailed to the author of these annals by a respectable
member of congress then present.

CHAP. VI of manners, took him in his arms, and placed him in the presidential
1 7 7 5 chair.

[215] This sudden elevation might place the fortunate candidate in a similar situation with the celebrated pope Ganganelli, who observed of himself, that after putting on the triple crown, he often felt his own pulse, to see if he was the same identical person he was a few years before. Mr. Hancock continued in the presidential chair until October, one thousand seven hundred and seventy-nine, when he took a formal leave of congress, and never again rejoined that respectable body. His time however was fully occupied in his own state in the various employments, to which he was called by a majority of voices in the Massachusetts, where his popular talents had a commanding influence, during the residue of his life.* But in the progress of the revolution, several men of less consequence than Mr. Hancock, and far inferior claims to patriotism, were raised to the same dignified station.

In the effervescence of popular commotions, it is not uncommon to see the favorites of fortune elevated to the pinnacle of rank by trivial circumstances, that appear the result of accident.

Those who mark the changes and the progress of events through all revolutions, will frequently see distinctions bestowed, where there are no [216] commanding talents, and honors retained, more from the strong influence of popular enthusiasm, than from the guidance of reason, which operates too little on the generality of mankind.

It may be observed, that public commotions in human affairs, like the shocks of nature, convulse the whole system, and level the lofty mountains, which have arisen for ages above the clouds, beneath the vallies; while the hillock, unnoticed before, is raised to a pitch of elevation, that renders it a land-mark for the eye of the weary seaman to rest upon.

All revolutions evince the truth of the observation of a writer, that "Many men great in title, have the spirit of slaves, many low in fortune, have great spirits, many a Cicero has kept sheep, many a Caesar followed the plough, many a Virgil folded cattle."†

---

* See Appendix, Note, No. XIII.

† Sir Francis Osborne's Memoirs. [Probably Francis Osborne, *Historical Memoires of the Reigns of Queen Elizabeth and King James* (London, 1658); also in *The Works of Francis Osborne, Esq.* (7th. ed., London, 1673), pp. 409–547. The statement quoted does not appear, but similar sentiments appear in *Advice to a Son. Or, Directions for*

The sudden rotations in human affairs are wisely permitted by CHAP. VI
Providence, to remind mankind of their natural equality, to check 1 7 7 5
the pride of wealth, to restrain the insolence of rank and family
distinctions, which too frequently oppress the various classes in society.

The late proclamation of general Gage was considered as a prelude
to immediate action, [217] and from all intelligence that could be
obtained from the town, there appeared the strongest reason to expect
a second sally from the troops lying in Boston. Uncertain on which
side the storm would begin, the provincials thought it necessary to
guard against surprise, by fortifying on both sides of the town, in the
best manner they were able. They threw up some slight entrenchments
at Roxbury, and several other places on the south side of Boston; at
the same time, on the night of the sixteenth of June, they began
some works at the extreme part of a peninsula at the north, running
from Charlestown to the river, which separates that town from Boston.
They executed this business with such secrecy and dispatch, that the
officers of a ship of war then in the river, expressed their astonishment
in the morning, when they saw some considerable works reared and
fortified in the compass of a few hours, where, from the contiguous
situation,* they least expected the Americans would look them in the
face.

The alarm was immediately given, and orders issued, that a continual
fire should be kept [218] playing upon the unfinished works, from
the ships, the floating batteries in the river, and a fortified hill on the
other side; but with unparralleled perseverance, the Americans continued to strengthen their entrenchments, without returning a shot
until near noon, when the British army, consisting of ten companies
of grenadiers, four battalions of infantry, and a heavy train of artillery,
advanced under the command of general Pigot and major general
Howe. A severe engagement ensued: many men and several brave
officers of the royal army fell on the first fire of the Americans. This
unexpected salute threw them into some confusion; but by the

---

your better Conduct through the various and most important Encounters of this Life (London,
1673) and *Works*, esp. pp. 70–99.]

* These works were erected on Breed's hill. This was the spot that cost the British
army so dear through the glorious action of that day, generally styled the battle of
Bunker hill. After the Americans retreated, the British left Breed's hill, took their
stand, and strongly fortified Bunker hill, about a fourth of a mile distant. Thus has
the name of the place of action been frequently confounded.

firmness of general Howe, and the timely assistance of general Clinton, who, with a fresh detachment arrived in season, the troops were immediately rallied, and brought to the charge with redoubled fury. They mounted the ramparts with fixed bayonets, and notwithstanding the most heroic resistance, they soon made themselves masters of the disputed hill.

Overpowered by numbers, and exhausted by the fatigue of the preceding night, and all hope of reinforcement cut off by the incessant fire of the ships across a neck of land that separated them from the country, the provincials were obliged to retreat, and leave the ground to the British troops. Many of their most experienced officers acknowledged the valor of their opponents; and that in proportion to the forces engaged, [219] there had been few actions in which the military renown of British troops had been more severely tried. Their chagrin was manifest, that the bravery of British soldiers, which had been often signalized in the noblest feats of valor, should be thus resisted; that they should be galled, wounded, and slaughtered, by an *handful of cottagers*, as they termed them, under officers of little military skills, and less experience, whom they had affected to hold in ineffable contempt.

There is a certain point of military honor, that often urges against the feelings of humanity, to dip the sword in blood. Thus, from the early maxims of implicit obedience, the first principle of military education, many men of real merit hazarded fortune, life, and reputation, in the inglorious work of devastation and ruin, through the fields and villages of America. Yet such was the reluctance shewn by some to engage with spirit in the disagreeable enterprise of this day, that their officers were obliged to use the utmost severity towards them, to stimulate others to persevere. The town of Charlestown was reduced to ashes by the fire of the shipping, while the land forces were storming the hills. Thus, in concert, was this flourishing and compact town destroyed, in the most wanton display of power. There were about four hundred dwelling-houses in the centre of Charlestown, which, with the out-houses adjacent, [220] and many buildings in the suburbs, were also sunk in the conflagration. The fate of this unfortunate town was beheld with solemnity and regret, by many even of those who were not favorably disposed to the liberties of the western world. The ingratitude which marked the transaction aggravated the guilty deed. We have recently seen the inhabitants of that place, prompted by humanity, opening their doors for the relief, and

pouring balm into the wounds, of the routed corps on the nineteenth CHAP. VI
of April. This in the eye of justice must enhance the atrocity, and 1 7 7 5
forever stigmatize the ingratitude, which so soon after wrapped the
town in flames, and sent out the naked inhabitants, the prey of
poverty and despair.

There are few things which place the pride of man in a more
conspicuous point of view, than the advantages claimed in all military
rencontres that are not decisive. Thus, though at the expense of many
lives, and the loss of some of their bravest officers, the British army
exulted much in becoming masters of an unfinished entrenchment,
and driving the Americans from their advanced post. Upwards of one
thousand men, including the wounded, fell in this action on the royal
side. Among the slain was lieutenant colonel Abercrombie, an officer
much esteemed by his friends and his country, and a major Pitcairn,
a gentleman of so much merit, that his fall was lamented even by his
[221] enemies. His valor on this occasion would have reflected glory
on his memory, had it been signalized in a more honorable cause.*

While this tragedy was acting on the other side of the Charles river,
the terror and consternation of the town of Boston are scarcely
describable. In the utmost anxiety, they beheld the scene from the
eminences. Apprehensive for themselves, and trembling for their
friends engaged in the bloody conflict, they were not less affected by
the hideous shrieks of the women and children connected with the
king's troops, who beheld their husbands, their friends, and relations,
wounded, mangled, and slain, ferried over the river in boat-loads,
from the field of carnage.

On the other side, though the Americans were obliged to quit the
field with very considerable loss, yet they gloried in the honor they
had this day acquired by arms. They retired only one mile from the
scene of action, where they took possession of an advantageous height,
and threw up new works on Prospect hill, with the enthusiasm of
men determined to be free. [222] They soon environed the town of
Boston on all sides with military parade, and though they wept the
fall of many brave men, they bade a daily challenge to their enemies.

But a cloud was cast over every face by the death of the intrepid

---

* It may be observed, that his zeal in the cause in which he was engaged, had hurried
  him previous to this action to some steps that could not easily be forgiven by
  Americans, particularly by those who believed him to have been the officer, who
  first gave the order for the king's troops to fire on the militia assembling at Lexington,
  on their appearance.

major general Joseph Warren, who, to the inexpressible grief of his countrymen, lost his life in the memorable action usually styled the battle of Bunker hill. He fell covered with laurels, choosing rather to die in the field, than to grace the victory of his foes by the triumph they would have enjoyed in his imprisonment. He had been chosen president of the provincial congress, when Mr. Hancock repaired to Philadelphia, and was an active volunteer in several skirmishes that had taken place since the commencement of hostilities, which in the minds of his enemies would have sanctioned the severest indignities their resentment might have dictated, had he fallen into their hands at this early period of the war.

This gentleman had been appointed a major general only four days previous to the late action: he was educated in the medical line, and was much respected for his professional as well as his political abilities. He possessed a clear understanding, a strong mind, a disposition humane and generous, with manners easy, affable, and engaging; but zealous, active, and sanguine, in the cause of his oppressed country, it [223] is to be lamented, that he rather incautiously courted the post of danger, and rushed precipitately on his fate, while more important occasions required his paying some regard to personal safety. Yet, if the *love* of *fame* is the strongest passion of the mind, and human nature pants for distinction in the flowery field, perhaps there was never a moment of more unfading glory, offered to the wishes of the brave, than that which marked the *exit* of this heroic officer.

He was the first victim of rank that fell by the sword in the contest between Great Britain and America: and the conflagration of Charlestown, enkindled by the wanton barbarity of his enemies, lighted his *manes* to the grave. These circumstances ensure a record in every historical annal, while his memory will be revered by every lover of his country, and the name of *Warren* will be enrolled at the head of that band of patriots and heroes, who sacrificed their lives to purchase the independence of America.

After the late action, the British troops appeared to be in no condition for further operations; weakened by the severe engagement near Bunker hill, sickly in the camp, and disheartened by unexpected bravery, where they had feared no resistance; straitened for provisions, and destitute of forage, except what was piratically plundered from the neighbouring [224] shores, they kept themselves shut up in Boston the remainder of the summer. Here they continued in so quiet a manner, that had they not sometimes for their own amusement saluted

the country with the sound of a useless cannonade, or the bursting
of a shell, the people might have forgotten, that the monarch of
Britain had several thousand soldiers cooped up within the walls of a
city that still acknowledged him as their sovereign. The inhabitants
of the town were held in duress, but their military masters did not
presume to enlarge their own quarters.

While this interesting scene had been acting in the field, the
congress of the Massachusetts had sent on to Philadelphia for the
opinion of the united delegates relative to their assumption of a regular
form of government. Articles of confederation had been agreed to in
general congress, in which a recapitulation of grievances, and the
reasons for taking up arms were subjoined in terms little short of a
declaration of war. These had been published in May, one thousand
seven hundred and seventy-five; but their ratification by legislative
bodies, or provincial congresses, had not yet generally taken place.
But as the independence of America was not yet formally declared,
it was in contemplation with many members of congress, as well as
others of equal judgment, that when all should be convinced, that
the breach [225] between the two countries was totally irreconcileable,
that the same modes of legislation and government should be adopted
in all the colonies. It was then thought that a similarity of manners,
police, and government, throughout the continent, would cement the
union, and might support the sovereignty of each individual state,
while yet, for general purposes, all should be in subordination to the
congressional head.

An elegant writer has observed, that it is no easy matter to render
the union of independent states perfect and entire, unless the genius
and forms of their respective governments are in some degree similar.
The judicious body assembled at Philadelphia were fully convinced
of this; they were not insensible that a number of states, under
different constitutions, and various modes of government and civil
police, each regulated by their own municipal laws, would soon be
swayed by local interests that might create irreconcileable feuds
tending to disjoint the whole.* It was therefore judged best, to

* Congress had about this time adopted the resolution to advise each of the colonies
   explicitly to renounce the government of Great Britain, and to form constitutions
   of government for themselves, adequate to their exigencies, and agreeable to their
   own modes of thinking, where any variation of sentiment prevailed. This was acted
   upon, and a representative government, consisting of one or more branches, was
   adopted in each colony.

CHAP. VI recommend [226] to the Massachusetts, the resumption of a regular
1 7 7 5 form of government in the present exigence, on the plan of the old
charter of William and Mary, which gave authority to the majority of
counsellors, chosen by an house of representatives, to exercise all
governmental acts, as if the governor was really absent or dead.

On this recommendation, James Warren, Esq. president of the
provincial congress, by their authority, issued writs in his own name,
requiring the freeholders in every town to convene, and elect their
representatives, to meet at Watertown on the twentieth of July, one
thousand seven hundred and seventy-five. This summons was readily
obeyed, and a full house appeared at the time and place appointed;
the late president of the provincial congress was unanimously chosen
speaker of the new house. Regardless of the vacant chair, they selected
a council, and the two branches proceeded to legislation and the
internal police of the province, as usually had been the practice in
the absence of the governor and lieutenant governor.*

Thus, after living for more than twelve months without any legal
government, without law, and without any regular administration of
justice, but what arose from the internal sense of moral obligation,
which is seldom a [227] sufficient restraint on the people at large, the
Massachusetts returned peaceably to the regular and necessary subordination of civil society. Reduced nearly to a state of nature with
regard to all civil or authoritative ties, it is almost incredible, that the
principles of rectitude and common justice should have been so
generally influential. For, such is the restless and hostile disposition
of man, that it will not suffer him to remain long in a state of repose,
whether on the summit of human glory, or reclined on his own native
turf, when probable contingencies promise him the acquisition of
either wealth or fame. From the wants, the weakness, and the ferocity
of human nature, mankind cannot subsist long in society, without
some stable system of coercive power. Yet amidst the complicated
difficulties with which they were surrounded, the horrors of anarchy
were far from prevailing in the province: vice seemed to be abashed
by the examples of moderation, disinterestedness, and generosity,
exhibited by many of the patriotic leaders of present measures.

It has been observed already, that not a drop of blood had ever
been spilt by the people in any of the commotions preceding the
commencement of war, and that the fear of popular resentment was

---

* See Appendix, Note, No. XIV.

undoubtedly a guard on the conduct of some individuals. Others, chap. vi checked by the frowns of public virtue, crimes of an atrocious nature 1 7 7 5 had seldom been perpetrated: all classes seemed to be awed by the magnitude [228] of the objects before them; private disputes were amicably adjusted or postponed, until time and events should give the opportunity of legal decision, or render the claims of individuals of little consequence, by their being ingulfed in the torrent of despotism, generally poured out by the conqueror, who fights for the establishment of uncontrolled power.

C H A P T E R V I I

A Continental Army • Mr. Washington appointed to the Command • General Gage recalled—succeeded by Sir William Howe • Depredations on the Sea Coast • Falmouth burnt • Canadian Affairs • Death and Character of General Montgomery

CHAP. VII [229] Freedom, long hunted round the globe by a succession of
1 7 7 5 tyrants, appeared at this period, as if about to erect her standard in America; the scimitar was drawn from principles, that held life and property as a feather in the balance against the chains of servitude that clanked in her disgusted ear. The blood of innocence had already crimsoned over the fields which had teemed for the nourishment of Britain, who, instead of listening to the groans of an oppressed country, had recently wrung out the tears of anguish, until the inhabitants of the plundered towns were ready to quit the elegancies of life, and take refuge in the forest, to secure the unimpaired possession of those privileges which they considered as a grant from heaven, that no earthly potentate had a right to seize with impunity.

The bulk of mankind have indeed, in all countries in their turn, been made the prey of ambition. It is a truth that no one will contest, [230] though all may regret, that in proportion to the increase of wealth, the improvement in arts, and the refinements in society, the great body of the people have either by force or fraud, become the slaves of the few, who by chance, violence, or accident, have destroyed the natural equality of their associates. Sanctioned by time and habit, an indefeasible right has been claimed, that sets so mischievous a creature as man above all law, and subjects the lives of millions, to the rapacious will of an individual, who, by the intoxicating nature of power, soon forgets that there are any obligations due to the subject, a reptile in his opinion, made only for the drudgery necessary to maintain the splendor of government, and the support of prerogative. Every step taken by the British government, relative to the colonies,

confirmed this truth, taught them their danger, and evinced to the
Americans the necessity of guarding at all points, against the assumed
jurisdiction of an assembly of men, disposed to innovate continually
on the rights of their fellow subjects who had no voice in parliament,
and whose petitions did not reach, or had no influence on the ear of
the sovereign.

The success of the last supplicatory address offered to the parliament
of Britain by the United States, still hung in suspense; yet the crisis
appeared so alarming, that it was thought necessary by many, to
attend immediately to the establishment of a continental army on
[231] some stable and respectable footing. But there were some
influential members in congress, who dreaded the consequence of a
step so replete with the appearance of hostility, if not with the avowed
design of independence; they observed, that such a measure would
be an inevitable bar to the restoration of harmony.

Some, who had warmly opposed the measures of administration,
and ably advocated the rights of the colonies, were of this opinion.
The idea of dissevering the empire, shocked their feelings; they still
ardently wished, both from the principles of humanity, and what they
judged the soundest policy, to continue if possible, the natural
connexion with Britain. Others of a more timid complexion, readily
united with these gentlemen, and urged, notwithstanding the contempt poured on all former supplications, that even, if their late
petition should be rejected, they should yet make one effort more for
conciliation and relief, by the hitherto fruitless mode of prayer and
remonstrance. Men of more enlarged and comprehensive views,
considered this proposal as the *finesse* of shallow politicians, designed
only to prevent the organization of a continental army.

The celebrated Machiavel, pronounced by some the prince of
politicians, has observed, "that every state is in danger of dissolution,
whose government is not frequently reduced [232] to its original
principles." The conduct of the British administration towards the
colonies, the corruption of the government in every department, their
deviations from first principles, and the enormous public debt of the
nation, evinced not only the necessity of a reform in parliament, but
appeared to require such a renovation of the British constitution, as
was not likely soon to take place. Thus circumstanced, many thought
it the interest of America, to dissolve the connexion with such a
government, and were utterly opposed to delay, or any further
application to the British king or parliament, by petition or concession.

CHAP. VII   After a long debate on the subject, the last description of persons

1 7 7 5 were obliged reluctantly to accede to a measure which they thought promised nothing but delay or disgrace. By a kind of necessary compromise, a most humble and loyal petition directly to the king of Great Britain, was again agreed to by the delegated powers of the United States. At the same time, it was stipulated by all parties, that military preparations should be made, and an army raised without farther hesitation. A decided majority in congress, voted, that twenty thousand men should be immediately equipped and supported at the expense of the United States of America. The honorable William Penn, late governor of Pennsylvania, was chosen agent to the court of Britain, and directed to [233] deliver the petition to the king himself, and to endeavor by his personal influence, to procure a favorable reception to this last address.

The command of the army, by the unanimous voice of congress, was vested in George Washington, Esq. then a delegate from the State of Virginia. He received this mark of confidence, from his country, with becoming modesty, and declined all compensation for his services, more than should be sufficient to defray his expenditures, for which he would regularly account.

Mr. Washington was a gentleman of family and fortune, of a polite, but not a learned education; he appeared to possess a coolness of temper, and a degree of moderation and judgment, that qualified him for the elevated station in which he was now placed; with some considerable knowledge of mankind, he supported the reserve of the statesman, with the occasional affability of the courtier. In his character was blended a certain dignity, united with the appearance of good humour; he possessed courage without rashness, patriotism and zeal without acrimony, and retained with universal applause the first military command, until the establishment of independence. Through the various changes of fortune in the subsequent conflict, though the slowness of his movements was censured by some, his character suffered little diminution to the conclusion of a war, that [234] from the extraordinary exigencies of an infant republic, required at times, the caution of Fabius, the energy of Caesar, and the happy facility of expedient in distress, so remarkable in the military operations of the illustrious Frederick.* With the first of these qualities, he was endowed

---

* The late king of Prussia, well known for this trait in his character, by all who are acquainted with the history of his reign.

by nature; the second was awakened by necessity; and the third he CHAP. VII
acquired by experience in the field of glory and danger, which 1 7 7 5
extended his fame through half the globe.

In the late war between England and France, Mr. Washington had
been in several military rencounters, and had particularly signalized
himself in the unfortunate expedition under general Braddock, in the
wilderness on the borders of the Ohio, in the year one thousand seven
hundred and fifty-five. His conduct on that occasion raised an *eclat* of
his valor and prudence; in consequence of which many young
gentlemen from all parts of the continent, allured by the name of
major Washington, voluntarily entered the service, proud of being
enrolled in the list of officers under one esteemed so gallant a
commander.

General Washington arrived at the camp at Cambridge in the
neighbourhood of Boston, the beginning of July, one thousand, seven
hundred [235] and seventy-five. He was accompanied by several
officers of distinction from the southern states, and by Charles Lee
and Horatio Gates, both natives of Great Britain, appointed now to
high rank in the American army. There appeared much expectation
from his abilities, and a general satisfaction in the appointment of
Mr. Washington to the chief command. A congratulatory address,
expressive of their esteem, with the strongest assurances of their aid
and support, to enable him to discharge the duties of his arduous and
exalted station, was presented him from the provincial congress of
Massachusetts, through the hand of their president, James Warren.
To this gentleman, general Washington brought letters of importance,
and to him he was referred for advice by the delegates of the
Massachusetts, as "a judicious, confidential friend, who would never
deceive him."

In his reply to this address, general Washington observed,

> That in leaving the enjoyments of domestic life, he had only emulated
> the virtue and public spirit of the whole province of Massachusetts Bay;
> who with a firmness and patriotism without example in history, had
> sacrificed the comforts of social and private felicity, in support of the rights
> of mankind, and the welfare of their country.

Indeed all ranks were emulous to manifest their respect to the
commander of the army. Multitudes [236] flocked from every quarter
to the American standard, and within a few weeks the environs of
Boston exhibited a brave and high spirited army, which formed to

order, discipline, and subordination, more rapidly than could have been expected from their former habits. Fired with an enthusiasm arising from a sense of the justice of their cause; ardent, healthy, and vigorous; they were eager for action, and impatient to be led to an attack on the town of Boston, where the British army was encamped. But they were still ignorant that both private and political adventurers, had been so negligent of their own and the public safety, as to pay little attention to the importation of powder, arms, and other warlike stores, previous to the prohibition of Britain, restricting the shipment of those articles to America, but for the immediate use of the king's troops.

Thus when hostilities commenced, and a war was denounced against the colonies, they had innumerable difficulties to surmount. Several of the most formidable powers of Europe had been invited by Britain to aid the cruel purposes of administration, either by the loan of auxiliaries, or by a refusal of supplies to the infant states, now struggling alone against a foe, whose power, pride and success, had often made the nations tremble. On a retrospect of the critical situation of America, it is astonishing she did not fall at the threshold; she had new [237] governments to erect in the several states, her legislatures to form, and her civil police to regulate on untrodden ground. She had her armies to establish, and funds to provide for their payment: she had her alliances to negociate, new sources of trade to strike out, and a navy to begin, while the thunder of Britain was alarming her coasts, the savages threatening her borders, and the troops of George the third, with the sword uplifted, pushing their execrable purpose to exterminate the last vestige of freedom.

But as Providence had led to the period of independence, the powers of industry and invention were called forth. Not discouraged by the magnititude of the work, or the numberless obstacles to the completion of their design, no difficulties damped the ardor and unanimity of their exertions, though for a time it appeared, as if their magazines must be furnished by the nitre from heaven, and the ore dug by their own hands from the bowels of the earth. The manufacture of salt-petre, at first considered as the ideal project of some enthusiast for freedom, was not only attempted, but became the easy occupation of women and children. Large quantities were furnished from many parts of America, and powder-mills were erected, which worked it with success. Sulphur, lead, and iron ore, are the natural productions of the country, and mountains of flint had recently [238] been

discovered and wrought for use. As nature had thus furnished the CHAP. VII
materials, every hand that was not engaged in arms was employed in 1 7 7 5
arts, with an alacrity and cheerfulness that discovered a determination
to be free. Precipitated into a conflict that probably might light half
Europe in flames, the demand was too great, and the process too
slow, to rely entirely on the efforts of genius and industry.

When general Washington became fully apprized of the astonishing
deficiency in the article of powder, having been led into a misappre-
hension of the stock on hand, by irregular returns, his embarrassment
was great; he immediately applied for advice to the speaker of the
house of representatives, who judged that the most prompt measures
were indispensably necessary. They agreed that the speaker should
communicate the circumstance to a few members who might be
confidentially entrusted: the result was, that committees were immediately sent by the assembly to many towns in the province, in a
cautious, guarded manner, to require the stocks of powder on hand
in their several magazines. This was expeditiously effected, and with
little difficulty; but the collection was very inadequate, yet sufficient
to relieve the anxiety of the present moment. Happily they were not
apprized within the walls of Boston, of the poverty of their antagonists
without, particularly in this article, until they had time [239] to collect
the small stocks from the neighbouring towns, and to receive some,
though far from an ample supply, from the southern colonies. At this
crisis, had general Gage ventured without his entrenchments, both
the American army and the people, must have been involved in
extreme distress.

Several vessels had been privately sent both to the Dutch and
English islands to procure arms and ammunition; but so narrowly
were they watched by the British cruisers, that they had returned
with little success.

These circumstances accelerated a spirited measure, before contemplated only by a few; the arming and equipping of ships to cruize on
British property, was a bold attempt, that startled the apprehensions
of many, zealously opposed to the undue exercise of British power;
but necessity impelled, and the enterprize was pursued. The general
assembly of the Massachusetts soon resolved to build, equip and arm,
a number of vessels suitable for the purpose, to cruize and capture
any British ships that might be found on, or near their coasts. They
granted letters of marque and reprisal to several adventurers, and
appointed courts of admiralty for the trial and condemnation of any

CHAP. VII captures within those limits. By these means, the seasonable capture,
1 7 7 5 in the beginning of this enterprise, of a British ship, laden with
ordnance, and an assorted cargo of warlike stores, sufficiently [240]
supplied the exigencies of the army, and dissipated the fears of those,
who had suffered the most painful apprehensions for the safety of
their country.

These naval preparations may perhaps be said, not to have been
merely of a defensive nature, the line yet avowedly observed by the
Americans; but they had advanced too far to recede; sophistical
distinctions of words, or names, were laid aside. It is a fact, of which
every one is sensible, that successful opposition to arbitrary sway,
places a civic crown on the head of the hero that resists; when
contingencies that defeat confer an hempen cord instead of a wreath
of laurel. The success and catastrophe of the infant navy of America,
will be shewn in the succeeding pages.

The naked state of the magazines had been kept as secret as
possible, and every preparation for attack or defence, had been made,
as if no deficiency was felt, while there were not three rounds of
powder in the American camp. Lines of circumvallation had been
formed from Mystick river to Roxbury and Dorchester. But, notwithstanding the appearance of strength, the collection of numbers, and
the hostile disposition of both parties, nothing of consequence was
attempted by either, after the action of the seventeenth of June,
during the remainder of Gage's [241] administration. This inactivity
was heavily censured by the more ardent spirits both within and
without the camp; it was thought disgraceful on the one side, nor
would it have been less dishonorable on the other, had not their
inability from the causes just mentioned prevented more vigorous
movements. Yet, from the circumstances of the colonies, their petition
to the king still pending, and their allegiance not formally renounced,
it was judged by many, most prudent for the American army, to
remain for the present only on the defensive.

Governor Gage obtained leave to repair to England in the autumn
of one thousand seven hundred and seventy-five. It was indeed
unfortunate for him, that he had been appointed to the command of
an army and the government of a province, without the talents that
qualified for the times. He was naturally a man of a humane disposition,
nor had his courage ever been impeached; but he had not the intrigue
of the statesman to balance the parties, nor the sagacity necessary to
defeat their designs; nor was he possessed of that soldierly promptitude

that leaves no interval between the determination and the execution CHAP. VII
of his projects. Glad to quit the thorny field, he bade adieu to a 1 7 7 5
country he had not the ability, and perhaps not the inclination to
subdue, and the command of the army devolved on Sir William Howe.

[242] General Oglethorpe, his senior in office, an experienced
veteran, grown old in military *fame* without sullying his laurels, had
the prior offer of this command. He agreed to accept the appointment
on condition the ministry would authorize him to assure the colonies,
that justice should be done them. His proposal at once appeared the
result of humanity and equity; he declared, that "he knew the people
of America well; that they never would be subdued by arms, but that
their obedience would be ever secured by doing them justice."* A
man with these ideas was not a fit instrument for the designs of the
British government: he was therefore, agreeable to his own request,
permitted to remain at home, where he was a quiet spectator of the
folly of his country through a seven years war with the colonies.† On
his declining the appointment, the important and hazardous command
was given to general Howe, a man of pleasure and a soldier; but the
predominancy of the [243] first trait in his character often interfered
with the vigour and decision necessary to complete the last. Early on
his promotion, his severity and indiscretion erased the favorable
impression which many in America yet cherished for his name and
family.

In the beginning of his administration, he published a proclamation,
condemning to military execution any of the remaining inhabitants of
Boston, who should attempt to leave the town; he compelled them
to form themselves into bodies under officers he should appoint, and
to take arms in case of an attack, against their brethren in the country.
Yet for a certain sum of money, he promised an exemption from the
cruel task of imbruing their hands in the blood of their friends. But
the most memorable event that took place, while he presided in the

* British Annual Register.
† General Oglethorpe had been distinguished for the benevolence of his disposition
through all his transactions in America, where he had resided several years. His
mildness and equity towards the natives in the early settlement of the state of
Georgia, and his conduct both in a civil and military capacity, had won the esteem
and affection of the inhabitants of the southern colonies, the approbation of his
sovereign and the applause of his native country.

Modern Universal History, vol. XL.
[*Modern Universal History*, 40: 455–463.]

CHAP. VII province, previous to the evacuation of Boston, was the cannonade
1 7 7 5 and destruction of Falmouth, a flourishing and well-built town in the
eastern part of the Massachusetts.

Alarm and depredation had spread from shore to shore through all
the sea coasts of America; their shipping were seized, their islands
plundered, their harbors infested by the landing of marauding parties,
and many places threatened with immediate conflagration. Bristol,
near Rhode Island, had been attacked in a dark [244] stormy night,
and an hundred and twenty cannon fired on the defenceless town
within an hour. Many houses were injured, and some set on fire; a
remarkable sickness had raged in the town for some time, and the
languishing inhabitants were now hurried into the streets in their
beds, to preserve them from immediate death in the conflagration of
their houses.* This was an uncivil mode of demanding a tax of cattle,
sheep, and hogs, for the supply of the squadron of captain (afterwards)
Sir James Wallace, who had for many months harassed and distressed
the state of Rhode Island.

This rude attack upon Bristol, took place only eight days previous
to the wanton desolation which on the eve of winter stripped the
inhabitants of Falmouth, both of shelter and provisions, and drove
them naked into the wilderness, uncertain of any accommodations to
secure them from the inclemency of the season. One captain Mowatt,
who had recently been a prisoner there, and had received the most
hospitable treatment from the inhabitants, was the instrument to
execute this deed of unprovoked barbarity. It is true he notified the
town, that

> he would give them two hours [245] to remove the *human species*, at the
> period of which term, a red pendant would be hoisted at the main-top-
> gallant-mast head, and that on the least resistance he should be freed from
> all humanity dictated by his orders or his inclination.†

* The Rev. Mr. Burt, distinguished for his piety, benevolence, and attachment to
the liberties of his country, was found dead in a field the morning after the
conflagration. He had fled from his bed where he was confined by sickness, to
escape the flames that consumed his house.

† The above is an exact copy of Mowatt's letter. See British Remembrancer.
[*Remembrancer* II (1776): 125. See John Sullivan to George Washington, October 29,
1775, in Sparks, *Correspondence*, I: 71; Nathanael Greene to Governor Ward, October
23, 1775; George Washington to President of Congress (Hancock), October 24
(November 1), 1775; Nathanael Greene to Governor Cooke, October 24, 1775; "To
the Inhabitants of New York," November 14, 1775, in Force, *Archives*, 4th. ser., 3:
1145–1147; 1151–1152; 1168; 1552–1554.]

Three gentlemen repaired on board his ship to inquire the reason CHAP. VII
of this extraordinary summons. Mowatt replied, that   1 7 7 5

> he had orders to set on fire all the sea-port towns from Boston to Halifax,
> and that he supposed New-York was already in ashes.

He said,

> he could dispense with his orders on no terms but the compliance of the
> inhabitants to deliver up their arms and ammunition, and their sending on
> board a supply of provisions, four carriage-guns, and the same number of
> the principal persons in the town, as hostages, that they should engage
> not to unite with their country in any kind of opposition to Britain.

He assured them that on a refusal of these conditions, he should lay the town in ashes within three hours.

Unprepared for such an attack, and intimidated by the roar of cannon, which began to play on the town, the people supplicated a suspension till the morning before they replied to the humiliating proposal. They improved the [246] short reprieve which with difficulty they obtained, in removing their families and effects; after which they made no further resistance, not even to the marines who landed with lighted torches to make the devastation complete. In this defenceless situation, the inhabitants considered opposition only as a useless waste of human life, and many of them stood on the heights, the passive spectators of the fire that played on the town through the day. They beheld with varied emotions, a conflagration that reduced many of them to penury and despair; thus, were they prepared for the occupation of soldiers, and driven to the field from the double motive of resentment and the necessity of immediate subsistence.

New York, Stonington, Newport, and many other places were threatened, but did not experience a similar fate. The last, situated on an island, was obliged to stipulate for a weekly supply, to save their town from the fury of the piratical corsairs that surrounded them, who proudly boasted of the civility and generosity of their nation. England has indeed been long celebrated for magnanimity, clemency, and humanity; but it is with nations as with individuals, when human nature falls from virtue, it generally sinks into the extremes of vice, in proportion as it was before conspicuous for superior excellence.

[247] Thus, the monarch divested of compassion, and the ministry of principle, the naval strength of Britain, the mistress of the seas, and the terror of Europe, was employed to interrupt the commerce, lay waste the cities, destroy the towns, and plunge the inhabitants of

America in misery and despair; forgetful that she was ever contributing
by the acquisitions of her industry to the strength of Britain. Nor was
America yet sufficiently irritated, to renounce her allegiance to the
king, or relinquish her connexion with England, cemented by the
strong ties of habit and consanguinity, language, religion, and manners.
Yet, though there was no formal dissolution of the legal bands that
had united them, the frequent outrages experienced by Americans,
convinced them of the necessity of some effectual naval preparations
on their part. This was so obvious, that Congress no longer delayed
acting with decision on a measure that had been balanced by various
opinions. They directed general Washington to contract for a number
of armed vessels to cruise abroad, to defend the sea coasts at home,
and as far as it was practicable, to capture British property wherever
it might be found.

Many gentlemen, sanguine in opinion, that an American navy was
no *Utopian* project, but that her marine might rapidly rise to a
respectable height, engaged with an energy that seldom [248] fails of
carrying into execution any attempt the human mind, on principles
of reason, is capable of forming. They accordingly built on the large
rivers from Portsmouth to Pennsylvania, a number of vessels, row-
gallies, and frigates, from four to forty guns; fitted, manned, and
completely equipped them for sea in the course of a few months. All
encouragement was given both to public and private adventurers who
engaged in the sea service; success was equal to expectation; many
very valuable prizes, and a vast number of provision vessels from
England, Ireland, and Nova Scotia, were captured, and by this means
the Americans were soon supplied, not only with the necessaries for
war, but with the conveniences and the luxuries of life.

While things remained in this situation in Boston, and along the
Atlantic shore, a very busy and important scene was acting in another
quarter of America. The conquest of Quebec by the immortal *Wolfe*,
in conjunction with the bold and hardy New Englanders, is a story
well known in the annals of Britain. On the peace concluded with
France at Fontainbleau, in the duke of Bedford's administration, the
whole province of Canada was ceded to the crown of England, in lieu
of more valuable acquisitions relinquished to France. Most of the
inhabitants of the country were French, some of them noblesse, and
all of them attached to their former [249] master. The Roman Catholic
faith was the established religion of the country, yet the Canadians
were in all respects to be governed according to the laws of England,

until the Quebec bill, the subject of much political disunion in CHAP. VII
England, passed into an act, in one thousand seven hundred and 1 7 7 5
seventy-four. This act cut the Canadians off from the privileges of
English subjects, denied them an assembly of their own on the
principles of the British constitution, deprived them of the trial by
jury in civil processes; the laws of France were restored, and the
boundaries of the province were extended far beyond the just limits:
the Roman Catholic religion also was not only to be tolerated, but
was established by act of parliament. This was very offensive both to
the French and the English inhabitants, who found their interests
inseparably connected. These new regulations were made with a view
of fixing the Canadians more firmly in the interest of the ministry;
but as they had tasted the advantages of a less despotic government,
the people in general had adopted more liberal modes of thinking,
both in civil and religious matters; and most of the inhabitants were
equally dissatisfied with the late parliamentary regulations.

The Quebec act, unpopular in England, and alarming in America,
was particularly disgusting to all the English settlers in Canada, except
[250] a few individuals employed by the crown. Neither the authority
of administration, nor the address of governor Carleton, was sufficient
to quiet the disorders that arose, or to induce the Canadians in this
early stage of the dispute, to take arms to assist in the subjugation of
the other colonies. They murmured loudly at the measures of the
British government; they refused peremptorily to act against the
United States, and several of the principal English inhabitants corresponded with some of the members of Congress; and encouraged
the measures that were taken to bring the province of Canada into
an union with the thirteen colonies.

Thus it required no small intrigue to instigate even the savages
who delight in blood, to the commission of unprovoked hostilities,
which would interrupt the traffic carried on between them and the
frontiers of the other provinces. It has been justly observed,

that the introduction of barbarians and savages into the contests of civilized
nations, is a measure pregnant with shame and mischief, which the interest
of a moment may impel, but which is reprobated by the best principles of
humanity and reason.*

* Gibbon on the decline and fall of the Roman empire. [Edward Gibbon, *The
History of the Decline and Fall of the Roman Empire* (6 vols.; London, 1776–1788).
Gibbon discusses barbarians throughout the six volumes, though most pointedly
in I, Chapter X. The quotation does not appear.]

CHAP. VII But these were not the principles on which the American war was
1 7 7 5 conducted. Congress had authentic information, that every method
was used to induce the savages [251] to take up the hatchet against
the Americans. Several conferences had been held the preceding
summer, with many of their chiefs assembled at Montreal. This was
in consequence of the machinations of colonel Johnson, a famous
Indian partisan in the last war, whose influence among them was very
extensive. In these conferences he gave each of them a war belt and
a tomahawk; invited them to drink the blood, and feast on the body
of a *Bostonian*, and to sing the war-song over a roasted bullock and a
pipe of wine he had prepared for the purpose; but several of them
declined either to eat, drink, or sing the barbarous song. They
afterwards delivered up the black belt with the hatchet depictured
thereon, to some of the American officers.*

These transactions were considered as incontestable proof, that
administration was determined to employ as their allies, the fierce
and numerous *hordes* of the wilderness, to subdue and butcher the
Americans, even before they had thrown off their allegiance to the
crown of Britain. It had also been recently discovered, that governor
Carleton had received a commission, authorizing him to muster and
arm all persons residing within the province of Canada, and,

> as occasion should require, to march and embark the levies to any of the
> provinces of [252] America, to pursue and prosecute either by sea or land,
> all enemies, pirates, or rebels, either in or out of the province; and if it
> should so please God, them to vanquish, to take, and so apprehended,
> according to law, them to put to death, or to preserve alive, at his
> discretion.†

A detail of the sufferings of one family will evince the wretched
situation of all in that province who had the courage to complain of
the measures of administration, or indulged a favorable opinion of the
exertions of the other colonies. The singular mode of bending the
minds of men of liberal opinions to the designs of government, was
first experimented on Mr. Walker, an English gentleman of fortune

---

* General Schuyler's letter, Dec. 14th, 1775, published by order of congress. [See
Force, *Archives*, 4th. ser., 4: 260–261; JCC, 3: 456.]

† The whole of general Carleton's extraordinary commission may be seen in the
parliamentary register of Nov. 2d, in the second sessions of the then parliament.
[Force, *Archives*, 4th. ser., 2: 403–408 (Commission dated April 1775). See *Annual
Register* (1776), "History of Europe," pp. 2–3.]

and abilities, who had been many years a resident at Montreal. His CHAP. VII
avowed dislike of the Quebec bill, drew on him the resentment of 1 7 7 5
the officers of government, and involved him in altercation and danger.
He had, in answer to the servile maxim—*"Qui le roi, est maitre"*—
repeated by one Rouvelle, coolly replied, that "with regard to monsieur
Rouvelle, it might by so, as he ate his majesty's bread;" but added,
"I deny that the king is *my master:* I respect him as my lawful
sovereign, and am ready to pay [253] due obedience to his lawful
commands; but I cannot acknowlege any one as *my master* while I live
by my own industry; when I receive pay from the king, perhaps my
acknowledgments may be equally submissive." Rouvelle immediately
informed general Carleton of this conversation; his prudence was
commended, and he was soon after appointed one of the judges of
the supreme court at Montreal. This appointment was equally astonishing to the French inhabitants, as it was disgusting to the English.
Men of all descriptions had a very ill opinion of Rouvelle. The recent
conversation between him and Mr. Walker was misrepresented and
exaggerated. The partisans of the crown and the officers of the army
were highly exasperated against him; and soon after, resentment was
carried so far as to attempt the assassination of Mr. Walker.

A number of soldiers under the command of a captain Disney,
entered his house in the evening, when at supper with a few friends.
On a sudden noise at the door of the hall, Mrs. Walker imagined it
to be some Canadians, who had been the preceding day on business
with Mr. Walker, as an officer of justice. Without any hesitation she
pronounced *entrez;* but to her inexpressible surprise, the next moment
she saw through the glasses of the inner door, a number of faces,
some of them blacked, others covered with a vizard of crape, all rising
on the steps, and rushing with [254] precipitation into the room: in
an agony of surprise she exclaimed, "Good God, this is murder!" Mr.
Walker sat with his back to the door, and before he had time to rise,
he received from one of the ruffians, a violent stroke of a broad sword
on his head; he attempted to recover his arms and defend himself,
but wounded in a most cruel manner, he sunk motionless on the
floor, when one of the villains kneeled on his breast, and cut off his
right ear, while he so far retained his senses as to hear one of them
say, "damn him, he is dead."

After recovering from his wounds, he commenced a civil process
against Disney and his party. The crime was proved with all its
atrocious aggravations, but justice had not its operation, either in

CHAP. VII compensation to the sufferer, or punishment of the guilty. Mr. Walker
1 7 7 5 finding himself unsafe in the city, retired to his country-house,
determined to amuse himself with his books and his farm, without
farther attention to political or public scenes; but his persecution was
not at an end; he had not long resided in his villa, before he was
molested in a still more barbarous manner.

A party of thirty soldiers was sent by governor Carleton, to bring
him dead or alive to Quebec. They surrounded his house just before
day, and summoned him to surrender. Instead of a compliance, he
courageously endeavoured [255] to defend himself and his family,
until the party without set fire to his house in several places, when
he was obliged to escape the flames by throwing himself from the
third story. In the fall from a window of such a height, one of his legs
was broken, which left him to the mercy of his antagonists, who made
him their prisoner, and conducted him to Quebec, where he was
loaded with irons, denied the use of pen, ink, and paper, and
forbidden even the light of a taper in his darksome cell.

Mrs. Walker, a lady of great elegance and sensibility, had in the
terror of the night, leaped from a second story window, and walked
through the snow till exhausted by fear and fatigue, she was overtaken
by one of the party, who had the compassion to throw his cloak over
her, and conduct her to a neighbouring house. She soon after made
her escape from that part of the country over the lakes, accompanied
by the commissioners, congress had some time before sent on, to
confer with and secure the interest of the Canadians. The boat in
which she crossed one of those inland seas, passed another almost
within call, which conveyed her husband a prisoner to Quebec.

It has already been observed, that an address had been sent by
Congress to the inhabitants of Canada, couched in nervous, friendly
and pathetic terms, reminding them of their common [256] danger,
and urging them to a union with the other colonies in defence of their
common rights. But the mixture of French, British, American, and
savage inhabitants of that country, rendered it very uncertain how far
the other colonies might depend on the aid or friendship of the
Canadians. Congress apprized of the situation of affairs there, judged
it prudent to endeavour to engage the people of all descriptions in
that quarter, more firmly to the interest of the union. It was thought
a favorable crisis for this purpose, when the flower of the British
troops then in America, were shut up in Boston; and when the
governors of the southern provinces, interrupted in their negociations

with the Indians, had taken refuge on board the king's ships, either
from real or imagined personal danger. This was an important business,
as whoever possesses Canada will in a great measure command the
numerous tribes beyond the lakes. A respectable delegation was sent
to Montreal, to treat with the white inhabitants, and as far as possible
to conciliate or secure the copper-colored nations.

The importance of possessing Canada, strongly impressed the minds
at this time, of gentlemen of the first penetration. A very respectable
committee was sent by congress into the country, with Dr. Franklin
at the head of the mission; whose talents as a statesman, perfect
knowledge of the French language, extensive [257] literary acquaintance with that nation, urbanity of manners, courteous deportment,
united with a prudent reserve, marked him as a suitable character to
negociate with, and endeavour to attach the Canadians of all descriptions to the American union. Mr. Carrol of Maryland, a clergyman of
the Roman Catholic profession, was sent on with the delegation, to
administer the ordinances of religion, baptism, absolution, &c., which
they had been denied for some time by their clergy under British
influence; who, instead of bestowing the blessings of the church, had
denounced their anathemas, to the great grievance of many tender
consciences, and threatened the vengeance of heaven, as well as
earth, on failure of due submission to parliamentary mandates.

These efforts to engage and fix the Canadians to a certain point
failed; the committee returned with little success. Words and professions are of little avail when the sword is, or is about to be, lifted for
decision. Congress now found that a force sufficient to strengthen the
hands of their friends in that province, was the only mode to be relied
on. In consequence of this necessity, they directed two regiments of
New York militia, and a body of New Englanders, consisting in the
whole of about three thousand men, to proceed under the command
of the generals Schuyler and Montgomery, by the lake [258] Champlain
to the river Sorel, which empties itself into the St. Lawrence, and
immediately attempt the reduction of Quebec. They arrived at the
Isle Noix, which lies at the entrance of that river, in the autumn of
one thousand seven hundred and seventy-five.

The commander there published a declaration announcing the
reasons of this movement, and inviting the inhabitants of every
description to arrange themselves under the banners of liberty, and
unite in the common cause of America. After this, they immediately
pushed on through woods, swamps, and morasses, to a fort about

twelve miles distance: here, an unexpected attack from a large body of Indians, obliged them to retreat to their former post, and wait the arrival of reinforcements.

On this retreat to the *Isle Noix,* general Schuyler immediately returned to Albany; the ostensible reason was, the broken state of his health, which indeed was so impaired, as to render him unfit for the fatigue of such a service. Thus the whole weight of the war in that quarter, was left to the intrepid Montgomery; who though qualified by his courage, capacity, and military experience, was not in force sufficient for so great an undertaking. He, however, notwithstanding the vigilance of general Carleton, made himself master of the forts of Chamblee and St. John's, and with various other successes [259] arrived at Montreal, about the middle of November. General Carleton had arrived there some time before, and had made every exertion for the preservation of all the posts in the neighbourhood, as well as those above mentioned; but the people disaffected, and his army weak, his efforts were blasted, and he thought himself happy to escape the vigilance of Montgomery; who had placed guards at every post for his interception: he, however, in a dark night, in an open boat, fortunately passed them all, and arrived at Quebec in safety.

When general Montgomery arrived at Montreal, the inhabitants, both French and English, wished to surrender by capitulation; but with a spirit and dignity consistent with his usual character, he refused this, though at the same time he gave them the strongest assurances of justice, security, and personal safety. He pledged his honor for their peaceable possession of their property, and the free exercise of their religion: he expressed in liberal terms, his disposition to protect the inhabitants on the same footing with the other American colonies. He then demanded the possession of the gates, and the keys of all the public stores, and ordered them to be delivered by nine o'clock the ensuing morning. Accordingly the gates were thrown open, and his troops entered at the appointed hour: thus without the smallest resistance, he took possession of this important post. He treated every [260] class of inhabitants with that lenity and politeness, which at once attached them to his person, strengthened their prejudices against the British government, and cherished the favorable ideas many had before imbibed, both of the Americans, and the cause in which they were engaged.

When Montgomery had made all proper arrangements for the security and peace of Montreal, he prepared immediately to go forward

and invest Quebec, then in a weak defenceless condition, their CHAP. VII
governor absent, the inhabitants disaffected, and but an handful of 1 7 7 5
troops in the garrison. When general Carleton left the neighbourhood
of Montreal, he made the utmost dispatch to reach and put the capital
of Canada in a proper state of defence; but he found Quebec in the
greatest consternation and danger, from a quarter not apprehended,
and scarcely conceived possible, from the novelty and hazard of the
undertaking.

A detachment of upwards of one thousand men had been marched
from the army near Boston. The command of this little band had
been given to colonel Arnold, a young soldier of fortune, who held
in equal contempt both danger and principle. They took passage at
Merrimack, and arrived at the mouth of the Kennebeck on the twenty-
second of September. There, finding it probable their provisions [261]
might fall short, when there could be no possibility of a fresh supply,
Arnold sent back three hundred of his men.* Most of the remainder
embarked in batteaux prepared for the purpose: a small division of
the troops marched slowly, and kept the banks of the river.

They encamped together every night, though frequently interrupted
in their progress, by rocks, falls, rapids, and carrying-places, where
they were obliged to carry their boats for several miles together on
their shoulders. With incredible perseverance, they traversed woods,
mountains, swamps, and precipices, and were obliged alternately to
cut their way where no human foot had trodden, to ford shallows, or
attempt the navigation of a rapid stream, with a rocky bottom, which
seemed not designed as a passage for any human being to attempt.
At the same time their provisions were so reduced, that they were
obliged to eat their own dogs, and convert their shoe-leather into
food.

But with astonishing resolution, they surmounted every obstacle,
and near two thirds of the detachment completed a *route* of several
hundred miles, through an hideous wilderness, unexplored before but
by the beasts and savages of the forest. It was at the time thought,
that if the historian did justice to the heroic firmness [262] of this
little party, that it would be as honorable a testimony of the exertions
of human intrepidity, as the celebrated march of the renowned
Hannibal: but the enterprising spirit of America has since taught her

---

* These appeared ready to desert with a field officer at their head, if they had not
been permitted to return.

sons to tread over a track of the forlorn desert so much more extensive, that this now appears but an epitome of their hardihood.

Colonel Arnold with his little army almost exhausted by hunger and fatigue, reached the Canadian settlements on the third of November. He was received in a friendly manner, and a liberal supply of provisions was collected for his relief. By the alacrity of the inhabitants, he was in a few days furnished with boats to cross the St. Lawrence, and by favor of the night he effected his passage, in spite of the vigilance of several frigates that lay in the river. When he sat down before Quebec, he found all the batteries manned from the shipping; but having no artillery, he could do little more than parade before the city, and wait the arrival of general Montgomery.

In the mean time, general Carleton was not idle; every preparation that courage or vigilance could dictate, was made for the reception of Montgomery. He ordered by proclamation, all who refused to take arms, immediately to quit the city with their wives and children, on peril of being treated with the utmost severity, [263] as rebels and traitors to their king. Many of them obeyed, and abandoned their residence and property. The Scotch inhabitants and the French *noblesse*, he could at that time firmly rely on; all others, disgusted with the Quebec act, and alienated by the severity of the governor, were in a temper to renounce their loyalty, and join the Americans. Yet the fear of losing their property in the confusion that might ensue, if the city was obliged to change its masters, operated on some, and caused them to arm, though with great reluctance. The consideration of pecuniary losses will always have a powerful influence on the minds of men: thus, the zeal which had been nurtured for the defence of liberty, soon began to abate; and both English and Canadians, actuated by the principle of immediate self-interest, concealed their former defection to the British government. Many of them were wealthy and opulent, and became daily more disposed to unite in defence of the town, which contained more families in opulent circumstances, than all the province besides.

After placing a garrison in Montreal, new clothing his troops, and stationing some small detachments in the out-posts in the neighbourhood, general Montgomery sent a few troops to different parts of the province, to expedite farther supplies of provisions, clothing, and other necessaries. He then pushed on his march beneath the fall of snows, embarrassed [264] with bad roads, a severe winter, an inhospitable climate, and the murmur of his little army. The term of their enlistment was nearly expired; nothing kept them together but their

attachment to their commander, and that zeal in the public cause, CHAP. VII
which had already prompted them to encounter perils and endure 1 7 7 5
hardships, which the human constitution seems not calculated to
surmount, after being softened by the habits of civilized life. But by
the address of the commander, and the resolution of the troops, they
with incredible expedition arrived at Quebec, notwithstanding the
impediments that lay in their way.

The soldiers in garrison, with the marines from the king's frigates,
that had been placed therein, and the armed militia, both French and
English, did not amount to more than two thousand men when the
army arrived from Montreal; but by the intrepidity of general Carleton,
and the activity of his officers, they had prepared for defence with
the spirit of veterans. They rejected with disdain a summons from
Montgomery to surrender the town, to prevent the fatal consequences
of its being taken by storm; fired on the flag that offered to convey
letters with proposals for capitulation, obliged it to retire, and all
communication was forbidden by the inflexible Carleton.

[265] General Montgomery after this, sent a second letter* by
colonel Arnold and Mr. Macpherson, his aid-de-camp, to general
Carleton. He upbraided him with personal ill-treatment, with the
cruelty exercised towards the prisoners that had fallen into his hands,
and with the unparallelled conduct, except among savages, of firing
at a flag of truce. He warned him not to destroy either public or
private stores, as he had done at Montreal, and kept up a tone of
superiority as if sure of success. The messengers reached the walls of
Quebec, but were ordered to decamp with speed, and informed that
the governor would receive no letters or hold any intercourse with
rebels.

Thus circumstanced, general Montgomery judged that immediate
and decided action, was the only means of serving his country, and
securing to himself that renown, which the lustre of his former conduct
had acquired. Thus, depending too much on his own good fortune,
and too little acquainted with the arrangement and vigor within the
walls, he resolved on the dangerous and desperate measure of an
effort to take the city by *escalade*. He made his dispositions accordingly,
and under the cover of a violent snow-storm, his army in four separate
divisions, [266] began the arduous work at the same moment, early
on the morning of the thirty-first of December.

But the enemy had gained intelligence of his movements, the alarm

* See general Montgomery's letter, December 6, 1775. Appendix, Note No. XV.

had been given, and a signal made for a general engagement in the
lower town, some time before Montgomery had reached it. He however
pushed on through a narrow passage, with a hanging rock on the one
side, and a dangerous precipice of the banks of the river on the other,
and with a resolution becoming his character, he gained the first
barrier. Warmed with the spirit of magnanimity and a thirst for glory,
the inseparable companions of exalted minds, he met undaunted the
fire of his enemies, and accompanied by some of his bravest officers,
he rushed on to attack a well-defended barricade. But to the regret
of the army, the grief of his country, and the inexpressible sorrow of
his numerous friends, the valiant Montgomery, with the laurels fresh
blooming on his brow, fell at the gates by a random shot from the
frozen walls of Quebec.

Connected with one of the first families in New York,* happy in
the highest enjoyment of domestic felicity, he was led by principle
to quit the occupations of rural life; and animated with an ardent zeal
for the cause of human nature, the liberties of mankind, and the glory
of America, [267] both his active life, and his heroic death, verified
his last expression to his amiable lady. . . . *"You shall never blush for
your Montgomery"*†

His philosophic taste, his pleasing manners, his private virtues, and
his military abilities, were acknowledged and revered even by his
enemies, who cannot but pronounce the Canadian fields are marked
with peculiar glory. It is there the choicest flowers of fame may be
culled to crown the memory of a Wolfe and a Montgomery. Yet, while
one of those illustrious names, written in characters of blood, reflects
lustre on the glory of a British monarch, the other will announce to
posterity, the efforts of virtue to resist the tyranny of his successor.

General Montgomery was justly considered as an early martyr in
the cause of freedom, and the premature stroke that robbed his
country of an officer of tried bravery and decided merit, was not only
bewailed by his friends, but excited the tear of generous compassion
from all those who were susceptible of the nobler feelings of the soul,
among such as were opposed to him in political opinion. The
animosities of war, and the enmities created by different sentiments,
or rivalry in fame, should ever expire with the life of a hero. Yet the
obsequies of this great [268] and amiable man, were not attended

* He married a daughter of judge Livingston.

† The writer of these annals had the particulars of his last adieu, in a letter from his
lady immediately after his death.

with those honorary marks of respect, usually paid to illustrious CHAP. VII
military characters, when victory has satiated resentment: his body 1 7 7 5
was thrown into a sledge, and without even a coffin, conveyed to the
place of burial. The manner of general Montgomery's interment, was
at first reported much more to the honor of governor Carleton; but
the above account is from the testimony of several respectable
American officers then in Quebec.* By the persuasion of a lady who
afterwards married the lieutenant governor of Quebec, who had
formerly served in the British army with general Montgomery, the
body of this worthy officer was taken up, and again interred in a rough
coffin, but without any particular marks of respect. The other officers
who fell, were indiscriminately thrown with their clothes on, into the
same grave with their soldiers.

The death of general Montgomery decided the fate of the day,
though colonel Arnold and his party with great bravery kept up the
attack; nor did they quit the field until after Arnold was obliged to
retire, having received a dangerous wound. Notwithstanding this
accident, added to the unspeakable loss of their brave commander,
this small resolute party kept [269] their ground, until galled on every
side, attacked in the rear, and their retreat cut off by a British party,
who found means to secure a passage that prevented even the attempt,
yet they kept up an obstinate defence for several hours, but at last
were obliged to surrender themselves prisoners of war.†

Though the manes of their commander in chief had not been
treated with that generosity which is usually the result of true
magnanimity, yet general Carleton treated the prisoners that afterwards
fell into his hands, with more humanity; their wounds were dressed,
their wants relieved, and his own physicians sent to visit the sick. He
also endeavoured to recal those, who, after the defeat, had taken
shelter in the woods, or such as had been left sick or wounded on
the way, after the retreat; and by proclamation, he promised liberty
to all the unhappy stragglers, when they should be cured of their
wounds and diseases.

---

* Particularly captain, afterwards general, Dearborn; taken prisoner at the attempt on
the second barrier.

† Most of the American officers distinguished themselves by their intrepidity and
vigilance on this fated day; but none more than colonel Morgan, who seemed to be
adapted by nature, by his strength of body, vigor of mind, and unconquerable
resolution, for the severe conflicts of war. This was afterwards exemplified in the
many rencounters he met in the ravage of the Carolinas.

CHAP. VII   After the death of Montgomery, the retreat of Arnold, and a
1 7 7 5 surrender of a considerable [270] part of his troops, the broken forces
collected and retired about three miles from the city. There they kept
up a kind of blockade through the winter; and by the spirit of Arnold,
on whom the command had devolved, and the vigilance of his party,
they prevented in a great measure, additional recruits and supplies
for the relief of the city. This there was every reason to expect would
be attempted, not only from the difficulties of their situation within
the city, but from the fickleness of the Canadians without, and their
manifest disposition to enlist under the banner of success. From their
local circumstances, this change of temper might from the beginning
have been apprehended, from those pretended allies of the United
States. Their neighbourhood and connexion with the savages, their
long habit of oscillating between England and France, and their
ignorance in general of the grounds of the dispute, must naturally
render their fidelity to the states, under the jurisdiction of Congress,
very uncertain.

But we leave the lakes, the wilderness, the savages, and their
employers in that quarter, for the present, to observe for a time, the
interesting movements on the borders of the Atlantic, and the
disposition discovered by the ancient parent of the colonies, which
soon produced consequences of the highest moment. It may, [271]
however, be proper to observe here, that general Arnold extricated
himself in a remarkable manner from his embarrassments in this
quarter; and lived to be conspicuously distinguished through the
American war, for his bravery and address, his activity, and his villany.

CHAPTER VIII

Dissensions in the British Parliament • Petition of Governor Penn rejected • Boston evacuated • Sir Henry Clinton sent to the Southward—Followed by General Lee—His Character • Sir Peter Parker's Attack on Sullivan's Island • General Howe's Arrival at Sandy-Hook • General Washington leaves Cambridge • Observations on the Temper of some of the Colonies

[272] While as above related, a busy and important scene was exhibited at the northward, the southern colonies were parrying the embarrass- ments created by the royal governors, some of whom had recently left America. The people were gradually laying aside the prejudices which mankind generally imbibe for old established governments, and were preparing themselves for new modes, if necessity should impel, whenever the delegates with whom they had entrusted their rights, should judge affairs fully ripened for a declaration of independence, and a final separation from Britain. The American congress was yet waiting the result of their late petition to the throne, with a degree of temper and moderation scarcely paralleled, among men possessing the unlimited confidence of their country on the one side, and on the other irritated by the neglect and contempt of their oppressors, and the rude insults of ministerial menace.

[273] Thus suspended on the wing of expectation, or rather an unfounded and fruitless hope, every thing remained quiet at head-quarters, through the winter of one thousand seven hundred and seventy-six. No attempt was made against Boston by the American army, nor did general Howe shew any disposition to sally from the town, and interrupt the tranquility of the camp. In short, the British army, engrossed by the pleasures of the town, and the exhibition of *farces* composed by one of their general officers* became so inactive,

---

* General Burgoyne, whose genius for these literary productions was afterwards displayed more to his honor.

CHAP. VIII and appeared so inoffensive, that the Americans (little less disposed
1 7 7 5 to indulge in the pleasures of peace) enjoyed at Cambridge the
conviviality of the season. The ladies of the principal American officers
repaired to the camp. Harmony and hospitality, united with that
simplicity which had hitherto been characteristic of the domestic taste,
style, and manners of the most respectable Americans, reigned among
them for several months, without the smallest interruption. Civility
and mutual forbearance appeared between the officers of the royal
and continental armies, and a frequent interchange of flags was
indulged, for the gratification of the different partisans.

[274] But notwithstanding the reluctance to action, observable in
two powerful and contiguous armies, the wheels of revolution were
rolling on in swift progression. The approach of spring lowered with
the fate of empire, the birth of nations, and the painful convulsions
experienced by every state, struggling to retrieve and permanently
secure the rights of nature, seized or curtailed by the strong hand of
power.

Through the last ten years, the British ministry had been repeatedly
changed, and though none of them, except the duke of Grafton and
the marquis of Rockingham,* who had figured at the head of
administration, had shewn any disposition to do justice to America,
yet the counsels of the cabinet had been kept in continual fluctuation.
From the retirement of lord Bute, in one thousand seven hundred
and sixty-six, there had been an extraordinary variety and succession
of characters in the colonial department. The lords Grenville, Rockingham, North, Hillsborough, and Dartmouth, had alternately taken
the lead in this thorny path: several others had labored in the road
for a time, and retired equally successless and chagrined; particularly
the duke of Grafton.†

[275] From the religious deportment of lord Dartmouth, he had
secured the partiality of a party; but it soon appeared from the
inefficacy of his measures, and the want of stability in his conduct,
that he was a very unfit person for a place, that required deeper
intrigue, more energy, and stronger abilities than he possessed. Tired
of the burthen himself, and his employers weary of his administration,
he resigned his office in the summer of one thousand seven hundred
and seventy-five.

---

* The marquis of Rockingham was through his whole life uniformly opposed to the
American war.

† The duke of Grafton was very explicit with his majesty in his reasons for resignation.

On his resignation, lord George Germaine, "the *hero* of *Minden*," CHAP. VIII
entered a field which did not brighten his laurels, though he engaged 1 7 7 5
with a boldness and temerity of spirit, that he had not on all occasions
discovered. Zealous for the honor of his sovereign, the interest and
superiority of his nation, the dignity and supremacy of parliament, he
undertook the conduct of the American war, and the subjugation of
the colonies, with a temper and resolution more sanguine than discreet.
Early in his administration, and through the whole course of this
eventful year, proposals for an accommodation with the colonies, were
offered from various quarters; but conciliation with America, had no
place in the system of the new minister.

The first bill that appeared for this purpose, was from the hand of
lord Chatham, whose energetic abilities and dignified policy, had
recently [276] rescued the empire from ruin. But not even the talents
of a man who had been courted by his sovereign, admired by his
enemies, and adored by the nation, had any influence on a ministry,
deaf to every thing but an American revenue, and the supremacy of
parliament. After the failure of the efforts of this distinguished
statesman, Burke, Franklin, Fothergill, Hartley, and others, anxious
to prevent the wanton waste of human blood, brought forward their
proposals to procure a reconciliation with the colonies, either on the
terms of equity, or partial concession. They supported them with the
most interesting pathos, and with great strength of argument: but
neither the persuasive eloquence of the orator,* the reasoning powers
or conclusive arguments of the philosopher,† nor the mild simplicity
and humane interference of the upright quaker,‡ were listened to
with the smallest attention, by a predetermined administration,
sanctioned by the approbation of royalty. Every suggestion that wore
any appearance of lenity, or re-union with the colonies, was rejected
on the principle of the supremacy of parliament. Tenacious of their
power, and the right to alter, or resume at pleasure, all colonial
charters, and to regulate and tax as consistent with the convenience
of the [277] parent state, the late petition from congress, met the
usual neglect that had been shewn to every former application.

Before it was totally rejected, the duke of Richmond suggested the
propriety of questioning governor Penn, who presented the petition,
relative to the strength, the resources, the disposition, and the designs

* Edmund Burke.
† Dr. Franklin.
‡ Dr. Fothergil. . . All well known in the literary world.

CHAP. VIII of America. Mr. Penn was a gentleman whose talents were equal to
1 7 7 5 the business he was sent to negociate. When called on the floor of
the house of commons for examination, he gave a clear and decided
statement of the situation and the views, the expectations, the wishes,
and the final determination of his countrymen, if they failed in their
present attempt to be heard by their sovereign.* But it was immediately
asserted, that congress was an illegal body; that no parley could be
held with rebels; that while the Americans in hostile array were
preparing armies for opposition to parliamentary authority, it was
beneath the dignity of the supreme legislative, to hold treaties with
men who denied their supremacy; that coercion alone was the proper
line of action for the nation; and that it was necessary this system
should be pushed with redoubled vigor. Consequently, after much
debate, it was agreed in the house, that foreign auxiliaries should be
[278] hired, at an immense expense, to assist in the complete
subjugation of the colonies. A treaty with the landgrave of Hesse,
and a price for payment for the loan of his slaves was voted and
several other similar steps adopted to facilitate the designs against
America.

These measures appeared to many in the house, replete with
absurdity, particularly the calling in of foreign mercenaries, to assist
in a work that discovered little liberality, less humanity, and no wise
policy. It was observed, that no language or act could justify the
authors or supporters of this project. It was replied, "that foreign
troops, inspired with military maxims and ideas of implicit obedience,
would be less liable to be biassed by that false lenity, which national
soldiers might indulge at the expense of national interest."† This was
an unusual and bold assertion to be made in a British house of
commons, and seemed tinctured with a spirit of despotism, that had
not always been characteristic of Englishmen: and indeed now, the
minority in opposition to this and several other high-handed measures,

---

* When the petition was presented by Mr. Penn and Arthur Lee, Esq. they were told
by the Minister that no notice would be taken of it.

† British Annual Register. [The quotation does not appear. Warren may have pieced
together her account at pp. 277–281 from *Annual Register* (1775), "History of Europe,"
pp. 94–120 and "State Papers," pp. 248–252; *Annual Register* (1776), "State Papers,"
pp. 252–255. For Governor Penn's petition (p. 277), see *Annual Register* (1776),
"History of Europe," pp. 45–47. A very lively debate over the use of foreign
mercenaries arose in both houses of Parliament. See *Cobbett*, XVIII: 798–836
(November 1775: use of foreign troops without consent of Parliament); 1167–1186
(February 1776: debate over the treaties with German states); 1188–1228.]

was too respectable to be frowned into insignificance, even by the CHAP. VIII
disapprobation of kings.* 1 7 7 5

The noble names of Rockingham, Scarborough, Abingdon, Effingham, and Ponsonby; [279] the dukes of Manchester, Devonshire, Richmond, and Grafton, with many others of equal rank and consideration, appeared on the protests against the sanguine, summary, and dangerous proceedings of parliament. Their opinions were supported even by some of the royal family: the efforts of the duke of Cumberland were strenuous; he reprobated in the most explicit terms, the whole American system; he lamented in pathetic language, the employing of foreigners; he observed, that he much regretted "that *Brunswickers*, who once to their honor, had been employed in defence of the liberties of the subject, should now be sent to subjugate a distant part of the British empire."†

But in spite of *protests*, arguments, reason, or humanity, the parliament of Britain proceeded as expressed in the dissent of the lords, to "a *refinement* in *tyranny*." Towards the close of the year, they interdicted all trade with America, declared the colonies out of the royal protection, licensed the seizure of their property on the high seas, and by an act of parliament, gave the forfeiture to the captors, and directed an indiscriminate compulsion of all persons taken on board any American vessel, to serve as common sailors in his majesty's navy.

[280] This mode of procedure was opposed and criminated with all the powers of language, by some members of the first consequence in the house of commons. They pronounced it the last degree of wretchedness and indignity to which human nature could be subjugated. They observed that

this was an instance of tyranny worse than death, thus to compel the unfortunate captives who might fall into their hands, after being plundered themselves, to assist their enemies in plundering their brethren.

They asserted

that such modes of severity were without example, except among pirates, outlaws and the common enemies of civil society.

Yet, notwithstanding these sensible remonstrances, there were some

* See Appendix, Note No. XVI.
† See the speech of his royal highness at large in the British Annual Register. [See *Annual Register* (1775), "State Papers," pp. 251; 269–271.]

CHAP. VIII   of the most distinguished characters in England, so heated by party
1 7 7 5   spirit, national pride, and the high claims of parliamentary dignity
and superiority, as shamelessly to avow the necessity of leaping over
the boundaries of equity, and winking out of sight the immutable
laws of justice. It is painful to record, as an evidence of this assertion,
a single instance, that must cause a blush for the weakness or
wickedness of man. Even the great lord *Mansfield*, whose superior
talents, profound erudition, law knowledge, and philosophical abilities,
should have elevated him above all local or party prejudices, declared
publickly, "that the original question of *right* ought no longer to be
considered; that the justice of the cause must give way to the present
situation; [281] that they were engaged in a war, and must use every
effort to obtain the end proposed thereby."* If the politician can
justify this sophistical reasoning, the dictates of justice must lead the
upright to revolt at the idea: a declaration so devoid of the principles
of rectitude, from a man of his lordship's celebrity, at once shocks
the feelings of equity and wounds the sensations of humanity.

The passions of some were irritated by this extraordinary speech
of lord Mansfield, and the judgment of others convinced, that America
had nothing to expect either from the justice or clemency of parliament,
under the influence of men of such abilities and principles. Yet still
the chimerical project of conquest and subjugation, continued to be
uniformly opposed by the dissenting lords in one house, and a
melioration of the American system urged in the other, on the strongest
grounds of reason, justice, policy, and humanity; but a ministerial
majority was astonishingly kept up in both, and on a division on every
question relative to the colonies, the minority bore no proportion to
the names in the other scale.

A war with America did not at this period appear to be the general
wish of the nation at [282] large; but engaged in their own pleasures
and pursuits, they seemed rather inattentive to the object in dispute,
as a matter that very little concerned them. There was indeed some
clamor among the great body of the merchants, on the total destruction
of the American trade, and some of the manufacturing towns were
disposed to be riotous on the occasion; but the danger of a foreign
war, or a final dismemberment of the empire, was not generally
apprehended by the people, though these consequences were pre-

* Debates in parliament, and lord Mansfield's speech in the house of lords, December,
1775. [*Cobbett*, XVIII: 1100–1103. Lords and Commons debated the Prohibitory Bill
at length. *Ibid.*, 1056–1106.]

dicted by some sagacious heads, and the hearts of the patriotic and
compassionate were hurt by the anticipation of the impending evils.
Calling in the aid of foreigners, and introducing a large body of
German mercenaries in British pay, to settle a domestic quarrel with
the colonies, was mortifying to the pride and valor of every uncorrupted
Englishman. But the torrent of secret influence was irresistible; the
expensive system was precipitated: prerogative and conquest was the
ministerial creed; *power* the princely object: and on the approbatory
speech of the monarch, when all was at hazard, there appeared a
coolness that bordered on *apathy*. Silence and submission were enjoined
on the friends of America in the house of commons; and the liberty
of writing their names, and witnessing their uneasiness by their own
signature, was all the consolation of the [283] protesting lords, while
these important questions were in agitation.*

The debates in parliament relative to colonial measures, the king's
speech, and the rejection of the late petition of the continental
congress, arrived in America before the month of March, one thousand
seven hundred and seventy-six. These were accompanied with the
intelligence of the Hessian treaty, and that foreign auxiliaries from
various other nations were to be employed in the compulsory system,
and that the barbarous strangers were to assist in the entire subjugation
of the colonies, if not otherwise reduced to unworthy submission.

On this information, the indignation of all ranks can scarcely be
described. The king's speech was condemned, and ordered to be
burnt in the centre of the camp at Cambridge. The wavering were
resolved, the timid grew bold, the placid and philosophic lovers of
peace left the retired haunts of literary felicity, and beneath the
helmet and the buckler, courted the post of danger:—vigorous action
was now the [284] only line of conduct to be observed through every
department. Previous to any other movement, it was judged important
that the British forces should be immediately removed from their
strong hold in the town of Boston, lest the work should be rendered
more difficult on the arrival of fresh troops from Great Britain, now
daily expected.

General Washington, sensible of this necessity, and that no more
time was to be lost, opened a severe cannonade on the western side,

* On the prohibitory, the restraining act, the interdiction of trade, and all other
coercive bills, the usual rate of voices in favor of them, was from an hundred and
twenty to an hundred and fifty—the number of the minority seldom more than
thirty or forty; when they amounted to forty, it was thought a considerable acquisition.

CHAP. VIII not far distant from the town, on the evening of the fourth of March.
1 7 7 6 This was designed rather to divert attention within the walls, than for any important consequences expected from this manoeuvre without. The Americans kept up a constant fire through the night, while several smaller works were erected for the annoyance of the besieged; but the principal effect was expected from the heights of Dorchester. By the greatest industry and dispatch, a strong battery, very unexpectedly to the enemy, appeared there on the morning of the fifth, from whence the Americans played their artillery with ease on the town. The assailants under the direction of general Thomas, erected and extended their works in such a judicious manner, as to command the peninsula leading to Boston, Castle-William, and at the same time a considerable part of the harbor.

[285] General Howe, mortified that such an advantageous post should have been so long neglected by himself, and astonished at the appearance of such strong and defensible works, rising as it were in a night, without noise or alarm in that quarter, did not long hesitate on the part necessary for him to act in this critical conjuncture. There remained no alternative between a bold and vigorous attempt to dislodge the Americans, or an immediate evacuation of the town. To fly on the first appearance of danger, was humiliating to the pride of the soldier, lessening his military honor, and sinking the dignity of the commander in chief.

A choice of difficulties lay before him. He was short of provisions; the soldiers had become discontented with the service, and fatigued with continual watching: an immediate retreat might appear to him less disgraceful, than the consequences of resistance under many apparent disadvantages. On the other hand, chagrined at the idea of drawing off seven or eight thousand of the best troops the king his master had in service, without striking a blow, and relinquishing the only American town they then had in possession, to the *undisciplined peasantry* of the country, was still a more humiliating thought. From these considerations he made all possible preparation to dislodge the American troops, the evening after they were discovered on the heights of Dorchester. But [286] the intervention of the elements disconcerted his operations: a tremendous storm of wind and rain prevented the dangerous enterprise, and saved the expense of much blood.

General Howe finding his design impracticable, in consequence of this disappointment, ordered an embarkation to begin as soon as the

tempest should subside. But embarrassed by a crowd of refugees and CHAP. VIII
other delinquents, who, conscious they could not rely on their country 1 7 7 6
for safety, had thrown themselves on his protection; encumbered with
women, children, furniture, soldiers, officers, and camp equipage;
the inconveniences and dangers of a voyage at the equinoctial season;
the sterility of the country* and the coldness of the clime to which
he must repair, with a discontented army and a *group* of miserable,
disappointed tories, rendered the situation of the British commander
in chief truly pitiable. To add to the confusion of the scene, the
strictest harmony did not exist between the officers of the army and
navy; this increased the difficulty of accommodation on this unexpected
emergency, when so many useless persons claimed protection and
subsistence.

When the Americans saw the British troops about to depart, they
did not offer to impede [287] their design in the smallest degree; the
cannonade was suspended, and they beheld with an eye of compassion,
the extraordinary emigration of some hundreds of disaffected Americans, whom they suffered to depart with the successless army, without
a wish to retard their flight. These unhappy people took with them
such of their effects as the hurry of the occasion and their military
masters would permit. General Washington with a few troops entered
Boston, with the ensigns of triumph displayed, and beheld the rear
of the panic-struck army of Britain, precipitately flying from a town
that had long been the object of ministerial vengeance.

This bloodless victory on the one side, and the disgraceful flight
on the other, was viewed with pleasure and surprise, or with astonishment and grief, in proportion to the political hopes and fears that
agitated the various parties, who all considered the transactions of the
day replete with important consequences. Every mark of respect was
externally shewn to general Washington, even by those who were not
well affected to the cause in which he was engaged. Many of this
class, more culpable than some who went off with the British army,
chose to stay and cast themselves on the mercy of their countrymen,
rather than to hazard the danger of a voyage, the loss of property,
and a separation from their families.

Some, much less criminal than these, and many really inoffensive
persons, suddenly struck [288] with imaginary fears, abandoned their
habitations and their country, which by a little address they might

* General Howe went from Boston to Halifax, Nova Scotia.

quietly have possessed. Several very doubtful characters not only acted with decent civility and condescension, but confidently assumed merit to themselves as friends of the revolution: some of these were afterwards promoted to places and offices of high trust. Indeed the loyalists in general who stayed in Boston, and chose to run all hazards rather than quit their native country, experienced much clemency from the opposite party; yet, perhaps not in the full latitude that policy might have dictated: but the impressions of danger and insult to which the victors had long been exposed, operated more powerfully in the minds of many, than the laws of forgiveness, or the distant view of political consequences.

Thus a kind of inquisitorial court was erected in Boston, and some persons more warm than discreet, and more zealous than judicious, were appointed to decide on the criminality of state delinquents, several of whom were adjudged to punishments rather ridiculous than severe. This step tended only to strengthen the alienation of those who had, either from interest, treachery, timidity, or a passion for the splendor of monarchy, enlisted under the banners of royalty, without any fixed principles in religion or politics. Had the new government at this period, passed an act of indemnity and oblivion, [289] and proclaimed pardon to all who had incurred the public resentment, excepting a few who had notoriously deserved proscription, it is probable many would have returned to the bosom of their country, and become faithful subjects to the United States, when they could have done it without the imputation of being rebels to their sovereign. This consideration before the declaration of independence, had a conscientious influence on the minds of some who disapproved of the ministerial encroachments, yet scrupled the right of resistance while the legal subjects of the British crown; but the line of separation soon after drawn, the doubts of many well-disposed persons were entirely dissipated.

After the evacuation of Boston, the succession of important events was too rapid for the mind to dwell long on single incidents. It remained for some time uncertain where the British army and navy would next direct their operations. Though they sailed immediately for Halifax, it was only to disembark their useless hands, and secure a rendezvous until fresh reinforcements should arrive from England.

The situation of the southern colonies at this time commanded the attention of every well-wisher to the American cause. Some time before the British troops left Boston, general Clinton had been sent

southward to the assistance of [290] governor Martin and lord William
Campbell. We have seen that before they left their governments,
they had instigated a number of the back settlers in the Carolinas to
create disturbances. These people formerly aggrieved by their own
government, had styled themselves *Regulators*, had embodied for
opposition, had resisted authority, and had suffered severely. They
were now persuaded, that the same persons who had some years
before oppressed them, were at this time in rebellion against their
sovereign. This opinion was strengthened by governor Martin, who
kept up a correspondence with their leaders, and invited them to
repair to the royal standard at Brunswick, where they should be
supported by a large body of the king's troops.

Though as observed, these people had been compelled to submission, and had remained quiet a number of years, yet their old
antipathies were not obliterated. Ignorant of the causes of the general
uneasiness of the colonies, and mistaken in character, they united
under the very men who had formerly exercised every severity against
them and their leaders.* These were joined by the Highlanders, who
had migrated [291] in shoals after the rebellion in Scotland, in one
thousand seven hundred and forty-five: they had suffered too much
not to dread a second opposition to the authority of the king of
England. These descriptions of men were for a time very troublesome
on the southern borders, more particularly of North Carolina; but by
the spirit and activity of some continental troops, under the command
of brigadier general More, the whole party was defeated. Their
commanding officer Macdonald, and most of their other officers
imprisoned, the unhappy remnant who escaped imprisonment or
death, retreated to the woods; and all hope or fear from this quarter,
was extinguished before the arrival of sir Henry Clinton at Cape Fear.

As soon as it was discovered at Cambridge, that general Clinton
had left Boston, general Lee was ordered to set forward to observe
his manoeuvres, and prepare to meet him with advantage in any part
of the continent he might think proper to visit. No man was better
qualified at this early stage of the war, to penetrate the designs, or to
face in the field an experienced British veteran, than general Lee.

* Particularly a colonel Fanning, a violent partisan of the crown, who had been in the
former insurrection, the executioner of most of their principal leaders, without even
the form of a trial. [Probably Edmund Fanning, a leader of the Regulator movement
in North Carolina in the 1760s and of "Fanning's Regiment," a band of New York
Tories, in 1776.]

CHAP. VIII He had been an officer of character and rank in the late war between
1 7 7 6 England and France.* Fearless of danger, and fond of glory, he was
[292] calculated for the field, without any of the graces that recommend
the soldier to the circles of the polite. He was plain in his person
even to ugliness, and careless in his manners to a degree of rudeness.
He possessed a bold genius and an unconquerable spirit: his voice
was rough, his garb ordinary, his deportment morose. A considerable
traveller, and well acquainted with most of the European nations, he
was frequently agreeable in narration, and judicious and entertaining
in observation. Disgusted with the ministerial system, and more so
with his sovereign who authorised it, he cherished the American cause
from motives of resentment, and a predilection in favor of freedom,
more than from a just sense of the rights of mankind.

Without religion or country, principle, or attachment, gold was his
deity, and liberty the idol of his fancy: he hoarded the former without
taste for its enjoyment, and worshipped the latter as the patroness of
licentiousness, rather than the protectress of virtue. He affected to
despite the opinion of the world, yet was fond of applause. Ambitious
of fame without the dignity to support it, he emulated the heroes of
antiquity in the field, while in private life he sunk into the vulgarity
of the clown. Congress did wisely to avail themselves of his military
experience in the infancy of a confederated army, and still more
widely in placing him in a degree [293] of subordination. He was on
the first list of continental officers, and only the generals Washington
and Ward were named before him; but though nominally the third in
rank, as a soldier he was second to no man. The abilities of general
Ward were better adapted to the more quiet disquisitions of the
cabinet, than on the hostile and dangerous scenes of the field or the
camp, both which he soon left and retired to private life, when nothing
remained to prevent this singular stranger from taking the command
of the armies of the United States, but the life of Washington.

General Lee with his detachment from Cambridge reached New
York, and put it in a state of defence, before sir Henry Clinton arrived
there, though he had sailed from Boston several days previous to its
being known at Cambridge. While at New York, Lee drew up a list
of suspected persons, and disarmed them. He carried his military
authority so high, that the congress of that state thought proper to

---

* He had served with reputation in Portugal, under the command of the count de la
Lippe.

check his career: they informed him, that the trial and punishment CHAP. VIII
of their citizens belonged to themselves, and not to any military 1 7 7 6
character. He apologized by observing, that

> when the enemy were at the door, *forms* must be dispensed with; that his
> duty to them, to the continent, and to his conscience, dictated the measure;
> that if he had done wrong, he would submit himself to the shame of being
> imputed rash; [294] but that he should still have the consolation in his
> own breast, that pure motives of serving the community, uncontaminated
> by individual resentment, had urged him to those steps.

The movements of general Lee were so rapid, that to the surprise
of sir Henry Clinton, he was in Virginia before him. But as the object
of the British armament was still farther south, Lee with uncommon
celerity, traversed the continent, met general Clinton in North
Carolina, and was again ready for the defence of Sullivan's Island,
near Charleston in South Carolina, before the arrival of the British
troops under the command of general Clinton.

Sir Peter Parker had appeared off Cape Fear in the month of May,
one thousand seven hundred and seventy-six, with a considerable
squadron of line-of-battle ships, and a number of transports containing
several regiments of land forces, and a heavy train of artillery. A body
of troops commanded by lord Cornwallis and general Vaughan were
soon after landed on Long Island: the design was to unite with general
Clinton, and reduce Charleston, the rich capital of South Carolina.
This state had thrown off their allegiance, assumed a government of
their own, and chosen John Rutledge, Esq. their chief magistrate,
under the style and title of *President*.

[295] Notwithstanding the parade of immediate attack, near a month
elapsed in total inaction, before the assault on Sullivan's Island was
begun by the British naval commander: in the mean time, the
Americans were strongly posted there. The engagement took place
on the twenty-ninth of June, and was conducted with great spirit and
bravery on both sides; the highest encomiums are justly due to the
valor and intrepidity of the British officers and seamen; and notwithstanding the courage and ability of general Gadsden, the vigor,
activity, and bravery of general Moultrie, and the experience and
military knowledge of general Lee, it is probable the action would
have terminated more to the honor of the British navy, had they been
properly supported by the land forces.

It remains yet to be investigated, why no attempt was made by the troops on Long Island, to cause a diversion on the other side, which would doubtless have altered the whole face of the action. But whether from a series of unexpected resistance, their imaginations had become habituated to view every thing through the medium of danger, or whether from a degree of caution that sometimes betrays the brave into the appearance of timidity, or from any jealousies subsisting between the commanders, is uncertain. However, this neglect occasioned loud complaints among the officers of the navy; nor was it easy for lord Cornwallis [296] and general Clinton, though high on the rolls of military fame, to wipe off the aspersions thrown on their conduct. Even their apologies for their own inactivity, instead of exculpating themselves, were rather a testimony of the skill, ability, and vigor of their antagonists; who, in so short a time, were prepared to bid defiance to the combined force of Britain, though commanded by sea and land, by officers of acknowledged merit in the line of their profession.

Many brave officers of the navy fought with valor and spirit, that would have been truly glorious in a more honorable cause. One instance of this, among many others of the unfortunate who fell on the occasion, was the valiant and spirited captain Morris of the Bristol: he lost an arm by a ball in the beginning of the engagement, and while retired to dress his wounds, two of his surgeons were killed by his side, before they had finished the operation. On this, the captain with his usual intrepidity, resumed his command; when he immediately received a shot through the body, and had time only to observe before he expired, that "he consigned his family to his God and his country." After an obstinate engagement of ten or twelve hours, the sailors disheartened, and their officers wounded,* the shattered fleet with difficulty [297] retired to the distance of three or four miles from the fort, and in a few days put themselves in a condition to withdraw to the general rendezvous before New York.

The triumph of the Americans in this success, who had always justly dreaded the naval power of Britain, was in equal proportion to the chagrin of their enemies, thus repulsed in a quarter where, from the locality of circumstances, they least expected it. The multitude of manumitted slaves, and the aristocratic spirit of many of the principal planters, had flattered them with the idea, that in the

---

* Lord William Campbell, governor of South Carolina, who had taken refuge on board one of the king's ships, was mortally wounded in the attack on fort Moultrie.

southern colonies they should meet but a feeble resistance. Lord
Dunmore, who had joined in the expedition, continued several weeks
after the repulse, to cruise about the borders of Virginia, and the
Carolinas, with his little fleet of fugitives and slaves. But, as the mid-
summer heats increased, a pestilential fever raged on board, which
carried off many of the refugees, and swept away most of the miserable
negroes he had decoyed from their masters. Forbidden admittance
wherever he attempted to land, and suffering for provisions, he burnt
several of his vessels; the remainder, except one in which he sheltered
himself and family, and two other ships of war for his protection, he
sent laden with the wretched victims of his folly and cruelty, to [298]
seek some kind of subsistence in the Floridas, Bermudas, and the
West Indies.

Lord Howe had been long expected with his motley mercenaries
from Hesse, Hanover, and Brunswick. His brother sir William, after
a disagreeable residence of two or three months at Halifax, did not
think proper to wait longer there the arrival of his lordship. Miserably
accommodated, and painfully agitated by the recollection of his
disgraceful flight from Boston, anxious for intelligence from Europe,
and distressed by the delay of recruits and supplies, without which
little could be done to retrieve his suffering fame, he quitted that
station, accompanied by admiral Shuldham, and arrived at Sandy
Hook the twenty-ninth of June. On his passage to New York, he
accidentally fell in with a few scattering transports from England,
which he took under his protection, while many less fortunate were
captured by the American cruisers.

General Howe was, soon after his arrival at New York, joined by
the repulsed troops from the southward, and the broken squadron
under the command of sir Peter Parker; by a regiment from St.
Augustine, another from Pensacola, also by a few troops from St.
Vincents, some small additions from other posts, and a considerable
party of loyalists from New Jersey, and from the environs of Philadelphia and New [299] York, which by great industry had been
collected and embodied by governor Tryon. Notwithstanding this
acquisition of strength, he found the continental army so strongly
posted on Long Island and New York, that he did not immediately
attempt any thing of consequence.

Immediately after the evacuation of Boston, general Washington
had sent on the army in detachments, and when he had made some
necessary arrangements for the future defence of the eastern states,

CHAP. VIII   he hastened on himself to New York, where he had made all possible
1 7 7 6   preparation for the reception of general Howe. It has just been
observed, that the British commander had collected all his strength,
and called in the forces from every quarter of America except Canada,
where, under the direction of the generals Carleton and Burgoyne,
measures were ripening for a junction at Albany, with the expected
conquerors of the more southern colonies. But in the present circumstance of affairs, general Howe thought proper to land his troops at
Staten Island, and wait more favorable appearances, which he had
reason to expect on the arrival of his brother, an event hourly and
anxiously looked for.

His lordship was considered by many in America, as the harbinger
of peace, though advancing in all the pride and pomp of war,
accompanied by the ready executioners of every [300] hostile design.
It was reported, that the commander of a formidable equipment both
for sea and land service, came out in a double capacity; that though
prepared for offensive operations, lord Howe had yet a commission
from his royal master to accommodate the disputes, and to restore
tranquillity to the colonies, on generous and equitable terms. The
augurs of each party predicted the consequences of this ministerial
manoeuvre, and interpreted the designs of his lordship's commission,
according to their own hopes, fears, or expectations.

In the infancy of her emancipation, America was not such an adept
in the science of political intrigue, but that many yet flattered
themselves, that an accommodation might take place, and that halcyon
days might be restored by the interposition of the two brothers, lord
and general Howe, joined in the commission of peace under the
sanction of royal indulgence; but more judicious men saw through,
and despised the bubble of policy, which held a pardon in one hand
and a poniard in the other, with the detestable offer of assassination
or slavery. They considered the mode of pacification proposed, as at
once an insult to the feelings, and an affront to the understandings
of a people, too serious for trifling when all was at stake, and too wise
to be cajoled by superficial appearances. Yet, those best acquainted
with the situation and character, the genius and connexions of the
[301] inhabitants of the middle colonies, were not surprised to find
many among them, who seemed ready to embrace such humiliating
conditions, as the safety, the interest, the honor, and justice of
America, were bound to reject.

It was well known, that from the beginning of the grand contest,

the lamp of liberty had not burnt so bright in New York, New Jersey,
and Pennsylvania, as in some other parts of America. Though there
was a party in New York strongly attached to the cause of the colonies,
there had been early reason to suppose, that some men of high
consideration in that state were not entirely proof against the influence
of ministerial gold. New Jersey was the retreat of the timid, the
disaffected, and the lovers of inglorious ease, from each corner of
America. They there thought they might rest secure from the ravages
of war, as the torch which was lighted at both ends, might be
extinguished before it penetrated to the centre.

The quakers and the proprietary interest, long hung as a dead
weight on the spirited measures of the genuine friends of freedom
and of their country, both in Pennsylvania and Maryland; but the
incidents of a few months connected every interest, and brought
almost every dissentient voice into union, and hastened on an event
that every one considered as decisive of the fate of America. The
necessity of a declaration of [302] independence was acknowledged
by all: even Maryland, the last state in the union that came into the
measure, and whose delegates seceded on the question of independence, was among the first who erected their own government, and
established their own modes of legislation, independent of proprietors
or kings.

"The dread of slavery in free nations, has at all times produced
more virtues than the principles of their political institutions."* This
dread hung heavily on the most sober and judicious, the most wise
and virtuous part of the inhabitants of America. They were sensible
that both public and private virtue sink with the loss of liberty, and
that the nobler emulations which are drawn out and adorn the soul
of man, when not fettered by servility, frequently hide themselves
in the shade, or shrink into littleness at the frown of a despot. They
felt too much for themselves, and feared too much for posterity,
longer to balance between either complete or partial submission, or
an unreserved and entire claim to absolute independence.

* Travels of Anacharsis. [Jean Jacques Barthélemy, trans., *Travels of Anacharsis the
Younger in Greece. During the Middle of the Fourth Century, Before the Christian Aera*
(4 vols.; 1st. ed. Paris, 1785; 1st Am. ed., Philadelphia, 1804). Anacharsis is
known to modern scholars as a Scythian of the sixth century B.C. who traveled
widely and was considered one of the seven wise men. After studying the laws
of Athens at Solon's side, he attempted to introduce Athenian-style government
in Scythia, for which he was put to death by his brother, his country's ruler.]

These ideas precipitated the important *era* when a connexion was
dissolved, the continuance of which both nature and affection seemed
to require. Great Britain the revered parent, and America the dutiful
child, had long been [303] bound together by interest, by a sameness
of habits, manners, religion, laws, and government. The recollection
of their original consanguinity had always been cherished with an
amiable sensibility, or a kind of mechanic enthusiasm, that promoted
mutual felicity when they met on each other's shores, or in distant
lands saluted each other in the same language.

A dereliction of old habits of friendship and attachment was far
from the wish of many, who had yet strongly opposed the ministerial
system: but the period was now arrived, when America felt her wrongs,
without hope of redress, and supported her own rights by assuming
her rank as a distinct nation on the political theatre. We shall see her
relinquish at once all hopes of protection, or fears of control, from
the sovereignty of Britain. The reverential awe with which she had
formerly viewed her potent parent, was laid aside, and every effort
made to forget her fond attachment for a people, that from her earliest
infancy she had looked up to as fathers, brothers, and friends.

The severities of the British government towards the American
colonies, had not yet taught them to express themselves in any other
modes of language, but what indicated their firm attachment to the
mother country; nor had they erased the habitual ideas, even of
tenderness, conveyed in their usual modes of expression. [304] When
they formed a design to visit England, it had always been thus
announced, "I am going home." Home, the seat of happiness, the
retreat to all the felicities of the human mind, is too intimately
associated with the best feelings of the heart, to renounce without
pain, whether applied to the natural or the political parent.

CHAPTER IX

Declaration of Independence • Lord Howe's Arrival in America • Action on Long Island • Retreat of the Americans through the Jersies, and the Loss of the Forts Washington and Lee • Affairs in Canada • Surprise of the Hessians at Trenton • Various Transactions in the Jersies • General Howe's Retreat—Makes Head-Quarters at Brunswick—His Indecision— Some Traits of his Character

[305] The commissioners who had been announced as the messengers of peace, were now hourly expected; but the dubious aspect of their mission, and the equivocal character in which they were about to appear, was far from lulling to inattention the guardians of the cause of America. Their errand was ostensibly, to restore peace to the colonies; but many circumstances combined to evince, that the design was in reality, to furnish new pretexts for the prosecution of the war, with redoubled vigor. Thus was the continental congress fully convinced of the impropriety of longer holding themselves in suspense, by delusory hopes, or the uncertain termination of their expectations or their fears. They were sensible the step they were about to take, would either set their country on the pinnacle of human glory, or plunge it in the abject state into which turbulent and conquered colonies have [306] been generally reduced. Yet they wisely judged, that this was a proper period to break the shackles, and renounce all political union with the parent state, by a free and bold declaration of the independence of the American States. This measure had been contemplated by some gentlemen in the several colonies, some months before it took place. They had communicated their sentiments to the individual members of congress, but that body had been apprehensive, that the people at large were not prepared to unite in a step so replete with important consequences. But the moment of decision had now arrived, when both the congress and the inhabitants of the colonies advanced too far to recede.

CHAP. IX   Richard Henry Lee, Esq., a delegate from the state of Virginia, a
1 7 7 6 gentleman of distinguished abilities, uniform patriotism, and unshaken
firmness and integrity, was the first who dared explicitly to propose,
that this decided measure, on which hung such mighty consequences,
should no longer be delayed. This public and unequivocal proposal,
from a man of his virtue and shining qualities, appeared to spread a
kind of sudden dismay. A silent astonishment for a few minutes
seemed to pervade the whole assembly: this was soon succeeded by
a long debate, and a considerable division of sentiment on the important
question.

[307] After the short silence just observed, the measure proposed
by Mr. Lee was advocated with peculiar zeal by John Adams, Esq.,
of the Massachusetts Bay. He rose with a face of intrepidity and the
voice of energy, and invoked the *god* of *eloquence*, to enable him to do
justice to the cause of his country, and to enforce this important step
in such a manner, as might silence all opposition, and convince every
one of the necessity of an immediate declaration of the independence
of the United States of America.

Mr. John Dickinson, of Pennsylvania, took the lead in opposition
to the boldness and danger of this decided measure. He had drawn
the petition to the king forwarded by Mr. Penn, and though no man
was more strenuous in support of the rights of the colonies, he had
always been averse to a separation from Britain, and shuddered at the
idea of an avowed revolt of the American colonies. He arose on this
occasion with no less solemnity than Mr. Adams had recently done,
and with equal pathos of expression, and more brilliance of epithet,
he invoked the *Great Governor* of the *Universe*, to animate him with
powers of language sufficient to exhibit a view of the dread consequences to both countries, that such a hasty dismemberment of the
empire might produce. He descanted largely on the happy effects
that might probably ensue from more patient and conciliatory dispositions, [308] and urged at least a temporary suspension of a step, that
could never be revoked. He declared that it was his opinion, that
even policy forbade the precipitation of this measure, and that
humanity more strongly dictated, that they ought to wait longer the
success of petitions and negociations, before they formally renounced
their allegiance to the king of Great Britain, broke off all connexion
with England, plunged alone into an unequal war, and rushed without
allies into the unforeseen and inevitable dangers that attended it.

The consequences of such a solemn act of separation were indeed of serious and extensive magnitude. The energy of brilliant talents, and great strength of argument, were displayed by both parties on this weighty occasion. The reasons urging the necessity of decision, and the indubitable danger of delay, were clear and cogent; the objections, plausible, humane, and important: but after a fair discussion of the question, an accurate statement of the reasons for adopting the measure, and a candid scrutiny of the objections against it, grounded either on policy or humanity, a large majority of the members of congress appeared in favor of an immediate renunciation of allegiance to the crown, or any future subjugation to the king of Great Britain.

[309] A declaration* of the independence of America, and the sovereignty of the United States, was drawn by the ingenious and philosophic pen of Thomas Jefferson, Esq., a delegate from the state of Virginia.† The delegates from twelve‡ of the American States, agreed almost unanimously to this declaration; the language, the principles, and the spirit of which, were equally honorable to themselves and their country. It was signed by John Hancock, then president of congress, on the fourth of July, one thousand seven hundred and seventy-six.

The allegiance of thirteen states at once withdrawn by a solemn declaration, from a government towards which they had looked with the highest veneration; whose authority they had acknowledged, whose laws they had obeyed, whose protection they had claimed for more than a century and a half—was a consideration of solemnity, a bold resolution, an experiment [310] of hazard: especially when the infancy of the colonies as a nation, without wealth, resources, or allies, was contrasted with the strength, riches, and power of Great Britain. The timid trembled at the ideas of final separation; the disciples of passive obedience were shocked by a reflection of a breach of faith to their ancient sovereign; and the enemies to the general freedom of mankind, were incensed to madness, or involved in despair. But these classes bore a small proportion to those who resented the rejection of their petitions, and coolly surveyed the impending dangers,

---

* See Appendix, Note No. XVII.

† This wise and patriotic statesman was afterwards appointed ambassador to the court of France. On the adoption of the present constitution of government, he was appointed secretary for foreign affairs, was chosen vice-president, and afterwards president of the United States of America.

‡ The members from Maryland seceded, but in a short time after joined the confederation.

that threatened themselves and their children, which rendered it clear to their apprehension, that this step was necessary to their political salvation. They considered themselves no longer bound by any moral tie, to render fealty to a sovereign thus disposed to encroach on their civil freedom, which they could now secure only by a social compact among themselves, and which they determined to maintain, or perish in the attempt.

By the declaration of independence, dreaded by the foes, and for a time doubtfully viewed by many of the friends of America, every thing stood on a new and more respectable footing, both with regard to the operations of war, or negociations with foreign powers. Americans could now no more be considered as *rebels*, in their proposals for treaties of peace and conciliation with Britain; they were a distinct people, [311] who claimed the rights, the usages, the faith, and the respect of nations, uncontrolled by any foreign power. The colonies thus irretrievably lost to Great Britain, a new face appeared on all affairs, both at home and abroad.

America had been little known among the kingdoms of Europe; she was considered only as an appendage to the power of Britain: the principles of her sons were in some respects dissimilar, and their manners not yet wrought up to the standard of refinement reigning in ancient courts: her statesmen in general were unacquainted with the intrigues necessary for negociation, and the *finesse* usually hackneyed in and about the cabinets of princes. She now appeared in their eyes, a new theatre, pregnant with events that might be interesting to the civil and political institutions of nations, that had never before paid much attention to the growth, population, and importance of an immense territory beyond the Atlantic.

The United States had their ambassadors to create, or to transplant from the bar or the compting-house. Their generals were many of them the yeomanry or the tradesmen of the country; their subordinate officers had been of equal rank and fortune, and the army to be governed was composed of many of the old associates of the principal officers, and were equally tenacious of personal liberty. The *regalia* of [312] power, orders of nobility, and the splendor of courts, had been by them viewed only at a distance. The discipline of armies was entirely new; the difficulty of connecting many distinct states to act as it were by one will, the expenses of government in new exigencies, and the waste of war had not yet been accurately calculated by their politicians and statesmen. But their senators, their represen-

tatives, and their magistrates, were generally sagacious and vigilant, CHAP. IX
upright and firm; their officers were brave, their troops in spirits, and 1 7 7 6
with a full confidence in their commander in chief: hope was exhilarated
by the retreat from Boston, and the repeated successes of their arms
at the southward; while new dignity was added to office, and stronger
motives for illustrious action, by the rank America had now taken
among the nations. Thus, by the declaration of independence they
had new ground to tread; the scene of action was changed, genius
was called forth from every quarter of the continent, and the public
expectation enhanced by the general favorable appearance in all their
military operations.

In this situation stood affairs, both in the cabinet and the field,
when lord Howe arrived at Staten Island, with a formidable squadron
under his command, on the twelfth of July, one thousand seven
hundred and seventy-six. At the head of this hostile arrangement, his
[313] lordship came in full confidence of success: yet amidst the
splendor and parade of war, while he held out his potent arm, he still
cherished the delusory hope of peace.

By a pompous declaration, he early announced his pacific powers
to the principal magistrates of the several colonies, and promised
pardon to all who, in the late times, had deviated from their allegiance,
on condition, that they would speedily return to their duty, and gave
encouragement that they should, on compliance, hereafter reap the
benefit of royal favor. Lord Howe observed in his declaration,

> that the commissioners were authorized in his majesty's name, to declare
> any province, colony, county, district, or town, to be at the peace of his
> majesty: and that due consideration should be had to the meritorious
> services of any, who should aid or assist in restoring the public tranquillity;
> that their dutiful representations should be received, pardons granted, and
> suitable encouragement to such as would promote the measures of legal
> government and peace, in pursuance of his majesty's most gracious
> purposes.*

[314] Congress ordered the declaration to be immediately published
in all the American gazettes, that the people of the United States
might be fully informed of the terms of peace; that they might see

---

* This declaration, and the consequent resolves of congress, may be seen at large in
the public journals of the session of one thousand seven hundred and seventy-six.
[See Howe's Proclamation, November 30, 1776, in Force, *Archives*, 5th. ser., 3:
927–928; also see JCC, 5: 567, 574–575, 592–593, 597.]

CHAP. IX for themselves, that the business of the commissioners was to amuse,
1 7 7 6   disunite, and deceive them; and that those who still continued in
suspense, from hopes founded either on the justice or moderation of
the court of Great Britain, might now be fully convinced, that their
own valor, virtue, and firmness, must rescue and preserve the freedom
of their country.*

The next advance his lordship made for the execution of his
commission, was by a flag sent on shore within a few days after his
arrival, with a letter directed to George Washington, Esq. By their
principles and their professions, the Americans were taught at this
period, to look down on titles and distinguished ranks; yet, in this
instance, they did not think proper to pass over the implicit denial of
either, to their commander in chief. It was viewed as a designed
affront, from those who consider such [315] adventitious circumstances
of so much consequence, as carefully to avoid all honorary epithets
in their addresses to the first officers of the United States. It was
thought more becoming the dignity of his station, both as a soldier
and a patriot, for the chief commander to refuse an address that tacitly
denied the legality of his commission and the right now claimed of
negociating on terms of equality: this letter was therefore, by the
advice of the principal officers, returned unopened.

This drew out a second advance from the hands of the British
commissioners, when major Patterson, adjutant general of the army,
was charged with a letter directed to George Washington, &c. &c.
&c. He was received in military state, and treated with great politeness
in the American camp. His lordship in this second address, expressed
the highest respect for the private character of general Washington,
but as he did not yet condescend to acknowledge the commander in
chief of the American troops, as any thing more than a *rebel* in arms,
this letter was also returned without breaking the seal.

Many civilities passed in this interview with Mr. Patterson, who
did not forget to insinuate his own wishes for the restoration of
friendship and harmony between the two countries. He, with due
propriety, made several observations [316] on the extensive powers
vested in the commissioners for this salutary purpose: this introduced

* The American congress were not remiss at this time, in exerting their efforts to
  detach foreigners from the service of Britain, and alluring them to become inhabitants
  of the United States, by promising them a quiet residence, an allotment of lands,
  and a security from all interruptions in the enjoyment of their religious opinions,
  and the investiture of all the privileges of native citizens.

some general conversation relative to the treatment of prisoners on
both sides. The conference was of some length, but as no circumstance
indicated a happy result from the negociation, general Washington in
the most explicit terms, informed the British adjutant general, that
the inhabitants of the American States were generally of opinion, that
a people armed in defence of their rights, were in the way of their
duty; that conscious of no criminality, they needed no pardon; and
as his lordship's commission extended no farther, nothing important
could be expected from protracting the negociation.

In the mean time, reinforcements were daily dropping in to the
assistance of the British army. The scattered divisions of Hessians,
Waldeckers, &c. designed for the summer campaign, had been
somewhat retarded by not knowing with certainty, the spot destined
for head-quarters. They had some of them sailed directly for Halifax:
this occasioned a delay of any energetic movement, until the latter
part of the month of August, when the British army began to act with
vigor.

General Washington had rather incautiously encamped the bulk of
his army on Long Island, a large and plentiful district, about two
miles from [317] the city of New York. This island contained many
settlements, through an extent of one hundred and twenty miles in
length. It was inhabited principally by loyalists, and persons generally
disaffected to the American cause. Many were at a loss for a reason,
nor indeed could any conjecture, why the commander of the American
army should hazard his troops on an island, liable at any moment to
be surrounded by the British navy. However it was, several thousand
Americans were there posted, under the command of the generals
Putnam, Sullivan, and William Alexander, lord Stirling.

Sir William Howe very wisely judged, that it was a less arduous
and a more promising undertaking to dislodge the Americans from
their encampment on the island, than a direct attempt to reduce New
York. The royal army at that time consisted of about thirty thousand
men: these he found no difficulty in landing from Staten Island, and
in detachments posted them from one end of Long Island to the
other, separated from the Americans by a ridge of hills covered with
woods. Very fortunately for the enterprise of the British, one of the
American out-guards early fell into the hands of general Clinton. In
consequence of some intelligence gained by this accident, he, before
day-light on the morning of the twenty-seventh of August, possessed
himself of some very advantageous heights, and made such a judicious

CHAP. IX arrangement [318] of his troops, as might have insured success, even
1 7 7 6 had the Americans been better prepared for the attack, which at that
time was rather unexpected.

The assault was begun by the Hessian general de Heister. He
opened the cannonade in front of the American lines, early on the
morning of the twenty-eighth. A general engagement speedily ensued.
Nearly the whole of the British forces were called in to action, under
the command of sir Henry Clinton, earl Percy, and lord Cornwallis.
By some fatal neglect, a very important post was left unguarded by
the American, which was seized by the British troops, who fought on
this occasion with a spirit and bravery becoming the experienced
commander and the hardy veteran. The American troops were early
deranged. Apprized of their danger, they with great resolution endeavoured to recover their camp; but nearly surrounded by the British,
and pushed in the centre by the Hessians, they were so far from
effecting their design, that their retreat was nearly cut off: yet many
of them desperately fought their way through some of the British
lines, and again bravely stood on their defence; others entangled in
the woods and marshes through which they endeavoured to escape,
were either captured, or perished in the attempt.

[319] In the midst of the general anxiety for the danger and distress
of the little army on Long Island, general Washington, undoubtedly
anxious to retrieve his mistake in thus exposing them, passed over
from New York to endeavour to secure the retreat of the surviving
troops. This was executed in the night of the twenty-ninth, without
noise or tumult. The remainder of the broken regiments that had
outlived the fatal action, abandoned the island with a considerable
part of their baggage, some artillery, and military stores, and without
molestation reached the city of New York. They had made a bold
and resolute stand, against far superior numbers and discipline; and
it may be deemed fortunate that any of them escaped, as on an island
they might easily have been hemmed in by a small number of British
ships. Perhaps the commanders on both sides were afterwards sensible
of their error, the one in hazarding his troops in such an exposed
situation, the other in suffering a single American to escape either
captivity or death.

The loss of men in this action was not inconsiderable on either
side, but it fell most heavily on the Americans. Many brave men
perished by the sword, others, as was observed, were lost in the
morasses and swamps to which they had fled on the defeat. Three

general officers, and a large number of inferior rank, were made CHAP. IX
prisoners. A regiment of valiant young men [320] from Maryland, 1 7 7 6
many of them of family and fortune, commanded by the gallant
colonel Smallwood, were almost to a man cut off. The misfortune of
the day was severely felt by them, but without checking the ardor of
the American army, the people, or the continental congress. The
same uniform dignity, and unruffled superiority of mind, appeared in
the judicious determinations of the united delegates, in the conduct
of the state departments, and in the subsequent firmness of most of
the military officers, as before this defeat. But the success of their
arms, and the acquisition of Long Island, exhilarated the spirits of
the British, and gave hopes of more compliant dispositions, and a
more ready acquiescence in the requisitions of ministers, or the *veto*
of kings: and that the business of the commissioners might now be
brought forward without farther impediment.

Not many days after the retreat from Long Island, congress was
called upon to exhibit a new proof of their firmness. General Sullivan,
one of the captured officers, was dispatched on parole with a message
to that assembly, in the joint names of lord and general Howe. The
purpose of the message was, that they had full powers, and that they
were disposed to treat on terms of accommodation and peace. At the
same time they intimated, that as congress was not considered in the
eye of majesty, as a legal assembly, they only desired a private
conference [321] with a few individuals belonging to that body, in
the character and capacity of private gentlemen. To this extraordinary
request, which threw them into a very delicate situation, congress
replied, that as delegates of a free and independent people, they
could with no propriety send any of the members of congress in a
private capacity, on an errand so replete with public consequences;
but they would depute a committee from their body, to inquire by
what authority and on what terms, his lordship and brother were
empowered to negociate.

The insidious message received had no tendency to eradicate the
previous opinion of congress, that this was but a ministerial pretext
to palliate their injurious designs. They were convinced, that the
commission of the agents was derogatory to the great national councils,
and to that high authority which had vested the British commissioners
with no powers, but to pardon those who deemed themselves guiltless,
and with no conciliatory proposals at which freemen would not spurn,
unless driven to despair. Yet they condescended so far to this political

CHAP. IX trifling, as to depute every respectable committee to meet lord Howe,
1 7 7 6 and confer on the subject. The celebrated doctor Franklin, the
honorable Mr. Rutledge of South Carolina, and John Adams, Esq. of
the Massachusetts, [322] were the persons chosen for this singular
interview.

On a stipulated day they met his lordship on Staten Island,
accompanied only by Mr. Strachey his secretary. He received them
with much civility, but conversed equivocally; and though careful not
to be explicit, it did not require the penetration of men of far less
superior abilities, to discover that he was restricted to very narrow
limits, for a negociator between contending nations. It was evident
that he had no plan of accommodation, or any proposals for amity, on
any terms but those of absolute and unconditional submission. Yet
these gentlemen patiently attended to the circumvolutions of his
lordship, who observed neither precision or perspicuity in his modes
of conversing; nor could he disguise an apparent embarrassment,
under the display of affability and good humor. It was even painful
to see a British nobleman, endowed with talents for the most honorable
employments, thus reduced to act under a veil of intrigue, inconsistent
with the character of the gentleman or the man of business.*

This conference continued three or four hours, when a short and
frugal repast concluded [323] a negociation that had fed many well-
meaning people with delusory hopes, and for several months had
been the subject of political speculation both in Europe and America.
This singular interview had indeed little other effect, than, on the
one side, to rivet that strong disgust which before existed, against the
treacherous councils of the British ministry and parliament, and on
the other, to convince more perfectly the agents of monarchy, of the
determined spirit of America, and the ability of the men with whom
she had entrusted the security of her rights. However, when the
parties took leave of each other, it was not without some tender
emotions. Dr. Franklin had been in long habits of friendship and
intimacy with lord Howe. They had in England frequently conversed,
and afterwards corresponded, on the parliamentary dispute with
America. Their regard for each other was mutual, and as there was
now every reason to suppose, this would be the last personal interview
between them, the idea was painful, that this political storm might
sweep away all remains of private friendship.†

* The above detail of the interview on Staten Island, was soon after verbally related
to the author of these annals, by one of the committee of conference.
† In the familiar conversation between lord Howe and doctor Franklin, his lordship

[324] It was not long after all ideas of negociation were relinquished, CHAP. IX before the commissioners and their sovereign had the most positive 1 7 7 6 proofs, that though the villages might be distained with the crimson tide that threatened to deluge the land, yet freedom in her last asylum, would resist the designs of all who had sighed for her annihilation, to the last moment of her existence.

The late defeat of the Americans, and the entire possession of Long Island, threw accumulated advantages into the hand of the British commander, who made immediate preparation to attack, and take possession of the city of New York. In consequence of these movements, general Washington, advised by the most judicious of his officers,* thought it prudent to evacuate the city without further delay. It would indeed have been madness to have attempted a longer defence with his diminished numbers, against a potent army flushed with recent success. The American army was drawn off from above Kingsbridge, on the twenty-first of October, but a day before the British took possession of the city. General Washington encamped his retreating troops on the heights of Haerlem, about nine miles distance from Kingsbridge. [325] When general Howe took possession of the evacuated post, he must from this event undoubtedly have felt some consolation for the mortification he had suffered on recollecting the circumstances of his flight from Boston. The alternate triumph or chagrin, from the uncertain chances and events of war, are generally of short duration: the Americans, now in their turn experienced the pains of anxiety, disappointment, and want, through a rapid flight from post to post, before a victorious army, who despised their weakness, and ridiculed their want of discipline.

General Howe placed a strong detachment in the garrison for the defence of the city of New York, and immediately marched with the main body of his army in pursuit of Washington. He crossed East River, seized a point of land near West Chester, and made himself master of the lower road to Connecticut, with design to impede the intercourse between the northern and southern states. By this movement, he also hoped to impel the American commander, at every

---

expressed a regard for the Americans, and the pain he felt for their approaching sufferings. Doctor Franklin, in his easy, sententious manner, thanked him for his regards, and assured him, that "the Americans would shew their gratitude, by endeavouring to lessen as much as possible, all pain he might feel on their account, by exerting their utmost abilities in taking good care of themselves."

* General Lee particularly, who had just arrived from Georgia. He, by urging this advice, may be said to share in the merit of saving the American army.

CHAP. IX hazard, to risk an engagement that might probably have been decisive.
1 7 7 6 But general Washington was too well acquainted with human nature,
to suffer his troops, though ardent for action, and impatient of delay,
to trust to the impulse of constitutional courage, and expose the
reputation of the American arms, and the decision of the great contest,
[326] to the uncertain events of a day, under the present disadvantages
of number and discipline. A second defeat in so short a time, would
undoubtedly have spread dismay, and perhaps a defection that might
have been fatal to the independence of America.* He was sensible
his troops, though naturally brave, were not sufficiently inured to
danger, and hardened by experience, to raise the mind to that sublime
pitch of enthusiasm and inflexibility, necessary to stand their ground
against superior strength, discipline, and numbers. He therefore
determined, by cautious and guarded marches, to keep in flank with
the British army, until circumstances might put it in his power to
combat on more equal terms.

He placed a strong party in fort Washington, a fortress near
Kingsbridge, which, though well provided, was at the time judged
not tenable by some of his best officers. This opinion was over-ruled,
and between three and four thousand men were left there. This was
considered by many a second fatal mistake of the renowned [327]
Washington.† With the remainder of the army the commander in
chief decamped, and moved towards the high grounds on the upper
road to Boston. The possession of this part of the country was an
important object; of consequence, the Americans were closely pursued
by general Howe, who did not yet relinquish his hopes of a decisive
action.

Frequent skirmishes had taken place on the *route*, without material
advantages on either side; but on the twenty-eighth of October, the
British overtook the American army near the White Plains, thirty
miles distant from New York city, when an action of moment ensued.
The attack was begun by the Hessians, the forlorn hope of the British
army. They were commanded by general de Heister and colonel
Rhal. Equal resolution animated both parties, and a considerable

---

* This opinion was corroborated by the behaviour of the Americans, when the British
landed from Kepp's Bay, Sept. 15. They discovered a timidity that nothing can
excuse, but their recent sufferings on Long Island, their inferior numbers, and their
dread of the superior discipline of British troops.
† General Washington, however, was undoubtedly advised to this step, by several of
his best officers.

slaughter among the troops on both sides took place.* The Americans CHAP. IX
unable to bear these losses, fully apprised of the strength of their 1 7 7 6
enemy, and that reinforcements had recently arrived under lord Percy,
both the American commander and the army, [328] were equally
willing to take a more distant position.

The British army had gained several very important advantages,
among which was the command of the river Brunx, which was passed
by colonel Rhal, who by this means acquired a very important post,
which enabled him essentially to annoy the American army.

The action on the White Plains was a well-fought battle on both
sides; but the Americans had neither the numbers, the experience,
nor the equipments for war, at that time, which rendered them equally
able to cope with the strength, the numbers, the preparation, and the
valor of the British army, under officers whose trade had long been
that of war. And though the American commander made his escape
with his small armament, and retreated with all the prudence and
firmness of a general who had been longer tried in the field of action,
the British had certainly a right in this affair, to boast a complete
victory.†

After the engagement, general Washington found it necessary to
quit the field. He drew [329] back in the night to his entrenchments,
and the next day took possession of some higher grounds, about the
distance of two miles.

General Howe, after parading a few days near the late scene of
action, and indiscriminately plundering the neighbourhood, ordered
his tents to be struck, and a movement of his whole army to be made
towards New York. As his troops had long been kept in continual
motion, were fatigued and harassed by sudden alarms, and the season
far advanced, it was rationally concluded, that his design was to repair
immediately to winter-quarters. But by a stroke of generalship, little
expected where no remarkable superiority in military knowledge had
yet been discovered, affairs took a most unfavorable turn for the
Americans, and reduced the little, resolute continental army to dangers
and distresses, to exertions and vigor, scarcely to be paralleled in
history.

---

* Among the slain was the valiant colonel Smallwood, whose regiment was nearly cut
  to pieces in the action on Long Island.
† The town of White-Plains was set on fire after the action, and all the houses and
  forage near the lines burnt. This the British writers charge to the account of the
  American commander.

CHAP. IX   The numbers that had already fallen on both sides, by the rapid
1 7 7 6 movements and frequent skirmishes for the space of three or four
months, cannot be ascertained with exactitude. It was computed that
not less than five thousand, principally Hessians, either perished or
deserted from the ministerial army, after the action of Long Island to
the middle of November, when general Howe laid the estimate before
lord [330] George Germaine.* The Americans undoubtedly suffered
in more than equal proportion, and from many causes were much less
able to bear the reduction. The peculiar mode of raising troops hitherto
adopted by the United States, had a tendency to retard the operations
of war, and in some measure to defeat the best concerted plans, either
for enterprise or defence. The several colonies had furnished their
quota of men for a limited term only; and the country unused to
standing armies, and the control of military power, impatient at the
subordination necessary in a camp, and actuated by a strong sense of
the liberty of the individual, each one had usually returned to his
habitation at the expiration of his term of service, in spite of every
danger that threatened the whole. This had occasioned frequent calls
on the militia of the country, in aid of the army thus weakened, and
kept in continual fluctuation by raw recruits, raised and sent on for a
few months at a time.

In addition to these embarrassments, animosities had sometimes
arisen between the southern and eastern troops, occasioned by the
revival of some old *local* prejudices. The aristocratic spirit [331] that
had been formerly characteristic of the south, frequently appeared in
airs of assumed superiority, very disgusting to the feelings of their
eastern brethren, the bold and hardy New Englanders; the *full-blooded*
Yankees, as they sometimes boasted themselves; who, having few
slaves at their command, had always been used to more equality of
condition, both in rank, fortune, and education. These trivial causes
sometimes raised animosities to such a height, that in the present
circumstances of the army, the authority of the commander in chief
was scarcely sufficient to restrain them.

General Washington was also obliged often in his retreat through
the Jersies, to press for provisions, forage, and clothing, in a manner

---

* In general Howe's letter to the secretary for American affairs, he acknowledged he
had lost upwards of three hundred staff and other officers, and between four and
five thousand privates. [See two letters of Howe to Lord George Germain, November
30, 1776, in Force, *Archives*, 5th. ser., 3: 921–927. Also see Howe, *Narrative*.
Warren's troop estimates are more optimistic than Howe's.]

new to the inhabitants of America; who, as their misfortunes seemed CHAP. IX
to thicken, grew more remiss for a time, in voluntary aids to the army. 1 7 7 6
Their grain was seized and threshed out for the use of the troops,
their blankets, provisions, &c. forcibly taken from their houses, with
a promise of payment in paper bills, when the exigencies of the
country should permit: but it always appeared to the people the act
of some subordinate officers, rather than the order of the commander
in chief. Thus was his popularity kept up; and thus were the inhabitants
of the Jersies plundered by each party; while many of them disaffected
to both, were uncertain on which side to declare.

[332] General Howe, well acquainted with these embarrassing
circumstances, and apprized that Congress were taking measures to
remedy the evils in future, wisely judged, that as he could not force
Washington to a general engagement, it would be more advantageous
for the present, to suspend his pursuit, and dislodge the Americans
from their strong holds in the environs of New York. He was too
sensible from the causes above related, that the continental army
would diminish of itself, as soon as the term of their enlistment
expired. From these considerations, he drew back his army, with the
determination to invest fort Washington immediately.* This fortress
on the one side of the North River, and fort Lee on the opposite
shore, commanded the whole navigation of the river, at the same
time that it impeded the communication with New York by land.

General Washington could not rationally suppose, that a post of so
much importance would remain long unmolested, or that the garrison
could be defended against the whole force of the British army. General
Lee afterwards boasted in a letter to a friend, that he had advised the
evacuation of both fort Washington and fort Lee, previous to the main
body of the American army leaving the neighbourhood of New [333]
York. However this might have been, it was indeed a great mistake
that it was not done; general Washington might then have had the
assistance of the brave men who fell there.†

* Near Kingsbridge, fifteen miles from the city of New York.
† An officer of the army wrote to general Lee after the surrender of fort Washington,
and expressed himself thus:

We have all additional reasons for most earnestly wishing to have you where the
principal scene of action is laid. I have no doubt had you been here, the garrison
of Mount Washington would now have composed a part of this army; every
gentleman of the family, the officers and soldiers generally, have a confidence in
you; the enemy constantly inquire where you are, and seem to me to be less

CHAP. IX   General Knyphausen with six battalions, suddenly crossed the
1 7 7 6 country from Rochelle to Kingsbridge, where, joined by the light
infantry and grenadiers, the one commanded by lord Cornwallis, the
other by earl Percy, the fort was on all sides attacked with vigor, and
defended with bravery. On the sixteenth of November, colonel Magaw
the commanding officer, was summoned to surrender without farther
delay. He requested that he might be allowed [334] to consider till
nine o'clock the next morning, before he gave a decisive answer. It
was replied, that two hours only were granted. At the expiration of
this short *parley*, the adjutant general of the British army, who waited
the reply, was informed, that the fort would be defended to the last
moment. Accordingly a resistance was made with astonishing valor
for several hours; but to prevent the farther effusion of blood, the
Americans yielded to necessity, and surrendered themselves prisoners
of war, at the moment when the Hessian and British troops were on
the point of storming the garrison.

Near three thousand continental troops were lost by this disaster.
These unhappy victims of war, notwithstanding the inclemency of
the season, were stripped of their apparel and thrown naked into the
jails of New York; where, after suffering the extremes of misery from
cold, hunger, and sickness, most of them perished. The remnant who
escaped immediate death, were after some months imprisonment,
sent on parole to visit their friends, many of them infected with the
small-pox, and all of them in such a languishing, emaciated condition,
as proved a useful lesson to their countrymen; who, by this instance
of severity towards the brave and unfortunate, were universally
convinced, that death in the field of battle, was much to be preferred
to the cruelties they had [335] reason to expect, if they fell into British
hands, though a nation once famed for the virtues of justice, generosity,
and clemency.

After the surrender of fort Washington, no time was lost; the
advantages gained by the British troops were pushed with spirit. With

---

confident when you are present. We are informed by an officer lately liberated,
that the enemy have a southern expedition in view; that they hold us very cheap
in consequence of the late affair at Mount Washington, where both the plan of
defence and execution were contemptible: if a real defence of the lines was
intended, the number was too few; if the fort only, the garrison was too numerous
by half.

Extract from general Reed to general Lee.

[See Joseph Reed to Charles Lee, November 21, 1776, and Lee to Reed, November
24, 1776, both in *Lee Papers*, II: 293–294, 305–307; Force, *Archives*, 5th. ser., 3: 793.]

the utmost ease they took possession of fort Lee: the American
garrison fled on the first apprehension of an attack, without offering
the smallest resistance. General Howe embraced these favorable
circumstances to prosecute his designs, stimulated by the hope of
reaching and surprising Philadelphia, before the American army could
be reinforced. Thus, near the close of the campaign, when the
continental troops were daily dropping off, and a severe winter setting
in, he had every reason to cherish his most sanguine hopes. He for
some time pushed his purposes with vigor and alacrity, and obliged
general Washington with an handful of men, to retreat from town to
town, until hunted through the state of New Jersey, and even over
the Delaware, which he had time to cross only six hours before the
whole body of the British army, consisting of ten or twelve thousand
men, were on the opposite banks.

The reasons why general Howe did not sooner overtake the
distressed fugitives, or why he cantoned his troops, without crossing
the river and taking possession of the city of Philadelphia, remain
[336] yet to be investigated. The retreat was conducted with ability,
but the remnant that escaped was too small to intimidate the enemy,
or to encourage the friends of the American cause. A great part of the
inhabitants of the city, either from fear, affection, or interest, were
at that time disposed to receive with open arms the British commander;
and the consternation of all parties operated in favor of erecting the
king's standard in the capital of America.

Congress, by advice of some military characters, precipitately
removed to Baltimore, in the state of Maryland. The public concern
was also heightened at this critical period, by the recent capture of
general Lee. He had been collecting a number of militia in the
neighbourhood of Morristown, with a design to fall on the rear of the
British army, while in chase of Washington through the Jersies. It is
not known why he was thus unguarded, but he incautiously lodged
at the little village of Baskenridge, four miles from the troops he had
collected, and about twenty from the British army. Here he was
betrayed, surprised, and taken prisoner. Colonel Harcourt of the light
horse, conducted the enterprise with so much address, that with a
very small party, he without noise passed all the American guards on
his way, surrounded the house, and took possession of his prisoner
without the smallest resistance. In the hurry of the business, Lee was
not suffered to take [337] either hat or cloak, and thus in a ruffian-
like manner, was he conducted to the British headquarters.

A peculiar triumph was enjoyed by his enemies in the capture of

CHAP. IX this single officer. They considered his services at that period, of the
1 7 7 6 greatest consequence to the American army: in addition to this, he
was viewed as a rebel to the sovereign of Britain in a double sense,
both as a deserter from the king's service, in which he had long held
an honorable rank, and as an abettor of the American defection, and
one of the first officers in their army: he was of course confined in
the strictest manner, and threatened with military execution as a
traitor to the king. The Americans at that time had no British prisoners
of equal rank, yet they made the most strenuous efforts for his release.
A colonel Campbell with five Hessian field-officers, were soon after
offered for the exchange of general Lee: when this was refused,
general Washington advertised sir William Howe, that their blood
must atone for his life, if Lee fell a sacrifice to the resentment of his
enemies.

Humanity recoils at the sufferings of individuals, who by the laws
of retaliation, are deemed the legal victims of policy; but though the
mind of the gentle may be wounded by the necessity, habit, in time,
too often learns it to acquiesce [338] in the cruel policy of nations.
Public emergencies may require the hand of severity to fall heavily
on those who are not personally guilty, but compassion prompts, and
ever urges to milder methods. However, general Lee was not executed,
nor suddenly released. Colonel Campbell was closely imprisoned, and
treated with much severity, and a considerable time elapsed before
either of them were relieved, except by some mitigation in the manner
of colonel Campbell's confinement, which was carried to an extreme
not warranted even to a notorious felon.*

Perhaps at no period of the great struggle for independence, were
the affairs of the United States at so low an ebb as at the present.
The footsteps of the British army in their route through the Jersies,
were every where marked with the most wanton instances of rapine
and bloodshed: even the sacred repositories of the dead were not
unmolested by the sacrilegious hands of the soldiery;† while the
licentiousness [339] of their officers spread rape, misery, and despair,
indiscriminately through every village.

Thus, while human nature was disgraced, and the feelings of
benevolence shocked, by the perpetration of every crime; when the

---

* General Lee was also treated very severely until the defeat of Burgoyne. After this
he was permitted to repair to New York on parole, and soon after liberated by an
exchange of prisoners.

† This usage of the dead is authenticated by the accounts of several gentlemen of
respectability near the scene of action.

army spared neither age or sex, youth, beauty, or innocence; it is CHAP. IX
observable, that the distresses of war had fallen principally on that 1 7 7 6
state, which at that time contained a greater proportion of persons
attached to the royal cause, than could have been found in any other
part of America. But so intermixed and blended were persons, families,
and parties of different political opinions, that it was not easy to
distinguish, in the wanton riot of victory, their friends from their foes,
or the royalists from the whigs, even had the royal army been disposed
to discriminate. It was indeed impossible for their foreign auxiliaries
to make any distinction among Americans, though some British officers
would gladly have checked the insolence of triumph, unbalanced by
any principle of religion, honor, or humanity. A neglect of strict
discipline prevented the melioration of crime and misery, and filled
up the measure of censure which afterwards fell on the commander
in chief of the British forces, even from those who wished to give his
military operations the most brilliant cast.*

[340] Had general Howe persevered in his pursuit, and have crossed
the Delaware, he would inevitably have destroyed even the vestige
of an American army. The remnant of the old troops drawn into
Philadelphia, was too small for resistance, the citizens were divided
and intimidated, congress had retreated to Baltimore, the country was
dispirited, and Washington himself, ready to despair, had actually
consulted some of his officers, on the expediency of flying to the back
parts of Pennsylvania, or even beyond the Allegany mountains, to
escape the usual fate of unsuccessful rebels, or as himself expressed
it, "to save his neck from a halter."†

Thus, without an army, without allies, and without resources, the

* See sir William Howe's defence of his conduct in his letters to administration,
   published in London. [See Howe, *Narrative*. Also see Lord George Germain to
   Howe, August 22, 1776 ("I am not at all surprised by the lively mortification which
   you suffered on account of your tedious detention at Halifax. . . ."), Force, *Archives*,
   5th. ser., 1: 1102.]

† This was confidentially said to an officer, who reported, that the general put his
   hand to his neck, and observed, that it did not feel as if made for a halter. *See
   Stedman's History*. It is probable if ever general Washington really expressed himself
   in this manner, it was uttered more from the momentary ebullition of distress, than
   from the serious contemplation of despair. It discovered more a determination to
   live free, than any timidity from sudden dismay. Had general Howe overtaken the
   American troops, and have secured their commander, he would doubtless have been
   made a victim of severe vengeance. [Charles Stedman, *The History of the Origin,
   Progress, and Termination of the American War. By C. Stedman, who Served under Sir
   W. Howe, Sir H. Clinton, and the Marquis Cornwallis* (2 vols.; London, 1794). Quoted
   statement not found.]

CHAP. IX gloom of disappointment overspread not only the brow of the com-
1 7 7 6 mander in chief, but expanded wide, and ruin from every quarter
lowered on the face of American freedom. The Newport and the adjacent
[341] islands were taken possession of by a part of the British army
and navy, under the command of commodore sir Peter Parker and sir
Henry Clinton. The whole colony of Rhode Island was not able to
make the smallest resistance to the seizure of their capital: and to
complete the climax of danger which this melancholy winter exhibited,
the irruptions of the natives in various parts, was not the least. Many
tribes of those aborigines, stimulated by their native fierceness,
wrought up still higher by British influence, and headed by some
American desperadoes in the service of Britain, were making the most
horrid depredations on the back settlements of some of the southern
states: nor did the affairs of America at the northward wear a more
favorable aspect.

General Carleton had conducted the campaign of this year, with
the ability of the statesman, and the courage of the soldier; and
notwithstanding the severity of his general character, he, with a degree
of humanity honorable to himself, and exemplary to his military
associates, had been disposed to commiserate the unfortunate. It has
been observed, that all who fell into his hands after the death of
general Montgomery, were treated with lenity and tenderness. He
was doubtless sensible, that a war enkindled more to satiate a spirit
of resentment [342] and pride, than to establish the principles of
justice, required every palliative to mitigate the odium of the disgraceful design of subduing America by the aid of savages, who had
hutted for ages in the wilderness beyond the distant lakes. General
Carleton with the most extraordinary vigilance and vigor, had conducted the pursuit of the Americans, until Arnold and his party were
chased out of the province of Quebec: nor did he ever lose sight of
his object, which was to make himself master of the Hudson, and
form a junction at Albany with general Howe, whose troops in detached
parties were wasting the middle colonies, and cooperating in the same
design.

By uncommon exertions, Carleton obtained a fleet in the wilderness,
of such strength and superiority, as to destroy the little American
squadron on the Lake Champlain, one of the smaller navigable basons
in the woods of that astonishing country. The lakes of America are
among the wonders of the world. They are numerous and extensive,
deep, and navigable at many hundred miles distance from the ocean.

A view of this part of creation is sublime and astonishing. There are chap. ix five of those lakes of principal magnitude. The smallest of them, *Lake* 1 7 7 6 *Ontario*, is more than two hundred, and the largest, *Lake Superior*, is five hundred leagues [343] in circumference.* Happy might it have been for the Atlantic states, had they been contented within these boundaries of nature, and not at an after period, have wasted the blood of their citizens in attempting to wrest from the natives a vast extent of territory, which it is very improbable they will be long able to govern, unless a remarkable coincidence of events should give them a commanding influence, superior to any European power.

The bravery of Arnold was on his retreat, equally conspicuous with the outset of his extraordinary undertaking: but notwithstanding his vigilance, and the valor of his soldiers, they were reduced to the utmost distress before he blew up the remainder of his fleet, which Carleton had not captured, and run his last ship on shore, without acknowledging the superiority of the British flag, by the servile signal of striking his colors. Obliged to relinquish every post of advantage, Arnold and the remnant of his troops, were driven naked, defenceless, and despondent, from forest to forest, and from lake to lake, until they reached Ticonderoga. The garrison there had been reinforced by some [344] militia from the eastern states, but they were in no condition to meet general Carleton, whose advancement they had every reason to expect, with superior numbers, and the double advantage of discipline and success, and his exertions aided by tribes of copper-colored savages.

General Thomas had been sent from Cambridge in the spring, one thousand seven hundred and seventy-six, with a detachment of the continental army, to endeavour in conjunction with the eastern militia, to retrieve the wretched state of affairs in Canada. He was a man of cool judgment, possessed of courage the result of principle, rather than bravery the impulse of passion. He was respected by the citizens, beloved by the soldiers, and well qualified by the firmness of his mind, and the strength of his constitution, to face the dangers of a campaign in the wilderness. But unfortunately for him, he was deputed to the northern command to oppose the conjoined forces of the native barbarians and their British allies, at a time when the remains of the American army were dismayed by defeat, worn out by fatigue, and

---

* The principal of these inland seas are, Lake Superior, Huron, Michigan, Erie, and Ontario. The description of these and the smaller sheets of water spread over the vast western territory, may be found in every geographical work.

CHAP. IX   in addition to their distresses, a pestilential disorder, then fatal to
1 7 7 6   New Englanders, had spread through the camp. The small-pox, by
the ill policy of the country, had been so long kept from their doors,
that there was scarce a man among them, who was not more afraid of
an attack from this kind of pestilence, than the [345] fury of the
sword: but no caution could prevent the rapidity of the contagion; it
pervaded the whole army; and proved fatal to most of the new raised
troops.

The character of the military officer who dies in his bed, however
meritorious, is seldom crowned by the *eclat* of fame, which follows
the hero who perishes in the field. Thus this good man, qualified to
reap the fairest laurels in a day of battle, was immediately on his
arrival at the scene of action, cut down by the hand of sickness, and
his memory almost extinguished by a succession of new characters
and events that crowded for attention. By the death of general
Thomas, and the reduced state of the Americans, they were far from
being in any preparation for the reception of general Carleton, whose
arrival they momently expected. They had nothing to hope—an
immediate surrender to mercy was their only resource. On this they
had determined; when to their surprise and joy they were informed,
that all further pursuit was relinquished, and that the Canadians and
British troops had precipitately retreated.

Thus the remnant of the broken continental army was left at full
liberty to escape in the best manner they could from other impending
dangers. From the nature of the grounds, [346] and from the
neighbourhood of the savages, from their weak, sickly, and reduced
state, their retreat was extremely difficult; but in scattered parties
they reached Crown Point in a very feeble condition. After this series
of successless efforts, all farther thoughts of the reduction and conquest
of Canada, were for the present laid aside. General Carleton had
repaired to Quebec. General Phillips with a considerable force made
winter-quarters at Montreal; and general Burgoyne took passage for
England. Both these officers had been very active in aid of Carleton,
through the campaign of one thousand seven hundred and seventy-
six.

The defeat of the Americans in Canada, and the advantages gained
by the British arms in the Jersies, and indeed for some months in
every other quarter, gave to the royal cause an air of triumph. The
brilliant hopes formed from these circumstances, by the calculators of
events for the ensuing spring, led the ministry and the army, the

nation and their sovereign, to flatter themselves that the completion CHAP. IX
of the war was at no great distance; and that only one more campaign 1 7 7 6
would be necessary for the entire subjugation of America. The
vicissitudes of fortune, that hourly cloud or brighten all human affairs,
soon convinced them that this was but the triumph of a day. The
new year opened in a reversive view. A spirited movement of general
Washington at this important crisis, [347] had a most happy effect: a
single incident gave a different face to the affairs of the colonies, in
a shorter time than could have been imagined, after the ruinous
appearance of every thing at the close of the campaign.

On the evening of the twenty-fifth of December, general Washington
in a most severe season, crossed the Delaware with a part of his army,
then reduced to less than two thousand men in the whole. They very
unexpectedly landed near Trenton. Colonel Rhal, an officer of decided
bravery, commanded a detachment of twelve hundred Hessians
stationed there, where they lay in perfect security. It was near morning
before they were alarmed: the surprise was complete; the resistance
small: Rhal was mortally wounded, and his whole corps surrendered
prisoners of war. After the fatigue, the hazards, and the success of
the night, general Washington with his party and his prisoners,
consisting of the three regiments of Rhal, Losbourg, and Knyphausen,
recrossed the river before eight in the morning, with little or no loss.

This adventure gave an astonishing spring to the spirits of the
American army and people, a short time before driven to the brink
of despair. They had viewed the Hessians as a most terrific enemy,
and in conjunction with the veterans of Britain, as an invulnerable
foe. To [348] see such a body of them surprised in their camp, and
yielding themselves prisoners to the shreds of an American army,
inspired them with a boldness that an action of the greatest magnitude
might not have awakened in different circumstances. General Washington did not sit down in Philadelphia satisfied with the *eclat* of this
enterprise, but in a few days again passed the Delaware, and took
post at Trenton.

The British army elated by success, had lain carelessly cantoned in
small divisions, in a line extending through New Jersey to New York.
General Howe was afterwards severely censured by his employers,
for his neglect in not crossing the Delaware, while he had the promise
of the most brilliant success from his own arms. The panic of the
Pennsylvanians had inspired most of them with a disposition to
succumb to any terms he should impose, which ought to have been

CHAP. IX an additional stimulus to have pursued his good fortune. Nor was he
1 7 7 6 less censured for his unguarded cantonments, through such an extensive line as the whole length of the Jersies.*

General Washington moved on from Trenton to Princetown by a
circuitous march, to avoid engaging the British or being hemmed in
near Trenton. He suddenly attacked the [349] British encampment
at Princetown, while the main body of the British army had marched
to Trenton, with design to dislodge the Americans from that post.
From Princetown the American army moved to Elizabethtown. Animated by success, warmed by bravery, and supported by fortitude,
they gathered strength as they moved, and gained some signal
advantages in several places on the Jersey side of the river; and in
their turn pursued the king's troops, with as much rapidity as they
had recently fled before them; while the British, as if seized with a
general panic, made but a feeble resistance.

After many marches, counter-marches, and skirmishes, the strength
of the British force was collected at Brunswick, a town in the Jersies,
about sixty miles from Philadelphia, and thirty-five from New York.
They continued their head-quarters there the remainder of the winter;
but they were not without apprehensions for the safety of their troops
and their magazines, even at this distance from Philadelphia, notwithstanding the contempt with which they had but a short time
before, viewed the broken, disheartened remains of a continental
army, which they had pursued into the city.

The British were indeed very far superior to the Americans, in
every respect necessary to [350] military operations,· except the
revivified courage and resolution, the result of sudden success after
despair. In this, the Americans at the time yielded the palm to none;
while the confidence of their antagonists apparently diminished, and
victory began by them to be viewed at a distance.

The waste of human life from various causes, through the vicissitudes
of this winter, was not inconsiderable on either side: but the success
of the American arms through the Jersies, was in some measure
damped by the death of the brave general Mercer of Virginia, who
fell at Princetown, in an action made memorable by the loss of so
gallant an officer. His distinguished merit was gratefully acknowledged
by congress, in the provision afterwards made for the education and
support of the youngest son of his family.

* See trial and defence of general Howe. [See Howe, *Narrative*, pp. 7–12, 67–68.]

The fortunate movements of the Americans at this critical era, had
the usual effect on public opinion. Such is human nature, that success
ever brightens the talents of the fortunate commander, and applause
generally outruns the expectations of the ambitious. General Washington, popular before, from this period became the idol of his country,
and the admiration of his enemies. His humanity to the prisoners who
fell into his hands, was a contrast to the severities suffered by those
captured at [351] fort Washington, and the victims in other places,
that fell under the power of either Hessians or Britons. In a book of
general orders belonging to colonel Rhal, found after the action at
Trenton, it was recorded, that "His excellency the commander in
chief orders, that all Americans found in arms, not having an officer
with them, shall be immediately hanged." * This instance may serve
as a sample of the cruel designs, and summary modes of proceeding
to execution among military masters, who hold themselves above the
censure or control of civil authority, or the restraints of humanity.

On the contrary, the lenity shewn by general Washington towards
the loyalists captured by his soldiers, disarmed the prejudices of many,
and multitudes flocked to the American standard, who, in the
beginning of the dispute, were favorers of the royal cause, and within
a few months had been ready to throw themselves into the arms of
Great Britain. But every favorable impression was erased, and every
idea of submission annihilated, by the indiscriminate ravages of the
Hessian and British soldiery in their *route* through the Jersies. The
[352] elegant houses of some of their own most devoted partisans
were burnt: their wives and daughters pursued and ravished in the
woods to which they had fled for shelter. Many unfortunate fathers,
in the stupor of grief, beheld the misery of their female connexions,
without being able to relieve them, and heard the shrieks of infant
innocence, subjected to the brutal lust of British grenadiers, or *Hessian
Yaughers*.

In short, it may be difficult for the most descriptive pen, to portray
the situation of the inhabitants of the Jersies, and the neighbourhood
of their state. The confusion of parties, the dismay of individuals,
who were still serving in the remnant of the American army, whose
dearest connexions were scattered through the country, and exposed
to the danger of plunder and misery, from the hostile inroads of a

---

* The intimation of lord Cornwallis afterwards, to the commander of a party sent out,
  much superior to the Americans they expected to meet, was not more humane. His
  lordship observed, that "he wanted no prisoners."

victorious army, can be imagined only by those whose souls are susceptible at once of the noblest and the tenderest feelings. Many of this description were among the brave officers, who had led the fragments of a fugitive army across the Delaware, and sheltered in the city of Philadelphia, had by flight escaped a total excision.

But after escaping the perilous pursuit, there appeared little on which to ground any rational [353] hope of effectually counteracting the designs of their enemies. They found congress had retreated, and that the inhabitants of the city were agitated and divided. Several of the more wealthy citizens secured their property by renouncing the authority of congress, and acknowledging themselves the subjects of the crown: others availed themselves of a proclamation of pardon, published by the British commander, and took protection under the royal standard, for personal security.

Several officers of high character and consideration, were on the point of pursuing the same steps, previous to the action at Trenton, from the anxiety they felt for their families, despair of the general cause, danger of the city, or the immediate military executions that might take place, when the victorious army should cross the river, which they momently expected. Why this was not done, remains involved among the fortuitous events, which often decide the fate of armies, or of nations, as it were by accident. The votaries of blind chance, or indeed the more sober calculators on human events, would have pronounced the fortune of the day was in the hands of the British commander. Why he did not embrace her tenders while it was in his power, no one can tell; nor why he stopped short on the borders of the [354] river, as if afraid the waters of the Delaware, like another Red Sea, would overwhelm the pursuers of the injured Americans, who had in many instances as manifestly experienced the protecting hand of Providence, as the favored Israelites.

The neglect of so fair an opportunity, by a single effort, to have totally destroyed or dispersed the American army, or in the language of administration, to have cut off the *hydra head* of *rebellion*, by the subjugation of the capital city, was viewed in the most unpardonable light by his employers. They were not yet fully apprised of the spirit of Americans: their ideas did not quadrate with those of a distinguished military officer, well acquainted with the country, who observed in a letter to a friend,*

* See a letter from general Charles Lee to the duke of Richmond, October, one

it was no exaggeration to assert, that there were two hundred thousand
strong-bodied, active yeomanry, ready to encounter all hazards and dangers,
ready to sacrifice all considerations, rather than surrender a tittle of the
rights which they have derived from God and their ancestors.

Subsequent events will prove that he had not formed a mistaken
opinion of the resolution and prowess of the Americans. It will be
seen, that they were far [355] from relinquishing their claim to
independence, by the ill success of a single campaign. The tardy
conduct of sir William Howe was reprehended with severity; nor was
he ever able to justify or vindicate himself, either to administration
or to the world.

From these and other circumstances, the character of sir William
Howe depreciated in proportion to the rising fame of the American
commander in chief, his rival in glory, and his competitor for the
crown of victory, on a theatre that soon excited the curiosity, and
awakened the ambition of the heroes and princes of Europe.

Indeed it must be acknowledged, that general Howe had innumerable difficulties to surmount, notwithstanding the number of his
troops. He was at a distance from his employers, who were ignorant
of his situation, and unable to support him as emergencies required.
He was in an enemy's country, where every acquisition of forage or
provisions, was procured at the expense or hazard of life or reputation.
A considerable part of his army was composed of discontented
foreigners, who, disappointed of the easy settlements they had been
led to expect, from the conquest of rebels, and the forfeiture of their
estates,—their former poverty not mitigated, nor their yoke of slavery
meliorated, in the service of their new masters, [356] —they were
clamorous for pay, and too eager for plunder, to be kept within the
rules of discipline: and their alien language and manners disgusting
to their British comrades, a constant bickering was kept up between
them.

Nor was the British commander less embarrassed by the tories, who
from every state had fled from the resentment of their countrymen,
and hung upon his hands for subsistence. On their fidelity or their
information, he could make little dependence. Many of them had
never possessed property at all, others irritated by the loss of wealth;
both were continually urging him to deeds of cruelty, to which he

---

thousand seven hundred and seventy-four. [Lee to Duke of Richmond, October
19, 1774, in Force, *Archives*, 4th. ser., 1: 949–950.]

CHAP. IX did not seem naturally inclined. At the same time, he was sensible
1 7 7 6 that the hopes of his nation would sink by the protraction of a war,
which they had flattered themselves might be concluded with the
utmost facility and expedition.

There were many concurring circumstances to lead the world to
conclude, that sir William Howe was not qualified, either by education
or habits of life, for the execution of an object of such magnitude, as
the restoration of the revolted colonies to obedience, and dependence
on the crown of Britain.

> He fought as a soldier and a servant to his king, without other principle
> than that of passive obedience. The immensity of the prospect before him
> embarrassed his mind, clouded his understanding; [357] and, too much
> engrossed by his bottle and his mistress, he frequently left his orders and
> his letters to be fabricated by subordinate officers: and seemed at some
> times to sink into stupor or indolence, at others, brave and cool as Julius
> Caesar.

If these traits of the character of the British commander are just
and impartial, as said to be by one of his former associates,* the world
need be at no loss why such instances of shameful outrage and rapine
appeared wherever his army entered; or why, when he had driven
the Americans over the Delaware, he did not pursue and complete
the business, by a triumphal entrance into Philadelphia, and the total
destruction of general Washington and his remaining troops.

No military character ever had a fairer opportunity (as observed
above) to place the martial laurel on his brow, than was presented to
general Howe on the banks of the Delaware; but he suffered it to
wave at a distance, without the resolution to seize it: and instead of
a chaplet of glory, he reaped only the hatred of America, the loss of
esteem and reputation in England, and disgrace and censure from his
parliamentary masters.

[358] The negligence of sir William Howe gave an opportunity to
the Americans, to recover the energies of their former courage. The
hopeless prospect that had beclouded their minds, vanished on the
successful termination of a single enterprise projected by the commander in chief, and executed with resolution and magnanimity, by
officers who had been almost reduced to despondency.

The surprise of Trenton saved the army, the city, and in some

---

* See letter of general Lee, Appendix, Note No. XVIII, which discovers the temper
and character of the writer, as well as of sir William Howe.

degree, the reputation of the commander in chief, which frequently
depends more on the fortunate exigencies of a moment than on
superior talents. The world ever prone to neglect the unfortunate,
however brave, amiable, or virtuous, generally pays its idolatrous
homage to those elevated by the favors of the ideal deity to the
pinnacle of honor: yet real merit usually commands the plaudit of
posterity, however it may be withheld by contemporaries, from rivalry
or envy.

Perhaps there are no people on earth, in whom a spirit of enthusiastic
zeal is so readily enkindled, and burns so remarkably conspicuous, as
among the Americans. Any fortuitous circumstance, that holds out
the most distant promise of a completion of their wishes, is pushed
with an ardor and unanimity that seldom fails of success. This
characteristic trait may in some measure account for the rapidity [359]
with which every thing has been brought to maturity there, from the
first settlement of the colonies.

The energetic operation of this sanguine temper, was never more
remarkably exhibited, than in the change instantaneously wrought in
the minds of men, by the capture of Trenton at so unexpected a
moment. From a state of mind bordering on despair, courage was
invigorated, every countenance brightened, and the nervous arm was
outstretched, as if by one general impulse, all were determined to
drive the hostile invaders, that had plundered their villages, and dipt
the remorseless sword in the bosom of the innocent victims of their
fury, from off the American shores.

But we shall see in the subsequent pages of these memoirs, that
they had yet many years to struggle with the dangers, the chances,
and the miseries of war, before an extensive country, convulsed in
every part, was restored to tranquillity. Agonizing amidst the complicated difficulties of raising, paying, and keeping an army in the field,
it is easy to conceive it was not with much facility, that money was
drawn from the pockets of the rich, for the support of the public
cause, at the hazard of receiving a scrip of depreciated paper, in lieu
of silver and gold.

[360] A nominal substitute for specie has often its temporary
advantages, and when not extended too far, its permanent ones; but
is oftener attended with a great balance of evil. Its deceptive value
often plunges a great part of the community into ruin, and corrupts
the morals of the people before they are apprehensive of the danger.
Yet without the expedient of a paper currency, the Americans could

CHAP. IX   never have supported an army, or have procured the necessaries of
1 7 7 6   life from day to day. Experience had before taught them the pernicious
effects of a paper medium, without funds sufficient for its redemption;
but the peculiar exigencies of their situation, left them no other
resources.

The United States had engaged in an hazardous enterprize, in
which all was at stake. Deficient as they were in the means necessary
to support a war, against a wealthy and potent nation, they yet stood
alone, uncertain whether any other power would aid their cause, or
view them with that degree of consideration, that might obtain a
credit for foreign loans. It was an interesting spectacle to all such
nations as had colonies of their own, to view such an unexpected
spirit of resistance and revolt in the Americans, as might be contagious,
and probably produce commotions as much to be dreaded by them,
as the alienation of the thirteen colonies was by England. The most
judicious statesmen [361] in America were sensible, that much time
must elapse, and many events take place, before any foreign stipulations could be effected. They were therefore impelled by the
peculiar circumstances of their situation, to resort to this dangerous
expedient, or relinquish the contest. No wise legislator, no experienced
statesman, no man of principle, would have recourse to a measure
fraught with such uncertain consequences, but from that necessity
which in human affairs, sometimes precludes all deliberation between
present utility, and distant events which may accrue.

In consequence of this dilemma, congress had emitted sums to a
vast amount in paper bills, with a promise on the face of the bill, of
payment in specie at some distant period. This circumstance was
alarming to the avaricious and the wealthy, who immediately withdrew
their gold and silver from circulation. This and other combining
circumstances, among which the immense sums counterfeited in New
York by the British, and thrown into the colonies, produced an
immediate and an astonishing depreciation. At the same time, the
widow and the orphan were obliged to receive the interest of their
property, deposited for security in the public treasuries, according to
the nominal sum on the face of the bills; by which they and other
classes, were reduced to [362] extreme necessity. The operative
effects of this paper medium, its uses, its depreciation, and total
annihilation, will be seen hereafter, when the credit of the circulating
paper had sunk so low, that no one presumed to offer it in barter for
any commodity. All public demands were consolidated by government

at a very great discount, and public securities given to those who had CHAP. IX
demands for services or loans, and the faith of congress pledged for 1 7 7 6
their payment in full value, as soon as practicable.*

The honor and the fate of the commander in chief, had been daily
hazarded by the unrestrained license of soldiers, with whom it was
optional to stay a few days longer, or to withdraw after the short term
of their enlistment had expired, however imminent the dangers might
be that threatened their country. Yet the establishment of a permanent
army was not more ardently wished by general Washington, than by
every judicious man in America: but the work, though not insurmountable, was attended with complicated difficulties. The reluctance
felt through that class of men from which an army was to be drawn,
to enlist for an indefinite term, was apparent to all. The precarious
resources for the support of an army, which at that time depended
[363] only on a depreciating medium, could not be concealed, and
were discouraging indeed: at the same time, it was a subject too
delicate to expatiate on, as the more it was conversed upon, the
greater was the danger of defeating the desired object. But, the
firmness of congress unshaken, and the legislatures of the individual
states equally zealous, while the people at large were convinced of
the utility of the measure, the object was in time obtained, though
not so rapidly as the exigencies of the day required.

* See Appendix, Note No. XIX.

CHAPTER X

Desultory Circumstances • Skirmishes and Events • General Howe with-
draws from the Jersies—Arrives at the River Elk—Followed by Washington • The Battle of Brandywine • General Washington defeated, retreats
to Philadelphia—Obliged to draw off his Army • Lord Cornwallis takes
Possession of the City • Action at Germantown, Red Bank, &c • The
British Army take Winter-Quarters in Philadelphia • The Americans
encamp at Valley-Forge • General Washington's Situation not eligible
• De Lisle's Letters • General Conway resigns • The Baron de Steuben
appointed Inspector General of the American Army

CHAP. X   [364] In the beginning of the year one thousand seven hundred and
1 7 7 7   seventy-seven, the spirits of the Americans were generally re-animated
by fresh hopes, in consequence of the measures taken by congress to
establish a permanent army, until the conclusion of the war, and still
more by their sanguine expectations of success from the negociations,
and prospects of an alliance with France.

A solemn confederation, consisting of a number of articles by which
the United States should in future be governed, had been drafted,
discussed, and unanimously signed by all the delegates in congress,
in the month of October, one thousand seven hundred and seventy-
six. This instrument was sent to each legislature [365] in the thirteen
states, and approved and afterwards ratified by the individual governments. After this, the congress of the United States thought proper
to appoint commissioners to the court of France, when fortunately a
loan of money was negociated on the faith of the United States, and
permission obtained for the reception of American ships of war, and
the sale of prizes that might be captured by them, and carried into
any of the ports of France. They were also encouraged to hope for
still further assistance from the generosity of that nation.

The growth of the infant marine of the United States had been so rapid, and so successful had been the adventurers in this early stage of the war, that it was rationally concluded, it could not be many years before the navy of America might make a respectable figure among the nations.

It was not expected in Great Britain, that the colonies could thus early have acquired a naval force of the least consideration. In consequence of this idea, a great number of British ships and transports, that went out slightly armed, or not armed at all, were this year captured on their way to America. So bold and adventurous were the American privateers, and their public ships, that the domestic trade of Britain was rendered insecure; and a convoy [366] became necessary to protect the linen ships from Dublin to Newry: a circumstance that never before took place.* The successful depredations also on the British West India trade, were felt through Great Britain in an alarming degree; and shocked their commerce so far, as to occasion sudden and frequent bankruptcies in London, Bristol, and almost all the great marts of the nation.

Thus the colonies were filled with every thing necessary for carrying on a war, or that furnished them the luxuries of life. But the sudden acquisition of wealth, which in consequence of unexpected success, flowed into the lap of individuals, so much beyond their former fortune or ideas, was not indeed very favorable to the virtue or manners of the possessors. It had a tendency to contract the mind, and led it to shrink into selfish views and indulgencies, totally inconsistent with genuine republicanism. The coffers of the rich were not unlocked for the public benefit, but their contents were liberally squandered in pursuit of frivolous enjoyments, to which most of them had heretofore been strangers.

This avaricious spirit, indeed, somewhat retarded the measures contemplated by congress, who had determined, that the army in future [367] should stand on a more stable footing. They had directed that eighty-eight battalions should be raised, and kept in full pay until the close of the war; and as an encouragement to enlist, they promised a certain allotment of lands to both officers and soldiers, at the commencement of peace; yet the recruiting service went on heavily for a time, and at an immense expense to the United States. But among a people whose personal liberty had been their proudest

* British Annual Register, 1777. [See *Annual Register* (1777), "History of Europe," pp. 24–27.]

CHAP. X boast, the above was not the sole cause of the difficulty of raising a
1 7 7 7 permanent army: the novelty of being enchained to a standing army
was disgusting; they generally revolted at the idea of enlisting for an
indefinite term: thus the army still remained incomplete, and the
militia were again called out as before. In that mode there was no
want of zeal and alacrity; great numbers always appeared ready for
any temporary service.

During the winter of this year, the British commander did not
attempt any thing of greater magnitude, than the destruction of the
American magazines. He effected his purpose at Peekskill, at Court-
land Manor; and about the middle of April, he sent on a detachment
under the command of governor Tryon, to the little town of Danbury,
on the borders of Connecticut, where a considerable quantity of
provisions and other articles had been deposited, for the use of the
American army. He considered [368] it of great importance to cut off
these resources, before the opening of the spring campaign.

In conjunction with sir William Erskine and brigadier general
Agnew, governor Tryon, who had embodied near two thousand
royalists, was vested with the principal command, on the trivial
expedition to Danbury. He executed his orders with alacrity. They
destroyed a few hogsheads of rum and sugar, a considerable quantity
of grain and other provisions, about seventeen hundred tents, and
plundered and burnt a number of houses in the town of Danbury.
But their retreat to their shipping was intercepted by the militia of
the country, drawn out by the generals Wooster and Silliman. A small
detachment of continental troops commanded by general Arnold, with
a party of recruiting officers joined them, and a rencounter ensued,
when much bravery was exhibited on both sides. General Wooster,
an aged and experienced officer, and a very worthy man, was mortally
wounded. General Arnold had his horse shot under him at the moment
a soldier had his bayonet lifted for his destruction; but with surprizing
agility, he disengaged himself from his horse, and drew a pistol that
laid his enemy dead at his feet. On the third day after his landing,
governor Tryon again reached the shipping, and re-embarked his
troops with inconsiderable loss, though exceedingly fatigued [369] by
a march of thirty miles, harassed the whole time by an enemy arranged
on each hand, and pressed in the rear by recruits hourly coming in to
the assistance of his opponents.*

---

* It has been acknowledged by some British historians, that their loss more than
counterbalanced the advantages gained in this expedition to Danbury.

Within a few days, reprisals were made for this successful feat of
Tryon, by the more brilliant enterprise of colonel Meiggs; who, with
only one hundred and seventy men, landed on the southern part of
Long Island, surprised the enemy lying at Sag Harbour, burnt twelve
armed vessels, captured the sailors, destroyed the forage and stores
on the east part of the island, and returned to Guilford, about ninety
miles distance, within thirty hours from the time of his departure
from thence. He brought with him the trophies of his success, without
the loss of a man. As no action of importance was exhibited for several
months, these smaller depredations and inconsiderable skirmishes,
served only to keep the spirits in play, and preserve the mind from
the lethargic state, which inaction or want of object creates.

The plan digested for the summer campaign, among the British
officers, was, to gain possession [370] of Philadelphia, to command
the central colonies, and to drive the Americans from all their posts
in the province of Canada. Some circumstances had taken place that
seemed to favor these designs. Confident of his success from his
superior numbers in the field, general Howe for a time, exercised all
the articles of an experienced commander, to bring general Washington
to a decisive engagement: but, from a perfect command of his temper,
and a judicious arrangement of the few continental troops, and the
militia he had in aid, the American chieftain defeated every measure
practised to bring him to a general action. He placed about two
thousand men in Princeton, and with the main body of his army, took
his stand on the high and advantageous grounds in the neighbourhood,
and made all possible preparation for defence. This determined line
of conduct in general Washington, gave a new turn to British operations.
On the nineteenth of June, general Howe decamped from Brunswick,
and removed to Amboy, with every appearance of a speedy embarkation. His troops as usual committed every outrage on their way,
and as if instigated by despair of becoming masters of the country,
and envious of the progress of arts and sciences in America, the
colleges and public libraries were burnt, all public buildings and places
of worship swept away, and nothing that had the appearance of
distinguished elegance escaped. But the mind and the [371] pen
weary of the detail of destruction, it is enough to observe, that the
British army in their retreat, left every trait of desolation and barbarism
behind them.

The manoeuvres of the British commander led to the belief, and
every thing wore the strongest appearance, that he was about to take
a final leave of the Jersies. The illusion succeeded so far, as to induce

CHAP. X general Washington to send a body of three thousand men, commanded
1 7 7 7 by the generals Maxwell, Conway, and lord Stirling, with design to
attack the rear of their march. General Howe apprised of this
movement, hastily returned to the charge. He dispatched lord Cornwallis on a circuitous route, who soon came up with lord Stirling,
strongly posted in a wood.

The Americans determined to dispute the ground with Cornwallis;
but the ardor of the British troops, and the rivalry of the Hessians,
obliged them soon to quit their advantageous post, and retreat with
precipitation. The loss the Americans sustained was not inconsiderable;
they suffered greatly, both from the extreme heat of the season, and
the valor of their antagonists. From this and some other circumstances,
it was for a time generally believed, that the late movement of general
Howe and his army, was but a feint to draw general Washington to
an action, rather than from a fixed [372] design immediately to
evacuate the state of New Jersey. Convinced of this, Washington
drew in his lines, and recovered his camp on the hills, determined to
persevere in his defensive system, until some more advantageous
opportunity should justify the hazard of a general engagement.

It would undoubtedly have been highly imprudent for general
Howe at this time, to have persisted in pushing his way to the
Delaware, through a country disgusted and alienated by the barbarity
of his troops. Most of the inhabitants of this state were now armed
for defence. Inflamed by resentment from the sufferings of the last
year, impelled by necessity from the impediments in the way of all
private occupations, and fired by a love of glory, they were now ardent
for action, in proportion as they had been heretofore remiss; and came
to the field prepared to conquer or die in defence of their country.
At the same time, general Washington was daily gaining strength by
the arrival of fresh troops, from various other quarters.

The British commander accordingly thought proper about mid-
summer, to decamp in earnest. He drew off his whole force as privately
as possible to New York; thence embarked, and sailed from Sandy
Hook the twenty-third of July. The destination of the fleet and army
[373] was kept so profoundly secret, that for some time after their
embarkation, every capital on the continent was apprehensive that
they should be the object of the next visit from a potent armament,
that seemed at a loss where to direct their operations. This expectation
occasioned a general anxiety until the latter part of August, when the
fleet appeared in the Chesapeak, and the army soon after landed at

the head of the river Elk. On his arrival there, general Howe
immediately published a proclamation, in which he assured the
inhabitants every where of safety and protection, provided they were
not found in arms, and promised pardon to all officers and soldiers
who should surrender to the royal army.

Indeed his disposition to clemency appeared so conspicuous on his
first arrival, that it prevented the entire depopulation of the adjacent
parts of Maryland, Pennsylvania, and the lower counties of Delaware;
the inhabitants of which, on the first appearance of so formidable a
foe in their neighbourhood, were struck with consternation, and on
the point of abandoning their habitations.

It was now obvious, that the possession of the city of Philadelphia
was the stake for which both armies played. General Washington had
moved with the greatest part of his troops for the defence of that
elegant city, and had by detached [374] parties, embarrassed the
march of the British army from the river Elk to the Brandywine. In
the neighbourhood of the last the two armies met, and on the eleventh
of September came to a general engagement. The battle was fought
with bravery, and sustained with spirit on both sides; but the fortune
of the day declared against the Americans, yet not so decidedly as
the sanguine expectations of their antagonists had led them to hope
from such an event. But it gave them an astonishing advantage in the
minds of the people through all the district of Pennsylvania; and
enabled general Howe with more facility to complete his enterprise.
Many officers of high rank on both sides, suffered much in the spirited
action at the Brandywine. A few days after this affair, general Wayne,
who had concealed himself in a wood, with fifteen hundred men, in
order to harass the rear of the British, was discovered and attacked
by brigadier general Grey, who had given orders that no alarm should
be made by the use of fire-arms. He made the onset about one o'clock
in the morning; and by the more cruel exercise of the bayonet, several
hundred Americans were killed and wounded; the remainder with
difficulty escaped by flight.

Among others who suffered in the battle of Brandywine, the marquis
de la Fayette, a young nobleman of France, was dangerously wounded.
[375] Warmed by an enthusiastic love of liberty, and animated by a
laudable ambition, this amiable young gentleman had left the court
of France without leave of the king: and quitting the pleasures of
domestic felicity, he embarked at his own expense, and engaged in
the service of the United States at an early period of the war, when

CHAP. X the affairs of America wore the darkest aspect. His zeal and his
1 7 7 7 heroism to the conclusion of the contest, placed the well-earned laurel
on his brow, and procured him the love, respect, and best wishes of
the people throughout America. Indeed all the French officers in the
continental army, among whom were many of high consideration,
acquitted themselves with distinguished gallantry on this and many
other occasions, where the courage of the soldier, and the humanity
of the officer, were called into exercise.

General Washington obliged to retreat in disorder, and closely
pursued after the action, retired to Chester. He soon after with his
army reached Philadelphia; but the British commanders directed their
operations with so much judgment and success, that before the twenty-
sixth of September, Washington thought proper to evacuate the city.
Lord Cornwallis with the British grenadiers, and two battalions of
Hessians, on that day made a triumphal entry, and took possession
of the capital of the United States.

[376] The era was truly critical. Congress again found it necessary,
a second time to desert the city, and now repaired to York-Town for
safety. Dissensions ran high among the inhabitants of Philadelphia.
Some of the most opulent families were disaffected, and renounced
all adherence to the union: and several persons of different descriptions, emboldened by the absence of congress, and the success of the
British arms, took this opportunity to declare in favor of the royal
cause. One of principal consideration among them, went out, and
conducted the king's troops into the city. Others declared themselves
zealously attached to the measures of administration, and equally
disgusted with the opposition of the colonies. Among these was Joseph
Galloway, a member of congress, and speaker of the house of
representatives in Pennsylvania. He soon after repaired to England;
where he indefatigably exerted his abilities and his influence against
his native country, on all occasions.

Besides those individual apostates, the quaker interest had long
embarrassed every public measure in that colony. They were a large
and powerful body in the state of Pennsylvania; and, notwithstanding
their pacific principles, though not actually in arms, they at this time
took a decided part against the American cause. Their previous
conduct had drawn upon themselves many severities. Several of the
[377] principal leaders had been imprisoned, and others sent out of
the city of Philadelphia, on the approach of the British army. Yet still
they refused the smallest submission to the present government, and

appealed to the laws, by which they claimed personal safety. But
whether from a consideration of the necessity of a temporary suspension
of law, in times of public and imminent danger, or whether from the
sanguine resolutions which operate on all parties, when their favorite
system totters on the brink of ruin, little regard was paid even to the
legal claims of this body of citizens. Several persons of the first
distinction and character among them, notwithstanding their just and
sensible remonstrances, were sent off to Virginia, to prevent the
influence they might have through a state, then the principal seat of
war.

From these political dissensions, the partial defeats, the loss of
Philadelphia, the slowness of recruits for permanent service, the
difficulty of obtaining supplies for the army from various causes, and
particularly from the monopolizing and avaricious spirit that was fast
gaining ground in America, and from *delay*, "the betrayer of all
confederations," a lowering aspect was cast over the operations of
America on every side. On the contrary, the British government, the
army, and their adherents, [378] had much reason to flatter themselves
with an idea of the speedy completion of their designs against the
United States. They were now in possession of the first city in the
union; general Clinton was in force at New York; general Vaughan
on the North River, with troops sufficient to sweep away the inhabitants
on both sides, and to keep the adjacent country in awe. A large
detachment of the British army still held the possession of Newport:
colonel Losbourg with a Hessian brigade in conjunction with them,
was piratically plundering the neighbouring coasts, and burning the
scattered villages of the state of Rhode Island.

It is proper here to observe, that soon after the British troops had
taken possession of Rhode Island, some animosities had arisen between
general Howe and lord Percy, who commanded there. This was
occasioned by a requisition from sir William Howe to his lordship, to
send him on fifteen hundred men for the better defence of New York,
and to aid his operations in that quarter.

Lord Percy declined a compliance with this order, alleging as a
reason for this refusal, that the Americans were rapidly collecting and
strengthening themselves in the town of Providence; that the number
of troops already there, gave them reason to be apprehensive for the
safety of Newport. General Howe resented [379] the refusal; threatened earl Percy with a trial for disobedience of orders, and reprimanded
him in language which the earl thought derogatory to an officer of his

CHAP. X rank, character, and consequence. On this usage, which lord Percy
1 7 7 7 considered very affrontive, he immediately wrote to his father the
duke of Northumberland, requesting him, without delay, to obtain
his recal from the American service. Soon after this he embarked for
England, having resigned his command to general Prescott.

His advance to the chief command of the troops on Rhode Island,
was not long enjoyed by general Prescott, before a circumstance took
place which was sufficiently mortifying to himself and the British. In
the beginning of July, one thousand seven hundred and seventy-
seven, colonel Barton, a provincial officer, and several others, accompanied by only thirty-eight men, embarked in several boats from
Warwick Neck, eluding the vigilance of the British ships and guard-
boats, he and his party passed them in the dark, and landed on Rhode
Island about twelve o'clock at night.

Colonel Barton had received some intelligence, of the insecure
situation in which the British commander frequently lodged on the
island. On this information, he formed the bold design of surprising
and seizing him: this he effected with a facility beyond his own most
[380] sanguine expectations. Having first secured the centinel at the
door, he surprised general Prescott in his bed. One of his *aids* leaped
from a window in hopes of escape, but was prevented. Their design
accomplished, the little party hastened to their boats with all possible
expedition. Signals were made for an alarm on shore; but it was too
late: Barton and his party were out of danger. When they reached the
spot from whence they had set out on this adventure, a chariot was
prepared for the reception of general Prescott, in which he was
escorted safely from Warwick to Providence.

Colonel Barton received great applause from his countrymen, for
his spirited and well-executed enterprise. It was not indeed an object
of much magnitude; but the previous circumstances of general
Prescott's conduct had been such, as to render his capture a subject
of much exultation to the Americans. He had, while in command at
Newport, insulted and abused the inhabitants, ridiculed the American
officers, and set a price upon some of their heads, particularly on that
of general Arnold, which Arnold retaliated with the advertisement of
a small price for the head of general Prescott.

The similarity of circumstances that attended the capture of the
generals Prescott and Lee, and their rank in the armies to which they
respectively belonged, rendered it highly proper [381] that an exchange
should have taken place immediately. It was however for a time

delayed; but finally, general Lee obtained his liberty in consequence
of this business.

The discouraging circumstances above related with regard to the arrangements, military posts, and operations of the British, from Newport to New York, and from New York to Philadelphia, gave very promising prospects of success to the British in that part of America. At the same time general Burgoyne, with the flower of the British army, the Canadian provincials, and hordes of savages that poured down from beyond the lakes, was making advances, and in the language of bombast and self-confidence, threatened destruction and vengeance to any who should have hardihood enough, to endeavour to stop his progress, or to oppose the authority under which he acted.

But notwithstanding the general wayward appearance of the affairs of the United States, the legislatures as we shall see, lost not their magnanimity, the people their ardor, nor the army their valor. Not disheartened by the circumstances of the late action at the Brandywine, or the loss of Philadelphia, general Washington with his brave troops, in numbers comparatively inconsiderable, kept the British army in play, until the setting in of winter. Within a few days after the surrender of Philadelphia, [382] the Americans attacked the royal camp at Germantown, situated about six miles from the city, where the main body of the British army had taken their stand.

This was a very unexpected manoeuvre. The attempt was bold, and the defence brave. The Americans for a time, seemed to have greatly the advantage; but the enterprise finally failed. They were obliged to retreat in great confusion, after the heavy loss of many officers and men. The disappointment of the Americans, was in consequence of the address and ability of colonel Musgrove, who judiciously stood on the defensive, and checked the progress of the continental troops, until general Grey and brigadier general Agnew, with a large detachment, came to his relief. A warm, but short action ensued: when the Americans were totally routed, and driven out of the field of action.

General Lee, who had not the highest opinion of general Washington's military abilities, observed on this occasion, "that by a single stroke of the *bathos*, the partial victory at Germantown was corrupted into a defeat."* This was however, too severe a censure. A number

---

* General Lee's letters. [The quoted statement does not appear in *Lee Papers*. Lee's letters are dotted with scurrilous references to Washington's deficiencies as com-

CHAP. X of circumstances co-operated to blast the hopes of the Americans,
1 7 7 7 after the early [383] promise of success. The Britons themselves have
given testimony to the bravery and good conduct of Washington and
his army on this occasion. One of their writers has attested,

> in this action the Americans acted upon the offensive; and though repulsed
> with loss, shewed themselves a formidable adversary, capable of charging
> with resolution, and retreating with order. The hope therefore entertained
> from the effect of any fair action with them, as decisive, and likely to put
> a speedy termination to the war, was exceedingly abated.

The highest expectation had been formed on the reduction of
Philadelphia, both by the foreign and internal foes of America. Though
both armies were fired with equal ardor, and on all occasions were
equally ready for action, yet the repeated skirmishes for several weeks
in the neighbourhood of the city, were not productive of any very
important consequences, except the loss of many brave men, and
several officers of great merit. None of these were more distinguished
and lamented, than general Nash on the American side, and brigadier
general Agnew and colonel Bird of the British line, who lost their
lives in the battle of Germantown.

It was very important to the British commander after the above
transactions, to open a [384] free passage to Philadelphia by the
Delaware, in order to obtain supplies of provisions by water for their
army. This was impeded by the American shipping, and by several
strong posts held by the Americans on the river; the principal of which
was Red Bank. Here they had an opportunity of retrieving the recent
disgrace of their arms at Germantown. The Hessians under the
command of colonel Donop, had the principal hand in this business.
He crossed the Delaware with fifteen hundred men, at Cooper's ferry
opposite Philadelphia, and marched to attack the redoubts at Red
Bank.

A cannonade was opened: the camp was attacked with spirit, and
defended with equal gallantry by colonel Greene of Rhode Island;
who replied to the summons of count Donop to surrender, "that he
should defend the place to the last extremity." On this, the Hessians

---

mander in chief. He was, however, a prisoner of the British from December 13,
1776 (when he was captured at Basking Ridge after delaying too long) until December
25, 1777, more than two months after the Battle of Germantown (October 4, 1777).
He was exchanged for general Richard Prescott in April 1778 and rejoined the
American troops in May. He wrote few letters during his captivity; none of them
mentions Germantown. See *Lee Papers* IV for biographical sketches.]

attempted to storm the redoubts; but the assailants were obliged to CHAP. X
retreat in their turn. One Hessian brigade was nearly cut to pieces in 1 7 7 7
the action, and count Donop mortally wounded and taken prisoner,
as were several other officers of consideration. The remainder retreated
with great precipitation through the night, leaving one half of their
party dead, wounded, or prisoners to the Americans; crossed the river
the next morning; and in this mortified situation, the remnant who
escaped entered Philadelphia. This important pass was [385] a key
to the other posts on the river; and for its brave defence the officers
and soldiers were justly applauded, and colonel Greene complimented
by congress, with a present of an elegant sword.

After the action at Red Bank, the vigilance and caution of general
Washington could not be overcome by the valor and advantages of
his foes, so far as to induce him to hazard any action of consequence.*
The design of opening the Delaware, was now the principal object
with the British commander. This was effected without much difficulty, after the reduction of Mud Island. From this strong post, the
Americans were obliged to retreat, after a very manly resistance. They
did not evacuate their works until reduced to despair, by some British
ships advantageously playing upon them. From the very superior
advantages of their enemies in many respects, they were induced to
set fire to every thing within reach; and after [386] great slaughter
they abandoned a place, which had already cost them too much in its
defence.†

In the struggle to open the Delaware, the Augusta and the Merlin
on the part of Britain, were lost; but the losses of the Americans were
far beyond those of the British. The Delaware frigate and some others
were captured, and several ships burnt by themselves, to prevent
their falling into the hands of their enemies.

Nothing more decided than the above transactions took place this
season. The Delaware river thus cleared, and eligible winter-quarters
secured for the king's troops, and the cold season fast advancing,

---

* For this general Washington was very severely censured by some; and even the
  legislature of the state of Pennsylvania remonstrated to congress, and expressed
  their uneasiness, that the American commander should leave the capital in possession
  of the enemy, and retire to winter-quarters. But his little army destitute of every
  necessary, without the possibility of a supply at that season, was a sufficient apology.
† The writer of this work does not aim at a particular description or detail of all the
  engagements, battles, and rencounters, between the two contending armies. A
  general sketch of the most material military movements, completes her design; the
  primary object of which, is not a dry narrative of military havoc.

general Howe gave up the pursuit of the cautious and wary Washington.
He found it impossible with all his efforts to bring him to another
general action, while his own judgment, and that of the most judicious
of his officers, forbade it, and common prudence dictated the probable
disadvantages of such a movement. His numbers were too small, and
[387] the wants of the army too many, to hazard any thing. The most
guarded and prudent defence was the only line of conduct left to the
American commander.

These circumstances induced general Howe, about the middle of
December, to draw the main body of his army into the city of
Philadelphia. They were indeed unable longer to keep the field,
being very destitute of tents and other equipage necessary for the
army in a cold climate, at this inclement season.

Thus after the proud vaunts of victory and conquest, and the loss
of many gallant officers and brave men, the British commander had
little to boast at the conclusion of the campaign, but the possession
of a city abandoned by the best of its inhabitants, and the command
of the adjacent country, circumscribed within the narrow limits of
twenty miles. This was but a small compensation for the waste of life
and treasure. It was a gloomy picture of the termination of a campaign,
for sir William Howe to convey to his master and to his countrymen,
after the exultation for some partial successes had flattered them with
the highest hopes of speedy and complete victory. Yet, notwithstanding
these vauntings over a people, among whom there did not yet appear
a probability of complete subjugation by the sword, nor the smallest
traces of a disposition among the people [388] of America, to yield
obedience to the laws and requisitions, which the government of
Great Britain were attempting thus to enforce at the point of the
bayonet.

After sir William Howe had retired and taken winter-quarters in
the city, a novel scene, considering the weakness of the continental
army, was exhibited without. To the surprise and wonder of their
foes, and to the admiration of all mankind acquainted with the
circumstances, the Americans, nearly destitute of tents, poorly supplied with provisions, almost without shoes, stockings, blankets, or
other clothing, cheerfully erected themselves huts of timber and
brush, and encamped for the winter, at a place called Valley-Forge,
within twenty-five miles of the city of Philadelphia. Thus in the
neighbourhood of a powerful British army, fearless of its numbers and
strength, a striking proof of their intrepidity in suffering, and their

defiance of danger, was exhibited by a kind of challenge bidden to CHAP. X
their enemies, not very usual in similar situations. The commander 1 7 7 7
in chief, and several of the principal officers of the American army,
in defiance of danger, either to themselves or to such tender connexions, sent for their ladies from the different states to which they
belonged, to pass the remainder of the winter, and by their presence
to enliven the gloomy appearance of a hutted [389] village in the
woods, inhabited only by an hungry and half-naked soldiery.*

The resolution and patience of this little army surmounted every
difficulty. They waited long, amidst penury, hunger, and cold, for
the necessary supplies, which in spite of the utmost exertions of the
several states, came in but too slowly. Such was the deficiency of
horses and waggons, for the ordinary as well as extraordinary occasions
of the army, that the men in many instances, cheerfully yoked
themselves to little carriages of their own construction: others loaded
the wood and provisions on their backs for present supply, in their
extreme necessity. General Washington informed a committee sent
from congress to inquire into the state of the army, that some brigades
had been some days without meat, and that the common soldiers had
frequently been at his quarters, to make known their distresses.
Unprovided with materials to raise their cold lodgment from the
ground, the dampness of the situation, and the wet earth on which
they lay, occasioned sickness and mortality to rage among them to an
astonishing degree:—"Indeed, nothing could surpass their suffering,
except [390] the patience and fortitude with which it was endured by
the faithful part of the army. Those of a different character deserted
in great numbers."†

In this weak and dangerous situation, the American army continued
encamped at Valley-Forge, from December till May; while the British
troops in high health and spirits, lay in Philadelphia, without once
attempting to molest them. For this want of vigor and enterprise,
general Howe was severely and justly censured in Britain, blamed by
those interested in his success in America, and ridiculed by the
impartial observer in every quarter. By his negligence this winter, he

* Nothing but the inexperience of the American ladies, and their confidence in the
  judgment of their husbands, could justify this hazard to their persons, and to their
  feelings of delicacy.
† See a letter from the committee sent from congress, to Mr. Laurens the president.
  [See the excellent account in LDC, 8: 501. Numerous letters written by delegates
  to the Continental Congress during 1777 make Warren's point.]

CHAP. X   again undoubtedly lost the fairest opportunity of executing the designs
1 7 7 7   of his *master*, and acquiring to himself much military fame. But by
wasting his time in effeminate and reprehensible pleasures, he sunk
his character as an officer; and few scrupled to assert, in the arms of
a handsome adulteress. Many of his officers followed his example,
and abandoned themselves to idleness and debauchery; while the
soldiers were left to indulge their own licentious habits.

At this period, though not attacked by a foreign foe, the situation
of the American commander in chief was really not very enviable.
[391] It required the utmost prudence and address, to keep together
the appearance of an army, under the complicated miseries they must
feel, in the depth of winter, hungry and barefooted, whose fatiguing,
circuitous marches over the snowy path, had been marked by their
bleeding feet, before they, in such a destitute predicament, pitched
their tents in the valley. The dilatory spirit of some, and the peculating
dispositions of other officers in the various public departments,
increased every difficulty with regard to clothing and subsistence.
The deplorable state of the sick, the corrupt conduct in some of the
hospitals, the want of discipline among the soldiers, the inexperience
of officers, the slowness of recruits, the diminution of the old army
from various causes, were circumstances discouraging indeed; and
might have been considered, if not a balance, at least a weight in the
scale, against the advantages and the pride of high station. Yet these
were not all the embarrassments which the commander in chief had
to encounter;—general Washington had his personal enemies to
combat: nor was he without his rivals for power and fame.*

[392] In all communities there are some restless minds, who create
jealousies and foment divisions, that often injure the best cause, and
the most unimpeachable character: and it may be observed, that there
is ever a spirit of intrigue and circumvention, that runs parallel with
the passions of men. Thus the fortune of war is frequently changed
by dangerous emulations, and the best systems of social and political
happiness overthrown, by the envy and resentment of little minds,
or the boundless ambition of more exalted souls. Nor was it many
years, before America discovered she had in her bosom, her Caesars
and her Catilines, as well as her Brutuses and her Catos.

* Both the conduct and letters of general Lee, had in several instances confirmed the
opinion, that he was ambitious of obtaining the chief command of the army of the
United States; and doubtless he had a party that for a short time flattered these
expectations. At this time indeed he was a prisoner, but his correspondencies were
extensive.

Many persons were disgusted with the dictatorial powers vested in CHAP. X
general Washington, after the action at Trenton, which they alleged 1 7 7 7
were at his own request. These were ample indeed. He was empowered
by congress "to reform and new model the military arrangements, in
such manner as he judged best for public service." He was also vested
with several other discretionary powers.* Congress had indeed limited
his power to six months; but exigencies of the highest necessity, had
urged him sometimes to exercise it in a manner too arbitrary for the
principles and dispositions of Americans, unused to the [393] impress-
ment of their property for the use of armies.

In this state of affairs, the commander was attacked by anonymous
letters, fictitious signatures, and incendiary suggestions: he was
censured for his cool operations, defensive movements, and *Fabian*
slowness. Disadvantageous impressions were made on the minds of
some, and others were led to believe, that general Washington was
not without his weaknesses and his foibles. It was observed by one
of his principal officers:†

> That decision is often wanting in minds otherways valuable:—That an
> indecisive mind in a commander, is one of the greatest misfortunes that
> could befal an army:—That he had often lamented this circumstance
> through the campaign:—That they were in a very awful situation, in an
> alarming state, that required the utmost wisdom and firmness of mind.

A wish at this time undoubtedly prevailed, among some distinguished characters,‡ for a supercedence [394] of his command: but

---

* See resolves of congress. [Force, *Archives*, 5th. ser., 3: 1606 (Resolves, December
  12, 1776) and 1479–1480, 1613 (Resolves, December 27, 1776) concerning the
  augmentation of Washington's powers. Benjamin Rush wrote to Richard Henry Lee,
  December 30, 1776 that "General Washington must be invested with dictatorial
  powers for a few months, or we are undone. The *vis inertiae* of the Congress has
  almost ruined this country." *Ibid.*, p. 1488.]

† See a letter from general Reed to general Lee, afterwards published. [See Reed to
  Lee, November 21, 1776, *Lee Papers* II: 293–294. Also see Lee to Reed, November
  24, 1776, *Ibid.*, pp. 305–307.]

‡ Samuel Adams of Boston, general Mifflin, and several other characters of distinction,
  were suspected of unfriendly designs towards the commander in chief. But there
  never were sufficient grounds to suppose, that Mr. Adams ever harbored any
  disaffection to the person of general Washington: on the contrary, he respected and
  esteemed his character, and loved the man. But zealous and ardent in the defence
  of his injured country, he was startled at every thing that appeared to retard the
  operations of war, or impede the success of the revolution; a revolution for which
  posterity is as much indebted to the talents and exertions of Mr. Adams, as to those
  of any one in the United States.

General Mifflin was a young gentleman of a warm and sanguine disposition. Active

CHAP. X   Washington, cool, cautious, and more popular than any man, his good
1 7 7 7   genius was ever at hand to preserve his character invulnerable: yet,
several circumstances confirmed the opinion, that even some members
of congress at this period, were intriguing for his removal. It might
indeed at this time, have had a fatal effect on American affairs, had
general Washington fallen beneath [395] a popular disgust, or the
intrigues of his enemies.

Perhaps few other men could have kept together the shadow of an
army, under such a combination of difficulties as the young republic
had to encounter, both in the field and the cabinet. Many men of a
more active and enterprising spirit, might have put a period to the
war in a shorter space of time; yet perhaps not ultimately so much in
favor of America, as the slow, defensive movements of the officer
then vested with the chief command.

This line of conduct was thought by some, to be not so much owing
to his superior sagacity and penetration, as to a constitutional want of
ardency, at times when energy appeared most necessary to many
persons. A predilection in favor of a connexion with Britain, seemed
united with this disposition. It had appeared clearly by many circumstances in conversation with his confidential friends, that he was not
in the beginning of opposition, fond of a final separation with the
parent state; and that he wished to move defensively, until some
events might take place, that would bring back, and with honor and
dignity re-unite, the revolted colonies to the bosom of their ancient
parent.*

[396] But the public opinion always in his favor, with a happy talent

---

and zealous, he engaged early in opposition to the measures of the British parliament.
He took arms, and was among the first officers commissioned, on the organization
of a continental army. For this he was read out of the society of quakers, to which
himself and his family had belonged. But Mr. Mifflin's principles led him to consider
himself under a moral obligation, to act offensively as well as defensively, and
vigorously to oppose the enemies of his country; and from his character and
principles, he undoubtedly wished to see a commander in chief of the united armies,
who would admit of no delay in the acceleration of the object in which they were
engaged.

* In the early period of the war, many very worthy characters opposed to the British
system, besides general Washington, wished for a reconciliation with Great Britain,
if it could be procured consistently with honor, and with sufficient pledges of security
to the just claims of the colonies, rather than an irrevocable separation. But time
convinced all, that nothing but independence, and a total dismemberment, could
secure the liberties of the United States.

to secure the confidence of the people, he commanded in a remarkable CHAP. X
manner, their affections, their resources, and their attachment, to the 1 7 7 7
end of the war; and had the good fortune to parry every charge
brought against him, with the firmness of the soldier, though not
without the sensibility of the man who found his reputation at stake.
He complained heavily to his private friends, yet took no public
notice of the vague imputations of slander, that fell from the pen of
a French officer of distinction, under the signature of De Lisle.

These letters were fraught with the most severe strictures on the
general's military character and abilities. Some other letters in the
same style and manner, without a name, were directed to gentlemen
of character and consideration in several of the states. Some addressed
to Patrick Henry, the governor of the state of Virginia, he immediately
transmitted to congress, and to the general himself. However boldly
some of the charges were urged, they [397] made little impression on
the public mind: the transient tale of the day passed as the pathless
arrow, without leaving a trace behind. His enemies shrunk from the
charge; and general Washington, by the current of applause that
always set in his favor, became more than ever the idol of the army
and the people.

General Conway, the reputed author of the letters signed De Lisle,
was a gentleman of great military talents and experience, with an
ambition equal to his abilities. He had left France with high expectations of rank in the service of the United States. Not satisfied with
the appointment of inspector general of the American army, his pride
wounded, and disappointed that he did not sustain a higher grade in
office, which he had been led to flatter himself with before he left
his country, and disgusted by the suspicions that fell upon him after
the publication of De Lisle's letters, he resigned his commission, and
returned to Europe.

Conway was not the only officer of his country, that suffered similar
mortifications. The credulity of men of talents, family, and merit,
had been imposed on by the indiscretion of one* of the American
agents, and their imaginations fired by ideas of *rank* and preferment
in America, to which no foreigner was entitled. [398] Thus, chagrined
from the same cause, it was thought the valiant Coudray, an officer
of distinguished name and merit, who was a brigadier general and
chief engineer in the French service, leaped voluntarily to his watery

---

* Silas Deane, the first agent sent by congress to France.

CHAP. X grave. His death indeed, was attributed to the fleetness of his horse,
1 7 7 7 which it was said he could not command. Having occasion to cross
the Schuylkill, in company with some other officers, he entered a
boat on horseback. The career was swift; the catastrophe fatal: he
leaped in on one side of the boat, and with equal celerity, out on the
other. Thus both horse and rider were irretrievably lost. Coudray was
beloved and lamented by all who knew him; and the loss of Conway
was regretted by many who esteemed him for his literary abilities,
and his military talents.

The important office of inspector general relinquished from necessity
by general Conway, was immediately conferred on the baron de
Steuben, an officer with the best credentials, who had recently arrived
from Germany. The essential services of this celebrated disciplinarian,
were in a very short time felt throughout the army. New regulations
took place, and new arrangements were made in the hospitals, in the
commissary's, the quarter-master's, and other departments, which had
been shamefully abused, not from a want of capacity or integrity in
the preceding inspectors, but from the ignorance, [399] inexperience,
or peculation of many of the subordinate officers. From the date of
the baron's advancement, a more thorough knowledge of *tactics* was
acquired by the officers; more system, discipline, and order appeared
in the army; more equitable and permanent regulations, and a stricter
adherence to the rules and laws of war, took place, than had been
observed at any period before. The merits of this officer, universally
acknowledged, were afterwards generously rewarded by the congress
of the United States.

It may not however be improper to observe, before we pass on to
the subsequent circumstances of the war, that though the baron de
Steuben had been promoted to the rank of inspector general, by the
approbation of congress and the army, yet general Conway had a
considerable party attached to him, among the military officers. Many
persons thought that his dismissal from office, and permission to
return to France, under the degradation of character which fell upon
him, without any specified charges of delinquency in office, or any
solid proofs that he really had been the author of the anonymous
reproaches thrown on the character of general Washington, was at
once affrontive both to himself and his nation. These ideas are more
clearly exhibited in a [400] sketch of the life of Conway, by another
hand.*

* See Appendix, Note No. XX.

We shall only further observe, that the French nation was not CHAP. X disposed to resent individual flights, or even public neglects, at this 1 7 7 7 interesting period: a nation who viewed the resistance of the American colonies to the overbearing power of Britain, on a broad scale. They considered their opposition, if successful, as at once redounding to their own interest, and to the promotion of the liberties of mankind in general.

It had for many years been a primary object with the house of Bourbon, to humble the pride and power of Britain. No contingencies that had arisen among the nations for near a century, appeared so likely to produce this effect, as an alienation from, and a total loss of their colonies. This consideration heightened the natural ardor, and quickened the constitutional energies of every Frenchman, to lend his hand to the work. Their characteristic impetuosity always appeared conspicuous in politics and war, as well as in the intrigues of love and gallantry. They were ever restless under any appearance of slowness that might retard the execution of their object: but the critical situation [401] of the American army at this period, rendered an attempt to lessen the influence and the character of the commander in chief, dangerous and inexcusable.

Notwithstanding the freedom of opinion, and the license of the press, which should never be too much restrained in a free country, there are times and circumstances which require silence; and however disposed any one might be to censure the conduct of general Washington, either for the want of enterprise, alacrity, or military skill, yet perhaps no man in the United States, under the pressure of so many difficulties, would have conducted with more discretion and judgment.

If there was any error in the dismissal of general Conway, it might be in not observing a due degree of delicacy, or furnishing any testimonials of his having acquitted himself well in his military capacity, a point on which all in that line are very tenacious. The displacing of a single officer of any rank, is not sufficiently important to dwell upon long; and the apology for having done it at all, must be the danger at this time, of disgusting a foreign corps belonging to a court whose assistance was necessary, and whose aid had been courted, though their faith was not yet absolutely pledged to promote the emancipation of the United States.

[402] France however, was looking with too eager and steady an eye, on the operations and success of the resistance of the colonies, to the measures and mandates of the crown and parliament of England,

CHAP. X to be moved by any partial considerations, from the line of political
1 7 7 7 conduct which they had adopted. This was to embrace the first
favorable opportunity, when contingent circumstances might promise
success, to support the claim of independence, and render the breach
complete and durable between the United States and Great Britain;
and thereby deprive that rival nation of the immense advantages they
had already reaped, and might again recover by a revival and
continuance of the connexion.

That part of the American army immediately under the command
of general Washington, must now be left encamped at Valley-Forge
for the winter. Their situation impels the mind to throw over them
that veil of compassion, which a season of perplexity, though not of
absolute despair, requires. We must now look over, and survey with
an anxious eye, and in the succeeding pages view the humiliating
events, which for a time, attended the fortune of war in the northern
department; and trace the footsteps of the soldier, through the forlorn
desert, which was ultimately the path to victory and glory.

END OF VOL. I.

HISTORY

OF THE

RISE, PROGRESS AND TERMINATION

OF THE

AMERICAN REVOLUTION.

INTERSPERSED WITH

Biographical, Political and Moral Observations.

IN THREE VOLUMES.

BY MRS. MERCY (OTIS) WARREN,

OF PLYMOUTH, (MASS.)

..........Troubled on every side..............
perplexed, but not in despair ; persecuted, but not forsaken ;
cast down, but not destroyed.   ST. PAUL.

O God ! thy arm was here.........
And not to us, but to thy arm alone,
Ascribe we all.   SHAKESPEARE.

VOL. II.

BOSTON :

PRINTED BY MANNING AND LORING,

FOR E. LARKIN, No. 47, CORNHILL.

1805.

C H A P T E R   X I

Northern Department • General Carleton superseded • General Burgoyne vested with the Command for Operations in Canada • Ticonderoga
abandoned by General St. Clair • Affair of Fort Stanwix—Of Bennington,
and various other important Movements of the two Armies, until the
Convention of Saratoga • General Burgoyne repairs to England on Parole—His Reception there • Reflections and Observations on the Event of
the Northern Campaign

[1] From the time that Quebec was invested by Montgomery and CHAP. XI
Arnold, at the close of the year one thousand seven hundred and 1 7 7 7
seventy-five, until the termination of general Burgoyne's campaign,
in the autumn of one thousand seven hundred and seventy-seven,
the successes, the expectations, and the disappointments from that
quarter, had been continually varying.

[2] Sir Guy Carleton, the governor of Canada, and who for a number
of years had been commander in chief of all the British forces through
that province, was an officer of approved fidelity, courage, and ability.
He had successfullly resisted the storm carried into that country by
order of congress; he had triumphed in the premature fall of the
intrepid, but unfortunate Montgomery; he had driven back the
impetuous Arnold to the verge of the lakes; he had defeated the
operations of general Thomson, in a bold and successless attempt to
surprise the British post at *Trois Rivieres:* general Thomson was there
made a prisoner, with all of his party who escaped the sword. This
happened about the time a detachment was marched northward,
under the command of general Thomas. He died of the small-pox,
as related above, when most of his army was destroyed by the sword,
sickness, or flight.

Though general Carleton had occasionally employed some of the
Indian allies of Great Britain, he had by his address kept back the
numerous tribes of savages, near and beyond the distant lakes. He

CHAP. XI   rather chose to hold them in expectation of being called to action,
1 7 7 7   than to encourage their ferocious inclination for war, which they ever
prosecute in those horrid forms, that shock humanity too much for
description. Whether his checking the barbarity of the savages, or
whether his lenity [3] to the unfortunate Americans that had fallen
into his hands, operated to his disadvantage, or whether from other
political motives, is yet uncertain; however, he was superseded in his
military capacity, and the command given to general Burgoyne, who
had re-embarked from England early in the spring, and arrived at
Quebec in the month of May, one thousand seven hundred and
seventy-seven, with a large and chosen armament.

General Carleton felt the affront as a brave officer, conscious of
having discharged his trust with a degree of humanity on one side,
and the strictest fidelity to his master on the other. He immediately
requested leave to quit the government, and repair to England. Yet
he did not at once desert the service of his king: his influence was
too great among the Canadians, and over all the Indian tribes, to
hazard his absence at this critical conjuncture. His return to Europe
was therefore postponed: he encouraged the provincials to aid his
successes, and exerted himself much more than heretofore, to bring
on the innumerable *hordes* of the wilderness. In consequence of this,
they poured down from the forests in such multitudes, as to awaken
apprehensions in his own breast of a very disagreeable nature; but he
cajoled them to some terms of restraint; acted for a time in conjunction
with Burgoyne, and made his arrangements in such a manner, as
greatly to [4] facilitate the operations of the summer campaign.

General Burgoyne was a gentleman of polite manners, literary
abilities, and tried bravery; but haughty in his deportment, sanguine
in opinion, and an inveterate foe to America from the beginning of
the contest with Britain: this he had discovered as a member of the
house of commons, as well as in the field. On his arrival in Canada
he lost no time, but left a sufficient force for the protection of Quebec,
and proceeded immediately across the lakes, at the head of eight or
ten thousand men, including Canadians, and reached the neighbourhood of Crown Point before the last of June.

There, according to the barbarous system of policy adopted by his
employers, though execrated by a minority in parliament, he summoned the numerous tribes of savages to slaughter and bloodshed. A
congress of Indians was convened, who met on the western side of
Lake Champlain. He gave them a war-feast, and though his delicacy

might not suffer him to comply with their usual custom, and taste
the goblet of gore by which they bind themselves to every ferocious
deed, he made them a speech calculated to excite them to plunder
and carnage, though it was speciously covered by some injunctions
of pity towards the aged and infirm, who might experience the
wretched [5] fate of becoming their prisoners. Yet, he so far regarded
the laws of humanity, as to advise the savages to tomahawk only such
as were found in arms for the defence of their country, and gave some
encouragement to their bringing in prisoners alive, instead of exercising
that general massacre usual in all their conflicts; nor would he promise
a reward for the scalps of those who were killed merely to obtain the
bounty.

Having thus as he supposed, secured the fidelity of savages, whom
no laws of civilization can bind, when in competition with their
appetite for revenge and war, he published a pompous and ridiculous
proclamation. In this he exhorted the inhabitants of the country,
wherever he should march, immediately to submit to the clemency
of his royal master. To quicken their obedience, he ostentatiously
boasted, that *"he had but to lift his arm, and beckon by a stretch thereof,"*
the innumerable *hordes* of the wilderness, who stood ready to execute
his will, and pour vengeance on any who should yet have the temerity
to counteract the authority of the king of England. He concluded his
proclamation with these memorable threats:

> I trust I shall stand acquitted in the eyes of God and man, in denouncing
> and executing the vengeance of the state against the wilful *outcasts*: the
> messengers of *justice* and of *wrath* await them in the field, [6] and devastation,
> famine, and every concomitant horror that a reluctant, but indispensable
> prosecution of military duty must occasion, will bar the way to their
> return.*

After these preliminary steps, general Burgoyne pushed forward
with his whole force, and possessed himself of Ticonderoga without
the smallest opposition. This was a strong post commanded by general
St. Clair, an officer always unfortunate, and in no instance ever
distinguished for bravery or judgment. Though the Americans here
were inferior in numbers to the British, they were not so deficient in

* See Burgoyne's speech to the Indians, and his singular proclamation at large, in the
British Remembrancer, the Annual Register, and in many other authentic records.
[*Remembrancer* (1777), pp. 211–212 (June 29, 1777). Burgoyne's speech was less
bloodthirsty than Warren reported.]

CHAP. XI   men as in arms, more particularly musquetry and bayonets: but their
1 7 7 7   works were strong, the troops healthy, and they had just received a
reinforcement of men, and a fresh supply of every thing else necessary
for defence. In these circumstances, there could scarcely be found a
sufficient excuse for calling a hasty council of war, and drawing off
by night five or six thousand men, on the first approach of the enemy.
The want of small-arms was the only plausible pretence offered by
the commander to justify his conduct. This deficiency St. Clair must
have known before the fifth of [7] July, when he in a fright fled with
his whole army, and left every thing standing in the garrison.*

It is not probable the Americans could have long kept their ground
against the superiority of the British officers, and the number and
discipline of their troops; yet undoubtedly measures might have been
early taken by a judicious commander, to have retreated if necessary,
without so much disgrace, and the total loss of their artillery, stores,
provisions, their shipping on the lake, and many valuable lives. The
order for retreat was unexpected to the army: they had scarce time
to secure a part of their baggage. The flight was rapid, and the pursuit
vigorous. The soldiers having lost all confidence in their commander,
the out-posts were every where evacuated, and a general dismay
pervaded the fugitives, who, in scattered parties, were routed in every
quarter, and driven naked into the woods.

[8] After two days wandering in the wilderness, the largest body of
the Americans who had kept together, were overtaken and obliged
to make a stand against a party that much outnumbered them,
commanded by colonel Frazer, who had been indefatigable in the
pursuit. The action continued three or four hours, when the Americans,
though they fought with bravery, were totally routed with very great
loss. Colonel Francis, the gallant commander of this party was killed,
with many other officers of merit; two or three hundred privates were
left dead on the field, thrice that number wounded or taken prisoners:
most of the wounded perished miserably in the woods. The British
lost several officers highly esteemed by them, among whom was major

* About this time a misfortune befel the Americans not far distant from Montreal, at
a place called the Cedars. There major Butterfield with his party, were compelled
to surrender prisoners of war. This party captured by captain Forster who commanded
the British, consisted of four or five hundred men. It was warmly disputed afterwards,
between congress and the British commanders, whether the Cedars men, who were
permitted to depart on parole, should be exchanged for British prisoners taken
under Burgoyne.

Grant, a man of decided bravery. Yet general Burgoyne found to his CHAP. XI
cost, his incapacity to execute the boast he had some time before 1 7 7 7
made in the house of commons, that "so little was to be apprehended
from the resistance of the colonies, that he would engage to drive the
continent with five hundred disciplined troops."

General St. Clair had made good his own retreat so far, as to be
six miles ahead with the van of the routed army. Such was his terror
on hearing of the defeat of colonel Francis, and some other successes
of the royal army, that instead of proceeding to fort Ann, as intended,
[9] he shrunk off into the woods, uncertain where to fly for security.
Another party of the Americans, who had reached fort Ann, were
attacked and reduced by colonel Hill, with one British regiment.
They set fire to the fortress themselves, to prevent its falling into the
hands of the victors, and fled with the utmost speed towards fort
Edward, on the Hudson. General St. Clair, and the miserable remains
of his army who escaped death, either by fatigue or the sword, after
a march of seven days, through mountainous and unfrequented
passages, harassed in the rear, and almost without provisions of any
kind, arrived at Fort Edward in a most pitiable condition.

General Burgoyne was too much the experienced officer to neglect
his advantages. He pushed forward with equal alacrity and success;
and in spite of the embarrassments of bad roads, mountains, thickets,
and swamps, he reached the neighbourhood of fort Edward, within a
few days after the broken remnant of St. Clair's army had posted
themselves there. On his approach, the Americans immediately
decamped from fort Edward, under the command of general Schuyler,
whom they found there, and withdrew to Saratoga. He had been
making some efforts to collect the militia from the country contiguous,
to aid and support [10] the routed corps; but on their advance, he did
not think it prudent to face the British troops.

A share of the public odium on this occasion fell on general Schuyler.
His conduct, as well as the delinquency of general St. Clair, was very
heavily censured. They were both ordered, with some other of the
principal officers of the late council of war at Ticonderoga, to repair
to congress to answer for the loss of that fort, and the command of
the Lake Champlain. On the other hand, it was no small triumph to
general Burgoyne and his army, thus to have chased the Americans
from the province of Canada, to find themselves in possession of all
the lakes, and to see the British standard erected on the Hudson,
which had long been an object of importance with administration.

CHAP. XI   Exaggerated accounts of the weakness of the Americans, the
1 7 7 7   incapacity of their officers, and the timidity of the troops, were
transmitted to England; and the most sanguine expectations formed
by people of every description through the island. They were ready
to imagine, that hunted from post to post, both in the northern and
southern departments, the spirits of the colonists must be broken,
their resources fail, and that the United States thus repeatedly
disappointed, would lose all energy of opposition, and soon fall a prey
to the pride and power of [11] Great Britain. But not withstanding
the unhappy derangement of their affairs at the northward, and the
successes of general Howe at the southward, there appeared not the
smallest inclination among the people at large, throughout the American states, to submit to royal authority. The untoward circumstances
that had taken place, neither exhausted their hopes, nor damped the
ardor of enterprise. The dangers that lowered in every quarter, seemed
rather to invigorate the public mind, and quicken the operations of
war.

On the defeat of St. Clair, and the advance of the British army,
the eastern states immediately draughted large detachments of militia,
and hastened them forward. Congress directed general Washington
to appoint proper officers, to repair to Saratoga and take the command.
They also appointed a court of inquiry to take cognizance of the
delinquency of the suspended officers: but their influence was too
great with the commander in chief, and some principal members of
congress, to subject them to that measure of *degradation* which it was
generally thought they deserved. They were dismissed, though not
with approbation, yet without any severe censure; but as the conduct
of St. Clair was disgraceful, and that of Schuyler could not be justified,
they were neither of them appointed to active service.

[12] General Gates, a brave and experienced officer formerly in
British service, a man of open manners, integrity of heart, and
undisguised republican principles, was vested with the chief command
to act against Burgoyne. On his arrival at Saratoga, he drew back the
army, and encamped at a place called *Stillwater*, where he could more
conveniently observe the motions of colonel St. Ledger, who was
advancing to the Mohawk River, to invest fort Stanwix. This post
was commanded by colonel Gansevoort, whose bravery and intrepidity
did honor to himself and to his country. General Arnold was sent on
with a reinforcement from the continental army, and a large train of
artillery, to the aid of general Gates. He was ordered to leave the

main body, and march with a detachment towards the Mohawk River
to the assistance of Gansevoort: but before there was time sufficient
for his relief from any quarter, this gallant officer found himself and
the garrison surrounded by a large body of British troops, in conjunction
with a formidable appearance of savages, yelling in the environs, and
thirsting for blood. At the same time he was threatened by their more
enlightened, yet not more humanized allies, that unless he immediately surrendered the garrison, or if he delayed until it was taken by
storm, they should all be given up to the fury of the Indians, who
were bent upon the massacre of every officer and soldier.

[13] St. Ledger by letters, messages, and all possible methods,
endeavoured to intimidate the commander of the fortress. He observed, that the savages were determined to wreak their vengeance
for the recent loss of some of their chiefs, on the inhabitants of the
Mohawk River, and to sweep the young plantations there, without
distinction of age or sex. He made an exaggerated display of his own
strength, of the power and success of Burgoyne, and the hopeless
state of the garrison, unless by a timely submission they put themselves
under his protection. On this condition, he promised to *endeavour* to
mitigate the barbarity of his Indian coadjutors, and to soften the
horrors usually attendant on their victories.

Colonel Gansevoort, instead of listening to any proposals of surrender, replied, "that entrusted by the United States with the charge of
the garrison, he should defend it to the last extremity, regardless of
the consequences of doing his duty." Their danger was greatly
enhanced by the misfortune of general Harkimer, who had marched
for the relief of fort Stanwix, but with too little precaution. At the
head of eight or nine hundred militia, he fell into an ambuscade
consisting mostly of Indians, and notwithstanding a manly defence,
few of them escaped. They were surrounded, routed, and butchered,
in all the barbarous shapes of savage brutality, after many of them
[14] had become their prisoners, and their scalps carried to their
British allies, to receive the stipulated price. A vigorous sally from
the garrison, conducted by colonel Willet of New York, and his
successful return with a number of prisoners, gave the first information
of the failure of Harkimer. This instead of discouraging, inspirited to
fresh enterprise. The valiant Willet, in contempt of danger and
difficulty, hazarded a passage by night through the enemy's works,
and traversed the unexplored and pathless wilderness for upwards of
fifty miles, to the more inhabited settlements, in order to raise the

CHAP. XI country to hasten to the relief of the garrison, and the protection of
1 7 7 7 the inhabitants scattered along the borders of the Mohawk River.

General Arnold had marched with a thousand men for the relief of
the besieged; but though in his usual character he made all possible
dispatch, the gallant Gansevoort had two days before his arrival,
repulsed the assailants, and obliged them to retreat in such disorder,
that it had all the appearance of a flight. In consequence of this, St.
Ledger was obliged to relinquish the siege with so much precipitation,
that they left their tents, stores, and artillery behind them, and their
camp-kettles on the fire. This movement was hurried on by the sullen
and untractable behaviour of the Indians; which rose to such a height,
as to give [15] him reason to be apprehensive for his own safety. His
fears were well founded: their conduct had become so outrageous,
that it was not in the power of sir John Johnson, Butler, and other
influential friends of the savages, to keep them within any bounds.
They frequently plundered the baggage of the British officer; and
when an opportunity offered the slightest advantage, they murdered
their British or German allies, with the same brutal ferocity with
which they imbrued their hands in the blood of Americans.

The next movement of importance made by general Burgoyne, was
an attempt to get possession of the little obscure town of Bennington,
lying in the Hampshire Grants among the Green Mountains, and
made considerable only by the deposit of a large quantity of cattle,
provisions, carriages, and other necessaries for the use of the American
army. For the purpose of seizing these, as well as to intimidate the
people in that quarter, by the magnitude of his power and the extent
of his designs, he detached a party of Hessians, with a few loyalists
and some Indians, to the amount of fifteen hundred, and gave the
command to colonel Baum, a German officer. He was commissioned,
after he had surprised Bennington, to ravage the adjacent country,
and if possible to persuade the inhabitants, that he was in force
sufficient, and that he designed to march on to Connecticut [16]
River, in the road to Boston. He was ordered to inform them, that
the main body of the British army was in motion for the same purpose,*
that they were to be joined at Springfield by a detachment from
Rhode Island, and that by their irresistible power, they meant to
bring the rebellious Americans to due submission, or to sweep the
whole country.

It is astonishing that a man of general Burgoyne's understanding

---

* See general Burgoyne's orders to colonel Baum, Appendix, Note No. I.

and military experience, should issue orders so absurd and impracticable. He must have been very little acquainted with the geography
of the country, and less with the spirit of the inhabitants, to have
supposed that a detachment of fifteen hundred men, could march
from Saratoga till they reached Connecticut River, take post at a
variety of places, levying taxes on the inhabitants, making demands
of provisions, cattle, and all other necessaries for the use of his army,
without any resistance; thence to proceed down the river to Brattleborough, and to return by another road and take post at Albany: and
this business to be completed in the short term of a fortnight. Nor
did he discover less ignorance, if he expected that a detachment was
to leave Rhode Island, and march through the country to Springfield
on the same design, and from thence to meet colonel Baum at Albany.

[17] It is impossible to suppose, that so renowned a commander as
general Burgoyne, could mean to deceive or embarrass his officers,
by his orders; but if he flattered himself that they could be executed,
he must still have cherished the opinion that he once uttered in the
house of commons, that four or five thousand British troops could
march through the continent, and reduce the rebellious states to a
due submission to the authority of parliament. In this march, Burgoyne
ordered all acting in committees, or in any other capacity under the
direction of congress, to be made prisoners.

These pompous orders and bombastic threats, were far from
spreading the alarm and panic they were designed to excite. The
adjacent country was immediately in motion, and all seemed animated
with the boldest resolution in defence of the rights of nature, and the
peaceable possession of life and property. When colonel Baum had
arrived within four miles of Bennington, appearances gave him reason
to apprehend, that he was not sufficiently strong to make an attack
on the place. He judged it more prudent to take post on a branch of
the river Hoosuck, and by express inform general Burgoyne of his
situation, and the apparent difficulty of executing his orders with only
fifteen hundred men.

[18] In consequence of this information, an additional party,
principally Waldeckers, were sent on under the command of colonel
Breyman. But before he could surmount the unavoidable impediments
of marching over bad and unfrequented roads, and reach the camp of
his friends and his countrymen, a body of militia commanded by
general Starks, had pressed forward, attacked, routed, and totally
defeated colonel Baum, in the neighbourhood of Bennington. General
Starks in his early youth, had been used to the alarm of war: his

CHAP. XI   birthplace was on the borders of New Hampshire, which had been
1 7 7 7   long subject to the incursions of the savages: when a child he was
captured by them, and adopted as one of their own, but after a few
years restored. He led a regiment to the field in one thousand seven
hundred and seventy-five, and distinguished himself as a soldier. On
the new arrangement of the army, he retired as a citizen. His manners
were plain, honest, and severe, excellently calculated for the benefit
of society in the private walks of life; but as a man of principle, he
again left the occupation of the husbandman, when his country was
in danger. On Burgoyne's approach, he voluntarily marched to the
state of Vermont, at the head of the militia, and immortalized his
name by his signal success at the Bennington, in one of the darkest
periods of the American war.

[19] Bennington, the present scene of action, was the first settlement
in the territory of Vermont, which was as recent as the year one
thousand seven hundred and sixty-nine. This was made by the
possessors of the tracts called the New Hampshire Grants, a robust
and hardy set of men, collected from the borders, and under the
jurisdiction, of the provinces of New Hampshire, Massachusetts,
Connecticut, and New York. Rough, bold, and independent, these
people, generally denominated the Green Mountain Boys, were brave
and active, not only in the present conflict, but were eminently useful
to their country by their intrepidity and valor, to the conclusion of
the American war.*

Governor Skeene, a singular character, who had been a colonel in
one of the king's regiments, had obtained a commission from the
crown, to act as governor at and about Lake Champlain, had assumed
a jurisdiction over the Hampshire Grants, and acted as companion
and guide to colonel Baum in the expedition. He fled on the first
appearance of danger, as did [20] the loyalists, the Canadian Provincials, and the Indians. Baum was wounded and taken prisoner, and
his whole corps captured by this small body of American militia.
Colonel Breyman, who arrived in the afternoon of the same day,
escaped a similar fate only by flight, after a short and brave defence,
and the loss of most of his men.

* General Burgoyne observed in a letter to lord George Germaine, "that the Hampshire
Grants, almost unknown in the last war, now abound in the most active and most
rebellious race on the continent, and hang like a gathering storm upon my left."
[Burgoyne to Germain, August 20, 1777 in Burgoyne, *Expedition*, "Appendix," pp.
xxiv–xxvi.]
See further particulars of the state of Vermont, Appendix, Note No. II.

This memorable event would perhaps at any other period, have CHAP. XI
appeared of less moment; but when so renowned a commander as 1 7 7 7
general Burgoyne, in the zenith of success and the pride of victory,
was threatening with the aid of his savage adherents, to execute all
the deeds of *horror* enjoined by his employers, a repulse from so
unexpected a quarter, was humiliating indeed: it gave a new turn to
the face of the campaign. The success at Bennington took place on
the sixteenth of August, one thousand seven hundred and seventy-
seven.

On the first rumor of this action through the country, the loyalists,
who in great numbers still resided among the opposers of royal
authority, affected every where to cast over it the shade of ridicule.
They alleged that the raw militia of Hampshire, and Starks their
commander, must have been too much awed by the name and prowess
of general Burgoyne, and his experienced veterans, to attempt any
thing of consequence: nor were [21] they convinced of the truth of
the report, until they saw the prisoners on their way to Boston. But
the people at large, who appeared to have been waiting with a kind
of enthusiastic expectation, for some fortunate event that might give
a spring to action, at once gave full credit to the account, and magnified
this success in strains of the highest exultation and defiance, and in
the warmth of imagination, anticipated new victories.

It is certain that from this moment, fortune seemed to have changed
her face. Whether the spirits of the British officers and troops flagged
in equal proportion, as the enthusiasm for glory and victory seemed
to rekindle in the bosoms of their antagonists, or whether general
Burgoyne was restricted by orders, that obligated him in some instances
to act against his own better informed judgment, his success terminated
with the capture of fort Edward.

By some of his letters written soon after this, to the minister of the
American department, the situation of the British army began to
appear to general Burgoyne exceedingly critical. He intimated his
apprehensions; and with an air of despondency, in one of them he
observed,

> that circumstances might require, that he and the army should be *devoted*;
> and that his orders were so peremptory, that he did not think himself
> authorised to call a council of [22] war, with regard to his present
> movements.*

* See general Burgoyne's own letters, in his defence and narrative. [Burgoyne to
Germain, October 20, 1777, in Burgoyne, *Expedition*, pp. xlvii–liii; "Narrative,"
p. 15.]

It was doubtless thought necessary at all hazards, to prevent the forces under general Gates, from being at leisure to join general Washington. It was also a favorite point with the ministry, that Burgoyne should push on to Albany. But however dubious the prospect might then appear to himself, or whatever might be his own expectations, general Burgoyne thought proper to pass the Hudson, and about the middle of September, he encamped on the heights and plains of Saratoga.

Supported by a number of brave, experienced, and most approved officers in British service, a large armament of British, Hessians, and provincials, with a prodigious train of artillery, and his copper-colored scouts and allies, he with all industry prepared to offer battle, and try the fortune of war in a general engagement. The Americans in equal readiness for action, marched from their camp on the nineteenth, and at a place called Stillwater, attacked the right wing of the British army, commanded by Burgoyne himself. Meeting a repulse, they turned their whole force to the left, commanded by the baron Redeisel, and supported by general Phillips, at the head of a formidable artillery. The Americans sustained the combat [23] for several hours, against officers of distinguished bravery, and more experience than themselves, who commanded some of the best troops the princes of Germany, or even the monarch of Britain could boast; but evening advancing, without decided advantage, the loss of men being nearly equal on both sides, the Americans retreated, and recovered their camp with little interruption.

The British troops lay on their arms through the night, and in the morning took an advantageous position, and spread themselves along a meadow, in full view, and almost within cannon-shot of the American camp. Here general Burgoyne received intelligence from sir Henry Clinton, that he had embarked for the North River, with several thousand troops, in order to make a diversion in his favor, that might greatly facilitate his operations. This account flattered the former expectations of Burgoyne; who judged that general Gates would be obligated to divide his army, to succour the distressed villages on each side the Hudson, now exposed to the most cruel ravages. Expectation was again raised, and the British army invigorated by fresh hopes, that a junction at Albany might soon be effected.

With these ideas, general Burgoyne found means to dispatch several messages by private ways, through the woods to general Clinton. [24] The purport of these was, "that if possible to remain unmolested, he should keep his present position a few days longer; when probably

the American army might be weakened by the necessity of detachments for other service." He was further strengthened in the ideas
of success, by a recent disappointment of the Americans in an attempt
to recover Ticonderoga. Had this enterprise succeeded, it would at
once effectually have prevented the retreat of the British army, which
began to be contemplated.

The business was principally committed to the direction of general
Lincoln, and prosecuted with vigor by the colonels Brown, Johnson,
Woodbury, and other spirited officers. They passed the mountains
between Skeensborough and Lake George, in so rapid and private a
manner, that before any intimation of the business was disseminated,
they seized the out-posts, captured the armed vessels and a number
of boats on the lake, and with four companies of foot and a party of
Canadians, they took possession of Mount Independence, and summoned the garrison in Ticonderoga to surrender. This was gallantly
refused, and the fortress bravely defended, by brigadier general
Powell. The Americans made several efforts to storm the garrison;
but repulsed with resolution and valor, they found themselves not in
force sufficient [25] for farther trial; and after a few days, they
relinquished the design, and retired.

Yet notwithstanding the rebuff and retreat from Ticonderoga, with
the advantages the British affected to claim from the action at
Stillwater, and the flattering encouragement received from sir Henry
Clinton, general Burgoyne was still involved in complicated difficulties.
The dangers he had to encounter, increased on every side. Fresh
troops of militia were continually reinforcing the army of his enemies;
while his own daily lessened by the desertion of the Canadian militia,
the provincial loyalists, and the defection of the Indians.

These last grew sullen from the disappointment of plunder, and
were irritated from the notice general Burgoyne was obliged in honor
to take, of the barbarous murder of a miss M'Crea; on which many
of them drew off in disgust. This beautiful young lady, dressed in
her bridal habiliments, in order to be married the same evening to an
officer of character in Burgoyne's own regiment, while her heart
glowed in expectation of a speedy union with the beloved object of
her affections, was induced to leave a house near fort Edward, with
the idea of being escorted to the present residence of her intended
husband, and was massacred [26] on the way, in all the cold-blooded
ferocity of savage manners. Her father had uniformly been a zealous
loyalist: but it was not always in the power of the most humane of

the British officers, to protect the innocent from the barbarity of their savage friends.

General Burgoyne was shocked by the tragic circumstances that attended the fate of this lovely, unfortunate girl; but he attempted to palliate the crime, though he did not neglect an endeavour to inflict due punishment on the perpetrators. Yet such was the temper of his Indian adherents, that instead of inflicting death, he was obliged to pardon the guilty chiefs, notwithstanding the cry of justice, and the grief and resentment of her lover.* The [27] best coloring that could be given the affecting tale was, that two of the principal warriors, under a pretence of guarding her person, had in a mad quarrel between themselves, which was best entitled to the prize, or to the honor of the escort, made the blooming beauty, shivering in the distress of innocence, youth, and despair, the victim of their fury. The helpless maid was butchered and scalped, and her bleeding corpse left in the woods, to excite the tear of every beholder.

In addition to the complicated embarrassments the British commander had to conflict, provisions grew short in the camp; he was obliged to lessen their rations, and put his soldiers on allowance. The most he could hope, as he observed himself in a letter to sir Henry Clinton, was to hold out to the twelfth of October, or effect a retreat before, in the best possible manner. The last expedient he soon found impracticable, by the precaution taken by general Gates, to guard all the passes, to cut off all supplies, and nearly to surround the British army. In this uncertain and distressed situation, general Burgoyne waited with all the anxiety of a faithful servant, and the caution and vigilance of an able commander, from the action on the nineteenth of September until the seventh of October, without any nearer prospect of a diversion in his favor. He then found it necessary to make a general movement, either [28] to decide the fate of his brave officers

---

* The earl of Harrington observed in evidence on Burgoyne's trial, that it was his opinion and that of other officers, that when general Burgoyne threatened the culprit with death, and insisted that he should be delivered up, that it might have been attended with dangerous consequences. Many gentlemen of the army besides himself believed, that motives of policy alone, prevented him from putting this threat in execution; and that if he had not pardoned the murderer, which he did, the total defection of the Indians would have ensued. He observed, that "the consequences on their return through Canada might have been dreadful: not to speak of the weight they would have thrown into the opposite scale, had they gone over to the enemy, which I rather imagine would have been the case."

and men in the field of battle, by a general engagement, or force a retreat.

General Gates equally prepared, either for attack or defence, a warm engagement ensued, which proved fatal to many of the best officers in the British line; but after a sharp conflict of several hours, and the highest exhibitions of military prowess, the British found it necessary to recover their camp before evening, which they did in some disorder. They had scarcely entered it when it was stormed on every side. Lord Balcarras with his light infantry, and a part of the British line, were ordered to throw themselves into the intrenchments, which they executed with spirit, and made a gallant and resolute defence. But the action led on by the ardent and undaunted Arnold, who acquitted himself with his usual intrepidity, was vigorously pushed in spite of the most valiant opposition, until almost in the moment of victory, Arnold was dangerously wounded, and his party obliged to retreat. The Americans were fortunate enough to carry the intrenchment of the German reserve, commanded by colonel Breyman, who was killed in the engagement. All the artillery and equipage of the brigade, and about two hundred officers and privates were captured.

[29] The engagement was continued through the whole of this fated day, which closed the scene of conflict and mortality on many brave men, and a number of officers of distinguished valor. The first in name who fell, was brigadier general Frazier.

> Before his death, general Frazier requested, that his body might be carried to his grave by the field-officers of his own corps, without any parade, and buried there. About sunset, the body was brought up the hill, attended only by the officers of his own family. They passed in view of the greatest part of both armies. Struck with the humility of the scene, some of the first officers of the army joined the procession, as it were from a natural propensity, to pay the last attention to his remains.
>
> The incessant cannonade during the solemnity; the steady attitude, and unaltered voice of the chaplain, though covered with the dust which the shot threw up on all sides; the mute, but expressive sensibility on every countenance; the growing duskiness of the evening, added to the scenery,— combined to mark a character, and to furnish the finest subject for the pencil of a master, that any field has exhibited.*

Colonel Breyman, and sir James Clark, aid-de-camp to general

---

* Extracted from a letter of general Burgoyne. [Burgoyne, *Expedition*, "Review of the Evidence," pp. 125–126; Burgoyne to Germain, October 20, 1777, "Appendix," p. l.

CHAP. XI Burgoyne, were also killed. [30] Major Ackland was dangerously
1 7 7 7 wounded, and taken prisoner. Lady Ackland, whose conjugal affection
had led her to accompany her husband through all the dangers and
fatigues of a campaign in the wilderness, was a woman of the most
delicate frame, of the genteelest manners, habituated to all the soft
elegancies, and refined enjoyments, that attend high birth and fortune.
Her sufferings exhibit a story so affecting to the mind of sensibility,
that it may apologize for a short interlude, in the most interesting
detail of military transactions.

She had accompanied major Ackland to Canada in one thousand
seven hundred and seventy-six. After which she traversed a vast
woody country, in the most extreme seasons, to visit her husband
sick in a poor hut at Chamblee. On the opening of the campaign of
one thousand seven hundred and seventy-seven, the positive injunc-
tion of her husband, prevented her risking the hazards expected
before Ticonderoga. There major Ackland was badly wounded, on
which she crossed the Champlain to attend him. She followed his
fortune and shared his fatigues, through the dreary way to fort Edward,
there lodged in a miserable tent, which by accident took fire by night,
when both major Ackland and herself were saved by an orderly
serjeant, who dragged them from the flames almost before they
awaked.

[31] Lady Ackland lost not her resolution or her cheerfulness by
the dangers she had encountered; but accompanied her soldier to the
action on the nineteenth of September. By his order, she had followed
the route of the artillery and baggage, where she would be least
exposed, until she alighted at a small uninhabited tent, which, when
the action became general, the surgeons took possession of to dress
their wounded.

Thus, within hearing of the roar of cannon, when she knew the
situation of her beloved husband was in the most exposed part of the
action, she waited some hours in a situation, and in apprehensions
not easily described. The baroness of Reidesel, and the wives of the
majors Harnage and Reynal were with her; but she derived little
comfort from their presence. Major Harnage was soon brought into
the tent dangerously wounded, accompanied with the tidings of the
death of the husband of Mrs. Reynal. Let imagination paint the
misery of this little group of distressed females. Here among the
wounded and the dying, lady Ackland with her usual serenity, stood
prepared for new trials, until the fatal seventh of October, when her
fortitude was put to the severest test, by the intelligence that the

British army was defeated, and that major Ackland was desperately chap. xi
wounded, and taken prisoner. Not [32] borne down by grief or anxiety, 1 7 7 7
she the next day requested leave to attend the wounded prisoner, to
the last moment of his life.

General Burgoyne, from whose narrative some circumstances of
lady Ackland's story are selected, observes,

> that though he had experienced, that patience and fortitude in a supreme
> degree, were to be found, as well as every other virtue, under the most
> tender forms, he was astonished at this proposal. After so long an exposure
> and agitation of the spirits, exhausted not only for want of rest, but
> absolutely for want of food, drenched in rain for twelve hours together,
> that a woman should be capable of delivering herself to the enemy,
> probably in the night, and uncertain what hands she should fall into,
> appeared an effort above human nature.

He adds, "he had not a cup of wine to offer her: all with which the
hapless lady could be furnished, was a little rum and dirty water, an
open boat, and a few lines to general Gates."

Thus this lady left the British lines, attended only by Mr. Brudenell,
chaplain to the artillery, the major's valet-de-chambre, and one female
servant. She was rowed down the river to meet the enemy, when her
distresses thickened anew. The night advanced before she met the
out-posts: the centinel would neither let the boat pass, nor the
passengers come on [33] shore, notwithstanding the singular state of
this heroic lady was pathetically represented by Mr. Brudenell:
apprehensive of treachery, the centinel threatened to fire into the
boat, if they attempted to stir until the appearance of day. Thus,
through a dark and cold night, far advanced in a state that always
requires peculiar tenderness to the sex, with a heart full of anxiety
for her wounded husband, she was obliged to submit, and in this
perilous situation, to reflect until the dawn of the morning, on her
own wretched condition, and the uncertainty of what reception she
should meet from strangers in hostile array, flushed with victory, and
eager to complete the triumph of the preceding day.

When general Gates in the morning was made acquainted with the
situation and request of lady Ackland, she was immediately permitted
to visit her husband, under a safe escort. The American commander
himself treated her with the tenderness of a parent, and gave orders
that every attention should be paid due to her rank, her sex, her
character, and the delicacy of her person and circumstances.* He

* Appendix, Note No. III.

CHAP. XI wrote general Burgoyne, and assured him of her safety and accom-
1 7 7 7 modation, [34] and informed him that this line of conduct would have
been observed, without a letter from the British commander, not only
to this lady, but to others of his unfortunate friends, languishing under
their wounds; that the American commanders needed not a *request*,
to excite their humanity to the unfortunate, who by the chances of
war, had been thrown on their compassion. In the same letter he
reminded general Burgoyne,

> that the cruelties which marked the late effort for the retreat of his army,
> were almost without a precedent among civilized nations; and that an
> *endeavour* to *ruin*, where they could not conquer, betrayed more the
> vindictive spirit of the *monk*, than the generosity of the soldier.*

Notwithstanding the misfortunes and the losses of the preceding
day, general Burgoyne did not yet totally despair of retrieving his
affairs and his honor, by another general engagement. This he
endeavoured to effect on the eighth, and in this he was again
disappointed. The utmost bravery was exhibited on both sides, but
no decided action. Several days passed on in desultory skirmishes:
spirit and intrepidity were not wanting on either side; while the one
had every thing to hope and inspirit [35] them, the other, nothing
left but a choice of insurmountable difficulties.

In this situation, the British commander judged the best expedient
was, a second effort to repass the Hudson, and retreat to fort Edward.
To this every impediment was thrown in his way. A retreat was
rendered impracticable, by the number and vigilance of the Americans:
the borders of the river were lined with troops; and detachments
pushed forward to cut off all hope of retreat on every side. The
condition of the British army grew hourly more desperate: winter was
approaching, their provisions spent, the troops exhausted by continual
fatigue; and not the smallest prospect of relief appeared from any
quarter.

In this deplorable situation, general Burgoyne summoned a grand
council of war, in which, as he stood in need of every advice, not
only the field-officers, but the subalterns had a voice. It was unanimously judged most prudent, in the humiliated and hopeless condition
to which they were reduced, to open a treaty of convention, and

---

* General Gates's letter to general Burgoyne, October 10, 1777. [Horatio Gates to
John Burgoyne, October 10, 1777, in Gates Papers, New York Historical Society,
reel 5: 1032. See Burgoyne, *Expedition*, "Review of the Evidence," pp. 127–129.]

endeavour to obtain some honorable terms of surrender. General CHAP. XI
Gates was acknowledged by all, not only the valiant, but the humane 1 7 7 7
and generous foe: they had no doubt he would mitigate their
mortification, as far as the laws of war or of honor would permit, from
the victor to the vanquished.

[36] In consequence of this determination, the solemn negociation
took place on the thirteenth of October. General Burgoyne intimated
to the American commander, that he wished to send a field-officer to
him, to confer on matters of the highest moment, and requested to
know when he might be received. General Gates really possessed
that humanity, which distinguishes the hero from the assassinator of
the feelings of wounded honor. He seemed touched by the request,
with that sympathy which ever resides in the bosom of generosity;
and replied instantly, that an officer from general Burgoyne should
be received at the advanced post of the army of the United States,
at ten o'clock the next morning.

Major Kingston was accordingly sent at the appointed time, and
was conducted to the headquarters of the American army. The purport
of the message was, that lieutenant general Burgoyne, having twice
fought general Gates, had determined on a third conflict; but well
apprised of the superiority of numbers, and the disposition of the
American troops, he was convinced, that either a battle or a retreat,
would be a scene of carnage on both sides. In this situation he was
impelled by humanity, and thought himself justified by established
principles of states and of war, to spare the lives of brave men, upon
honorable terms. Should general Gates be inclined to treat upon those
ideas, general Burgoyne would propose a cessation [37] of arms,
during the time necessary to settle such preliminaries, as he could
abide by in any extremity.

A convention was immediately opened. A discussion of some articles
proposed by the American commander, which appeared to the British
officers inadmissible, occasioned a delay of two or three days: these
being accommodated, a treaty of surrender was signed the seventeenth
of October, one thousand seven hundred and seventy-seven. The
substance of the treaty was,

That the troops under the command of general Burgoyne, should
march out of their camp with the honors of war, and the artillery of
the intrenchment, to the verge of a certain river, where the arms and
the artillery should be piled at the command of one of their own
officers:

That a free passage should be provided for the army to return to England, on condition that they should not serve again in America, during the present contest: that transports should enter the port of Boston for their reception, whenever general Howe should think proper to request it: and that they should be quartered near Boston, that no delay might take place, when an order for embarkation arrived:

[38] That the Canadians of every description, should be permitted to return immediately, on the sole condition of their not again arming against the United States:

That the army under general Burgoyne should march to the Massachusetts by the nearest route: they should be supplied with provisions, both on their route and in quarters, at the same rate of rations, by order of general Gates, as that of his own army;

That the officers should wear their side arms, and be lodged according to their rank; nor at any time be prevented assembling their own troops, according to the usual military regulations:

That passports should be granted to such officers as general Burgoyne should appoint, immediately to carry dispatches to sir William Howe, to general Carleton, and to England by the way of New York: and that general Gates should engage on the public faith, that none of the dispatches should be opened.

After the second article it was stipulated, that if a cartel should take place, by which the army under general Burgoyne, or any part of it, might be exchanged, the second article should be void, as far as such exchange should be made.

[39] These and several other circumstances of less moment agreed to, the convention was signed with much solemnity.

After the negociation was finished and completed, by the mutual signature of the officers, general Gates conducted not only as an officer of bravery, punctuality, and a nice sense of military honor, but with the fine feelings of humanity, and the delicacy of the gentleman. He carried these ideas so far, as to restrain the curiosity and pride of his own army, by keeping them within their lines, while the British were piling their arms. He did not suffer a man among them, to be a near witness to the humiliating sight, of a haughty and once powerful foe, disarming and divesting themselves of the *insignia* of military distinction, and laying them at the feet of the conqueror.

Thus, to the consternation of Britain, to the universal joy of America, and to the gratification of all capable of feeling that dignity of sentiment, that leads the mind to rejoice in the prospect of liberty

to their fellow-men, was the northern expedition finished. A reverse <small>CHAP. XI</small>
of fortune was now beheld, that had not fallen under the calculation <small>1 7 7 7</small>
of either party.

It is more easy to conjecture, than agreeable to describe, the chagrin
of a proud, assuming foe, who had imperiously threatened to penetrate
[40] and lay waste cities and provinces, thus humbled by the arms of
a people they had affected to hold in the utmost contempt, and their
laurels thus faded beneath the sword of the victorious Americans.

It was a tale without example in British annals, that so many
thousands* of their best troops, in conjunction with a large body of
German auxiliaries, commanded by generals and field-officers of the
first character, accompanied by many young gentlemen of noble family
and military talents, should be thus reduced, mortified, and led
captive, through a long extent of country, where they had flattered
themselves they should parade in triumph. They were obliged before
they reached their destined quarters, to traverse the pleasant grounds,
pass through many flourishing towns, and growing settlements, where
they had expected to plant the standard of royalty, in all the cruel
insolence of victory, to the utter extermination of every republican
principle.

The British army, with general Burgoyne at their head, was escorted
from the plains of Saratoga, to their quarters at Cambridge, about
three hundred miles, by two or three American [41] field-officers, and
a handful of soldiers, as a guard. The march was solemn, sullen, and
silent; but they were every where treated with such humanity, and
even delicacy, that themselves acknowledged, the civil deportment
of the inhabitants of the country, was without a parallel. They thought
it remarkable, that not an insult was offered, nor an opprobrious
reflection cast, that could enhance the misery of the unfortunate, or
wound the feelings of degraded honor. Yet they were destined to a
long captivity, from various circumstances that arose, relative to the
punctual observance of some of the articles of the treaty of convention,
which will be noticed in their place.

As soon as general Gates had finished the campaign of Saratoga,
which terminated with so much *eclat* to himself, and so much glory
to the arms of his country, he wrote a spirited letter to general
Vaughan, who had been for some months ravaging, plundering, and

---

* Five thousand seven hundred and fifty-two men surrendered, exclusive of Canadians.
Two thousand nine hundred and thirty-three had been previously slain.

CHAP. XI burning, with unparalleled barbarity, the settlements on the North
1 7 7 7 River. He informed him, that

> notwithstanding he had reduced the fine village of Kingston to ashes, and
> its inhabitants to ruin; that though he still continued to ravage and burn
> all before him, on both sides of the river; these instances of unexampled
> cruelty, but established the glorious act of [42] independence, on the broad
> basis of the general resentment of the people.

He added,

> and is it thus, sir, your king's generals think to make converts to the royal
> cause? It is no less surprising than true, the measures they adopt to serve
> their master, have the quite contrary effect. Abler generals, and much
> more experienced officers than you can pretend to be, are by the fortune
> of war now in my hands. This fortune may one day be your's; when it
> may not be in the power of any thing human, to save you from the just
> resentment of an injured people.*

After this letter, general Gates stayed only to make the necessary
arrangements, and immediately moved on to the relief of the sufferers
in that quarter. On the approach of the renowned conqueror of
Burgoyne, the marauding parties under general Vaughan, Wallace,
and governor Tryon, all retired to New York, there to give an account
to administration, of their barbarous exploits against the defenceless
villages.

General Clinton with three thousand troops, in conjunction with
commodore Hotham, had entered the Hudson in the beginning of
October. At a great expense of men on both sides, [43] they took
possession of Stoney Point, Verplanks, and the forts Montgomery and
Clinton.

The posts on the Hudson were defended by officers of dexterity
and skill. Governor Clinton of New York, a gentleman distinguished
for his patriotism, military talents, and unshaken firmness in the cause
of his country, commanded the forts Clinton and Montgomery. General
Putnam, an experienced and meritorious officer, was stationed lower
down the river. But though the works were strong, and defended
with courage and ability, by the American officers, they were overpowered by the number of the enemy, and obliged to retreat with

---

* General Gates's letter, published in British Remembrancer. [Gates to Major General
Vaughan, October 19, 1777, *Remembrancer* (1778), p. 58. See *Annual Register* (1777),
"History of Europe," p. 175.]

precipitation. After the storming of the forts Clinton and Montgomery, many of the soldiers, and some officers were made prisoners. The retreat of those who escaped, was effected with difficulty: governor Clinton himself had time only to escape by crossing the river in a boat.

The count Grabouski, a Polish nobleman, a volunteer in the British army, fell in the storm of the forts, as did major Sill, and several other officers of much military merit. General Clinton had laid waste the borders, dismantled the forts, burnt most of the houses, and spread terror and devastation on both sides of the Hudson. General Vaughan was left to finish the business. In one of his letters transmitted to [44] England by lord viscount Howe, he boasts that "he had not left one house, in the flourishing and industrious town of Esopus;" and offers no other reason for reducing it to ashes, but that "the inhabitants had the temerity to fire from their houses, on his advance" to rob them of liberty, property, and life. This is a mode of making war, that the politeness and civilization of modern Europe has generally agreed to criminate, though still practiced by many inhuman conquerors: but it was revived and adopted in the American system, with all the ferocity that stimulated the ancient barbarians, to sink in conflagration the Italian cities.

These instances of severity were not singular: the same mad fury was exercised in almost every place, where the strength and power of Britain obtained the advantage. This became the source of perpetual jealousies, and destroyed all confidence between Britons and Americans, even in the faith of treaties. Thus, some intimations from general Burgoyne while at Cambridge, that the terms of convention were not fully complied with on the part of America, and some equivocal conduct with regard to the embarkation of the troops, raised a suspicion, that the British officers intended to evade their engagement, and transport the captured army to New York, instead of [45] conveying them directly to England, as stipulated.

This was grounded on a proposal, that the convention troops should march to Newport, and there embark. This occasioned a resolve of congress, "that the troops should remain in their quarters at Cambridge, until an explicit ratification of the convention of Saratoga, should be properly notified to congress by the court of Great Britain." This was heavily complained of by general Burgoyne and his officers, who said that this step was sinking the dignity, and a breach of faith in that respected body. Political casuistry frequently palliates the deviations

CHAP. XI from rectitude in public bodies. Sound policy might justify the
1 7 7 7 measure, but it is yet doubtful whether there was sufficient reason to
believe, that Burgoyne meant to break his engagements, and throw
his troops into New York, to be immediately again employed against
the United States.

New causes arose to enhance the difficulties of their exchange, or
their return to their native country. Thus this idle and dissipated
army lay too long in the neighbourhood of Boston, for the advantage
of either side. While there in durance, they disseminated their
manners; they corrupted the students of Harvard college, and the
youth of the capital and its environs, who were allured to enter into
their [46] gambling parties, and other scenes of licentiousness. They
became acquainted with the designs, the resources, and the weaknesses of America; and there were many among them, whose talents
and capacity rendered them capable of making the most mischievous
use of their knowledge. After long altercations between general Phillips
and general Heath, who commanded in that quarter, relative to the
disorders that took place among the soldiery of both parties, and
mutual charges of breaches of the articles of convention, congress
directed that the British troops should march to Charlotteville in
Virginia. They accordingly left Cambridge November the tenth, one
thousand seven hundred and seventy-eight.

General Burgoyne had early requested leave to repair to England
on parole, pleading the broken state of his health, the deranged
situation of his private affairs, and the hazard of character, if not
present to defend himself on the tidings of his defeat. He was
permitted by congress to depart, and arrived in England in May, one
thousand seven hundred and seventy-eight. But he met a very
ungracious reception both from the people, the ministry, and his king.
Notwithstanding his abilities to serve, and his fidelity to his master,
he was refused an audience by majesty, a court of inquiry, or a court-
martial, and for some time a hearing in the house of commons.

[47] He had left England in the sanguine expectation of carrying
conquest before him, wherever he appeared, of subduing the Americans, and restoring tranquility to the revolted colonies; he had returned
on parole by the favor of that authority he had ever despised, and
left his army in the hands of his enemies. The debates in parliament
on the occasion, were warm and interesting. Some law-officers of the
crown insisted, that as a prisoner, he was bound by his first engagements: they said, to talk of a trial without the power to punish, was
a farce. It was urged,

that as a prisoner, he was not capable of acting in his personal capacity;
and that under his present obligations, he was totally incapacitated for the
exercise of any civil office, incompetent to any civil function, and incapable
of bearing arms in his country.*

Thus was the haughty Burgoyne affronted and mortified, after long
and faithful services to his king and country. He was ordered
immediately to repair to America as a prisoner, according to his
engagements; but as the ill state of his health prevented his compliance,
he was persecuted until he resigned all his employments under the
crown.

[48] After some time had elapsed, general Burgoyne was permitted
the opportunity of speaking for himself in the house of commons,
where he defended his own reputation and cause with ability and
spirit. In the course of his argument, he cast many severe censures
on the ministry; and did not scruple to pronounce them totally
incapable of supporting the weight of public affairs in the present
dangerous and critical emergency, into which they had brought the
nation. Nor was he without many powerful advocates, who both
ridiculed and reprobated the severity with which he was treated.
Strong intimations had been suggested, both within and without doors,
that it might be thought expedient, that the general should be
sacrificed, to save the reputation of the minister. Several expressions
of his previous to his capture, intimated his own apprehensions. In a
letter to the secretary of state he said, "my confidence is still placed
in the justice of the king and his council, to support the general they
had thought proper to appoint, to as arduous an undertaking, and
under as positive directions, as a cabinet ever signed." In the same
letter, he gave his opinion of the number and discipline of the
American troops, and the many difficulties he had to encounter,
without the liberty of acting at discretion.

General Burgoyne observed himself, with regard to American
bravery, when speaking of [49] the action of the nineteenth of
September,

few actions have been characterized by more obstinacy in attack or defence.
The British bayonet was repeatedly tried ineffectually. Eleven hundred
British soldiers, foiled in these trials, bore incessant fire from a succession

* Parliamentary debates. [See, *Cobbett*, XIX: 1176–1199, for debates on Mr. Vyner's
motion to inquire into Burgoyne's conduct and the Saratoga Convention (May 26,
1778). Also see Burgoyne, *Expedition*, "Evidence and Testimony." The quoted
statements do not appear, though very similar sentiments are recorded.]

of fresh troops, in superior numbers, for above four hours; and after a loss of about a third of their numbers, (and in one of the regiments above two-thirds,) forced the enemy at last. Of a detachment of a captain and forty-eight artillery-men, the captain and thirty-six men were killed or wounded. These facts are marked by a concurrence of evidence, that no man can dispute. The tribute of praise due to such troops, will not be wanting in this generous nation; and it will certainly be accompanied with a just portion of shame to those who have dared to depreciate or sully valor so conspicuous; who have their ears open only to the prejudice of American cowardice, and having been always loud upon that courtly topic, stifle the glory of their countrymen, to maintain a safe consistency.

He also adds, with regard to the action of the seventh of October,

if there can be any persons, who, after considering the circumstances of this day, continue to doubt, that the Americans possess the *quality* and *faculty* of fighting, (call it by whatever name they [50] please,) they are of a prejudice that it would be very absurd longer to contend with.

But no hazard or fatigue, bravery or misfortune, was thought a sufficient apology for the loss of his army.

The northern expedition had been a favorite object with the British administration. They were sanguine enough to suppose, and the nation was led to believe, that success in that quarter would reduce the turbulent spirits of Americans so low, as to prevent further energy of opposition, and bring the whole country to a due sense of subordination, and unconditional submission to the authority of parliament. The low ebb of American affairs at the southward, previous to the success of general Gates, gave some reasonable grounds for such an expectation. It is not strange that a disappointment in this object, which was calculated, if successful, to redound much to the glory of the British arms, should be equally mortifying to the pride of the ministry, and the high-spirited people of England, or that it threw the parliament and the nation into a ferment, that did not easily subside. Many gentlemen of distinguished talents, did honor to the feelings of the heart, and the sagacity of their understanding, while it was a subject of parliamentary debate, by their humane, sensible, and judicious speeches, interspersed with pointed wit, and brilliancy of sentiment.

[51] The conquest and capture of general Burgoyne, and the British army under his command, was undoubtedly the most fortunate circumstance for the United States, that had yet taken place. It was the most capital and eventful military transaction, from the com-

mencement to the close of the American war. The termination of this
expedition, opened new views to the philosopher, the politician, and
the hero, both at home and abroad. It disseminated a spirit, and
produced effects throughout America, which had been neither anticipated or calculated, until her sons paraded in the style of the
conqueror, before the humiliated bands of veteran British and German
prisoners.

So many thousands of brave men and distinguished officers, led
captive through the wilderness, the plains, and the cities of the United
States, was a spectacle never before beheld by the inhabitants; and
the impression it made on their minds, was in proportion to the
novelty of the scene, and the magnitude of its consequences. It was
viewed as a prelude to events of the highest moment, both to the
arms and to the future negociations of the United States. British
battalions were no longer deemed invulnerable, even by the most
timid and uninformed sons of America. That formidable power which
had spread dismay through the colonies, they now beheld as the
object of curiosity, and [52] her armies were viewed more in the light
of compassion than of terror.

Nor were the troops of the United States longer considered as a
mere undisciplined rabble, either by the parliament or the people of
England. Their armies began to appear formidable; and conciliation
was pressed from very respectable characters. From the moment of
their recent victory, the United States were beheld in a still more
honorable light by the other European powers. Most of them had yet
stood undecided and wavering: none of them seemed determined on
which side to declare, or whether to look coolly on, as uninterested
spectators, until Great Britain had sufficiently chastised her rebellious
children. It is true some loans of money had been obtained from
France previous to this period, and the sale of prizes had been
permitted in the Gallic ports; but this appeared to be more in
consequence of the benevolence and the enthusiasm of the people,
than the result of any governmental system to aid America *effectually*,
in her struggle for freedom and independence.

The consequences of the brilliant success of general Gates, the
influence of this event on the opinion of foreign nations, its operation
on the councils of Britain, its effects on the policy of several European
courts, and its important consequences throughout America, will be
[53] related concisely in the subsequent part of these annals.

But it is proper before we conclude the present chapter, to detail

CHAP. XI a few other circumstances relative to general Burgoyne. After some
1 7 7 7 time had elapsed, and the agitation of parties so far cooled, as to
permit him the public defence of his character, he gave an affecting
epitome of his feelings, his difficulties and embarrassments in the
northern expedition. He observed,

> the remembrance of what I personally underwent cannot easily be sup-
> pressed: and I am sure I shall not outgo the indulgence of the candid, if
> in delineating situations so affecting, I add feelings to justification. The
> defence of military conduct is an interesting point of professional honor;
> but to vindicate the heart, is a duty to God and to society at large.
>
> Few conjunctures in the campaign I have been describing, few perhaps
> upon military record, can be found so distinguished by exigencies, or
> productive of such critical and anxious calls upon public character and
> private affection, as that which now took place.
>
> In the first place, the position of the army was untenable; and yet an
> immediate retreat was impossible, not only from the fatigue of [54] the
> troops, but from the necessity of delivering fresh ammunition and provi-
> sions.
>
> The losses in the action were uncommonly severe. Sir Francis Clarke,
> my aid-de-camp, had originally recommended himself to my attention, by
> his talents and diligence. As service and intimacy opened his character
> more, he became endeared to me by every quality that can create esteem.
> I lost in him an useful assistant, an amiable companion, an attached friend:
> the state was deprived by his death, of one of the fairest promises of an
> able general.
>
> The fate of colonel Ackland, taken prisoner, and then supposed to be
> mortally wounded, was a second source of anxiety. General Frazier was
> expiring.
>
> In the course of the action, a shot had passed through my hat, and
> another had torn my waistcoat. I should be sorry to be thought at any
> time, insensible to the protecting hand of Providence: but I ever more
> particularly considered, (and I hope not superstitiously,) a soldier's hair-
> breadth escapes as incentives to duty, a marked renewal of the trust of
> being, for the due purposes of a public station; and under that reflection,
> to lose our fortitude by giving way to our affections, to be diverted by any
> possible self-emotion, from [55] meeting a present exigency with our best
> faculties, were at once dishonor and impiety.*

Perhaps no general officer ever experienced a greater variety of
untoward circumstances, than general Burgoyne before the convention,

---

* Burgoyne's defence. [Burgoyne, *Expedition*, "Review of the Evidence," pp. 124–
125.]

and the surrender of his army to the victorious Americans. It requires CHAP. XI
a lively imagination, to comprehend a full view of the difficulty of 1 7 7 7
marching an army, composed of heterogeneous materials, from Quebec
to Saratoga, to traverse a forlorn wilderness, pathless thickets and
swamps, extensive sheets of water, and navigable lakes defended by
a resolute enemy, covered by strong works, that cost the waste of
many of his troops to overcome.

It is true his German allies were brave, and the usual valor of British
troops needs no encomium; but the Canadians and the loyalists could
not be depended upon, and the hordes of savages that joined his
train, were more the objects of terror than assistance, even to the
masters under whom they had enlisted. They pillaged, plundered,
threatened, and occasionally murdered their friends, and when the
cause grew desperate, retreated in tribes to take shelter in their distant
forests.

[56] Of the loyalists, general Burgoyne thus observes:

Many of them had taken refuge in Canada the preceding winter, and
others had joined us as we advanced. The various interests which influenced
their actions, rendered all arrangement of them impracticable. One man's
views went to the profit he was to enjoy when his corps should be complete;
another, to the protection of the district in which he resided; a third was
wholly intent upon revenge against his personal enemies; and all of them
were repugnant even to an idea of subordination. Hence, the settlement
who should act as a private man, and who as an officer, or in whose corps
either should be, was seldom satisfactorily made among themselves; and
as surely as it failed, succeeded a reference to the commander in chief,
which could not be put by, or delegated to another hand, without
dissatisfaction, increase of confusion, and generally a loss of such services
as they were really fit for; viz. searching for cattle, ascertaining the
practicability of routes, clearing roads, and guiding detachments or columns
upon the march.

He further observed, that

the interests and the passions of the revolted Americans, concenter in the
cause of the congress, and those of the loyalists break and subdivide into
various pursuits, with which the cause of the king has little or nothing to
do.

[57] From these and other circumstances above detailed, even 1 7 7 8
prejudice itself ought to allow a due share of praise to general
Burgoyne, for maintaining his resolution and perseverance so long,

CHAP. XI rather than to wound his character by censure, either as a soldier, a
1 7 7 8 man of honor and humanity, or a faithful servant to his king.

But talents, valor, or virtue, are seldom a security against the vindictive spirit of party, or the resentment that results from the failure of favorite political projects. Thus, though the military abilities of general Burgoyne had been conspicuous, and his services acknowledged by his country, yet from the mortification of the monarch, the court, and the people of England, on the disgrace of their arms at Saratoga, he was not only suffered, but obliged to retire.

Though the marked resentment of administration was long kept up against this unfortunate officer, he did not spend all the remainder of his days in private and literary pursuits. It is true he never again acted in a military capacity; but time relieved the present oppression, when he again took his seat in parliament, and with manly eloquence, not only defended the rights and liberties of his native isle, against the arbitrary systems in vogue, but asserted the justice and propriety of American opposition. [58] This he did with becoming dignity, and an impartiality which he never might have felt, but from the failure of his northern expedition. The reputation the American arms acquired by this defeat, not only humbled the proud tone of many British officers besides general Burgoyne, but did much to hasten the alliance with France, and brought forward events that accelerated the independence of America.

CHAPTER XII

Observations on the Conduct of the British Parliament, previous to the Capture of Burgoyne • The ineffectual Efforts of the Commissioners sent to America, in consequence of Lord North's Conciliatory Bill—Their Attempts to corrupt Individuals and Public Bodies • Negociation broken off • Manifesto published by the Commissioners • Counter Declaration by Congress • Sir William Howe repairs to England

[59] While America gloried in her recent success against the northern CHAP. XII army, and was making all possible preparations for vigorous action at 1 7 7 8 the southward, the coercive system in Britain was so far from being relaxed, that the most severe measures were urged with bitterness and acrimony. The speeches of the king were in the same tone of despotism as formerly: the addresses of parliament were in the usual style of compliment and applause; as if they had little else to do, but to keep each other in good humor, until alienation was complete, and the colonies so far connected with other powers, that there could be no hope of reconciliation.

But though a unison of sentiment, and a perfect conformity to the royal will, previous to [60] the news of Burgoyne's defeat, appeared in the majority of both houses of parliament, yet the measures of the ministry were, as usual, warmly opposed by some gentlemen of the first abilities in the nation. Several of the principal nobility were in the minority, and urged an accommodation before America should be irretrievably lost. It was recommended to the minister, "rather to forge bands of amity for the minds, than chains for the bodies of Americans." The present moment of uncertainty with regard to success, was urged as the proper season for giving the most unequivocal proofs of cordiality, by requesting his majesty to order a cessation of hostilities, and the immediate adoption of measures for accommodation.*

* Debates in parliament, before the news of the termination of the northern campaign reached England. [See *Cobbett*, XIX: 1176–1199.]

CHAP. XII   Mr. Fox, whose powers of oratory were the admiration of the world,
1 7 7 8 not only reasoned against their measures, but ridiculed the ministry
in the most pointed manner, for their ignorance of America from the
outset of the controversy. He alleged, "that they had mistaken the
extent of the thirteen colonies, and considered the Massachusetts as
including the whole." Nor were they less mistaken in the weight of
opposition they had to encounter. He observed,

> they had ever been blind to the consequences of their own measures, or
> they [61] never would have rejected the most dutiful and loyal petitions;
> more especially that presented by Mr. Penn, late governor of Pennsylvania,
> even after the battles of Lexington and Bunker Hill.*

He expatiated on the absurdity and injustice of the bill for transporting
Americans to England for trial, the Quebec act, the restraining bill,
the declaratory act, and the Boston port bill.

All papers relative to America for three years past, were ordered to
be laid before the house; and the state of the army, and the
expenditures in the course of the war, loudly called for. But amidst
the severe scrutiny of the house, the anxiety of the nation, the
perseverance of the king, and the perplexity of the minister, all parties
were thunderstruck by the arrival of the intelligence of Burgoyne's
defeat, and the capture of the army at Saratoga.

A general gloom overspread every countenance: the severest censures were cast on the late measures of administration; indignation
burnt in the bosoms of those who opposed them: clamor raged without
doors; asperity, sarcasm, and reproach, from the lip of truth within:
and, notwithstanding his abilities and his firmness, the minister was
distressed, the minority [62] increased, and opposition was strengthened.

Lord Chatham rose with his usual energy, eloquence, and commanding spirit, and reprobated both the war and the mode of
prosecuting it; and with vehemence and acrimony asserted,

> that a court system of wickedness had been adopted for the last fifteen
> years, subversive of all faith and confidence, tending to extinguish all
> principle in the different orders of the community; and that an ascendency
> had been obtained by worthless men, the dregs of party, where no influence
> ought to exist. That a spirit of delusion had gone forth, the people had
> been deceived by ministers, and parliament had sanctioned the deception.
> False lights had been held out to the country gentlemen, imposed on by

* Appendix, Note No. IV.

the ideal project of an American revenue; but that the visionary phantom, CHAP. XII
conjured up for the basest purposes of deception, was about to vanish.   1 7 7 8

The minister,* though attacked, mortified, and embarrassed, retreated with ability and address from ground to ground, through the
debates, and endeavoured to shift the blame from himself, and cast
the failure of the system, and the odium of disappointment, on the
want of [63] capacity in the officers employed. He manifested his
regret for the unhappy differences between the two countries, in
passionate expressions, and urged, that the conciliatory plan he had
proposed some time before, might be immediately adopted; and that
commissioners should be sent to America, with powers to restore
tranquility, without further delay. He acknowledged that he began
to despair of reducing the colonies by arms, unless a disunion could
be effected, and the intervention of foreign powers in their behalf,
decidedly prevented.

But the people in several counties were so infatuated by the popular
theme of an American revenue, that subscriptions were opened in
London, Bristol, and other places, for raising and supporting a body
of troops at private expense, to supply the deficiencies in the army
by the convention of Saratoga. The legality of this measure was
contested in both houses of parliament; and a resolve was proposed
by the earl of Abingdon,

> that granting monies for private uses, and without the sanction of parliament,
> was against both the letter and the spirit of the constitution: that obtaining
> money by subscription, and applying it to his majesty's use, in such manner
> as he should think fit, was unconstitutional, and a direct infringement of
> the principles of the British constitution.

But the measure was not discountenanced [64] by authority, and the
subscriptions went on.

If not first suggested by them, these subscriptions were encouraged
by some of the most affluent of the American refugees, who had
repaired to England on the retreat of general Howe from Boston.
This appearance of settled rancor against their native country increased
the resentment of their countrymen; and in consequence thereof,
some of their estates, which had been only sequestered, were
confiscated and sold, and the monies arising therefrom deposited in
the public treasury. But many of this class of people, who laid their

* Lord North.

CHAP. XII real or pretended sufferings before administration, were afterwards
1 7 7 8 amply provided for by the liberality of the British government, though
not adequate to their own expectations.

All Europe had beheld with astonishment and applause, the
exertions and the struggles of the American colonies, against the
opulence, the arms, and the intrigues of Britain. It was now three
years that they had with uncommon resolution, and systematical
decision, supported their armaments by sea and land, without a single
ally.

The American congress had indeed, as early as the beginning of
the autumn, one thousand seven hundred and seventy-six, appointed
commercial [65] agents to several European courts, empowering them
to procure arms, ammunition, and clothing, on the credit of the
United States. They were received politely by the nation, though not
publicly countenanced by the court of France, on their first arrival.
Yet their negociations had been favorable to trade, and to the
condemnation of a vast number of prizes, that had been taken by the
Americans and sent into the several ports of France.

Doctor Franklin was soon after empowered to act as an American
plenipotentiary there, and arrived in France, December, one thousand
seven hundred and seventy-six. The celebrity of his character, and
the popularity of his mission, insured him the warmest reception from
all ranks; and the minister* gave him private encouragement to hope
for all necessary aid, and a full completion of the wishes of his
constituents. The Spanish ambassador likewise, at this time requested
copies of his instructions, and a sketch of the state of America, which
he forwarded to his catholic majesty, as the two courts were determined
to act in perfect unison, although no national compact was completed
between France and America, until early [66] in the year one thousand
seven hundred and seventy-eight.†

It required time to ripen a measure in a despotic court, to support
a struggle like the present; a struggle unparalleled in modern nations.

---

* The count de Vergennes.

† See doctor Franklin's letter to congress, March, one thousand seven hundred and
seventy-eight. [Franklin wrote several letters to Congress in March 1778, none of
which discusses precisely what Warren addresses here. See LDC, 9; Albert Henry
Smith, ed., *The Writings of Benjamin Franklin* (10 vols.; New York, 1905–1907);
Francis Wharton, ed., *The Revolutionary Diplomatic Correspondence of the United States*
(6 vols.; Washington, 1889); Jared Sparks, ed., *The Diplomatic Correspondence of the
American Revolution* (6 vols.; Washington, 1857).]

An effort for the liberties of mankind, by colonial opposition to the CHAP. XII
parent state, the proud and potent sovereignty of Britain, might 1 7 7 8
rationally be expected to have an influence on the political systems
of the greatest part of Europe. Besides, the intrigues of the British
cabinet, and the policy of France, might co-operate to postpone the
event of any foreign alliance with the colonies, until American firmness
had been tried in the ordeal of affliction, and her constancy and
success had rendered her more respectable in the eyes of older nations,
and long practised statesmen.

But the conquest and capture of a British army, commanded by
officers of distinguished name and abilities, was considered as a
decided proof of the importance of the connexion, and hastened the
determination of France to conclude a treaty, that might cut off all
hope of reconciliation between the colonies and the mother country.
Thus on the sixth of February, one thousand seven hundred and
seventy-eight, [67] a treaty of alliance, amity, and commerce, was
signed by the minister on the part of France, and by Benjamin
Franklin, Arthur Lee, and Silas Deane, esquires, on the part of the
United States of America. Doctor Franklin was immediately introduced
to his most christian majesty, as the minister plenipotentiary for the
American states: and on the May following, the Sieur Gerard arrived
on the continent, in quality of ambassador, and was introduced in
form to the American congress.

This mortifying event had for some time been predicted by the
minority in the British parliament; yet the minister affected to
disbelieve even the probability of its taking place; and as late as
March the eleventh, one thousand seven hundred and seventy-eight,
desired, "that it might be remembered he declared in his place, that
he knew of no such treaty, either in existence or contemplation."
Only eight days after this, the duc de Noailles, in the name of his
sovereign, announced the treaty in form; and a rescript thereof was
delivered to the king of Great Britain.

The ignorance or incapacity of the minister, in not obtaining more
early intelligence of the conduct of the house of Bourbon, or his
wickedness in concealing the information if he had received it, was
echoed from the house to the city, and from the city through the
nation. [68] But there was little reason to doubt, notwithstanding the
solemn declaration of the minister, that he had obtained more authentic
documents than he was willing to acknowledge, of the transactions
of the French cabinet. This was undoubtedly the reason, why the

CHAP. XII conciliatory bills were hurried through both houses, and sent over to
1 7 7 8 lord and general Howe, before the act was completed, or commissioners
named for the purpose.

Many distinguished members in both houses of parliament insisted,
that an immediate suspension of hostilities, and a direct acknowledgement of the independence of America, was the only medium of
safety. They justly observed, that the burning some of their fairest
towns, desolating their lands, plundering their houses, and abusing
their wives and daughters, had left such an acrimonious stamp on the
minds of Americans, as destroyed all faith and confidence in the
appearances of accommodation, or advances towards reconciliation.
Others still sanguine in prosecution of measures less derogatory to
the pride of Britain, urged a change of ministry, and a new arrangement
of officers, in both the civil and military departments. At the same
time they urged, that commissioners should be appointed to repair to
America, to confer with congress as a legal body, or with the state
legislatures in their present form; and that they should be authorised
to offer a [69] cessation of hostilities, a repeal of all obnoxious bills,
a free trade, a representation in parliament, and in short, almost every
thing they could wish, except an explicit acknowledgment of independence.

This mode was adopted, and commissioners appointed to make
overtures from the parent state, that would once have been received
with the highest tokens of gratitude. But that period was irretrievably
passed. Probably had administration taken a cool retrospect of the
natural operations of the human mind, and reflected on the insult and
mortification, of the repeated rejection of sincere and ardent petitions;
of the commencement of hostilities by staining the sword with the
blood of innocence; of the miseries that awaited the unhappy victims,
which the uncertain chances of war had thrown into their hands; and
the numberless instances of deception, that had been practised on
the less experienced politicians of America,—they must themselves
have been sensible, that all ideas of peace, on any conditions, but
the most decided acknowledgement of the independence of the
United States, were precluded.

But men impelled by a partiality for systems of their own fabricating,
whether they originated in passion, plausibility, or interest, can seldom
bend their pride to a generous dereliction [70] of their favorite object,
though reason or time might have brought to their view a full conviction
of its absurdity or impracticability.

Great Britain was at this time herself without allies; nor had she

any reason to expect the assistance of foreigners, to facilitate the CHAP. XII
subjugation of America, except the auxiliaries she had obtained at an 1 7 7 8
immense expense, from some of the petty princes of Germany. They
had some time before applied to the states of Holland, to send forward
a Scotch brigade in their service, in aid of their hostile operations
against the colonies; but by the single voice of one of their honest
republicans, it was prevented, and the proposal rejected in a style
characteristic of his nation. He observed, that "it was more proper for
Britain to hire janizaries for their purpose, than to apply to the
Batavians, who had so dearly purchased their own liberties." *

Thus, while a war with France was apprehended to be the immediate
and inevitable consequence of the weak, pernicious, and perverse
councils of the British cabinet, the opposition declared the nation had
every thing to fear from the house of Bourbon, and nothing to hope
from the assistance of other European [71] powers. These circumstances generally known, occasioned the most painful feelings to those
who were actuated by the principles of justice or humanity; nor were
the minds of such as were influenced only by the rancor of party,
much more tranquil. But the loss of the colonies, the independence
of America, her connexion with France their hereditary foe, could not
yet be digested by the king, the ministry, or the nation; and the
conciliatory proposals were voted to be carried forward on other
principles than those of humanity or equity. The army and navy
establishments were augmented; and the proud display of war, power,
and conquest, was again to accompany the soft voice of peace and re-
union.

The gentlemen appointed to undertake the arduous work of
conciliation with the American states, after the inhumanity and
irritation of a three years war, were the earl of Carlisle, sir William
Eden, governor Johnstone, and sir Henry Clinton. Qualified for
negociation, and determined if possible to re-unite the revolted
colonies with Great Britain, they left England with these flattering
expectations, and arrived in the Delaware the latter part of May,
amidst every preparation on both sides, for opening a vigorous
campaign.

During their residence in America, they faithfully executed their

---

* Speech of van der Capellen, in the assembly of Overyssel. [See Stevens, *Facsimiles*,
10: Nos. 934, 935 for an extract of Van der Capellen's "Memorial . . . to the States
of the Province of Overyssel on the Demand of the King of England for the Scotch
Brigade," March 14, 1776, and two letters to Benjamin Franklin, April 28 and
September 6, 1778.]

CHAP. XII trust; and by every [72] exertion, both in their joint and separate
1 7 7 8 capacity, they endeavoured to fulfil the expectation of their sovereign:
yet from the reception which congress had recently given to a previous
intimation of their designs, the commissioners could have no very
sanguine hopes of success.

General Howe had, as early as April the twenty-first, sent a flag to
general Washington, informing him of his own expectations: at the
same time, he transmitted him a copy of the conciliatory bill. These
the general immediately forwarded to congress, who appointed a
committee to consider the proposition. It did not take much time to
deliberate, before the committee reported a number of reasons, why
the proposals of the British court appeared to them fallacious; and
that it was

> their opinion, that the United States could with no propriety, hold any
> conference or treaty with commissioners on the part of Britain, unless, as
> a preliminary, they withdrew their fleets and armies, and in positive and
> express terms, acknowledged the independence of the United States.

This spirited language, before any account of the completion of
any treaty with France had arrived in America, discovered a due
dependence on their own magnanimity and firmness: and by the
dignity of their resolutions, congress [73] manifested a consciousness
of the justice of their cause, and a reliance on that providential
support, they had hitherto remarkably experienced.

Perhaps at no time since hostilities had commenced, between Great
Britain and the colonies, could the United States have been found
less disposed to negociate on the terms now offered by the British
government, than at the present.

When the commissioners arrived, they found the news of an alliance
with France, and a treaty of amity and commerce with that nation,
had reached York-Town, where congress was sitting, the second day
of May, a very short time after they had rejected the proposals sent
on by lord Howe.*

* These overtures were rejected on the twenty-eighth of April, one thousand seven
hundred and seventy-eight. *See journals of congress.* [See JCC, X: 369–371 (April 21,
1778); 374–380 (April 22, 1778); XI: 614–615 (June 17, 1778). Also see Richard
Henry Lee's Draft Letter to the Carlisle Commissioners, (June 16, 1778); Charles
Thomson's "Notes," (June 16, 1778); William Henry Drayton to the Carlisle
Commissioners, June 17, 1778; Henry Laurens to the Carlisle Commissioners, June
17, 1778; Henry Laurens to George Washington, June 18, 1778, in LDC, 10: 105;
111–112; 114–115 (and note, 115); 116–121 (and note, 121); 122–123; 131–132.]

All America was apprised of the divisions in the British parliament, CHAP. XII
and happy in their own unanimity. An ambassador had been appointed 1 7 7 8
to repair to America, and her independence was acknowledged by
one of the first courts in Europe. The brilliant successes of the last
year, [74] and the promising appearances on the opening the campaign
of the present, all co-operated to lead the congress and the state
legislatures, to continue the high tone of sensibility and dignity,
becoming a free and independent people, just emancipated from
foreign domination. The commander in chief, the officers of the army,
the soldiers in the field, and indeed every description of people, felt
a new degree of enthusiasm, enkindled from the sanguine expectation
of all necessary aid, in consequence of an alliance with France, which
was now completed to their wishes.

The commissioners on their arrival lost no time: they immediately
opened their correspondencies, both public and private. The secretary
to this commission was the celebrated doctor Ferguson, a gentleman
well known in the literary world, by his elegant historical and
philosophical writings. Yet the respect for his character and abilities,
which would have insured his welcome, on any occasion unconnected
with political considerations, could not influence congress to grant
him passports, as requested by the commissioners, only to deliver in
person the credentials for opening a treaty. In consequence of this
refusal, the king's commission, and a letter from the commissioners,
were both sent on by the usual military posts.

[75] The letter contained some flattering advances towards America,
and many complimentary expressions to individuals; but it was without
the smallest appearance of any recognition of the independence of
the United States. Many reproachful strictures on the insidious policy
of France, were interwoven in the letter: this rendered their address
still more exceptionable in the eye of congress; and their overtures
were generally disgusting to the people at large.

In the present crisis, it was not thought either polite or politic by
any one, to interlard the proposals for an accommodation with America,
with indelicate reflections on the new allies of the United States,
almost at the moment when congress had received the most indubitable
proofs of the friendship of the house of Bourbon; and when every
bosom glowed with hope and expectation, of the highest advantages
from an alliance just sealed by each party, and ratified by congress,
to the mutual satisfaction of both nations.

Yet allowances ought ever to be made for hereditary or national

CHAP. XII   prejudices, as well as for private disgusts. In both cases the soreness
1 7 7 8   of the human mind feels the keenest sensibility, when old wounds
are probed by a hand prepared to strike a mortal blow, the first
favorable opportunity. Thus the commissioners and the [76] British
nation, beheld with indignation and bitterness, the arm of France
their hated rival, stretched out to rescue *their colonies*, now the United
States, from the despotic views of the king and parliament of England.

When congress had given the proposals for peace, offered under
the sanction of royal authority, a fair and candid discussion, a reply
was concisely drawn up and signed by the honorable Henry Laurens,
president of the continental congress. It was observed in this answer
to the proposals, that

> both the late acts of parliament, and a commission empowering a number
> of gentlemen to negociate, and the letter received by congress from those
> gentlemen, all went upon the same mistaken ground, on the supposition
> that the people of America were the subjects of the crown of Britain.
>
> That such ideas were by no means admissible. Yet notwithstanding the
> injustice of the claim on which the war originated, and the savage manner
> of conducting it, congress was inclined to peace, whenever the king of
> England should manifest a sincere disposition therefor, by an explicit
> acknowledgment of the independence of America, and by withdrawing his
> fleets and armies: that they will then enter into a treaty of commerce, not
> inconsistent with treaties already existing.

[77] They also referred the commissioners to their resolves and
determinations of the twenty-third of April, a short time before the
arrival of the treaty of alliance with France.

This drew out a second letter from the commissioners, draughted
with much art, ability, and address. In this they observed, that

> they were not disposed to dispute about words: that a degree of inde-
> pendence was admitted in their letter of the tenth of June: that the people
> of America had the privilege of disposing of their own property, and to
> govern themselves without any reference to Britain, beyond what is
> necessary to preserve a union of force, in which mutual safety consists.

They added,

> that danger from their hereditary enemy, and gratitude to those who had
> hazarded much for their affection to Britain, must for a time prevent his
> majesty from withdrawing his fleets and armies; but that they were willing
> to enter on a discussion of circumstances, that might be necessary to secure
> and enlarge their independence: and that they wished for a full commu-

nication of the powers, by which congress was authorised to treat with foreign nations.

They intimated that there had been no resolutions of the particular assemblies, conferring this power. Thus an effort was made in the beginning of negociation, to diffuse jealousies, [78] and divide the people. In short, the sophistry that marked their public declarations, and the insidious proposals made to corrupt private persons, were very unbecoming the negociators for peace, and inconsistent both with the probity of individual character, and the dignity of their master.

It does not appear, that the conduct of any of these gentlemen singly, was equally reprehensible with that of governor Johnstone. By private letters to some of the members of congress,* he endeavoured to warp their integrity with the flattering promises of distinguished offices and emoluments, in proportion to their risk in promoting the present views of administration. He was bold enough to say, "Washington and the president would have a right to every thing a grateful nation could bestow, if they would be instrumental, once more in uniting the interests of Great Britain and America."†

His advances to Mr. Reed, an influential member of congress, were still more openly affrontive, by offering him a direct bribe, and naming [79] the conditions for the sale of his honor. Governor Johnstone doubtless thought he knew his men, when he selected Mr. Reed, Robert Morris, esquire, and Mr. Francis Dana, to open his correspondence with, and try the golden effects of secret influence, that had been so often successful in his native land. He might perhaps think it some extenuation of the affront offered to Mr. Reed, that he had formerly fallen under some suspicions from his countrymen.

He had been early and zealous in opposition to Britain; had repaired to Cambridge as aid-de-camp to general Washington; was afterwards appointed adjutant general; and continued in habits of intimacy and confidence with the commander in chief, until the retreat through

---

* The principal of these were Joseph Reed, and Robert Morris, Esq. of Pennsylvania, and Francis Dana, of Massachusetts.

† See governor Johnstone's letter to Robert Morris, Esq., laid before congress, June, 1778. [See Johnstone to Morris, June 1778, LDC, 9: 505n.1; Henry Laurens to George Johnstone, June 14, 1778; Joseph Reed to Robert Morris, June 14, 1778; Reed to Johnstone, June [15], 1778; William Henry Drayton to the Carlisle Commissioners, June 17, 1778, in LDC, 10: 91–92; 93–94; 96–97 (and note, 97–100); 116–121.]

CHAP. XII the Jersies, and the gloomy and desperate situation of American
1 7 7 8 affairs, towards the close of the winter of one thousand seven hundred and seventy-six. His fortitude then forsook him,* and despairing of brighter [80] prospects to his country, more from timidity than disaffection, he was on the point of relinquishing the public cause. It was asserted he absolutely applied to count Donop at Burlington, for a protection for himself and family, on condition of his forsaking his country, in the lowest stage of her distress, and his general and friend, at a period when he most needed his assistance.

But the brilliant action at Trenton, and the subsequent successes at Princeton, and other places in the beginning of the year one thousand seven hundred and seventy-seven, restored the tone of his nerves so far, as to enable him to act with distinguished firmness, fidelity, and bravery, on many trying occasions; and disposed almost every one to throw a veil over the momentary weakness of a mind, generally well disposed to his country.†

[81] These circumstances were known in the British army, and probably induced governor Johnstone to think Mr. Reed a proper subject for his designs. He proposed as an adequate reward for his treachery, if Mr. Reed would engage his interest to promote the object of their commission, that he should have any office in the colonies in the gift of his Britannic majesty, and the sum of ten

* See Cadwallader's letters to and of Mr. Reed. They exhibit strong suspicions, that agitated by fear in the most gloomy period of American affairs, he really contemplated security for himself and friends, under the protection of the British standard. This appeared at the time to be the apprehension of many of his connexions. However, if he was really as culpable as represented by some of those letters, he soon recovered his firmness, his character, and the confidence of his country, and the commander in chief. [See Cadwallader Collection, Cadwallader Papers, Vol. II, "Cadwallader-Reed Controversy," Historical Society of Pennsylvania.]

† Mr. Reed had publickly announced his regret that a letter written by him to general Lee, in the year one thousand seven hundred and seventy-six,* had been published to the world. He observed, that "that letter was written in haste, and written in a moment of great anxiety; not from any diminution of affection for general Washington," whom he justly styles, "a great and good man."

This letter was undoubtedly the result of Mr. Reed's apprehensions, at a period when there was the utmost danger, that all would be lost to America, from various causes that prevented more vigorous operations. But he ever after expressed the highest respect for the character of the commander in chief; and observed that his countrymen might rest in full confidence in the judgment, abilities, and discretion of general Washington.

* See vol. I, page 393. [Page 213 in Volume One of this edition.]

thousand pounds sterling in hand. This extraordinary proposal was CHAP. XII
made through a lady, who had some connexions in the British army. 1 7 7 8
Finding she expected an explicit reply, and being a lady of so much
respectability as to demand it, Mr. Reed answered, that "he was not
worth the purchasing, but such as he was, the king of Great Britain
was not rich enough to do it."

Mr. Johnstone knew Mr. Morris to be a commercial character, a
speculating genius, a calculator of finances, and a confidential friend
of general Washington. He might probably think, that if the commander in chief of the American army [82] could once be brought to
listen to proposals, or to barter his fidelity, no one could make a better
bargain for Britain than Mr. Morris, who had so much the ear and
confidence of general Washington.

From some circumstances in Mr. Dana's former conduct, Mr.
Johnstone might think himself sure of his influence, without bidding
very high; and though liberal of his master's gold, it does not appear
that he offered him a direct bribe. Mr. Johnstone's confidence in the
success of his attempt on the fidelity of this gentleman, was probably
grounded on a circumstance generally known. Mr. Dana had formerly
fallen under the suspicions of many of his countrymen, that he was
not friendly to their opposition of British measures.

This suspicion arose from his having repaired to England a short
time before the commencement of the war: but within a year after
the battle of Lexington, he had eradicated those prejudices by
returning to his native country, entrusted with some secret communications from the friends of America then in England. This recommended him to favor and reconciliation with his countrymen: they
laid aside their suspicions; and some characters of known integrity
brought him forward, and soon after he was chosen a member of the
general congress.

[83] The above traits of character might be thought proper materials
for a British commissioner to operate upon, but governor Johnstone
was mistaken in the character of Americans: for, notwithstanding their
passions, their foibles, or their weaknesses, there were few at that
time, who would not have spurned at the idea of being purchased.
They highly resented the effort to tamper with their integrity at any
price, when the liberty of America was the stake.

These letters and transactions were immediately laid before congress
by the several gentlemen, who thought themselves particularly insulted, by such unequivocal attempts on their honor and fidelity. This

CHAP. XII demeanor of one of the commissioners, was resented in a manner that
1 7 7 8 might be expected from that respectable body. The American congress
at this period, was, with few exceptions, composed of men jealous of
their rights, proud of their patriotism and independence, and tenacious
of their honor and probity. They resolved, that as they felt, so they
ought to demonstrate the most pointed indignation, against such
daring attempts to corrupt their integrity. They added, that "it was
incompatible with their honor, to hold any further intercourse with
George Johnstone, Esq., more especially to negociate [84] with him,
on affairs in which the cause of liberty was interested."*

This resolve announced in all the public papers, drew out a very
angry declaration from Mr. Johnstone. He intimated, that he should
decline acting in future as a commissioner, or in any other way
negociating with congress. He observed that

> the business would be left in abler hands; and that he should be happy to
> find no other impediment in the way of accommodation, after he was
> removed; but that he was inclined to believe, the resolutions of congress
> were dictated on similar motives to the convention of Saratoga.

Mr. Johnstone alluded to a resolve of congress in reply to the offer
of the commissioners, to ratify the convention of Saratoga. To this
offer they had replied,

> that no ratification that may be tendered, in consequence of powers that
> only reached the case by construction, or which may subject all transactions
> relative thereto, either to the future approbation or disapprobation of
> parliament, can be accepted by congress.

[85] To the resentful language of governor Johnstone, he added,
that congress acted a delusory part, contrary to the wishes of their
constituents: and after many very severe reflections on their connexion
with France, he avowed a total disregard either of the good or ill
opinion of such a body; but acknowledged, "that making a just
allowance for men acting under the heats of civil convulsions, he had
a regard for some individuals that composed it."

Doubtless, at the moment of this passionate declaration, Mr.

---

* For Mr. Johnstone's private letter to the president of congress, and Mr. Laurens'
reply, which was equally honorable to himself and to his country, and which breathed
that spirit of dignity, independence, and virtue, which uniformly marked the
character of this gentleman, the reader is referred to the journals of congress. [See
JCC, XI: 585 (June 11, 1778); Laurens to Johnstone, June 14, 1778, in LDC, 10:
91–92.]

Johnstone had forgotten the flattering epithets, even to adulation, CHAP. XII
that he had recently bestowed on the same body he now affected to 1 7 7 8
hold in sovereign contempt. But congress persevered in their usual
steady line of conduct, and took no further notice of the letters,
declarations, or addresses of the commissioners.

Thus closed their public negociations, yet they did not despair of
dividing the colonies. Letters and addresses were still circulated to
the governors of particular states, and to private gentlemen, and
inflammatory declarations were spread throughout America. The
poison of these new modes of overture for peace, between contending
nations, was effectually antidoted by the spirited publications of
several gentlemen of ability, in their private capacity.*

[86] The last effort made by these disappointed negociators, before
they left America, was the publication of a manifesto signed by three
of them, and dispersed throughout the continent. This address
appeared to be dictated more by resentment and despair, than
expectation or hope. It contained an endeavour to foment jealousies
between the several states; and insinuated that congress were not
authorized by their constituents, to reject the offers of Britain, or to
enter into alliances with foreign nations. Proposals were made for
separate treaties, either with the governors, the legislative bodies, or
individual gentlemen; and offers of pardon were held out to any in
civil or military departments, and to all descriptions of men, who
should, within forty days, desert the service of their country, and
enlist under the standard of Britain.

This was not the most offensive part of this extraordinary manifesto.
Vindictive threatenings were denounced against all, who should
continue deaf to these *gracious* and *generous* calls of their sovereign. It
finished by declaring, that if America still preferred her connexion
with the insidious and hereditary enemy of Britain, she must expect
the operations of war [87] would be continued in such modes, as
tended most to *distress, depopulate,* and *ruin.*†

Mankind are seldom driven into compliance, by the haughty threats
of powerful adversaries, unless they feel their own weakness to such

---

* W. H. Drayton, and others.

† See the manifesto at large in the British Remembrancer, and in the Annual Register,
as well as in the journals of congress. [See *Remembrancer* (1778), pp. 293–322, 330–
332; *Annual Register* (1778), "State Papers," pp. 328–332; Stevens, *Facsimiles*, 11:
No. 1104 (Commissioners to Laurens, June 9, 1778) and No. 1119 (same, after
being rebuffed).]

CHAP. XII a degree as to render them abject. But America, conscious of her own
1 7 7 8 internal strength, and sure of the assistance of foreign allies, rather
spurned at the virulent spirit of this declaration. It did not increase
their respect towards the negociators for peace. Nor were the Americans
alone offended at the style and manner of this address: it was considered
as deficient both in policy and humanity, even by some officers in
the British army. One of them, of high rank, immediately repaired
to England, and declared with honest indignation in the house of
commons, of which he was a member, that

> he could not bear the attempt to convert soldiers into butchers, assassins,
> and incendiaries; or the abominable idea of sheathing his sword in the
> bowels of age and innocence. Nor would he be instrumental in tarnishing
> the lustre of the British name, by acts of barbarity, in obedience to the
> mandates [88] of the most infamous administration, that ever disgraced a
> free country.*

But by the activity of officers of less delicacy and tenderness, the
theory of cruelty held out by the commissioners, was soon realized
by the perpetration of every crime: and the extreme rigor of war,
which in modern times has been meliorated by the general consent
of civilized nations, was renewed in America, in all the barbarous
shapes that the ingenuity, or the wickedness of man could invent.

Soon after the manifesto of the commissioners was published, a
declaration was issued by congress, though not in terms equally cruel
and threatening. They however discovered their resentment by the
severity of their language; and a sort of license was encouraged for
retaliation on individuals, if the British proceeded to murder the
inhabitants, and burn the houses of private persons. They thought
themselves justifiable in this from past sufferings, and the present
threatenings of officers commissioned to reconcile, instead of further
irritating the injured Americans.

Congress reproached them with meanness, in attempting to carry
their point by bribery, corruption, and deceit; and charged their nation
[89] with making

> a mock at humanity, by the wanton destruction of men; a mock at religion,
> by impious appeals to God, whilst in the violation of his sacred commands;
> and a mockery of reason itself, by supposing that the liberty and happiness
> of America could safely be entrusted to those who had sold their own,
> unawed by a sense of virtue or shame.

* See debates in parliament. [See *Cobbett*, XIX: 1176–1199.]

They appealed to the Searcher of Hearts for the rectitude of their CHAP. XII
intentions, and observed, that not instigated by anger or revenge, 1 7 7 8
they should, through every possible change of fortune, adhere to their
determinations.

In this state and temper of the congress, the people, and the
commissioners, sir Henry Clinton took the command of all the royal
troops in America. Previous to the opening of the summer campaign,
sir William Howe had obtained leave to repair to England. His
intended absence was much regretted by the British army, and as a
man of pleasure and address, by the gay part of the city of Philadelphia.
Every manifestation of respect was expressed on the occasion, and
the most superb display of modern luxury exhibited in an elegant
entertainment, which drew attention from the novelty of the style.
The *mischianza* was considered a new species of pleasure; but the
appellation [90] was only an additional decoration to an effort designed
to pay the highest compliment and respect, both to the military and
the private character of general Howe.

Notwithstanding this and other testimonials of the affection of his
officers and his army, he was censured by the ministry on his arrival
in England, and a public clamor prevailed against his general conduct,
during his command in America. In consequence of the ill temper
excited against him, he published a long narrative in his own defence,
and urged a free examination of his conduct in the house of commons.

But the minister appeared averse to strictures that might lay open
too many of the secrets of the cabinet. However, several distinguished
gentlemen of the army were at last called to examination, and on the
whole gave a favorable testimony to the military character and
operations of general Howe, and extenuated the failure of particular
manoeuvres, by the difficulty and embarrassment of his situation, in
a country where it was impossible for him to know, whether he was
surrounded by friends or foes, and where he often found himself
deceived by the misrepresentations of the loyalists. In order to
invalidate the evidence of lord Cornwallis and other respectable
characters, the party against sir William Howe procured the examination and evidence of Joseph Galloway, and [91] some others of the
most inveterate refugees, who had fled from America, and were
disappointed that the subjugation of their country was thus long
delayed.

Much censure fell on the ministry for their resorting to the testimony
of American refugees, pensioners, and custom-house officers, whose

CHAP. XII places, pensions, and existence, depended on their adherence to
1 7 7 8 ministerial measures, to invalidate the evidence of military men of
high rank and great professional knowledge.

Sir William Howe was not again vested with command during the
American war. Some other officers, either disgusted or discouraged,
returned to England after the summer campaign. Several of them
were advanced and sent out again in the succeeding spring, to pursue
the work of slaughter, or to humble the haughty spirit of Americans
at the feet of monarchy. A number of these ill-fated officers, whose
merits were conspicuous in their line, did not again return to the
bosom of their native country, the beloved island of Britain; where
their surviving friends were left to weep at the recollection of the
ashes of the brave, scattered over the heights and plains of the
American world.

CHAPTER XIII

Evacuation of Philadelphia • Battle of Monmouth • General Lee censured • General Clinton reaches New York • The Count de Estaing arrives there—Repairs to Rhode Island—Expedition unsuccessful • French Fleet rendezvous at Boston, to refit after the Damages sustained by a Storm • Lord Howe leaves the American Seas • Marauding Exploits of General Grey • Destruction of Wyoming • Expedition into the Indian Territories

[92] The new commission with which sir Henry Clinton was now vested, was prompt, arduous, and replete with consequences of the highest magnitude to his country, and to his own reputation. The Trident man of war had arrived in the Delaware early in the month of June, one thousand seven hundred and seventy-eight. In this ship came the British commissioners for conciliation; and through the hand of sir William Eden, general Clinton received peremptory orders to evacuate the city of Philadelphia, within six days after their reception. Accordingly the whole British army decamped, and began their march toward New York on the eighteenth of June.

The sudden desertion of a city that had been so much the object of their warmest [93] wishes, tended at once to dishearten the adherents to the royal cause, and to invigorate the operations of their antagonists. It could not be expected, that general Washington would remain a quiet spectator of this movement of the British troops. He immediately dispatched a reconnoitering party under general Maxwell, to harass their march.* The marquis de la Fayette also marched at the head of

---

* Before general Washington moved, he called a council of officers to consult on the expediency of attacking the British on their march. They were almost unanimously opposed to the measure, as the failure of success would be ruin to the American army. But the American commander, with two or three of his best officers, had no reluctance at hazarding the consequences of a general action.

CHAP. XIII a detachment, to meet them and impede their progress; and general
1 7 7 8 Lee with two brigades, was ordered to follow and support him.

The British commander prepared for this interruption, suddenly attacked and routed the cavalry under the marquis. By this the infantry were deranged: and general Washington, finding an action of moment was likely to ensue, posted himself, after several military movements, as advantageously as possible, near the heights of Monmouth.

The Americans spirited and courageous, the British resolute, brave, and desperate, a sharp [94] conflict succeeded. The military game of death and retreat, of recovery and slaughter, was kept up for several hours without decision. But a misunderstanding on a disobedience of orders by general Lee, occasioned such a derangement on the American side, as gave the opportunity for a safe retreat to the royal army, in spite of the valor and intrepidity of their opponents. Many on both sides fell by the intense heat of the weather. It was one of those days not unusual in the southern clime, when the stroke of the sun is instantaneously fatal to human life, without the agitation and fatigue inseparable from the hour of battle.

Some warm expressions in the heat of engagement from general Washington, drew several letters from Lee, that could not be passed over in silence. For these, and for his deportment through the events of the day of action, he was suspended from his command, and afterwards tried by a court-martial. The exigencies of affairs, as well as his misconduct, made it *necessary*, that he should lie under censure for disobedience, and disrespect to the commander in chief:* yet many of his brother officers advocated, or at least extenuated his conduct.

[95] Perhaps it might not have been either treachery, cowardice, envy, or any other unworthy motive, that influenced the conduct of general Lee. He had but recently recovered his liberty after he was captured at Hackinsack. Previous to that time, the American army was too justly considered by him, an undisciplined rabble. They had indeed, in his absence, made great improvements in the art of war, and the necessary arrangements of military discipline; however, he had not yet a proper confidence in the infant troops he commanded, when opposed to the superiority of British battalions, actuated by necessity in addition to constitutional bravery. He might retreat more

---

* The court-martial adjudged, that he should retire from the army, and lie under suspension for one year. [Proceedings of Lee's court martial are in *Lee Papers* III: 1–208.]

from the cautious prudence of an experienced officer, than from any CHAP. XIII
design to betray, or disobey the orders of the commander in chief: 1 7 7 8
but it is certain he did not on all occasions, discover a due respect,
either for the character or talents of general Washington.

General Lee was never again employed in American service; and
undoubtedly died a martyr to chagrin, disappointment, and personal
abuse, in consequence of the ingratitude of some of his former friends,
arising from the popularity of a more favored, fortunate, and meritorious
officer.

After his trial and suspension, general Lee retired to a little farm
in Baltimore, where he [96] lived in the most coarse and rustic manner.
Totally secluded from all society, he conversed only with a few
favorite authors and his dogs, until the year one thousand seven
hundred and eighty-two; when weary of his sequestered situation, he
left his retreat, and repaired to Philadelphia. But out of command,
he found himself without friends, without respect, and so far from
that independence congenial to his mind, and to his years, that he
was almost without the means of subsistence. In a short time, he
sickened and died in obscurity, though in a city where he had been
used to receive the highest marks of applause and respect.

After the battle of Monmouth, both parties boasted their advantages,
as is usual after an indecisive action. It is certain, Washington and his
brave troops gained only honor and applause,* whilst sir Henry Clinton
must have thought himself fortunate indeed; on the one [97] hand
he escaped a pursuing army, and on the other, a fleet commanded by
the count de Estaing, which had just arrived in the Chesapeake.

The design of the French admiral was to shut up the British army
in Philadelphia; but from the inclemency of the weather, and contrary
winds, a long passage prevented his arriving seasonably to effect so
desirable an object. When sir Henry Clinton left Philadelphia, he
could scarcely expect, or entertain a hope, that he could conduct his
army in safety, through such an extent of country, to their destination
at New York; but after surmounting many embarrassments, he arrived

---

* Even the British themselves acknowledged, that the Americans behaved with great
spirit and intrepidity. In this action, a corps commanded by colonel Dearborn,
acquitted themselves with such undaunted bravery, that they attracted particular
notice. A southern officer of rank rode up to Mr. Dearborn, and inquired "who they
were, and to what portion of America that regiment belonged?" The colonel replied
in this laconic and soldierly manner:—"*Full-blooded Yankees, by G–d, sir, from the
state of New Hampshire.*"

there with his troops, nearly at the same time when the French squadron appeared at the entrance of the Delaware.

It was a happy circumstance for Clinton, that the count de Estaing did not at first direct his course to New York: however, within a few days after the arrival of the British troops, he appeared unexpectedly off Sandy Hook; and to the inexpressible mortification of British pride, they found themselves blocked up in their own harbor, by the hereditary enemy of their nation. Old antipathies revived; irritation and resentment were wrought up to the [98] highest pitch, by new provocations; and nothing could exceed the indignation raised by the idea, that the king of France was sending out his fleets and armies, to aid and support the *rebellious colonies*.

From the situation of the two fleets before New York, an engagement was thought by all to be inevitable. A spirit was diffused through all ranks of the royal army and navy, expressive of the vigor, valor, and activity of British soldiers and seamen. Such was the popularity of lord Howe, the importance of the cause, and their resentment towards France, that the soldiers, scarce recovered from their wounds and fatigue, in the late action and retreat, were solicitous and impatient to face their Gallic enemy; and the British seamen in private service were equally emulous, and solicited eagerly, and even contested the honor of employment in the navy.

Prepared for action, and confident of success, they ostentatiously boasted, that the name of *Howe*, and the terror of the British flag, must intimidate Frenchmen in the moment of danger; as the recollection of former defeats would officiously obtrude, in spite of their most brilliant designs. This opinion was in some measure sanctioned by the inactivity of the count de Estaing, who, after lying eleven days without the smallest advance to action, left his [99] station at Sandy Hook, and proceeded northward.

It is difficult to say, whether the joy or the surprise of his enemies preponderated on this occasion. They justly considered it a very fortunate circumstance, as within two or three days, five ships of the line belonging to admiral Byron's squadron, arrived singly in so shattered a condition, that probably they, with the remainder of the fleet, must without a blow, have fallen into the hands of the French, had they continued before New York.

This unexpected manoeuvre of the count, was in consequence of a preconcerted plan, that all naval operations should be suspended at the southward, and that with all possible dispatch, the French fleet should repair to Rhode Island. This was in order to favor an expedition for the recovery of that beautiful spot, which had been seized October, one thousand seven hundred and seventy-six, and held by the British troops, now commanded by sir Robert Pigot. There, under cover of a number of frigates, they had rested in safety nearly two years. Detachments from the army at Newport and its environs, had frequently made incursions to the main, burnt a part of the town of Bristol, and greatly annoyed both Providence and all the adjacent country.

[100] The count de Estaing arrived before Newport the ninth of August; and within a few days, a large body of militia from the neighbouring states, commanded by general Hancock, and a detachment of continental troops under the command of general Sullivan, landed on the island.

The American troops, healthy, active, and vigorous, flushed with the hope of victory, not only from their own spirit and bravery, but from expectations derived from the presence of their new allies, with a powerful naval force to aid their operations, were sanguine, confident, and impatient for action. But to their unspeakable disappointment, the very day on which they landed, the French fleet again put to sea, their commander having received intelligence that lord Howe had left Sandy Hook, in full force to engage him, and to prevent the dislodgement of the royal troops, who were strong and well fortified in every part of the island.

Count de Estaing judged it prudent to meet and fight the British squadron at sea, rather than suffer lord Howe to make an effort to gain the harbor. His force was superior, his officers equally brave; there was a mutual ardor for engagement in the seamen, and a mutual ambition for glory, in both the British and French commanders. But the unforeseen operations [101] of nature, that so often impede the designs of man, again defeated the proud expectations of triumph in both parties. A severe storm that raged forty-eight hours, separated the two fleets; and such was the violence of a gale scarcely paralleled in those seas, that lord Howe in a very shattered and broken condition, was obliged to repair to New York to refit; and the French commanders thought themselves happy to reach Boston, in a very wretched and disabled state. The admiral's own ship was dismasted; the Caesar of seventy-four guns, commanded by monsieur de Booves, met the Isis, a British ship of war of only fifty guns; a sharp conflict ensued; but the Caesar having lost all her masts in the storm, darkness approaching,

CHAP. XIII most of his men being slain, and his own right arm shot off, monsieur
1 7 7 8 de Booves found it necessary to sheer off for Boston, where the whole
fleet arrived in a few days.

The count was opposed in the measure of leaving the harbor of
Newport, by all the American, and many of the French officers, but
by none more strenuously than the brave marquis de la Fayette, who
followed him to Boston with the utmost celerity, to endeavour to
expedite his return.* This misfortune [102] damped the ardor of the
militia, some of whom had, more from ostentation than bravery,
voluntarily engaged in this expedition. Near three thousand men
relinquished their posts, and left the island in a day. Many of them
were influenced to this precipitate desertion, by the conduct of major
general Hancock, who, in spite of the remonstrances of friends, and
forgetful of the hazard of popularity, left all in the moment of danger,
and repaired to Boston.

General Sullivan, not disheartened by these unexpected events,
nor discouraged by the untoward accidents that hitherto attended his
operations, kept his station fourteen days after the secession of so
large a part of his forces. Nor did he suffer his troops to be idle:
several skirmishes took place, that kept up apprehension on the one
side, and a military ardor on the other; but none of more importance
than an action on the morning of the twenty-ninth, when a cannonade
began early on both sides, and continued some hours with doubtful
success. A detachment of the British troops under colonel Campbell,
was routed and fled in confusion, leaving many dead on the field,
among whom a favorite nephew of the commander was killed by his
side. After this, [103] Sullivan and his officers, judging it not prudent
to attack a superior force entrenched within their lines, withdrew to
their own camp, while the British employed the ensuing night in
strengthening and fortifying theirs.

Within three days after this rencounter, an express arrived from
general Washington with information, that lord Howe had again sailed
from New York, and that sir Henry Clinton had himself embarked
with four thousand men, for the relief of Rhode Island. On the same
day the marquis de la Fayette returned from Boston, and reported it
impossible for the count de Estaing to arrive there again, timely for

---

* Zealous to promote the same object, the commissioners of the navy-board at Boston,
with great dispatch repaired, watered, victualled, and equipped the ships under the
command of the count de Estaing. It not being practicable to return to Rhode
Island, he in a few weeks after, sailed in complete order for the West Indies.

any operations of consequence: and as nothing effectual could be CHAP. XIII
done without the aid of naval force, general Sullivan thought proper 1 7 7 8
to withdraw his troops from the island.

His retreat was conducted with such secrecy, silence, and dexterity, as discovered the judgment and ability of the experienced commander. He had in his council some officers of distinguished name, who fully justified his conduct through the whole of this unsuccessful expedition. Greene, la Fayette, and Laurens,* [104] Fleury, Wade, Glover, Knox, Livingston, and Talbot, with many other excellent officers, had the mortification to quit the field, without the laurels so fair a prospect of military glory had waved in view.

This disappointment occasioned some temporary murmurings against the conduct of de Estaing, and even the connexion with France. A squabble soon after the fleet arrived at Boston, between some French and American sailors, heightened the uneasiness. But the most respectable people, disposed to view with a favorable eye, and to place the utmost confidence in their untried allies, all censure was hushed; and a discreet silence in the more prudent, prevented or counteracted all invidious observations from the less candid.

Lord Howe arrived in the harbor of Newport, with an hundred sail of ships of war and transports, the morning after Sullivan's retreat. [105] Admiral Byron was hourly expected to join him. Thus, so superior in strength, there was every reason to expect Boston would be the next object of attack. In consequence of this appearance, the count de Estaing, who found it would require time to victual, water, and equip his shattered fleet for a second cruise, judged it necessary to fortify several advantageous islands in the harbor, and thus be in readiness for the reception of the British fleets, if they should be again disposed to visit Boston.

Lord Howe before he returned to New York, went round and looked into the harbor of Boston; but finding most of the ships belonging to the French fleet repaired, and Castle William and the

* The noble, disinterested sentiments of this gentleman, who was then aid-de-camp to general Washington, were exhibited in his reply to congress, who for his distinguished bravery in this and other actions, had advanced him to the rank of lieutenant colonel. Mr. Laurens' acceptance would have superseded some officers in the family of the commander, earlier in commission. Apprehensive that it might create some uneasiness among them, he declined the honor. He observed, "that having been a spectator of the convulsions occasioned in the army by disputes of rank, he held the tranquillity of it too dear, to be instrumental in disturbing it."

CHAP. XIII islands in a defensible state, he did not think proper to make any
1 7 7 8   hostile attempt on the town. Not perfectly pleased with the American
war, and disgusted at some things relative to his own command, his
lordship resigned his commission soon after this, and repaired to
England. He left the American seas in September, one thousand
seven hundred and seventy-eight.

When his lordship arrived in England, he complained publicly, that
he had been deceived into the command, and deceived while in it.
Tired and disgusted with the service, he had [106] been compelled
to resign; and that he had suffered too much ever to risk a return to
any situation, that might terminate in equal mortification. He observed,
that he must be excused from any employment, while the present
ministry continued in office, being convinced by decisive experience,
that he not only risked his own honor and professional character in
the attempt, but that under such councils, he was as sensible as those
who had been earlier in opposition, that no essential service could be
rendered his country.

But though we see him no more on the American theatre, yet,
notwithstanding his dissatisfaction with the conduct of administration,
lord Howe again, before the conclusion of peace, acted a conspicuous
part under the renowned flag of Great Britain.

The celebrated Bougainville, who had before explored the other
side of the globe, was, with many other officers of high rank and
distinction, for the first time in the American seas. They were every
where welcomed as the generous friends of the United States, the
patrons of liberty, and the supporters of the rights of men. But, as
there had not yet been time to prove the sincerity of either party, the
old officers who remembered the late war between England and
France, when America hugged herself in the protection of Britain,
and adopted [107] all her opinions, looked as if they wished rather
than believed, all ancient prejudices obliterated.* They seemed
silently to half doubt the reality of that friendship which appeared in
the politeness of their reception, from a people of a different religion,
language, habits, and manners; and at first, seemed reluctantly to
hold back that flow of affection, which the Americans were ready to
return in full measure.

* Some jealousies had arisen while at Rhode Island, on some points of *etiquette* between
the count de Estaing and the commander of the American forces. These had been
amicably adjusted: yet the pride of older military characters, had been too much
hurt for the wound to be instantly healed.

As to the younger class, unconscious of injury, ambitious for glory, CHAP. XIII
and eager for the humiliation of Britain, hope danced in their eye; 1 7 7 8
every feature displayed the wish of mutual confidence; and with
honest joy, they extended their arms to embrace their new allies. Yet,
the squadrons of the house of Bourbon riding in the ports, and
fortifying the American harbors against their natural friends, the parent
of the once loyal and affectionate colonies, was an event which,
though precipitated by the folly of Britain, had out-run the expectations
of America: nor could such a circumstance fail to excite the most
serious recollections [108] and contemplations, both of the philosopher
and the politician.

The timely and judicious movement of general Sullivan, disappointed the expectations of sir Henry Clinton, who flattered himself
he should arrive soon enough to cut off the retreat of the American
army. When he found they had withdrawn, he immediately left the
neighbourhood of Rhode Island, and returned to New York, after he
had dispatched major general Grey at the head of a large detachment,
on a marauding expedition against some defenceless towns in the
Massachusetts.

The first attack was on Bedford, a small town on the river Acushnet.
He landed in the evening. The inhabitants alarmed at this unexpected
attack, most of them fled, and left their property a prey to their
enemies. When they returned in the morning, they found the Britons
retired; but to their inexpressible mortification, almost every thing of
value was destroyed or carried off. Houses, warehouses, magazines,
and stores, with near an hundred sail of shipping, were burnt on the
Bedford and Fairhaven sides of the river.

After this feat, Grey proceeded to Martha's Vineyard, laid the
inhabitants under contribution, and demanded a surrender of their
arms. From thence he visited Nantucket and the [109] neighbouring
isles: and with the plunder of fifteen or twenty thousand cattle and
sheep, for the use of the army at New York, he returned with his
party, exulting in depredations that would have been disgraceful to
an officer of much inferior character and abilities.*

Sir Henry Clinton pleased with the success of this expedition, sent
Grey immediately on to aid a similar mode of war on the Jersey coast.
Lord Cornwallis had with a large body of troops, taken post between

* A number of refugees from the state of Massachusetts, aided Grey in depredations
  on their countrymen and former friends. From a regard to the feelings of some of
  their connexions, still living in America, we forbear to name them.

CHAP. XIII the North River and the Hackinsack: general Knyphausen with another
1 7 7 8 division, was posted in a parallel position on the other side of the
North River. Thus were they conveniently situated to guard their
foraging parties, and distress the country by sudden depredations and
continual havoc, during the remainder of the autumn.

General Grey with his usual activity had gained intelligence of the
insecure situation, in which a regiment commanded by colonel Baylor,
had reposed themselves for the night of the twenty-fourth of September. A party sent on with orders to give no quarter, cut off the [110]
guards, and surprised the unhappy victims asleep in an out-house.
They awoke, submitted, implored quarter, and were massacred in an
hour. Only ten or twelve escaped with life, after they were barbarously
wounded, stripped, and left for dead. This remnant so far recovered
as, by favor of the darkness, to reach the post of their friends, and
detail the horrid transaction. They agreed on oath, that they and their
companions had all surrendered, as soon as they found themselves in
the enemy's hands, and asked only for life. But the savage cry was,
"kill them, kill them; we have orders to give no quarter:" and the
barbarous echo was kept up till every man was, or appeared to be
murdered.*

A repetition of the same cruel policy soon after took place on the
surprise of a party of Pulaski's light infantry. Some deserters had
betrayed them into the hands of the British. Several hundred of these
unhappy men were butchered without mercy, after the surrender of
their arms. The baron de Bose, a Polish nobleman, was among the
slain. An apology was afterwards attempted, by pleading that they
had received information, the count Pulaski in orders [111] to his
legion, had enjoined that no quarter should be given to any that might
fall into their hands. This was denied both by the count and his
officers. But had it been true, that a foreign nobleman, hardened
amidst the barbarities of Polish confederacies, could so far deviate
from the laws of humanity as to give such an order, the example
should never have been followed by the polite and gallant Englishmen.
But in this war, they seemed to have lost those generous feelings of
compassion to the vanquished foe, that must ever be deemed honorary
to the human character.

* See a particular detail of this transaction in the British Remembrancer, with the
affidavits of the few soldiers that escaped the massacre. [See Grey to Clinton,
September 18, 1778; Lord Sterling to ?, October 21, 1778; Affidavits; *Remembrancer*
(1779), pp. 36–38; 292–293; 294–298.]

A counterpart to the conduct of the more refined, though little CHAP. XIII
more humanized commanders of the predatory parties in the middle 1 7 7 8
and northern colonies, was exhibited in the southern borders, by their
savage allies of the wilderness.

This was dreadfully realized by the inhabitants of Wyoming, a
young settlement on the eastern branch of the Susquehanna. The
population of this once happy spot had been remarkably rapid, and
when the fury of civil discord first appeared among them, it contained
eight townships of five miles square each. They were situated in a
mild climate, in a country fertile, and beautifully displaying a pictur-
esque appearance of that kind of primitive simplicity, only enjoyed
before the mind of man [112] is contaminated by ambition or gold.
But party rage had spread its baneful influence to the remotest corners
of America, and political animosities had at this period poisoned the
peace, even of the most distant villages, where simplicity, friendship,
and industry had reigned, until the fell fiend which prompts to civil
war, made its frightful appearance, attended by all the horrors
imagination can paint.

The inhabitants of this favored spot, perhaps more zealous than
discreet, had so far participated the feelings of all America, as
voluntarily to raise and send forward one thousand men, to join the
continental army. This step disclosed the embers of opposition that
had hitherto lain concealed, in the bosoms of a number long disaffected
to the American, and warmly attached to the royal cause. A rancorous
spirit immediately burst from the latent spark, which divided families,
and separated the tenderest connexions. Animosities soon arose to
such a height, that some of the most active members of this flourishing
and happy society, abandoned their plantations, forsook their friends,
joined and instigated the neighbouring savages to molest the settlements, and assisted in the perpetration of the most unheard of
cruelties.

Several outrages had been committed by small parties, and many
threatening appearances [113] had so far alarmed the inhabitants, that
most of them had repaired to some fortresses early erected for their
defence against the native savages. Yet there was no apprehension of
a general massacre and extermination, till the beginning of July, one
thousand seven hundred and seventy-eight, when an army of near
two thousand men, made its appearance on the Susquehannah, and
landed on their borders. This body was composed of the motley
materials of Indians, tories, half-blooded Englishmen, and British

renegadoes, headed by one Butler, who had nothing human about
him, except a rough, external figure of a man.

All the inhabitants of those weak, defenceless settlements capable of bearing arms, embodied, and put themselves under the direction of a person of the same name, a near relation of the commander of the savages. This man, either through fear, weakness, or misplaced confidence, listened to the offers of treaty from his more artful kinsman, and suffered himself with four hundred men, to be drawn from fort Kingston by a delusive flag, that alternately advanced and retired, as if apprehensive of danger. Caught by the snare, he was completely surrounded before he had any suspicion of deception, and his whole party cut off, notwithstanding [114] they fought with a spirit becoming their desperate situation.

The victor immediately pushed on, invested the garrison thus indiscreetly left, and demanded a surrender. The demand was accompanied by the horrid display of a great number of scalps, just torn from the heads, and yet warm with the blood, of their nearest friends and relations. In this situation of wretchedness, embittered by impotent resentment, colonel Donnison, on whom the command had devolved, finding resistance impracticable, went out himself with a flag, to ask the terms of surrender. To this humiliating question, the infamous Butler replied, with all the *sang-froid* of the savage, and the laconism of an ancient Greek, "*the hatchet.*"

The unfortunate Donnison returned in despair; yet he bravely defended the fort until most of his men had fallen by his side, when the barbarians without, shut up this and a neighbouring garrison, where a number of women and children had repaired for safety, and setting fire to both, they enjoyed the infernal pleasure of seeing them perish promiscuously, in the flames lighted by their bloody hands.*

[115] After this catastrophe, the most shocking devastation was spread through the townships. Whilst some were employed in burning the houses, setting fire to the corn-fields, and rooting out every trait of improvement, others were cruelly and wantonly imbruing their hands in the blood of their parents, their brothers, and every near connexion, who had unfortunately held different political opinions. But a particular detail of the transactions of savages, stimulated by the agents of more refined and polished nations, with passions whetted

---

* The transactions at Wyoming are recorded above, agreeably to the most authentic accounts at the time.

by revenge, without principle to check its operation, is too painful to CHAP. XIII
the writer, and too disgraceful to human nature to dwell on. Nor is it 1 7 7 8
less painful to the impartial historian, to relate the barbarous, though
by them deemed necessary, vengeance, soon after taken by the
Americans.

The conflagration spread over the beautiful country of the Illinois,
by a colonel Clark of Virginia, equally awakes compassion, and was a
counterbalance for the sufferings of the miserable Wyomings. It is
true the Illinois, and other distant warlike tribes, were at the instigation
of governor Hamilton,* the British commander at Detroit, generally
assisting in the measures perpetrated under Butler and Brandt, nearer
the frontiers; and perhaps the law of [116] retaliation may, in some
measure, justify the depredations of Clark.

This intrepid ranger left Virginia in the course of this summer, with
a few adventurers hardy as himself, and traversed a country of eleven
or twelve hundred miles in extent: and surmounting all the hardships
that imagination can paint, through a wilderness inhabited only by
strolling hunters from among the savages, and the wild beasts that
prowled before them, through hunger, fatigue, and sufferings innumerable, they reached the upper Mississippi. The Indian inhabitants,
who had there long enjoyed a happy climate, and the fruits of a fertile
soil, under a high degree of cultivation, fearless of danger from their
distance from civilized neighbours, were surprised by Clark and his
party; their crops were destroyed; their settlements broken up; their
villages burnt, the principal of which was Kaskaskias. This town
contained near three hundred houses; and had it not been surprised
at midnight by these desperate invaders, bold, outrageous, and near
starving in the wilderness, the natives might successfully have defended their lives and their plantations; but not a man escaped
seasonably to alarm the neighbouring tribes.

A British officer, one *Rocheblave*, who acted as governor, and
paymaster for American scalps, was taken and sent to Virginia, with
many written proofs of the cruel policy of inciting [117] the fury of
savages against the American settlements. From Quebec, Detroit,
Michilimackinac, &c., these orders every where appeared under the
signature of the chief magistrates, acting in the name of the British
king. Some of their principal warriors were made prisoners; the
remainder who escaped the sword, had only to fly farther through a

---

* Governor Hamilton was afterwards captured by Clark.

CHAP. XIII   trackless wilderness, if possible to procure some new lodgement,
1 7 7 8   beyond the reach of civilized pursuers.

Nor did the Cherokees, the Muskingums, the Mohawks, and many
other savage tribes, feel less severely than the Illinois, the resentment
of the Americans, for their attachment to the British nation, and their
cruelties practised on the borders of the Atlantic states.

An expedition entrusted to the conduct of general Sullivan, against
the Six Nations, who had generally been better disposed toward
Americans than most of the savage tribes, was replete with circumstances that must wound the feelings of the compassionate heart;
while the lovers of cultivation and improvement among all mankind,
will be touched by a retaliation, bordering, to say the least, on savage
fury. The sudden and unexpected destruction of a part of the human
species, enjoying domestic quiet in the simplicity of nature, awakes
the feelings of the first: the second must be disturbed in his
philosophical pursuits of cultivation [118] and improvement, when he
contemplates fire and sword destroying all in their way, and houses
too well built to be the workmanship of men in a state of rude nature,
the prey of conflagration, enkindled by the hands of the cultivators
of the arts and sciences.*

The rooting up of gardens, orchards, corn-fields, and fruit trees,
which by their variety and growth, discovered that the industrious
hand of cultivation had been long employed to bring them to
perfection, cannot be justified; more especially where there is a mind
capable of looking forward to their utility, and back to the time and
labor it has cost to bring them to maturity. But general Sullivan,
according to his own account in his letters to the commander in chief,
to congress, to his friends and others, spared no vestige of improvement, and appeared little less proud of this war upon nature, than he
was of his conquest of the savages.†

The difficulties, dangers, and fatigues of the march, required
courage, firmness, and perseverance. Hunger and famine assailed
them before they reached the fertile borders of the [119] pleasant and

---

* By the testimony of British writers, this description is not exaggerated. See their
registers and histories.
† See general Sullivan's account of this expedition on the public records, dated Sept.
30, 1779. [For Sullivan's Official Report, September 30, 1779, see *Journals of the
Military Expedition of Major General John Sullivan Against the Six Nations of Indians in
1779* (Auburn, New York, 1887), pp. 296–306. Sullivan's report was republished
from the *Maryland Journal and Baltimore Advertiser*, October 19, 1779.]

well settled Indian towns; yet general Sullivan and his party finished chap. xiii
the expedition in as short a time as could be expected, and to all 1 7 7 8
public appearance, met the approbation of congress and of the
commander in chief.

Yet there were some things in the demeanor of general Sullivan,
that disgusted some of his officers, and raised a censure on his conduct
that made him unhappy, and led him to resign his military command.
His health was indeed broken, which he imputed to the fatigues
encountered on his hazardous march. Yet he lived many years after
this period, and was advanced to the highest stations in the civil
administration of the state of New Hampshire, and died with the
reputation of a brave and active officer, both in military and civil life.

General Sullivan had acquitted himself during his military command
with valor and reputation, in many instances. During the ravages of
the British on the Jersey shore, in the latter part of the summer of
one thousand seven hundred and seventy-seven, he had gained much
honor by an expedition to Staten Island, concerted by himself. This
he undertook without any orders from the commander in chief; and
for this a court of inquiry was appointed to examine into his conduct.
His reasons for such a step, without permission or command, were
thought justifiable. He brought off a great number of [120] prisoners,
officers, soldiers, and tories, who had frequently made incursions on
the borders of the Jersies, and harassed, plundered, and murdered
the inhabitants in their sudden depredations. It appeared that general
Sullivan had conducted this business with great prudence and success:
he was, by the court of inquiry, acquitted with honor and applause,
for planning and executing to great advantage, a design from which
so much benefit had resulted.

It may be thought by some, an apology sufficient for the invasion
of Clark and Sullivan, of Pickens, Van Schaick, and others, that the
hostile dispositions of the aboriginals had always led them to imbrue
their hands in the blood of the borderers. The warriors of the distant
tribes, either instigated by their own ferocity and resentment, or the
influence of Europeans inimical to the United States, were ever ready
to molest the young settlements. Jealous of their encroachments, the
natives viewed them with such an hostile eye, that no treaties were
binding: when a favorable opportunity presented, they always attacked
the whites, perhaps from the same impulse that in human nature
prompts all mankind, whether civilized or savage, to resist the invaders
of his territory.

CHAP. XIII   Indeed their condition and their sufferings, from the first emigration
1 7 7 8 of the Europeans, their corruptions in consequence thereof, their
[121] wars, and their extirpation from a vast tract of the American
continent, must excite a solemn pause in the breast of the philosopher,
while he surveys the wretchedness of savage life, and sighs over its
misery. Yet he is not relieved when he contemplates the havoc among
civilized nations, the changes in society, the prostration of principle,
and the revolutions permitted by Providence in this speck of creation.

The rivers of blood through which mankind generally wade to
empire and greatness, must draw out the tear of compassion; and
every sympathetic bosom will commiserate the sufferings of the whole
human race, either friends or foes, whether dying by the sword,
sickness or remorse, under the splendid canopy reared by their own
guilty hands. These with equal pity look into the wilderness; they
see the naked hunter groaning out his fierce soul on his native turf,
slain by the tomahawk of his own savage tribe, or wounded by some
neighbouring hordes, that prowl through an existence little elevated
above the brute. Both stages of society excite compassion, and both
intimate to the rational mind, that this is but the road to a more
improved, and exalted state of existence.

But the unhappy race of men hutted throughout the vast wilderness
of America, were the [122] original proprietors of the soil; and if they
have not civilization they have valor; if they have not patriotism they
have a predilection to country, and are tenacious of their hunting
grounds. However the generous or humane mind may revolt at the
idea, there appears a probability, that they will be hunted from the
vast American continent, if not from off the face of the globe, by
Europeans of various descriptions, aided by the interested Americans,
who all consider valor in an Indian, only as a higher degree of ferocity.

Their strenuous efforts to retain the boundaries assigned them by
nature and providence, are viewed with contempt by those descriptions
of persons, or rather as a sanction to their own rapacity, and a warrant
from heaven to exterminate the hapless race. But "the rivers, the
mountains, the deserts, the savages clad in armor, with other destroyers
of men," as well as the voice of heaven, and their natural boundaries,
forbid these encroachments on the naked forester, content with the
produce of nature in his own grounds, and the game that plays in his
own wild woods, which his ancestors have possessed from time
immemorial.

The ideas of some Europeans as well as Americans, that the rude
tribes of savages cannot be civilized by the kind and humane

endeavours of their neighbours, is absurd and unfounded [123]. What CHAP. XIII
were once the ancestors of the most refined and polite modern nations, 1 7 7 8
but rude, ignorant savages, inured to all the barbarous customs and
habits of present existing tribes? Nature has been equal in its
operations, with regard to the whole human species. There is no
difference in the moral or intellectual capacity of nations, but what
arises from adventitious circumstances, that give some a more early
and rapid improvement in civilization than others. This gradual rise
from the rude stages of nature to the highest pitch of refinement,
may be traced by the historian, the philosopher, and the naturalist,
sufficiently to obviate all objections against the strongest efforts, to
instruct and civilize the swarms of men in the American wilds, whose
only natural apparent distinction, is a copper-colored skin. When the
present war ceases to rage, it is hoped that humanity will teach
Americans of a fairer complexion, to use the most strenuous efforts
to instruct them in arts, manufactures, morals, and religion, instead
of aiming at their extermination.

It is true at this period, when war was raging through all the United
States, few of the tribes of the wilderness appeared to be contented
with their own native inheritance. They were every where stimulated
by the British government to hostility, and most of the inhabitants of
the wilderness seemed to be in array [124] against their former
colonies. This created a necessity in congress, to act offensively against
the rude and barbarous nations. Defensive war against any nation,
whether civilized or savage, is undoubtedly justifiable both in a moral
and political view. But attempts to penetrate distant countries, and
spread slaughter and bloodshed among innocent and unoffending
tribes, too distant to awaken fears, and too simple and unsuspicious
to expect approaching destruction from those they had never injured,
has no warrant from Heaven.

Even in the present war, instances may be adduced of the effects
of civilization, which often soften the most savage manners; one of
which may be here recorded. A part of the Muskingum tribe had
professed themselves Christians of the Moravian sect. They considered
war of any kind as inconsistent both with the laws of religion and
humanity. They refused to take any part with the numerous hostile
tribes of savages, in the war against the Americans. They observed
with more rationality and consideration than is generally discovered
in more civilized nations, "that the Great Spirit did not make men to
destroy, but to assist and comfort each other."

They persisted in this placid demeanor, until some of their savage

CHAP. XIII   neighbours were so enraged, that they forcibly removed them from
1 7 7 8   [125] their former settlement; and after committing great cruelties,
and destroying a number of them, placed the remainder near the
Sandusky. Their removal was in consequence of orders from the
British commander at Detroit. They remained for some time in the
enjoyment of their own simple habits; but some suspicions were
afterwards infused among the settlers on the Monongahela, that their
dispositions were not friendly to the Americans. It is painful to relate,
that on this slight pretence, a number of Americans embodied
themselves and marched to the Moravian town, where the principal
men had repaired by permission, to reap the harvest they had left
standing in the fields. The Americans followed them, and barbarously
murdered the whole of this innocent and inoffensive band.

The whites at first decoyed them by a friendly appearance, which
induced them to collect themselves together; when thus collected,
they, without resistance, suffered themselves to be bound and
inhumanly butchered. They died professing their full expectation,
that their troubles would soon be at an end. Thus they fell as martyrs
to religion, by the hands of a people who had much longer professed
themselves adherents to the principles of Christianity.

This instance of the treachery and cruelty of the whites, is one
among many other proofs, of [126] the truth of an observation made
by a gentleman* afterwards,

> that the white savages were generally more savage than the copper colored;
> and that nine times out of ten, the settlers on the borders were the
> aggressors: that he had seen many of the natives who were prisoners at
> fort Washington; that they appeared to be possessed of much sensibility
> and gratitude: that he had discovered some singular instances of this among
> them, very honorable to the human character, before the advantages or
> the examples of civilized nations had reached their borders.

In short, no arguments are necessary to adduce the truth, or impress
on the minds either of the philosopher or the politician, that it will
be the indispensable duty of the American government, when quietly
established by the restoration of peace, to endeavour to soften and
civilize, instead of exterminating the rude nations of the interior. This

---

* A young American officer of great sensibility and penetration, who fell at the battle
at the Miamis, one thousand seven hundred and ninety-one. [The reference is to
Winslow Warren, Mercy's favorite son, who served with General Arthur St. Clair's
corps against the Indians in Ohio. See editor's Foreword, p. xx.]

will undoubtedly be attempted in some future period, when uncultivated reason may be assisted; when arts, agriculture, science, and
true religion, may enlighten the dark corners which have been obscured
by ignorance and ferocity, for countless ages. The embrowned, dusky
wilderness, [127] has exhibited multitudes of men, little distinguished
from the fierce animals they hunted, except in their external form.
Yet, in a few instances, the dignity of human nature has been
discovered by traits of reason and humanity, which wanted only the
advantages of education, to display genius and ability equal to any
among the nations, that have hunted millions of those unhappy people
out of existence, since the discovery of America by Europeans. But
it is a pleasing anticipation, that the American revolution may be a
means in the hands of Providence, of diffusing universal knowledge
over a quarter of the globe, that for ages had been enveloped in
darkness, ignorance, and barbarism.

CHAPTER XIV

Foreign Negociations • Dissensions among the American Commissioners • Deane recalled • Mr. Adams appointed • Mr. Lee and Mr. Adams
recalled • Spain declares War against England • Mr. Jay sent to the Court
of Madrid • Sir George Collier's Expedition to Virginia—His sudden
Recal—Ravages on the North River • Depredations in the State of Connecticut, in aid of Governor Tryon and his Partizans • General Washington
seizes Stoney Point—Recovered by the British • Penobscot Expedition • Destruction of the American Navy

CHAP. XIV [128] It has already been observed, that in an early stage of the
1 7 7 8 American contest, some gentlemen were deputed to negociate, and
to endeavour to secure the assistance of several European nations.
This had had such an effect, that at the period we are now upon, the
United States were in strict alliance with France, and were considered
in a partial and respectful light by some of the first powers in Europe.
Yet difficulties both at home and abroad, which had scarcely been
viewed in theory, were now realized and felt with poignancy, by the
true friends of their country.

The objects that employed the abilities of congress at this period,
were of such magnitude, [129] as required the experience of ancient
statesmen, the coolness of long practised politicians, and the energies
of virtue.

The articles of confederation offered to the consideration of each
legislative in the several states, in one thousand seven hundred and
seventy-six, had been rejected by some, and suspended by others. It
is true they were now recently ratified by all of them, but were
scarcely yet established on a permanent basis.*

They had to arrange, harmonize, and support the new permanent
army, collected from every part of the union, and now interwoven
with foreign volunteers from different European nations: and in the

* See Appendix, Note No. V. _____

rear of every other difficulty at home, they had to guard with all
possible discretion, against the innumerable moral and political evils,
ever the inevitable consequence of a depreciating currency.

Abroad they had a task of equal difficulty, to heal the animosities
that existed, and to conciliate the differences that had arisen among
the American ministers at the court of France, or to prevent the fatal
consequences of their virulence towards each other. This was expressed
[130] in strong language in their letters to congress, nor was it a secret
in the courts of England or France, and in some instances, perhaps
it was fomented by both.

In the infancy of congress, in the magnitude of the new scenes that
were opening before them, and in the critical emergencies that sprung
up on untrodden ground, they, through hurry or inexperience, had
not in all instances, selected men of the most impeccable characters,
to negociate with foreign powers. Perhaps in some of their appointments, they did not always look so much at the integrity of the heart,
as at the capacity of the man for the arts of intrigue, the ready address,
and supple accomplishments necessary for the courtier, both to insure
his own reception with princes, and to complete the wishes of his
employers, in his negociations with practised statesmen.

Silas Deane, esquire, a delegate to congress from the state of
Connecticut, was the first person who had been vested with a foreign
commission. He embarked as a commercial agent in behalf of the
United States, in one thousand seven hundred and seventy-six; and
was afterwards named in the honorable commission for a treaty of
alliance with the court of France, in conjunction with doctor Franklin
and Arthur Lee, esquire.

[131] Mr. Deane had nothing to recommend him to such a
distinguished and important appointment, except a degree of mercantile experience, combined with a certain secrecy or cunning, that
wore the appearance of knowing things much beyond his ability, and
the art of imposing a temporary belief of a penetration far beyond his
capacity. His weakness and ostentation, his duplicity, extravagance,
and total want of principle, were soon discovered by his constituents:
but they placed the most unlimited confidence in the great abilities,
profound knowledge, and unshaken patriotism, of the venerable and
philosophic Franklin. His warm attachment to his native country, had
been evinced in numberless instances, during his long residence in
England as agent to the British court, both for the Massachusetts and
the state of Pennsylvania.

Before he left England in one thousand seven hundred and seventy-

CHAP. XIV five, he had taken unwearied pains to reconcile, on the principles of
1 7 7 8 equity and sound policy, the breach between Great Britain and
America. In the beginning of hostilities he repaired to Philadelphia,
was chosen a member of congress, and by his decided republican
principles, soon became a favorite in the councils of America, a stable
prop of her independence, and the most able and influential negociator
they could send abroad.

[132] The character and principles of Mr. Arthur Lee, gave equal
reason to expect his most energetic endeavours, to support the interest
and weal of America. He had resided in England for several years, as
agent for the state of Virginia. Invariably attached to his native country,
and indefatigable in his efforts to ward off the impending evils that
threatened it, he had communicated much useful intelligence and
advantageous advice, to the patriotic leaders in various parts of America;
and by his spirited writings and diligent exertions, he procured them
many friends in England. He was a man of a clear understanding,
great probity, plain manners, and strong passions. Though he loved
America sincerely, he had at this period great respect and affection
for the parent state; and his predilection in favor of Britain appeared
strongly, when balanced with the idea of an American connexion with
the house of Bourbon.

The celebrity of doctor Franklin has been so just and so extensive,
that it is painful even for the impartial historian, who contemplates
the superiority of his genius, to record the foibles of the man; but
intoxicated by the warm caresses and unbounded applauses of all
ranks, among a people where the art of pleasing is systematized, he
appeared, notwithstanding his age and experience, in a short time
after his residence [133] in France, little less a Gallican than an
American. This might be from policy. It was said however, that he
attached himself to the interest of the count de Vergennes, who,
though he countenanced the American revolution, and co-operated in
measures that completed it, yet it was afterwards discovered, that he
secretly wished to embarrass their councils, and dreaded the rising
glory of the United States. Whatever suggestions there might have
been, it was never supposed that doctor Franklin was led off from his
attachment to the interest of America: yet this distinguished sage
became susceptible of a court influence, that startled his jealous and
more frigid colleague, Mr. Lee.

Thus the trio of American agents at the court of France, were
designated by peculiar traits of character: yet the respectability of Dr.
Franklin and Mr. Lee was never lessened, either at home or abroad,

notwithstanding some variation of opinion. But Mr. Deane, immersed
in the pleasures of a voluptuous city, a dupe to the intrigues of deeper
politicians, not awed by the aged philosopher the tool of the French
minister, and the supple instrument of military characters, ambitious
of rising in the fair field of glory in America, he wasted the property,
and bartered away the honors of his country, by promising offices of
rank to fifty gentlemen at a time. He sent many of these on to [134]
America, with the most flattering expectations of promotion, and even
with ideas of superseding the previous appointments of congress.

Many of the French officers who arrived on the American continent
at this early period, with these fallacious hopes, were men of real
merit, military experience, and distinguished rank; but it was impossible for congress to provide for them all according to their views,
without deranging the whole army, and disgusting many of their best
officers. Thus disappointed, some of them returned to France, under
a cloud of chagrin that was not easily dissipated.

The indiscretion of Mr. Deane did not terminate with his engagements to individual strangers; for while he embarrassed congress and
the army with his contracts, and his country by squandering the public
monies, he had the audacity to propose in a letter to a person of
influence, that a foreign prince should be invited to the command of
the armies of the United States.*

From the outlines of these heterogeneous characters, it is not strange
that the most incurable [135] animosities took place among the
commissioners, and arose to such a height as to endanger the interests
of an infant republic.

Indeed the fate of America in some measure depended on the
vigor, integrity, prudence, and unanimity of her ministers abroad; but
dissension ran to such a pitch among them, that it exposed them not
only to the censure of their country, but to the derision of Britain.
Consequently, an immediate recal of some of the American commissioners became necessary, and an order passed in congress, December,
one thousand seven hundred and seventy-seven, that Silas Deane,
esquire, should immediately return to America. No reasons were
offered for his recal; and Mr. John Adams of the state of Massachusetts,
was chosen to succeed as commissioner in behalf of the United States,
at the court of France.

Mr. Deane arrived in America a short time after the treaty with

---

* Deane in this letter named prince Ferdinand of Brunswick, as a suitable commander
for the armies of the free Americans.

CHAP. XIV   France had been received, and ratified by congress. He assumed an
1 7 7 8   air of importance and self-confidence; and as guilt frequently sends a
hue and cry after justice, in order to hoodwink the multitude, and
calls loudly for vengeance on such as are about to detect its villany,
he offered a most inflammatory address to the public, complaining of
ill usage, and vilifying Mr. Lee in the grossest terms. He criminated
every part of his public [136] conduct, charged him with betraying
his trust, corresponding with gentlemen in England, impeding as
much as possible the alliance with France, and disclosing the secrets
of congress to British noblemen. At the same time, he cast the most
virulent and insidious reflections on his brother, William Lee, agent
for congress at the courts of Vienna and Berlin.

He claimed much merit relative to the treaty of alliance with France,
and complained heavily that congress delayed giving him an opportunity of vindicating his own character, by an immediate public
investigation. By these bold suggestions and allegations, so injurious
to congress and to their ministers, the public mind was for a time
greatly agitated. But the attack on individual character, was defeated
by the exertions of some very able writers,* who laid open the
iniquitous designs and practices of the delinquent and his abettors;
while congress parried the abuse, they defended their own measures,
and quieted the clamors of a party against themselves, by calling Mr.
Deane to a hearing on the floor of their house.

With the guise of innocence and the effrontery of guilt, he evaded
the scrutiny, by pleading [137] that his papers and vouchers were all
left in Europe, where, he alleged, the necessity of his own private
affairs required his immediate presence. In short, though it was
obvious that he had abused his commission, rioted long at the public
expense, and grossly slandered some of its most faithful servants, yet
by the influence of certain characters within, and a tenderness for
some without, who might be exposed by too strict an investigation,
congress were induced to suffer him again to leave the continent and
return to Europe, though not as a public character, yet without
punishment or judicial censure. He afterwards wandered from court
to court, and from city to city, for several years: at last, reduced to
the extreme of poverty and wretchedness, he died miserably in
England.

---

* Mr. Drayton and others. Also Mr. Paine, author of a pamphlet entitled Common
Sense. See some observations on his character, Appendix, Note No. VI.

Parties ran very high in congress, relative to the dissensions among CHAP. XIV
their ministers. Mr. Lee had many friends in that assembly; Dr. 1 7 7 8
Franklin had more; and it was necessary for some mercantile speculators in that body, to endeavour to throw a veil over the character of
Mr. Deane, that under its shade, the beams of clearer light might not
too deeply penetrate their own.

Mr. Robert Morris, a member of congress from the state of
Pennsylvania, had undoubtedly [138] been concerned in some very
profitable contracts, in company with several French and American
gentlemen, besides Mr. Deane; and under the sanction of public
negociations, the most lucrative trade was carried on, and the fortunes
of individuals accumulated beyond calculation.

Monsieur Gerard, the French minister residing in Philadelphia, was 1 7 7 9
warmly attached to Dr. Franklin and Mr. Deane, and not less disgusted
with Mr. Lee. It may be observed, that there are few public ministers
so tenacious of the dignity of their own character and conduct, as not
occasionally to descend to rank among partizans, and exert the
influence of public character to gratify private interest or resentment.
Thus Mr. Gerard, an idolizer of Dr. Franklin, supported Mr. Deane,
offered pensions to take off the defenders of Mr. Lee, and instead
of retaining the superiority of an ambassador from one of the first
monarchs in Europe, appeared the champion of a club of merchants
and speculators. He resided but a short time in America: the chevalier
de la Luzerne superseded him as ambassador to the United States,
in the summer of one thousand seven hundred and seventy-nine. The
reasons of his recal do not appear; but it was undoubtedly a prudent
measure in the court of France, not to suffer a minister to continue,
after he had discovered himself attached to a party.

[139] Within a few months after Congress had made a new
arrangement of ministers, and Mr. Adams had been sent on in the
room of Mr. Deane, both Mr. Adams and Mr. Lee were directed to
repair immediately to America; and Dr. Franklin was appointed sole
minister at the court of France. *Americans*, it is true, were early
initiated in the spirit of intrigue, but they were not yet so thoroughly
acquainted with the manoeuvres of courts, as to investigate the
necessity of the sudden recal of those gentlemen.

Mr. Lee had been very severely censured by many for his want of
address, and his unaccommodating spirit at the French court. Nor
had he been more successful in his negociations with Spain. He had
resided some months at Madrid, as commercial agent, with powers if

CHAP. XIV practicable to negociate a treaty, or to obtain a loan of money for the
1 7 7 9   use of the United States. But he was unacceptable to the court; and
though he had the abilities of a statesman, he was without the address
of a courtier; and his negociations in Spain redounded little to the
advantage of America. Yet such was his integrity, that he found it not
difficult on his arrival in his own country, to reinstate himself fully in
the good opinion of the public, and to wipe from his character the
aspersions of malice or prejudice.

[140] Mr. Adams returned rather disgusted at the early revocation
of his commission, and the unexpected order thus speedily to leave
the court of France. He did not himself repair to congress, but retired
privately to his seat in Braintree, where he employed himself for a
time, in preparing a concise statement of the situation and political
connexions of the different powers of Europe, which he laid before
congress, with his opinion of their interests and their views relative
to America, and recommended the pursuance of every step, that might
tend to strengthen the alliance with France. Nothing can more strongly
exhibit the pride Mr. Adams felt in the Gallican alliance, and his zeal
for supporting it, than the expressions contained in his own letters on
this subject, on his first residence at the court of France.

But in Mr. Adams's communications to congress, he advised them
strenuously and invariably "to guard against their principles in government, and the manners that were so opposite to the constitutions
of America, and the character of a young people, who might hereafter
be called to form establishments for a great nation."* Mr. Adams
continued in [141] this retired and mortified situation for some months;
but we shall see in its place, he was afterwards called upon to transact
affairs of a very high and important nature.

It was obvious to every one, that from the family interest and
connexion between the courts of France and Spain, the latter would
undoubtedly co-operate with the views and designs of the former;
but no treaty, alliance, or any public countenance had yet been given
to the Americans, by the court of Madrid. Spain had oscillated between
peace and war for several years. She had offered herself as mediatrix
among the contending powers: but insulted on the seas, and her
interference rejected by Britain, she appeared in June, one thousand

* This was under the despotism of kings. It was monarchic principles and manners
that Mr. Adams then admonished his countrymen to avoid. See his letter to congress,
August the fourth, one thousand seven hundred and seventy-nine. [Adams, *Works*,
VII: 99–110.]

seven hundred and seventy-nine, to act a more decided part. The CHAP. XIV
marquis de Almodovar, the Spanish ambassador in London, delivered 1 7 7 9
a rescript to lord Weymouth about this time, couched in language
that amounted to a declaration of war.

On these movements in Europe, congress thought proper again to
send an envoy to the court of Spain. John Jay, esquire, a gentleman
from the state of New York, was appointed to this mission, September
the twenty-seventh, one thousand seven hundred and seventy-nine.
His capacity was equal to the business: he was well received, and his
public character acknowledged: [142] yet his negociations were of
little consequence to America, while he resided in Spain. Perhaps
apprehensive that the spirit of freedom and revolt might extend to
her own colonies, Spain chose to withhold her assistance.

No treaty with the United States was effected by Mr. Jay's mission,
no concessions with regard to the free navigation of the Mississippi,
or any security for trade to the Bay of Honduras, were obtained. On
these important points he was directed to negociate, as well as to
solicit a loan of money, sufficient to assist the United States in the
pursuit of their measures. But no loan of money of any consequence,
was to be drawn from the frigid and wary Spaniards. Notwithstanding
the necessities of America were fully exposed by her minister, the
highest favor he could obtain was, the trivial loan of four or five
thousand pounds.

Spain had no predilection in favor of the independence of the
British colonies. She had always governed her own plantations beyond
the Atlantic, with a very arbitrary and despotic hand. Their contiguity
and intercourse with the North Americans led her to fear, that the
spirit of freedom might be contagious, and their own subjects there
so far infected, as to render it necessary to keep themselves in reserve
against future contingencies. This they had done for some time after
a war was announced [143] between Great Britain and France; but it
was impossible for them to continue longer neutral. France was now
involved in war, and decidedly supporting the Americans, and England, in expectation of a union of interests, and a modification of the
same line of conduct, in the courts of the several branches of the
house of Bourbon, had in various instances discovered a hostile
disposition, and stood in a menacing posture, as if both her sword
and her flag were ready to meet the conjoined forces of both France
and Spain.

His catholic majesty thought it impossible for him longer to delay

CHAP. XIV   an explicit declaration of his intentions. He published a long manifesto,
1 7 7 9   giving the reasons for a declaration of war. He ordered his ambassador
to retire from the court of London, without taking leave, and in a
schedule published by order, great moderation was professed. In a
paper delivered to lord Weymouth by the marquis de Almodovar, it
was observed, that

> the causes of complaint given by the court of London not having ceased,
> and that court shewing no dispositions to give reparation for them, the
> king has resolved, and orders his ambassador to declare, that the honor of
> his crown, the protection which he owes to his subjects, and his own
> personal dignity, do not permit him to suffer their insults to continue, and
> to neglect any longer the reparation [144] of those already received; and
> that in this view, notwithstanding the pacific dispositions of his majesty,
> and even the particular inclination he had always had and expressed, for
> cultivating the friendship of his Britannic majesty, he finds himself under
> the disagreeable necessity of making use of all the means which the
> Almighty has entrusted him with, to obtain that justice which he has
> solicited by so many ways, without being able to acquire it.
>
> In confiding on the justice of his cause, his majesty hopes, that the
> consequences of this resolution will not be imputed to him before God or
> man; and that other nations will form a suitable idea of this resolution, by
> comparing it to the conduct which they themselves have experienced, on
> the part of the British ministry.

While things stood thus in the courts of Great Britain, France, and
Spain, the indecisive movements for a time in the southern states of
America, engaged the public attention, and awakened anxious apprehensions for the result; at the same time that a scene of rapine and
plunder was spread through the central parts, Virginia, New York,
and Connecticut.

The predatory excursions of this year were begun early in the
summer. An expedition to [145] the Chesapeake, under the command
of sir George Collier of the navy and general Matthews of the army,
served no other purpose than to alarm, distress, and impoverish the
towns of Portsmouth, Suffolk, and other places in the state of Virginia,
that fell under their spirit of conflagration. They stayed but a short
time there: after enriching themselves with the spoils of the inhabitants, and leaving many of those who had once basked in the lap of
affluence, the houseless children of poverty, they left the state, by
order of the British commander in chief.

The pleasant line of towns bordering on Long Island Sound, in the

state of Connecticut, were the next who felt the severe consequences
of this mode of war, from British troops supported and covered by
the squadron under sir George Collier, who was recalled from the
Chesapeake to aid similar measures farther north.

About the beginning of July, governor Tryon with a number of
disaffected Americans, and general Garth with a ravaging party of
British troops and German *yaughers*, landed at New Haven, took
possession of the town with little resistance, plundered and insulted
the inhabitants, on whom every cruelty was perpetrated, except [146]
burning their houses: this was delayed from their thirst for plunder,
and the barbarous abuse of the hapless females who fell sacrifices to
their wanton and riotous appetites. Hurried afterwards by their avarice
for new scenes of plunder and misery, they left New Haven and
repaired to Fairfield, where they landed on the seventh of the month.

This place suffered a still more cruel and severe fate. Their landing
at Fairfield was but feebly opposed: the militia indeed made a faint
resistance, but soon retreated, and left their property and in many
instances their families, to the mercy of the enemy. This was not
altogether from the want of courage, but from a consciousness of their
own comparative weakness, and a strange delusive opinion, that the
generosity and compassion of the British would be exercised towards
them, when they found only a few women, children, and aged men
left, who seemed to have thrown themselves on their compassion.

The historian would willingly draw a veil over the wanton outrages
committed on the wretched inhabitants left in the town, most of them
of the feebler sex. Some of them, the first characters in the place,
from a wish to save their property, and an indiscreet confidence in
the honor of governor Tryon, with whom they had been personally
acquainted, and who had [147] formerly received many civilities at
their houses, risked their own persons and their honor, amidst the
fury of a conquering enemy, on a kind of sham protection from a man
who had forgotten the obligations of politeness, and the gratitude due
to those who had treated him with every mark of genteel hospitality.

The principal ladies of Fairfield, who from their little knowledge
of the world, of the usages of armies, or the general conduct of men,
when circumstances combine to render them savage, could not escape
the brutality of the soldiery, by shewing their protections from governor
Tryon. Their houses were rifled, their persons abused, and after the
general pillage and burning of every thing valuable in the town, some
of these miserable victims of sorrow were found half distracted in the

CHAP. XIV   swamps and in the fields, whither they had fled in the agonies of
1 7 7 9   despair.

Tryon endeavoured afterwards to exculpate his own character, and made some futile excuses for his conduct. He would have justified himself on the principles of policy, when he felt the indignation expressed against him for his want of humanity; but policy, reason, and virtue, equally revolt at modes of war, that eradicate from the mind not only the moral feelings, but the sense of decency, civility, and politeness.

[148] The avidity of this party was by no means satiated by the distresses of New Haven, and the total destruction of Fairfield: the neighbouring towns of Norwalk and Greenfield suffered a similar fate: the waste of property in shipping and merchandize, was there more complete. The whole coast equally defenseless and exposed to their ravages, expected to fall in the same way; but, whether from compunction or policy is uncertain, whichever it might be, sir Henry Clinton thought proper to check the career of depredation, so grateful to the feelings of Tryon and his partisans, by a sudden recal within ten days of their landing at New Haven.

Meantime general Washington had kept himself in a defensive and respectable situation, in the central parts of America, but without a movement for any very capital stroke, after the derangement of a well concerted plan for an attack on the city of New York. He had expected the aid of the French squadron from the West Indies, to facilitate this judicious measure: the militia of several states had been collected to assist in the design: the army was in high spirits; sanguine expectations were formed; and every thing promised success to the enterprise. But the count de Estaing, perhaps ambitious to subjugate one of the states to the arms of his master, and not dreaming of effectual resistance to a force, both by land and [149] sea, that might reasonably be thought sufficient for the most capital enterprise, instead of uniting first with general Washington, and covering his attempt on New York by a respectable necessary naval force, he thought proper to hazard the reduction of Georgia on his way, and then repair northward.

But his attack on Savannah, his unexpected repulse and retreat, not only retarded, but totally prevented the decisive stroke contemplated by Washington, nor less apprehended by Clinton, who was thereby induced to order the evacuation of Newport, and draw off all his troops from that quarter. Newport and its environs had been

infested with the inconvenience and misery of an army and navy on
their borders, from the seizure of that place by earl Percy, in one
thousand seven hundred and seventy-six, to their relief in the present
year.

The circumstances above related, put it out of the power of general
Washington to prosecute the feasible system he had meditated. The
militia were dismissed, and many of the continental troops returned
as usual, at the expiration of their term of enlistment. General Clinton
had made several attempts to draw the American commander from
his strong and defensible post in the Jersies, as well as to induce him
to divide his army, to oppose the desultory invasions and depredations
on the defenceless [150] sea-coast. But general Washington very well
knew the advantages he might lose by weakening the main body of
his army, and was too wise and judicious to be ensnared by the
manoeuvres of the British commander.

The first object of sir George Collier's speedy recal from the ravage
of the borders of Virginia, was to co-operate with general Vaughan,
in the important movements on the North River. The principal design
of this project was, to obtain some important posts on the Hudson.
General Vaughan, who had before been distinguished for his feats
there, still commanded on the Hudson, but higher up the river. On
the arrival of the squadron commanded by sir George Collier, they
united, and immediately made themselves masters of Stoney Point
on the one side, and Verplank's Neck on the other.

After these places had been dismantled the preceding autumn by
sir Henry Clinton, the Americans had in part repaired the works. In
each post they behaved with spirit and resolution; but as their numbers
were inconsiderable, and their works unfinished, they soon surrendered
prisoners of war, on the single condition of humane treatment.

Not many days after this event, general Washington ordered a
detachment of his most [151] active troops, under the command of
general Wayne, to attempt the recovery of Stoney Point. This bold
and vigorous enterprise was conducted in a manner peculiarly honorary
both to the officers and soldiers, but not altogether so consistent with
humanity. They were directed not to load their pieces, but to depend
on the bayonet: one who appeared discontented at the order, was
shot on the occasion. Though this summary mode of punishment is
severe, it was designed to prevent the effusion of blood: doubtless,
had the British been early alarmed by the fire of the American arms,
the carnage would have been greater.

CHAP. XIV   The works had been repaired and strengthened with great alacrity,
1 7 7 9 and two British regiments, some loyal Americans, and several companies of artillery, left in garrison by general Vaughan. On the evening
of the fifth of July, after a difficult and hazardous march, Wayne
reached, surprised, and recovered the post, in spite of the valiant
opposition within. Colonel Fleury, an amiable, ambitious, and spirited
young Frenchman, had the honor and peculiar pleasure of striking
the British standard with his own hand. This youthful officer had
received the thanks of congress, and the honorary rewards of the
soldier, for his distinguished bravery in several previous rencounters.

[152] General Wayne was himself slightly wounded in this enterprise; but the united applauses of the commander in chief, of congress,
and of his country, which he received, would have been ample
compensation for more painful wounds, or much severer fatigue. The
acquisition of this post was more honorary than important: an attempt
to have held it would have been fruitless: it had been previously
determined in a council of war, that on the success of Wayne, the
works should be demolished, and the stores brought off.

Sir Henry Clinton immediately set his whole army in motion for
the relief of Verplanks, which was momently expected to surrender
to the American arms, and for the recovery of Stoney Point. He
succeeded to his wishes; and after only three days possession, this
contested spot a third time changed its masters; and the command of
the whole river for a time, continued in the hands of the British.

Several other manoeuvres took place about this time near New
York, and the more central parts of the country, that kept up the
spirit of enterprise, and the honor of the arms of the states: but a
more consequential affair occupied the public attention, in the eastern
extreme of the American territory. A colonel Maclean had been sent
with a party of British troops from Halifax, to land at the mouth of
[153] the Penobscot, within the jurisdiction of the Massachusetts. He
erected a fort, and established a strong post in a convenient situation
for harassing the trade, and distressing the young settlements bordering
on the province of Nova Scotia. When this intelligence was received
at Boston, the hardy and enterprising spirit of the men of Massachusetts
did not hesitate to make immediate preparation to dislodge an enemy,
whose temerity had led them to encroach on their state.

It had been only four years since the commencement of hostilities
with Britain. America was then not only without a navy, but without
a single ship of war. The idea of constructing and equipping a maritime

force, was ridiculed by some, and thought chimerical and impracticable CHAP. XIV
by others: but the human mind is generally capable of accomplishing 1 7 7 9
whatever it has resolution to undertake.

By the industry and vigilance of public bodies and private adventurers, they had in this short period acquired a navy, that a century
before would have made a respectable figure among the most warlike
nations: and within ten days after Maclean's attempt was known at
Boston, the Warren, a handsome new frigate of force, commanded
by commodore Saltonstall, and seventeen [154] other continental,
state, and private ships, were equipped, manned, victualled, and
ready for sea. They were accompanied by an equal number of
transports, with a considerable body of land forces, who embarked in
high spirits, and with the sanguine expectation of a short and successful
expedition.

This business was principally conducted by the state legislature;
nor would the gentlemen of the continental navy board consent to
hazard the public ships, unless the commanding officers were positively
enjoined to execute their design immediately. They were apprehensive
that any delay might give opportunity to send a superior force from
New York. From the dilatory conduct of the Americans, after they
reached Penobscot, these apprehensions were realized; and before
any efficient movements had taken place, sir George Collier with a
heavy squadron under his command, appeared for the relief of Maclean.

General Lovell who commanded by land, was a man of little military
experience, and never made for enterprise sufficient to dislodge the
British from a post of consequence, or in any way complete an
undertaking, that required decision, promptitude, and judgment.
Commodore Saltonstall proved himself a character of as little enterprise, and in this instance, of [155] less spirit, than the commander
of the troops designed to act on shore.

Thus by the shameful delay of both, and to the mortification of
many brave officers who accompanied them, the expedition terminated
in the disgrace of both army and navy, and the total destruction of
the fleet. On the first appearance of sir George Collier, the American
shipping moved up the river, with a shew of resistance, but in reality
to escape by land, from an enemy they seemed not to have expected,
nor had the courage to face. Two of their best ships fell into the
hands of the British: the remainder, lighted by their own hands,
suffered a complete conflagration. The panic-struck troops, after
leaving their own ships, chagrined at the conduct of Saltonstall, and

CHAP. XIV disgusted with the inactivity, indecision, and indiscretion of Lovell,
1 7 7 9 made their escape through the woods, in small, indiscriminate parties
of soldiers and sailors. On their way they agreed on nothing, but in
railing at their officers, and suffering the natural ebullitions of
disappointment to spend itself in mutual reproaches. With fatigue,
hunger, and difficulty, they reached the settlements on the Kennebec,
and brought the intelligence of their own defeat.

It was not in the power of the infant states to repair their maritime
loss during the war; and to complete the ruin of their little navy,
[156] some of their best ships were lost in the defence of Charleston,
the year following, as will be seen hereafter. What added to the
mortification of this last stroke was, that these ships were prepared
and ready to sail, in order to prosecute a very flattering expedition
projected by the gentlemen of the navy board, in the eastern
department, when they received an express order from congress, to
send them to South Carolina.

Scarcely any single event during the great contest, caused more
triumph to Britain, than this total demolition of the beginning of an
American navy. So successful and enterprising had they been, that a
gentleman of the first information has observed, that "the privateers
from Boston in one year, would defray more than one half the expense
of that year's war."* By their rapid progress, they had given the
promise of a formidable appearance on the ocean, that in time they
might become a rival, even to the proud mistress of the seas: but this
blow gave a fatal stroke for the present to all farther attempts of the
kind.

After the loss of Charleston, the ship Alliance and the Deane
frigate, were the only remnants left of the American navy. These
were [157] soon after sold at public auction, the navy boards dissolved,
and all maritime enterprise extinguished, except by private adventurers. They were also much less fortunate after the loss of the public
ships, than they had been at the beginning of the war: it was calculated
that two out of three were generally captured by the British, after the
year one thousand seven hundred and eighty. Time may again revive
the ambition for a naval power there, as America is abundantly replete
with every thing necessary for the equipment of fleets of magnitude
and respectability.

* See letters of the honorable John Adams to Mr. Calkoen. ["Twenty-six Letters
upon Interesting Subjects Reflecting the Revolution of America, Written in Holland
in the Year MDCCLXXX [1780]," in Adams, *Works*, VII: 265–312.]

After all it may justly be considered, that the constructing a national
fleet, is but an addition to human misery; for besides the vast expense
of such equipments, the idle and licentious habits of a vast body of
sailors, a naval armament is only a new engine to carry death and
conflagration, to distant, unoffending, innocent nations. The havoc
of human life on the ocean, the great balance of evil resulting from
naval engagements, if duly weighed in the scale of equity or humanity,
might lead the nations, with one general consent, to their total
annihilation. Yet undoubtedly, the pride of empire and the ambition
of kings, will still induce them to oppress their subjects, for the
purpose of enhancing their own power, by this horrid instrument of
human carnage; and that they will continue to waft death and
destruction [158] to every corner of the globe, that their maritime
thunders can reach.

It is true the etiquette of modern courts usually introduces some
plausible apologies, as a sort of prelude to the opening of those real
scenes of war and destruction, which they are preparing to exhibit,
by that monstrous engine of misery, a naval armament.

They usually trumpet forth the godlike attributes of justice, equity, mercy,
and above all, that universal benevolence and tenderness to mankind, with
which their respective courts or sovereigns are supposed to be infinitely
endued; and deplore in the most pathetic strains, those very evils which
they are bringing on, and those miseries which they are exerting their
utmost powers to inflict.

But it is to be feared it will be long before we shall see a combination
of powers, whatever may be their professions, whose ultimate object
is the establishment of universal equity, liberty, and peace among
mankind. War, the scourge of the human race, either from religious
or political pretences, will probably continue to torment the inhabitants
of the earth, until some new dispensation shall renovate the passions,
correct the vices, and elevate the mind of mortals beyond the pursuits
of time.

[159] The world has so long witnessed the sudden and dreadful
devastation made by naval armaments, that it is unnecessary to
expatiate thereon: it is enough to observe, that the splendid display
of maritime power has appeared on the largest theatres of human
action. The proudest cities have unexpectedly been invaded, and the
inhabitants involved in misery, by the fire of those floating engines,
in too many instances to particularize, from the first building up a

British navy, to the early attempt of America to strengthen themselves
by following the example of the parent state, in building and equipping
ships of war, in the beginning of their opposition to British power.

The truth of this observation may be evinced by a single instance of surprise and capture, by a little squadron under the command of commodore Hopkins, only the second year after hostilities commenced between Great Britain and the colonies. The American commander of a ship of only thirty-six guns, and seven or eight smaller vessels, surprised New Providence, captured the governor, lieutenant governor, and other officers of the crown, seized near an hundred pieces of cannon, and carried off all the warlike stores on the island. But not habituated to the usual cruelties exercised on such occasions, though they continued there two or three weeks, they offered no insult to the inhabitants, and took possession of no private [160] property without paying for it. This was an instance of lenity that seldom falls under observation, where men have been longer inured to scenes and services that harden the heart, and too frequently banish humanity from the breast of man.

The small naval armament constructed by the United States, did not continue long enough in existence, either to attempt great enterprise, or to become hardened by the cruel achievements consequent on the invasion of cities, towns, and villages, and desolating them by the sudden torrents of fire poured in upon their inhabitants. Some future day may, however, render it necessary for Americans to build and arm in defence of their extensive sea-board, and the preservation of their commerce; when they may be equally emulous of maritime glory, and become the scourge of their fellowmen, on the same grade of barbarity that has been exhibited by some other nations.

CHAPTER XV

A Retrospect of some Naval Transactions in the West Indies, one thousand seven hundred and seventy-eight, and seventy-nine • Affairs in Georgia concisely reviewed • General Lincoln sent to take the Command at the Southward • The Count de Estaing's Arrival in Georgia • Savannah closely besieged by the Combined Forces of France and America • Repulsed by General Prevost • The Count de Estaing leaves the Southern Clime • The Count Pulaski slain in Georgia • Some Anecdotes of Count Kosciusko

[161] From the concise mode of narration hitherto observed in these annals, a particular detail of naval operations will not be expected. Yet it is necessary to look a little back, and observe that an insular war had raged between the British and French in the West Indies, during the winter of one thousand seven hundred and seventy-eight, though they had not yet received any intelligence, that a formal declaration of hostilities between those two potent nations had taken place.

The island of Dominica was seized by the marquis de Bouille, governor of Martinico, as early as September, one thousand seven hundred [162] and seventy-eight; but the terms imposed on the inhabitants by the conqueror, were so mild, that they scarcely felt the change of sovereignty. No licentious rudeness, or avaricious pillage, was permitted by the humane and honorable commander, who, through all his conduct in the West Indies, exhibited a specimen of that generous compassion always honorary to the conqueror and to human nature.

The loss of the island of Dominica was peculiarly mortifying to the court of St. James, as it had been ceded to Great Britain on the last peace, as a kind of balance of accounts, after a very expensive war with the house of Bourbon.

Admiral Barrington with a considerable force, lay at this time at

Barbadoes, in a very anxious and inactive state. He had yet no orders for hostile operations; but he was soon after relieved by the arrival of five thousand men commanded by general Grant, convoyed by six ships of the line and a number of frigates, under the direction of commodore Hotham. The want of instructions, and even of intelligence that might be depended on, had exceedingly embarrassed the British admiral: but on Hotham's arrival, an expedition to the island of St. Lucia was prosecuted with celerity and success.

[163] The chevalier de Micaud, the commandant, took all the precaution of a brave and judicious officer. The main point was to prevent the completion of the British success, until he should be relieved by the arrival of the French squadron from Boston, which he had the highest reason every moment to expect. The count de Estaing had formed the design, and was in force sufficient, to have swept all the leeward islands, before the junction of admiral Barrington and commodore Hotham. But interrupted in his military progress by a second violent gale in the American seas, and seldom a favorite of fortune, he did not appear in sight of St. Lucia until the last French flag was struck. He however made some spirited, but successless efforts for the recovery of the islands. The vigilance and valor of the British commander defeated this design: to which was added the mortification of repeated disappointment, in several valiant rencounters with the bold and resolute English.

Though the count de Estaing's ships were equal in force, and experience had shewn that neither his officers nor seamen were deficient in courage, yet after he quitted St. Lucia, he apparently declined a general engagement, and within ten days withdrew to Port Royal. He was frequently insulted while there by the appearance of challenge from the British flag; but he still adhered to his own system of inaction, [164] determined to undertake no capital stroke before the arrival of fresh reinforcements from Europe. It was not until the month of June, one thousand seven hundred and seventy-nine, that this event took place, when the arrival of monsieur de la Motte, with every thing necessary for the most vigorous naval operations, excited the count de Estaing to immediate enterprise.

The first object of attack was the valuable island of St. Vincents, which had formerly cost much British blood to arrest and secure, by the cruel attempt to exterminate the unfortunate and innocent Caraibs. After the easy acquisition of this island, the count proceeded to the Grenades. He there landed two or three thousand men under the

command of count Dillon, a brave Irish officer in the French service.
He also headed a strong column himself, and attempted to carry the
most defensible fortress by storm. His superiority of strength insured
his success; and lord Macartney was obliged to offer a surrender, on
the proposals of capitulation he had at first rejected; but the count
received and treated the governor's flag with an unbecoming *hauteur*.
He made new and severe proposals in such a tone of defiance and
contempt, that both the governor and the inhabitants chose rather to
surrender at discretion, than to bind themselves to such hard conditions, as neither the customs of nations nor the justice of courts had
usually required.

[165] There is much reason to believe, that the count de Estaing
did not exercise all the lenity that ought to be expected from a brave
and generous conqueror. On the contrary, after this new acquisition,
the inhabitants were plundered and distressed; an unbounded license
raged among the soldiery, till their excesses were checked by the
humanity of count Dillon, who paid every attention to the miseries
of the people; and supported by his own regiment, he rendered the
condition of the conquered island less deplorable.

The capture of St. Lucia was in a degree fatal to the conquerors.
The noxious air of an unhealthy island, in a burning climate, did
more than the sword of France to waste the veterans of Britain.
Sickness and mortality raged and cut down the troops; and the
squadron weakened by the departure of admiral Byron, to convoy the
homeward bound fleet of merchantmen, nothing of consequence was
attempted in his absence.

When he returned, both St. Vincents and the Grenades were in
the hands of the French; but so uncertain were the accounts at first
received, of the wretched situation of the Grenades, that the British
commander determined to hazard an attempt for their relief. This
brought on a general, though not a decisive action. It was supported
on both sides with laudable [166] spirit and bravery; but they finally
separated without victory on either. Yet the proud and gallant Britons,
whose island has long assumed the haughty style of mistress of the
seas, who have justly boasted their superiority in naval engagements,
could not forbear to claim the advantage in this doubtful conflict. But
it is certain the wounded fleets under the admirals Barrington and
Byron, found some difficulty in reaching St. Christophers, without
some of their ships falling into the hands of their enemy.

The count de Estaing returned to Grenada; and the lillies of France waved for a short time in the West Indies; and the English admirals were insulted in their turn, by the parade of the French fleet before St. Christophers, in the same manner lord Barrington had before manoeuvred in vain at Martinico, without provoking the Frenchmen to engage. After these partial successes, the count de Estaing soon left the tropical seas, and repaired again to the American continent, where the assistance of a naval force was by this time exceedingly wanted, to aid the operations of the Americans.

The southern campaign had been opened the preceding year, by the seizure of the capital of Georgia. Sir Henry Clinton, late in the autumn of one thousand seven hundred and seventy-eight, had ordered a large detachment of [167] Hessian, British and provincial troops, under the command of lieutenant colonel Campbell, to Savannah, to assist major general Prevost in further prosecuting some expected advantages he had already gained. They were escorted by a small squadron under the command of commodore Parker, and arrived in the Savannah the twenty-seventh of December.

The state of Georgia was at this time in a very weak and defenceless situation. Their frontiers were exposed to the depredations of the savages; and the rude incursions of the wild borderers who mixed with them, had often been so troublesome, as to require the call of the southern militia to check their outrages. Colonel Campbell landed his troops immediately on his arrival in the river, and by several spirited and judicious movements, possessed himself of the town of Savannah, the capital of the state, with little or no loss, and obliged general Robert Howe, a gentleman of North Carolina, who commanded a party of about eight hundred militia, to retreat with precipitation.

Orders had been previously given by sir Henry Clinton to major general Prevost, the commander in chief in East Florida, to repair with all possible expedition, to aid the invasion and reduction of Georgia. This active officer immediately collected his remote cantonments, and with dispatch and perseverance, pushed [168] his march through a hot and barren country of great extent. Surmounting innumerable difficulties and fatigue, he reached Sunbury, and took possession of the town and garrison, before Campbell had possessed himself of Savannah.

Both military skill and a great degree of humanity, marked this first important enterprise in the south. The British commander forbid that the inhabitants not in arms should be either molested or plundered; and by promises and proclamations, encouraged them to submit

quietly to the authority of the parent state. Some acquiesced by
inclination, and many impelled by necessity, appeared ready to enlist
under the British standard; others, of more bold and independent
sentiments, made their escape across the river, with the hope of an
asylum in South Carolina.

These successes again encouraged the disaffected and disorderly
people, who had long infested the back parts of North Carolina, to
renew their incursions. Those insurgents had been apparently subdued, their leaders cut off, and their spirits broken, in the beginning
of the American convulsions; but their aversion to the reigning powers
in that state, still rankled in their breasts: they had impatiently waited
an opportunity of displaying it, in all the fierce and cruel modes of
savage war, in conjunction [169] with the neighbouring Indians, to
whom they had attached themselves.

They considered this a favorable crisis, and again left their rural
occupations. They united with some scattering parties of the same
description, on the borders of South Carolina and Georgia, embodied
themselves, and in their progress committed every outrage, that might
be expected from an armed banditti. But on an attempt to join general
Prevost, their main body was attacked by the provincial militia, many
of them cut off, and others taken prisoners; the remainder fled to the
frontiers of Georgia, where, with their old associates of the wilderness,
and all others who could be collected in the back settlements, they
united to aid general Prevost in his future operations.

The hazardous situation of Georgia, and the imminent danger of
the wealthy state of South Carolina, had spread an alarm that awakened
to immediate exertion for the recovery of the one, and the security
of the other. General Lincoln had seasonably been sent forward to
take the command in the southern department. He reached Savannah
a short time after colonel Campbell's arrival there; but he found
himself not in so eligible a situation as might have been wished. The
number of troops under his command fell far short of expectation:
the artillery and stores were insufficient; and every [170] difficulty
was enhanced by the want of order and discipline in the militia, who
refused to submit to the necessary subordination of armies: they left
their posts and retired at pleasure.

General Lincoln however, consistent with his usual disposition on
all occasions, endeavoured to make the best of his situation. He
continued himself at Purisburgh, with the main body of his army,
and ordered general Ashe with a detachment of two thousand men,

to take a strong post at a place called Briar Creek. His design was to secure the upper part of the country against the loyalists, who were every where collecting their strength.

Soon after general Ashe had taken possession of the advantageous post, that in the opinion of the principal officers, promised perfect security, general Prevost formed and executed the design of surprising him there. To facilitate this judicious measure, he made such arrangements on the banks of the Savannah, as took off the attention of general Lincoln: at the same time, he ordered his brother, colonel Prevost, by a circuitous march of fifty miles, to fall unexpectedly on Ashe's party at the creek. The success of the enterprise justified the design; the whole detachment was routed, many of them killed or captured; and thus the way was opened for the loyalists, and their copper-colored allies in the back country, to join Prevost [171] without molestation. After this action which took place the third of March, the two parties separated by the river, continued quietly in their own posts, till the latter end of the month of April, one thousand seven hundred and seventy-nine. Savannah, Sunbury, and some other towns, were in the hands of the British, and the state by proclamation, laid under military government: yet the people in general considered themselves as belonging to the union.

General Lincoln, zealous to procure an election of delegates to congress from Georgia, which he expected would be impeded by violence, left his advantageous situation on the lower part of the river, and moved towards Augusta. This was rather an unfortunate movement, as, had he continued his first station, he might have secured Charleston for a time. Indeed, there was then little reason to apprehend any immediate danger in that quarter; yet he had the precaution to leave general Moultrie, with fifteen hundred men to guard the passes of the river.

The campaign in Georgia however, did not redound much to the advantage of the American arms, or to the honor of general Lincoln. It was thought by some, he did not discover himself a judicious and experienced commander, who had penetration to calculate on fortuitous events, or resources at hand to extricate himself when they unexpectedly took place. [172] Yet he supported a character, cool and brave, under a variety of disappointments. He was however, led a circuitous dance from place to place, by the rapid movements of general Prevost through the state of Georgia, until he was obliged to move with more serious prospects towards Charleston.

The loss of his party at Briar Creek, was no more than might have CHAP. XV
been expected from the activity and vigor of such an officer as Prevost, 1 7 7 9
attending more to his military renown, than to the political manoeuvres
of the state. While general Lincoln was canvassing for the election of
a delegate to congress,* the commander of the forces of his antagonist
was intent only on winning success in the field.

The active Prevost seized the moment of advantage; suddenly
crossed the river in different parts, and penetrated into South Carolina,
with little or no opposition. The party under Moultrie, consisting
chiefly of militia, on seeing themselves surrounded on all sides by
British troops, retreated hastily, and secured themselves within the
city of Charleston.

General Prevost having thus succeeded, even beyond his most
sanguine expectations, in several [173] enterprises of considerable
moment, inspired by his own wishes, and prompted by the importunities of the loyalists, he formed the bolder resolution of pushing
directly for Charleston. He arrived at the river Ashley on the eleventh
of May, crossed it, and within a few days summoned the city to
surrender. Nor had he any reason for some time, to regret the
determination. He had every assurance from the disaffected Americans, that Charleston would surrender without resistance, and that
they had the best authority for this decided opinion; nor did they in
this instance so totally disappoint the expectations of their British
friends, as they frequently had done, and continued to do in their
subsequent informations. It is true general Prevost did not immediately
succeed to the full completion of his hopes; but on the first summons
to surrender, the citizens assured him, that no opposition should be
made, provided they might be permitted to continue in a state of
neutrality to the conclusion of the war.

This was the only instance in America of an offer made so derogatory
to the honor of the union. No single state, whatever might be their
distresses, ever expressed a wish during the war, to be bound to a
neutral repose, while their sister states were bleeding at every pore,
in support of the general cause. The conduct of the citizens of
Charleston cannot be accounted [174] for, but from the momentary
panic to which the human mind is liable, when sudden danger presses,

* There was an effort to defeat this measure, which general Lincoln judged it necessary
to counteract, bearing in mind the interests of his country in civil as well as military
matters.

before it has time to collect its own fortitude, and to act with decision and dignity, consistent with previous principles.

South Carolina had been distinguished for the bold and active part, taken by that state against the measures of Britain. This was the first southern colony, after Virginia, who adopted the proposal of a general congress; nor was there now any reason to suspect any defection in the bulk of the inhabitants, though there were numbers in the city of Charleston, attached to the royal cause. Her patriots were unshaken, her officers brave; and the subsequent conduct of the people at large, and the sufferings of individuals, effaced the unfavorable impressions this proposal might have left, had it not have been wiped off by the vigorous opposition afterwards made to a successful foe, both in their councils and in the field, amidst the extremes of peril, personal danger, and public misery.

General Prevost, encouraged by success, and animated by his own personal bravery, united with the hope of subduing Charleston, rejected the offer of neutrality, and all further negociation ceased. The city immediately recovered its former spirit, and preparation was made on both sides for the most vigorous attack and defence.

[175] General Lincoln had been rather slow in his movements, having been deceived into an opinion, that Prevost had no farther design in crossing the river Savannah, than to procure forage and provisions. But soon finding more serious consequences were to be expected, he hastened on with his whole force, and made his arrangements with so much judgment and alacrity, that general Prevost thought it prudent to withdraw from before the city, lest his retreat should be cut off. He encamped his troops on the islands before the harbor, where he continued for some time, in anxious expectation of reinforcements from New York. This being delayed until the advance of the intense heats, and the sickly season of that country came on, which rendered it in some measure necessary to suspend all vigorous operations in that quarter, little else was done there this year, except the indiscriminate plunder of the wealthy inhabitants of the state, who were out of the reach of the protection of their friends.

Affairs in Georgia requiring his presence, general Prevost repaired there soon after the siege of Charleston was raised. He left a force sufficient in Port Royal to encourage his friends, by keeping up the appearance of some permanent establishment in that province, where he meant soon to return. But early in the autumn, the unexpected arrival of the squadron [176] commanded by the count de Estaing,

on the southern coast, gave the flattering promise of a new face to
the affairs of Georgia and the Carolinas.

The admiral on his arrival in the Savannah, landed his troops with all possible expedition, and in conjunction with the Americans, laid siege to the capital of Georgia. On the sixteenth of September, he demanded a surrender of the town to the arms of the king of France. The summons was in language that rather excited terror than allurement, and would have determined an officer of less courage and resolution than general Prevost, to defend the town to the last. The situation of Savannah was indeed scarcely defensible; but resolved not to yield but in the last extremity, Prevost returned a polite, but evasive answer to the French commander; and had the address to obtain a truce of twenty-four hours to deliberate.

In this fortunate interval, the arrival of colonel Maitland, with a body of troops from Port Royal, put an end to deliberation. All thoughts of surrender were laid aside, and a most gallant defence made. The town was bombarded for five days, to the great terror and distress of the inhabitants. In this predicament, general Prevost wrote and requested the count de Estaing, that the women and children, with his [177] own wife and family, might be sent down the river, and placed under the protection of one of the French ships. After some delay, he had the mortification to receive an unpolite and cruel refusal.

As this answer was signed by both the French and American commanders, censure for want of humanity fell equally on each. It is not improbable the severe language it contained, might be designed to intimidate, and hasten a surrender, and thereby prevent the further effusion of blood. Yet there appeared a want of generosity unbecoming the politeness of the Frenchman, and inconsistent with the well known humanity of the American commander. Of this they seemed to be sensible within a few days, when fortune began to change her face. Apologies were made both by general Lincoln and the count, for this indelicate refusal: great tenderness was therein expressed for the inhabitants, and every civility offered, particularly to the general's lady and family, and a ship assigned as an asylum for herself and friends. General Prevost replied to this offer of kindness, extorted by apprehension if not by fear, that "what had been once refused in terms of insult, could in no circumstances be deemed worth the acceptance."

[178] The little time gained by this short parley for the purposes

of civility, was improved by general Prevost to great advantage in every view. With indefatigable industry he strengthened his old works; and, assisted by the spirit and capacity of Mr. Moncrief, the chief engineer, he erected new ones with celerity and judgment, very honorable to his military talents, and consistent with his zeal and alacrity on all occasions.

The arrival of an officer of colonel Maitland's abilities, accompanied by a considerable reinforcement, was indeed a very fortunate circumstance at this period for the commander at Savannah. Stimulated by a recent affront, and urged on by a constitutional activity, and a thirst of military applause, general Prevost seemed to bid defiance to the combined forces of France and America, and repulsed them in every quarter.

On the eleventh of October, the besiegers attempted to storm the town, but were defeated with great slaughter. They however kept up the appearance of a blockade until the sixteenth, when they requested a truce to bury their dead, and take care of their wounded. This was readily granted by Prevost. The conflict had been bloody indeed, and both sides equally wished for time to perform this charitable and necessary [179] business. Soon after the melancholy work of interring many of their comrades, the French and the Americans took the advantage of a dark and foggy night, and retreated with all possible precipitation, breaking down the bridges as they passed, to impede the pursuit of their enemies, if they should be disposed to follow them.

The count de Estaing had now an opportunity to survey the condition of his fleet; when he found the sailors sickly and dispirited; nor was the army less so, from the unhealthiness of the climate, and the failure of their late enterprise. The count himself had been wounded in the course of the siege, and several of his best officers were either killed or wounded. The loss of very many of his men in this decided repulse, with the disgrace that every commander thinks he incurs, when the expectation of success from great designs is defeated, deeply affected the mind of the French commander. Thus unfortunately disappointed in the spirited attack on the town of Savannah, he found it necessary, from a combination of untoward circumstances, to abandon the design of recovering Georgia. In a short time after this, the French commander bade adieu to the American seas.

He had never been disgraced by any deficiency in military ability,

knowledge, or spirit, [180] while acting in behalf of the United States:
yet a series of disappointments had prevented his reaping the laurels,
the just reward of bravery, or rendering much service to his allies,
who had received him with the highest marks of cordiality and
expectation.*

The summons of the count de Estaing to the British commander,
to surrender the capital of one of the states to the arms of his most
christian majesty, was neither pleasing, prudent, or productive of
harmony and confidence, between the French under his command
and the Americans. It occasioned some discontent at the time; and
perhaps some jealous Americans did not regret, that the recovery of
Georgia was left to an officer of merit in their own corps, sent forward
afterwards by general Greene, who had been the favorite of fortune,
of the people, and of the commander in chief.

This was done at a period of complicated difficulties, when general
Greene could not leave the state of South Carolina himself, but in
the abilities of general Wayne he had the utmost confidence. The
event shewed that this confidence was not misplaced. We shall [181]
see hereafter general Wayne was sent on, and had the honor of
finishing the war in Georgia, and the pleasure of witnessing the
evacuation of the troops from their strong holds in that state,
annihilating the last remains of British authority there, and recovering
again the youngest of the sister states, to their former union.

In the repulse before Savannah, many valorous and gallant officers
fell. Among this number was the count Pulaski, a Polish nobleman
of great consideration. His bravery and enterprising spirit was celebrated, not only in America, but in his own country. He had once,
amidst the fierce contests of the miserable Polanders, in the height
of his zeal for the recovery and support of the liberties of that nation,
seized on the person of the king of Poland, and for a time held him
his prisoner; and though he had with him only two or three, whom
he deemed trusty associates, one of them relented, and betrayed him:
the king was saved, and the count obliged to fly.† A few years after,
he repaired to America, where he found a field ample enough for the

---

* The count de Estaing was some years afterwards, one of the proscribed victims who
  fell by the guillotine, amidst the distractions and misery of his own country, in the
  infuriated reign of Robespierre.

† A full narrative of this transaction may be seen in Coxe's Travels through Russia,
  &c. &c. [William Coxe, *Travels into Poland, Russia, Sweden, and Denmark* (5 vols.;
  4th. ed.; London, 1792).]

exercise of his soldierly talents, to cherish his love of freedom, and to support the military character of his ancestors and his family, many of whom survived this heroic officer.

[182] The count Pulaski was not the only officer of his nation who distinguished himself in the American war; but the count Kosciusko, for his firmness, his valor, and his sufferings, merits particular notice. He was amiable and virtuous, as well as brave, and supported a character that will seldom be passed over in silence, in a history of either Poland or America.

The kingdom of Poland had for years exhibited a most striking monument of human misery. Their struggles for liberty, the pride of the nobles, the ignorance and barbarism of the peasantry, their unstable confederacies, the usurpation of princes, and the interference of neighbouring monarchs, rendered it a scene of carnage, for several ages previous to the expulsion of Stanislaus Augustus, their ruin as a nation, and the partition of their country among the crowned despots that surrounded them. The sovereign of Poland was dethroned; the kingdom partitioned among the trio combined for that purpose, Frederick, Catherine, and Maria Theresa. Many of the inhabitants were sent to plant colonies in the cold and distant regions of Siberia, and other parts of the Russian domains. Some of the nobility survived under the heavy yoke of their victorious neighbours; others had fled, and lent their valorous arms to England, France, and America.

This melancholy termination of efforts grounded in nature and reason, might for a time [183] smother the spark of freedom implanted in every human breast, which yet almost every man, when ascending the pedestal of power, endeavours to extinguish in the bosom of all but himself. But the misfortunes of their country, or their own personal sufferings, could not deaden the flame of liberty and independence, that burnt in the bosoms of many noble-minded Polanders: though the distractions of their native country obliged them to abandon it, their enthusiasm was cherished amidst strangers, and they lent their veteran abilities to aid the emancipation of others from the degrading yoke of servitude.

The character of no one of this distinguished band became more conspicuous, than that of the count Kosciusko, who survived the fierce conflicts to which his bravery exposed him through the revolutionary war in America.* His subsequent transactions in his native

* See more of the count Kosciusko in Appendix, Note No. VII.

country, his valor, his misfortunes, and his renown, are too well CHAP. XV
known, and too replete with extraordinary events, to record in this 1 7 7 9
place.

While we admire the patriotism, bravery, and other virtues, that
adorned the characters of some individuals among the heroes of that
ill-fated country, the deplorable situation of Poland [184] should
forever stand as a *memento* to all other nations, who claim or maintain
any degree of freedom. By their private animosities, jealousies, and
dissensions, all confidence was destroyed, and all patriotism annihilated, except in the bosoms of a few, until their king was dethroned,
the nobility laid prostrate, the country drenched in blood, and the
people driven into banishment by thousands, and obliged to wear out
a miserable existence, under the authority of the arbitrary sovereigns
who had completed the ruin of their liberty, their government, and
their country.

The history of Poland is indeed an awful lesson to every republic,
where the seeds of dissension begin to spring up among the people.
Those symptoms, when nurtured by faction, and strengthened by
jealousies among themselves, render the people an easy prey to foreign
invaders, and too generally terminate in a tragic catastrophe, similar
to that of the Poles; who no longer continued a distinct nation, after
the æra which has stained the annals of Europe by the shameful
partition treaty, preconcerted in the cabinets of Russia, Prussia, and
Germany, and announced by the joint declaration of their sovereigns,
in one thousand seven hundred and seventy-three.

The inhabitants of Poland were now the subjects and slaves of
those usurping princes, who [185] had seized and divided the kingdom;
transplanted the inhabitants of the territory to distant regions, and re-
peopled the depopulated country with the soldiers of Prussia, Germany, and the northern potentates, who had long trained their own
subjects to bend in silence, under the yoke of servility.

The partition of Poland was a singular event in the history of
Europe, where the great powers, inattentive to the *balance* about
which they had for many years expressed so much solicitude, viewed
this extraordinary circumstance with little or no emotion. Whatever
may be the effect on the general state of Europe, it is yet uncertain,
whether the Poles lost so much by the change as has been apprehended.

It is difficult to say in what period of the history of Poland, they
had any proper claim to the honor of a free, republican form of
government. The people had long groaned under the unbridled

CHAP. XV oppresssion and power of a proud domestic aristocracy. The absurd
1 7 7 9 *veto*, designed as a check, only increased their discontents, jealousies, rancor, and confusion. They had indeed a nominal king, more the subject of a foreign power, than the sovereign of his own country. They are now under the iron hand of foreign despotism. Whether that, or the scourge of [186] aristocracy, is the most productive of vassalage and misery, is a problem yet undecided. We leave deeper politicians to determine if they can, which is the most abhorrent to the feelings of humanity. But the discussion of the constitution of the Poles, is not a part of the business of the present work. Yet the ruin of Poland may be viewed as an example and a warning to other nations, particularly to those who enjoy a free, elective, representative government.

C H A P T E R   X V I

Sir Henry Clinton and Admiral Arbuthnot sail for South Carolina • Charleston invested • Capitulates • General Lincoln and his Army
Prisoners of War • General Clinton returns to New York • Lord Cornwallis's Command and Civil Administration in Charleston • Mr. Gadsden
and other Gentlemen suspected, and sent to St. Augustine • Much Opposition to British Authority in both the Carolinas • The Count de Rochambeau and the Admiral de Tiernay arrive at Newport • British Depredations
in the Jersies • Catastrophe of Mr. Caldwell and his Family • Armed
Neutrality • Some Observations on the State of Ireland • Riots in England • Cursory Observations

[187] From the unavoidable inactivity of the Americans in some parts
of the continent, and the misfortunes that had attended their arms in
others, in the summer of one thousand seven hundred and seventy-
nine, sir Henry Clinton was left without any impediment, to prosecute
a well concerted expedition to the southern colonies. The opulence
of the planters there, the want of discipline in their militia, the
distance and difficulty of reinforcing them, and the sickly state of the
inhabitants, promised an easy conquest and a rich harvest to the
invaders.

[188] The summer and autumn passed off; and it was late in the
month of December, before general Clinton embarked. He had a
strong body of troops, and a forcible squadron commanded by admiral
Arbuthnot, who accompanied him; but they proceeded heavily on
their way; and it was not until the ensuing spring was far advanced,
that the admiral passed the bar, and made himself master of the
harbor of Charleston.

The Americans flattered themselves for some time, that they should
be able to make an effectual resistance to the passage of the British
fleet up the Cooper river: (this passes on one side, and the Ashley

runs on the other of the town of Charleston:) but they soon abandoned every ground to the potent English, except the town of Charleston, which they determined to defend to the last extremity.

Governor Rutledge was vested by the legislature with very extraordinary powers, which he was obliged to exercise in their full latitude. This gentleman had acted on all occasions with spirit and judgment becoming his character, both as a soldier and a magistrate. He immediately called out the militia; and published a proclamation directing all the inhabitants who claimed any property in the town, to repair immediately to the American standard, on pain of confiscation. Though couched in strong and [189] severe terms, this proclamation had little effect. The manifest reluctance of some to oppose the power of Britain, the dread that others felt of so potent an adversary, the ill success of the American arms in Georgia, the surprise of the cavalry and other parties that were coming to their relief, the arrival of British reinforcements, and the rapid advance they made to conquest, appalled the inhabitants, and obliged the citizens soon to abandon all hopes of even saving their town.

The first summons of surrender, on the sixteenth of April, was rejected by the American commander, though it announced the dreadful consequences of a cannonade and storm, which would soon be the unhappy fate of Charleston, "should the place, in fallacious security, or the commander, in wanton indifference to the fate of the inhabitants, delay a surrender." General Lincoln replied, that he had received the joint summons of general Clinton and admiral Arbuthnot; that

> sixty days had passed since it had been known, that their intentions against the town of Charleston were hostile; in which, time had been afforded to abandon it; but that duty and inclination pointed to him the propriety of defending it to the last extremity.

After this decided answer, the most vigorous operations ensued on both sides, but with great [190] advantage in favor of the British, till the eighth of May, when sir Henry Clinton again called on the American commander, to prevent the farther effusion of blood, by an immediate surrender. He warned him, that

> if he refused this last summons, he should throw on him the charge, of whatever vindictive severity an exasperated soldiery might inflict on the unhappy people: that he should wait his answer till eight o'clock, an hour beyond which, resistance would be temerity.

General Lincoln summoned a council on this occasion, who were CHAP. XVI
unanimously of opinion, that articles of capitulation should be pro- 1 7 8 0
posed.* The terms offered were several of them rejected, others were
mutilated; and all relaxation or qualification being refused by the
British commander, it was as unanimously agreed, that hostilities
should again re-commence on the ensuing day. Accordingly, an
incessant fire was kept up from the ninth to the eleventh, when an
address from the principal inhabitants of the town, and a number of
the country militia, expressed their satisfaction in the terms already
offered by general Clinton: at the same time, [191] the lieutenant
governor and council requested, that negociations might be renewed,
and that they might not be subjected to the horrors of a city taken
by storm.

The militia of the town had thrown away their arms; the troops on
the lines were worn down with fatigue, and their provisions exhausted:
thus closely invested on every side, a disaffected, factious party within,
no hopes of succor from without, and all possibility of retreat cut off,
general Lincoln again offered terms of surrender, little variant from
Clinton's proposals. They were acceded to, and signed the twelfth of
May.

Though the conditions were not the most favorable to the inhabitants, or honorary to the soldier, yet perhaps they were as lenient as
could be expected from an enemy confident of success, and as
honorable as could be hoped, in the desperate situation to which the
Americans were reduced. The continental troops were to retain their
baggage, but to remain prisoners of war until exchanged. Seven
general officers were among the prisoners. The inhabitants of all
conditions were to be considered as prisoners on parole; but they soon
experienced the severities usually felt by a conquered city. All who
were capable of bearing arms, were enrolled in the British service:
and the whole state laid under heavy contributions.

[192] The loss of Charleston, the great number of the captured,
and the shipping that fell in its defence, was a severe blow to America.
Much censure was cast on general Lincoln for neglecting a timely
retreat, and for attempting the defence of the town against such

* This general view of the siege and surrender of Charleston, is principally collected
  from general Lincoln's defence and apology in a letter to general Washington, which
  the author was favored with the perusal of in manuscript, by general Lincoln.
  [Benjamin Lincoln to George Washington, July 17, 1780, Benjamin Lincoln Papers
  (MHS microfilm, reel 13).]

CHAP. XVI   superior force, both by sea and land: but it must be acknowledged,
1 7 8 0   he did all that could be expected from an officer of courage, to save
the capital and the state; or from a man of humanity, to make the
best possible terms for the inhabitants. He afterwards justified the
measure by a full detail of the invasion, and the motives for his
conduct, to the satisfaction of the commander in chief, and of his
country.

General Lincoln certainly had great merit, in many respects: yet it
may be observed, few officers have been equally fortunate in keeping
up the *eclat* of character, who have so frequently failed in enterprize:
for, however unjust it may be, yet military fame more generally
depends on successful events, than on bold design, or judicious
system. Victory had seldom followed in the rear of any of his exploits:
yet from his known bravery and patriotism, from his acknowledged
integrity and honor, he escaped the censure frequently attached to
unfortunate heroes, and which might have fallen heavily on a general
of more doubtful character.

[193] Before sir Henry Clinton left Charleston, some new and
severe regulations took place, that could not well be justified, either
by the letter or the spirit of the capitulation. All persons in the city
were forbidden the exercise of their commercial pursuits, excepting
such as were the decided friends of the British government. Confiscation and death were threatened by proclamation, to any who should
be found in arms, unless in support of royal authority. All capable of
bearing arms were enrolled for British service: such as had families
were permitted to continue near them, and defend the state against
their American brethren; those who had none were required to serve
six months out of twelve, in any part of the southern states.

Many inhabitants of the principal towns, and indeed a great part
of the state of South Carolina, despairing of any effectual resistance,
and unwilling to abandon their connexions and their property, laid
down their arms and submitted either as prisoners of war, or subjects
to the king of Great Britain: and even congratulatory addresses were
fabricated, and signed by great numbers of respectable characters in
Charleston, and offered to the British commanders on the success of
their arms. Thus from motives of interest or fear, many who had
appeared [194] to be actuated by higher principles, stooped to the
servile homage of the sycophant, and flattered the victors on the
conquest of their country; an acquisition that reduced their countrymen
to beggary, and themselves to slavery.

Soon after these arrangements, sir Henry Clinton, vainly flattering

himself that he had entirely subdued one wealthy colony, at the
extremity of the continent, and that every thing was in a hopeful
train for other brilliant strokes of military prowess, left the command
of the southern department to lord Cornwallis, and repaired himself
to New York. His lordship immediately detached a strong body under
the command of lord Rawdon, to march, to subjugate, and guard the
frontiers, while he turned his own attention to the commercial
regulations, and the civil government of the newly conquered province.
But he soon found the aid of auxiliaries, impelled by fear, or stimulated
by the hope of present advantage, is not to be depended on, and that
voluntary compacts are the only social ties considered among mankind
as binding on the conscience.

On the first opportunity, many persons exchanged their paroles for
certificates of their being good subjects, and immediately returned to
the country, or to the neighbouring state, and stimulated their friends
to resistance. A [195] remarkable instance of this nature was exhibited
in the conduct of colonel Lisle, a brave American officer; who, after
an exchange of the parole, decamped from the British standard, and
carried off with him a whole battalion to the aid of colonel Sumpter,
and other spirited officers, who were in motion on the borders of both
the Carolinas.

The new regulations, and the hard conditions enjoined on them by
the conqueror, were highly resented by many of the principal inhabitants of Charleston. Their dissatisfaction was so apparent, that they
soon fell under the suspicion and displeasure of the commander.
Some allegations were brought against them, though far from being
sufficiently founded. They were charged with treasonable practices
and designs against government; arrested in their beds, sent on board
prison ships, confined and treated with great rigor, and in a short time
sent off to St. Augustine. Among this number was lieutenant governor
Gadsden, a gentleman early distinguished for his patriotism, his
firmness, his republican principles, and his uniform exertions to
emancipate his country from the shackles of British government.

Nothing appeared to justify the severities exercised towards these
gentlemen; nor was there any reason to believe they had forfeited
their honor. The rigorous policy of a conquering [196] foe, was all
that was offered in vindication of this step. But it is certain the
Carolinians in general evinced the difficulty of holding men by political
fetters, while the mind revolts at the authority that has no claim but
what arises from the laws of conquest.

Lord Rawdon was extremely active on the frontiers. No exertion

CHAP. XVI was wanting on the part of this valiant officer, to bring the whole
1 7 8 0 country to a united submission to royal authority; and a diversion was
made in the Chesapeake, under the command of general Leslie, in
favor of the operations in the Carolinas. Yet within two months after
the surrender of Charleston, opposition to British government again
resumed a stable appearance.

Marches, counter-marches, surprise, pillage, and massacre, had for
some months pervaded the frontiers; and whichever party gained the
advantage, the inhabitants were equally wretched. But a particular
detail of the miseries of the southern states through this period, would
be more painful than entertaining to the reader, and is a task from
which every writer of humanity would wish to be excused. Imagination
may easily paint the distresses, when surveying on the one side, a
proud and potent army flushed with recent success, and irritated by
opposition from an enemy they despised, both as Americans and as
rebels; their spirit of revenge [197] continually whetted by a body of
refugees who followed them, embittered beyond description against
their countrymen, and who were joined by a banditti who had no
country, but the spot that yielded a temporary harvest to their rapacious
hands: rapine and devastation had no check.

On the other side, little less severity could be expected from a
brave and high-spirited people, not softened by the highest refinements
of civilization, warmed by the impulse of retaliation, driven almost to
despair, and under every painful apprehension for their lives, their
property, their liberty, and their country: these were joined by the
soldiers of fortune, and the fierce borderers, who had not yet been
taught to yield quietly, either to military or civil subordination: the
most striking outrages were every where committed. But no partisan
distinguished himself more on either side, than a colonel Tarleton,
who made himself a character in the ravage of the Carolinas, equally
conspicuous for bravery and barbarity; and had the effrontery afterwards in England, to boast in the presence of a lady of respectability,
that he had killed more men, and ravished more women, than any
man in America.*

---

* This was so highly resented by the lady, who had before been his friend, that by
her influence, she defeated his hopes as a candidate for a member of parliament.
[Lt. Colonel Banastre Tarleton had been perceived in America as a vicious, ruthless
warrior since David Ramsay's *History of the Revolution of South-Carolina* (2 vols.;
Trenton, 1785). After returning to England, he lived for some years with Mary
Robinson, an actress and writer who had had a relationship with the Prince of Wales.

[198] But not the loss of their capital, the ravage of their country, chap. xvi the proscription of some of the principal inhabitants, and the total 1 7 8 0 ruin of some of the wealthiest families, could subdue the spirit of independence, and the aversion to British government, that had taken deep root in the bosoms of most of the inhabitants of the southern states.

Sumpter, Morgan, Marion, Lee, Caswell, Rutherford, and other brave officers, continually counteracted the intrigues of the loyalists; and attacked, harassed, and frequently defeated the British parties, that were detached to the various parts of the country to enforce submission. Nor did the repulse in Georgia, the loss of Charleston, nor the armament sent to the Chesapeake by sir Henry Clinton, in favor of lord Cornwallis's movements, in the smallest degree check the vigorous efforts of these spirited leaders, by whose assistance a new face to the affairs of their country was soon restored.

France had this year given a new proof of her zeal in favor of American independence. The count de Rochambeau arrived on the eleventh of July at Newport, with six thousand forces, under cover of a respectable squadron commanded by the admiral de Tiernay. They brought the promise and the expectation of farther and immediate support, both by land and sea. Some ineffectual movements were [199] made on both sides, in consequence of these expectations: and on the arrival of admiral Graves at New York, with six sail of the line and some transports, a feint was made by sir Henry Clinton, with the assistance of those fresh reinforcements, immediately to attack the French at Rhode Island. This plan was diverted by general Washington's preparation to embrace the favorable opportunity, to strike a decided blow by the reduction of New York.

All the states east of the Delaware discovered their readiness, by all possible exertions to cooperate in the design: but amidst all the preparation and sanguine hope of the Americans, an account was received, equally mortifying to the United States, and to their allies already in America, that admiral de Guichen had sailed from the West Indies directly for France, instead of repairing with all his forces, as

He ran for Parliament unsuccessfully in 1784, but was returned from Liverpool, with only a short break, from 1790 to 1812. He published an account of his service in America, *A History of the Campaigns of 1780 and 1781 in the Southern Provinces of North America* (2 vols.; London, 1787), which earned him enmity as an egotist and an ingrate. See *Dictionary of National Biography*; Robert D. Bass, *The Green Dragoon: The Lives of Banastre Tarleton and Mary Robinson* (New York, 1957).]

CHAP. XVI
1 7 8 0

was expected, to aid the united operations of Washington and Rochambeau. The admiral de Tiernay died soon after at Newport. It was thought by many, that this brave officer fell a sacrifice to chagrin and disappointment.

After the failure of these brilliant hopes, little more was done through the summer in the middle or eastern department, except by skirmishing parties, which served only to keep up the hope of conquest on the side of Britain, while it preserved alive some military ardor in [200] the American army. But so uncertain are the events of war, that the anticipation of success, the pride of victory, or the anguish of disappointment, alternately play on the passions of men, until the convulsion gives place to tranquillity and peace, or to the still solemnity of melancholy, robbed of all its joys.

General Washington found himself at this time unable to do much more, than to guard against the uncertain inroads of a powerful fleet and a hostile army. It could not be congenial to the feelings of the military character, endowed with a spirit of enterprise, to be placed in a situation merely defensive, while too many circumstances forbade any concentrated plan, that promised any decision of the important object for which the United States were struggling.

While thus situated, the British troops were frequently detached from New York and Staten Island, to make inroads, and by surprise to distress and destroy the settlements in the Jersies. The most important of their movements was about the twenty-fifth of June, when general Knyphausen with about five thousand regular troops, aided by some new levies, advanced upon the right wing of the American army, commanded by major general Greene. Their progress was slow until they arrived at Springfield, where they were checked by a party of the Americans.

[201] They had yet done little mischief on their march, but at Springfield they burnt most of the houses in the town, and retired from thence to Elizabethtown. After some time, they advanced from Elizabethtown with the whole of their infantry, a large body of cavalry, and fifteen or twenty pieces of artillery. Their march was then rapid and compact: they moved in two columns, one on the main road leading to Springfield, the other on the Vauxhall road. Major Lee with the horse and picquets, opposed the right column, and colonel Dayton with his regiment, the left; and both gave as much opposition as could have been expected from so small a force.

General Greene observed in a letter to congress, that the American troops were so extended, to guard the different roads leading to the

several passes over the mountains, that he had scarcely time to collect
them at Springfield, and make the necessary dispositions, previous to
the appearance of the enemy before the town; when a cannonade
commenced between their advance and the American artillery, posted
for the defence of the bridge.

Every prudent measure was taken by general Greene, to confront
and repel the invaders, protect the inhabitants, and secure the retreat
[202] of his own parties, when danger appeared from superior numbers.
The generals Maxwell and Dickenson, the colonels Shrieve, Ogden,
and others, at the head of their regiments, exhibited the highest
specimens of American bravery: but the enemy continued to press on
in great force. Their left column began an attack on colonel Angell,
who was posted to secure a bridge in front of the town. "The action
was severe, and lasted about forty minutes; when superior numbers
overcame obstinate bravery," and forced the American troops to retire
over the second bridge.

After various military manoeuvres, skirmishes, and retreats, general
Greene took post on a ridge of hills, from whence he detached parties
to prevent the burnings of the enemy; who spread conflagration
wherever it was in their power, and retreated towards Elizabethtown.
This detachment from the British army finished their marauding
excursion, and re-crossed to Staten Island, July the twenty-third.

The outrage of innocence in instances too numerous to be recorded,
of the wanton barbarity of the soldiers of the king of England, as they
patroled the defenceless villages of America, was evinced no where
more remarkably, than in the burnings and massacres that marked
the [203] footsteps of the British troops, as they from time to time
ravaged the state of New Jersey.

In their late excursion, they had trod their deleterious path through
a part of the country called the Connecticut Farms. It is needless to
particularize many instances of their wanton rage, and unprovoked
devastation, in and near Elizabethtown. The places dedicated to
public worship did not escape their fury: these were destroyed more
from licentious folly, than any religious frenzy or bigotry, to which
their nation had at times been liable. Yet through the barbarous
transactions of this summer, nothing excited more general resentment
and compassion, than the murder of the amiable and virtuous wife of
a Presbyterian clergyman, attended with too many circumstances of
grief on the one side, and barbarism on the other, to pass over in
silence.

This lady was sitting in her own house, with her little domestic

CHAP. XVI circle around her, and her infant in her arms; unapprehensive of
1 7 8 0 danger, shrouded by the consciousness of her own innocence and
virtue; when a British barbarian pointed his musquet into the window
of her room, and instantly shot her through the lungs. A hole was
dug, the body thrown in, and the house of this excellent lady set on
fire, and consumed with all the property it contained.

[204] Mr. Caldwell, her affectionate husband, was absent: nothing
had ever been alleged against his character, even by his enemies, but
his zeal for the rights, and his attachment to his native country. For
this he had been persecuted, and for this he was robbed of all that
he held dear in life, by the bloody hands of men, in whose benevolence
and politeness he had had much confidence, until the fated day, when
this mistaken opinion led him to leave his beloved family, fearless of
danger, and certain of their security, from their innocence, virtue,
and unoffending amiability.

Mr. Caldwell afterwards published the proofs of this cruel affair,
attested on oath before magistrates, by sundry persons who were in
the house with Mrs. Caldwell, and saw her fall back and expire,
immediately after the report of the gun. "This was," as observed by
Mr. Caldwell, "a violation of every tender feeling; without provocation,
deliberately committed in open day; nor was it ever frowned on by
the commander." The catastrophe of this unhappy family was completed within two years, by the murder of Mr. Caldwell himself, by
some ruffian hands.

His conscious integrity of heart had never suffered him to apprehend
any personal danger: and the melancholy that pervaded all, on the
tragical death of his lady, who was distinguished [205] for the excellence
and respectability of her character, wrought up the resentment of that
part of the country to so high a pitch, that the most timid were aroused
to deeds of desperate heroism. They were ready to swear, like
Hannibal against the Romans, and to bind their sons to the oath of
everlasting enmity to the name of Britain.

But we shall see too many circumstances of similar barbarity and
ferocious cruelty, to leave curiosity ungratified, or to suffer the tear
of pity to dry on the sympathetic cheek, as we follow the route of
the British army. Agitation and anxiety pervaded the eastern states,
while rapine and slaughter were spread over the middle colonies.
Hope was suspended in every mind; and expectation seemed to hang
on the consequences of the strong effort made to subdue the southern
provinces.

The present year was replete with the most active and important CHAP. XVI
scenes, both in Europe and America. We leave the latter to wait the 1 7 8 0
operation of events, and turn our eyes towards Great Britain, whose
situation was not less perplexed and embarrassed, than that of the
United States. The sources of concern which pervaded the patriotic
part of the nation, were innumerable. A remarkable combination of
powers against the British nation was unusually alarming. Spain had
now declared war, and acted [206] with decision: and many new and
great events among other nations, threatened both the maritime and
internal state of Great Britain, with checks to their pride and power
which they had not before experienced.

The despot of Russia, with haughty superiority, appeared at this
time, umpire of the *Armed Neutrality,* set on foot by herself.* The
novelty of this measure excited much observation, attention, and
expectation, both in Europe and America. Some writers have robbed
the empress of the honor of originating this humane project, which
was thought to be levelled at the imperious sway, and the insolent
aggressions of the British flag, which had long been vexatious to all
the nations.

This measure has been attributed to a stroke of policy concerted
by count Panin, in order to defeat the design of sir James Harris,
minister from Great Britain, who had been making every [207] effort
in favor of his court, to engage the empress to fit out a naval armament
against Spain. Prince Potemkin, the empress's favorite, was fond of
the measure of assisting the court of Spain: but the determined
opposition of the count Panin, against the interference of the court
of Russia in the war between Great Britain and the house of Bourbon,
in conjunction with the American colonies, was such, that the design
was not only defeated, but the court of Petersburgh took the lead in
a declaration to the belligerent powers, for setting the principles of
navigation and trade; and the armament in preparation for other
purposes, was sent out to support the armed neutrality.†

* Before this period, the wealth and inhabitants of the Turkish empire had been
diminished, and the power of the Sublime Porte so far crippled, by the ambitious
projects of Catharine, that they were unable to lend much assistance to any of their
distressed neighbours. For some time after the remarkable partition of Poland, the
hero of Prussia, the Germanic body, and the northern powers, breathed in a kind
of truce, as if paralysed by the recollection of recent slaughter and devastation,
rather than in the benign prospect of a permanent peace.
† See History of the Armed Neutrality by a German nobleman. A more recent work

[208] But such was the commanding genius of Catharine, and her predominant passion for the extension of her fame, that those who have studied her character will not deny her the capacity, nor the honor of originating this humane and novel system. She was a woman in whom were united, the most splendid talents, a magnificent taste, an unconquerable mind, the most beneficent virtues, and the most detestable crimes. But whoever was the prime mover of a system so benevolent, the idea was the greatest that ever entered into the head of a prince, since the days of Henry the fourth of France.* The design was glorious, as it might in time be so far improved, as to put a period to a great part of the distress brought on the trade of nations, by the ambition, interest, and proud usurpation of some maritime powers.

The empress forwarded an explicit declaration of the design and the nature of the combination, to the several European courts. By [209] this extraordinary treaty, all neutral ships were to be freely navigated from port to port on the coasts of nations at war, and the effects belonging to the subjects of any sovereign, were to be safe in all neutral vessels, except contraband merchandize. Thus the seas were to be left in the situation designed by God and nature, that all mankind might reap the benefits of a free and open intercourse with each other.

Several other articles, humane, just, and favorable to trade, were

---

has attributed the origin of this benevolent system, to the policy of the count de Vergennes, and has asserted that it was a plan of his own to counteract the operations of the British court against France, by this check to the power of their navy. But from the character of the count de Vergennes, as drawn by an American minister, his abilities were not equal to the comprehensive system. He observed, that

> notwithstanding the gazettes of Europe had been filled with pompous panegyrics of this minister, and sublime ideas of his power and credit, as well as his abilities, it was but mere puff and bubble: and that notwithstanding his long experience in courts, he was by no means a great minister: that he had neither the extensive knowledge, nor the foresight, nor the wisdom, nor the virtue, nor the temper of a great man.

[Johann Eustach von Goertz, *The Secret History of the Armed Neutrality. Together with Memoirs, Official Letters and State Papers, Illustrative of the Celebrated Confederacy . . . Written Originally in French by a German Nobleman* (London, 1792).]

* Every one acquainted with the history of France, will recollect the benevolent design formed by Henry the fourth and his sagacious minister, the duke of Sully, to put an end to the waste of human life by war, by a combination, great, extensive, and more humane than generally falls under the contemplation of princes. His design to settle the contests of nations by amicable treaty, was defeated by the hand of the assassin, which deprived him of life.

stipulated. Their security was guaranteed by a powerful fleet, directed CHAP. XVI
by a despotic female; while the neighbouring sovereigns, awed by 1 7 8 0
her prowess, strength, and stern authority, aided her measures.

Though this was a very unpleasant proposition to the court of Great
Britain, it was acceded to with alacrity by the northern powers, and
by most of the other courts in Europe. Thus Sweden, Denmark, and
Portugal, united with the potent court of Petersburgh, to guard and
protect the trade of nations, while war raged among so many of them.

This capital measure was equally pleasing to France, Spain, and
America; but to Great Britain it was a grievance of magnitude: and
what greatly enhanced their mortification, it [210] had originated with
a sovereign whom they considered as a friend and an ally; one to
whom they had looked forward as a powerful assistant, if the exigencies
of war should oblige them to seek the further aid of foreigners. But,
as a writer observed, "the solitary court of London was obliged to
suppress her indignation." Neither her resentment, chagrin, or address, could prevent a measure which Great Britain considered as
particularly injurious to herself.

The British minister expostulated warmly with the court of Petersburgh, on the constant attention and regard hitherto shewn on every
occasion, to the flag and commerce of Russia, by Great Britain. He
declared there was a continuance of the same disposition and conduct
in his court, and reminded the empress of the reciprocal ties of
friendship, and the commercial interests, by which the two nations
were mutually bound.

The confederacy too formidable for opposition in their present
situation, an equivocal, rather than an explicit reply to the declaration
of the empress, was sent by the court of Great Britain to the British
envoy resident at Petersburgh, dated April the twenty-third, one
thousand seven hundred and eighty.

While this indecisive mode of conduct was observed by the court
of Great Britain, the [211] other European powers had not only readily
agreed to the proposition for an armed neutrality, but appeared
generally pre-disposed to a friendly intercourse with America, if not
unequivocally to support her claim to independence.

A general state of danger from foreign combinations seemed to
threaten the empire of Great Britain, with a convulsion in almost all
its parts; at the same time, discontent and dissatisfaction, particularly
in Ireland, seemed to be on the point of rising to an alarming height,
and fast approaching to a crisis.

It was observed by one of their own writers, that

it was not to be expected that a country dependent on Great Britain, and much limited in the use of its natural advantages, should not be affected by the causes and consequences of the American war. The sagacious in that kingdom could not avoid perceiving in the present combination of circumstances, an advantage which was to be now improved, or given up forever.

There now appeared a remarkable revolution in the temper of the people of Ireland, that discovered strong symptoms of their weariness of their subordinate and depressed situation. These were doubtless quickened and brought into action, by the struggle of the Americans for independence.[212] Early in the opposition of the united colonies to parliamentary measures, congress had forwarded a friendly address to the inhabitants of Ireland. In this they had observed, that "the ministry had for ten years, endeavoured by fraud and violence, to deprive them of rights which they had for many years enjoyed:" that

at the conclusion of the last war, the genius of England and the spirit of wisdom, as if offended at the ungrateful treatment of their sons, withdrew from the British councils, and left that nation a prey to a race of ministers, with whom ancient English honesty and benevolence disdained to dwell. From that period, jealousy, discontent, oppression, and discord, have raged among all his majesty's subjects, and filled every part of his dominions with distress and complaint.

In this address to the inhabitants of Ireland, the American delegates had recapitulated their several grievances, which had driven them to opposition, and a suspension of all commerce with Great Britain, Ireland, and the English West India islands. After observing that they hoped from this peaceable mode of opposition to obtain relief, they made a friendly apology to the Irish, for including them in this restriction, assuring them,

that it was with the utmost reluctance we could prevail upon ourselves, [213] to cease our commercial connexions with your island. *Your* parliament had done us no wrong. *You* had ever been friendly to the rights of mankind: and we acknowledge with pleasure and with gratitude, that *your* nation has produced patriots, who have nobly distinguished themselves in the cause of humanity and America.

On the other hand, we were not ignorant, that the labors and manufactures of Ireland, like those of the silk-worm, were of little moment to herself, but served only to give luxury to those who neither *toil* nor *spin*. We

perceived that if we continued our commerce with you, our agreement CHAP. XVI
not to import from Britain would be fruitless; and were therefore compelled 1 7 8 0
to adopt a measure, to which nothing but absolute necessity could have
reconciled us. It gave us, however, some consolation to reflect, that should
it occasion much distress, the fertile regions of America would afford you
a safe asylum from poverty, and in time from oppression also; an asylum
in which many thousands of your countrymen have found hospitality,
peace, and affluence, and become united to us by all the ties of consanguinity, mutual interest, and affection.*

[214] We offer our most grateful acknowledgments for the friendly
disposition you have always shewn towards us. We know that you are not
without your grievances. We sympathize with you in your distress; and are
pleased to find, that the design of subjugating us, has persuaded administration to dispense to Ireland, some vagrant rays of ministerial sunshine.
Even the tender mercies of government, have long been cruel towards
you. In the rich pastures of Ireland many hungry parricides have fed, and
grown strong to labor in its destruction. We hope the patient abiding of
the meek may not always be forgotten: and God grant that the iniquitous
schemes of extirpating liberty from the British empire, may be soon
defeated!

But we should be wanting to ourselves; we should be perfidious to
posterity; we should be unworthy that ancestry from which we derive our
descent,—should we submit with folded arms, to military butchery and
depredation, to gratify the lordly ambition, or sate the avarice of a British
ministry. In defence of our persons and properties, under actual violation,
we have taken up arms: when that violation shall be removed, and
hostilities cease on the part of the aggressors, they shall cease on our part
also. For the achievement of this happy event, we confide in the good
offices of our fellow-subjects beyond the Atlantic: of their [215] friendly
disposition we do not yet despond, aware, as they must be, that they have
nothing more to expect from the same common enemy, than the humble
favor of being last devoured.

This energetic address to the Irish may be seen in almost every
public record of the transactions of congress, in one thousand seven
hundred and seventy-five. This, with other addresses of the same
determined body of men, to the inhabitants of England, of Canada,
of the United States, comprise an epitome of the grievances complained
of by Americans, of the existing opinions, and the cause of the
colonies taking arms against the parent state.

The similarity of sufferings which the Irish had long felt, oppressions

* See Appendix, Note No. VIII.

CHAP. XVI which had often driven them to the point of despair, a prospect of
1 7 8 0 successful resistance by the colonies to the overbearing measures of
the British crown and parliament, awakened in them a dawn of hope,
that relief might result from union and concert among themselves,
sufficient to check the present, and to prevent still greater burdens,
from the usurpations of power often exercised against them, without
equity or humanity.

The rising ferment in the Irish nation was justly alarming to the
court of Britain. This, with the weight of foreign combinations which
[216] pressed upon them, awakened apprehensions in the highest
degree, in the minds of the sober and judicious, who had the welfare
of the nation at heart. In addition to their concern from these causes,
their differences of opinion with regard to their own internal affairs,
on almost every subject, increased. This disunion of sentiment
appeared in the vast number of petitions laid on the table of the
house of commons, from the most respectable counties; not less than
forty at once. These brought on much debate and altercation, that
promised much reform and produced little.

The enormous influence of the crown, the abuse of contracts, the
corruption in all departments, were discussed, and the American war
again reprobated. The waste of human life, and the treasures of the
nation, were pathetically lamented in the course of parliamentary
debate; and this absurd and fruitless war criminated in strong language.

The strength of party was tried to its utmost, on a variety of
subjects. The increasing and dangerous influence of the crown, was
particularly dwelt upon: on this a member of the house* observed,
that nothing more strongly evinced its existence, than the minister's
keeping his place, "after so many years of loss, misfortune, [217] and
calamity, as had already marked the fatal course of his administration."
He asked,

> whether that noble lord had not lost America? whether he had not
> squandered many millions of the public money, and wasted rivers of blood
> of the subjects of Great Britain? And yet, though the whole country, with
> one voice, cried out against him, and execrated his American war, the
> noble lord still held his place. Could this possibly be ascribed to any other
> cause than to the overgrown influence of the crown, along with that daring
> exertion of it, which sets the voice and the interests of the people at
> nought?

* Sir Thomas Pitt.

He observed that the present minister by his measures,

had sunk and degraded the honor of Great Britain. The name of an
Englishman was now no longer a matter to be proud of: the time had been
when it was the envy of all the world; it had been the introduction to
universal respect; but the noble lord had contrived to sink it almost beneath
contempt. He had rendered his countrymen, and their country, despicable
in the eyes of every other person.

This session of parliament continued desultory, angry, agitated,
and inconclusive, till towards [218] the close; when all eyes were
opened to immediate danger, by the distracted and incoherent conduct
of lord George Gordon, at the head of the *London Associators*, who
had combined expressly to defend the Protestant religion. They had
taken the alarm from a motion made by sir George Saville, deemed
too favorable to the Roman Catholic religion, though received with
universal applause in the house of commons.

It is observable, that the pretext of religion had often rent in sunder
the bands of union, and interrupted the peace of the English nation,
from the conquest to the present day. Nor had persecution ever been
pushed with a more severe hand in any part of the world, than among
these islanders, all of whom professed themselves Christians, though
divided by a variety of denominations. The popish religion had been
particularly inhibited from the days of the Stuarts; but as many of the
nobility still adhered to the Catholic faith, a degree of liberality and
toleration was indulged, and religious distinctions, if not annihilated,
had generally lain dormant among a people highly improved in
politeness and erudition. Yet the same spirit of bigotry was concealed
in the bosoms of many, which wanted only the contact of a torch to
emblazon into the flames of persecuting fury.

[219] This the present moment presented; and no animosities of
this nature had for many years arisen to such a height of riot, confusion,
tumult, and danger, as raged in the city of London in consequence
of an act recently passed, entitled "an act for relieving his majesty's
subjects professing the popish religion, from certain penalties and
disabilities, imposed on them by an act made in the eleventh and
twelfth years of the reign of king William the third." The zealous
opposition in Scotland to any relaxation of the penal laws against the
Papists, seems to have originated the Protestant association in England.

Though not immediately connected with American affairs, it may
not be improper before we conclude this chapter, to notice, that no

CHAP. XVI heat of opposition among the *insurgents* of the *colonies*, as they were
1 7 8 0 termed, ever arose to such an atrocious height, as the mobs in London,
in the face of the parliament of England, and under the eye of their
sovereign.

The restless and turbulent spirit and conduct of lord George Gordon,
gave rise to the notorious outrages committed in and about London
in the month of June, one thousand seven hundred and eighty.
Enthusiastically bitter against the indulgence of the Roman Catholic
religion, he carried his designs and temper so far, as to spread the
same intolerant spirit through a large [220] body of his adherents.
Fifty or sixty thousand persons assembled in St. George's Fields,
under the appellation of the *Protestant Associators*, distinguished by
blue cockades in their hats, a badge which they endeavoured to affix
to many well-meaning persons, whom they compelled to move in
their train. The passions of the mad multitude inflamed by various
artifices, they paraded the city for several days, and set fire to many
elegant buildings, among which lord Mansfield's house, furniture,
library, and many valuable manuscripts, were destroyed.

Lord George Saville's house in Leicester Fields, fell under the
resentment and fury of the rioters, professedly for his preparing and
bringing a bill into parliament in favor of the Catholics. The bishop
of Lincoln, and several other dignified clergymen, felt the effects of
their ruffian and licentious hands: they were insulted, abused, and
treated with the utmost rudeness and indignity. In short, plunder,
rapine, anarchy, murder, and conflagration, spread in every quarter
of the city. The prisoners were released, and the jails set on fire:
Newgate, King's Bench, the Fleet Prison, and other public buildings
destroyed. Neither the civil authority, the remonstrances of the
moderate, nor the terror of the military, were able to quell the rioters,
or disperse the rabble, under four or five days, that the city blazed in
so [221] many different and conspicuous parts, as to threaten the
conflagration of that noble capital.

As soon as a degree of quiet was restored by a dispersion of the
inflamed multitude, lord George Gordon was taken into custody, and
committed to the tower. After six or seven months confinement, he
was tried; but as there appeared a derangement of his intellectual
faculties, bordering on insanity, he was acquitted and set at liberty.

It is no singular circumstance that a zeal for religion, or rather for
a particular mode of worship, should disgrace the Christian system,
by the wild fanaticism of its real or pretended votaries. It has been

observed, that this was the pretext for the licentious conduct of the CHAP. XVI
London Associators: their cry was *religion;* forgetful among the most 1 7 8 0
ferocious deeds of cruelty, that the religion they ostensibly pretended
to defend, was interwoven with the most rational morality, and the
most fervent piety.

The same illiberal spirit of superstition and bigotry, has been the
pretext for establishing inquisitions, for Smithfield fires, for massacres,
wars, and rivers of human blood poured out on the earth, which
groans beneath the complicated crimes of man. Thus, mistaken ideas
of religion have often led the multitude to deeds [222] of cruelty and
madness, enkindled the fury of the assassin to murder the monarch
amidst his guards, or the hapless maid in her devotional closet. The
ignorant, the artful, or the illiberal children of men, have often brought
forward the sacred name of religion, to sanction the grossest absurdities,
to justify the most cruel persecutions, and to violate every principle
of reason and virtue in the human mind.

It is a melancholy truth, that the Christian world too generally
forgets that the mild spirit of the gospel dictates candor and forgiveness
towards those who are dissentient in opinion. The example of the
good Samaritan was recorded, to impress the cultivation of the
benevolent affections towards all mankind, without restriction to
neighbour or to country: and the sword of Peter was ordered into its
scabbard, by the founder of that code of rational and just sentiment,
productive of order and peace in the present stage of weakness and
error.

The mild virtues of charity and brotherly kindness, are the distinguishing characteristics of this benign religion: yet it is not less
humiliating than wonderful, when we calmly reflect, that mankind
have seemed to delight in the destruction of their fellow-beings, from
the earliest records of time to the present struggles of America, to
maintain their rights at the point [223] of the sword, against a nation
long inured to the carnage of their own species.

This has been evinced, not only in the oppression of Great Britain
over her own colonies, and the civil convulsions on their own island,
but from the havoc made by their enormous naval armaments, which
have crimsoned the ocean with human blood, carried death to their
antipodes, and desolation round the globe.

To the universal regret of the most benevolent part of mankind,
they have witnessed, that the nabobs of India have been reduced to
slavery, and the innocent inhabitants of the eastern world involved

in famine, poverty, and every species of misery, notwithstanding the immense resources of the most luxuriant and fertile country on earth, by the innovating, ambitious, and insolent spirit of a nation, assuming the jurisdiction of the seas, and aiming at universal domination.

The black catalogue of cruelties permitted by the English government, and executed by their myrmidons in the east, against the innocent natives of India, will leave a stain on the character of the British nation, until the memory of their deeds shall be blotted from every historic page. Nor was the system of conquest there [224] relaxed in the smallest degree: while the Ganges and the Indus were reddened with the blood, and covered with the slaughtered bodies of men, their armies in the west were endeavouring to reduce their former colonies, to the same state of slavery and misery with the inhabitants of that distant region.

The attempted extermination of many of the primitive inhabitants, and the waste of human life through all Indostan and other parts of the eastern world, by the destroying sword of Britain, are recollections too shocking for the humane and benevolent mind to dwell on. Too melancholy a picture is exhibited, when the eye of compassion is turned towards that ill-fated country. It must in tears behold the zemidars and the nabobs in chains, their princes and princesses of every age immersed in poverty, stripped of their connexions, captured by the English, and dying in despair, without the cold solace of pity from their foes. All the ancient, well-informed, and ingenious inhabitants of that rich, populous, and favored spot of creation, involved in one common ruin, exhibit the most striking and affecting view of the cruelties of man, and of the vicissitudes of human affairs, that modern history presents.

These last observations indeed, may not appear to be connected with the design of the present work: nor have the cruelties which have [225] been exhibited in the East Indies by the arms of Great Britain, arisen from a spirit of religious intolerance. It may however be observed, when the mind has for a moment left the more sublunary pursuits of man, and adverted to the sacred theme of religion, that nothing can be a more insurmountable bar to the propagation of truth, either in the east, the west, or in the dark regions of African or Asiatic slavery, than the cruelties perpetrated by men, who profess a system of ethics more sublime than that of Zoroaster, morals more refined than taught by Socrates, and a religion pure and simple, inculcating the most benign dispositions, forbidding all injuries to the weakest of its fellow beings.

Observations on the moral conduct of man, on religious opinion or CHAP. XVI persecutions, and the motives by which mankind are actuated in their 1 7 8 0 various pursuits, will not be censured when occasionally introduced. They are more congenial to the taste, inclination, and sex of the writer, than a detail of the rough and terrific scenes of war. Nor will a serious or philosophic mind be displeased with such an interlude, which may serve as a temporary resting-post to the weary traveller, who has trodden over the field of carnage, until the soul is sickened by a view of the absurdity and cruelty of his own species.

[226] These reflections may justify a short digression, that only means to hint at the happy consequences that might result, if a nation which extends its power, and carries its arms to the extremities of the globe, would transmit with them, that mildness of manners, that justice, humanity, and rectitude of character, that would draw the inhabitants of the darker regions of the world, from their idolatry and superstition. Thus nations who had long been immersed in errors, might be led to embrace a religion, admirably adapted to the promotion of the happiness of mankind on earth, and to prepare a rational agent for some higher stage of existence, when the drama on this tragic theatre is finished.

A P P E N D I X
T O   V O L U M E   F I R S T

———————————— Note No. I. Page 7. ————————————

[403] The reader's curiosity may be gratified by the perusal of a few particulars relative to the Plymouth settlers, from their earliest memorials. One hundred and one persons left Holland, all of whom arrived at Plymouth in the month of December, one thousand six hundred and twenty. From the sufferings and hardships they sustained, more than half their number died before the end of March, one thousand six hundred and twenty-one.

On the borders of a forlorn wilderness, without any governmental restrictions, they thought it necessary to adopt some measures for order and subordination. They voluntarily on their arrival at Cape Cod, entered into covenant for this necessary purpose. It was a short code, but replete with rules of equity and authority, sufficient to maintain peace among themselves, in their infant state. Forty-one persons affixed their names to the instrument; but at the end of four months, only twenty of them were living. These were, John Carver their first governor, William Bradford the second, and Edward Winslow* the third, captain Miles Standish, who had been an experienced military [404] officer in the Netherlands, Richard Warren, eminently useful in the establishment of the new colony,† (he lived only to the year one thousand six hundred and twenty-eight,‡) John Alden, Samuel Fuller, William Brewster, Isaac Allerton, Stephen Hopkins, Gilbert Winslow, Peter Brown, Richard Gardner, John Howland, Francis Cook, John Billington, Francis Eaton, Edward Doty, George Soule, Edward Leister.

* Prince's Chronology, where may be found most of the particulars extant, relative to the first settlers at Plymouth. [Thomas Prince, *A Chronological History of New England, in the Form of Annals* (2 vols.; Boston, 1736–1755).]

† Prince's Chronology. [Thomas Prince, *A Chronological History of New England, in the Form of Annals* (2 vols.; Boston, 1736–1755).]

‡ The estates first purchased of the natives by Winslow, Warren, and Bradford, remain in the hands of their posterity to this day:—Warren at Plymouth, Bradford at Duxborough, and Winslow at Marshfield.

Several weeks elapsed after their arrival at Plymouth, before they saw any of the natives. About the middle of March, an Indian chief named Samoset appeared, and abruptly exclaimed, "welcome English." This Indian had formerly been a prisoner to some Europeans, and had learnt a little of their language. By him they found that a pestilence had raged among the bordering nations, that had swept them all off within the limits of Cape Cod and Braintree Bay, two or three years before. This was corroborated by the vast number of graves, and sepulchral mounds and holes they had observed, in which the dead were interred, in all the grounds they had explored. Samoset informed them, that Massasoit was a neighbouring chief, who held jurisdiction over several other tribes. This induced the English to send him a friendly message by Samoset, which was faithfully delivered. The great sachem soon came forward in an amicable manner, and entered into a treaty of peace with this handful of strangers.

In the next autumn, an addition of thirty-five persons from the Leyden congregation, arrived at Cape Cod. They soon found their associates at Plymouth, patient, pious, and contented, though they could set nothing on their board but a lobster, cold water, and a scanty pittance [405] of Indian bread, for the entertainment of their countrymen recently arrived, to share with them the difficulties and dangers of planting settlements in the wilderness, at a vast distance from the civilized world, and surrounded by hordes of hostile nations of terrific form and barbarous manners.*

———————————— Note No. II. Page 18. ————————

VIRGINIA RESOLVES

On the twenty-ninth of May, one thousand seven hundred and fifty-five, the house of burgesses of Virginia came to the following resolutions:—

WHEREAS the honorable house of commons in England, have of late drawn into question, how far the general assembly of this colony hath power to enact laws for

* New England Memorial. [Nathaniel Morton, *New England's Memorial: Or, A Brief Relation of the Most Memorable and Remarkable Passages of the Providence of God, Manifested to the Planters of New-England in America: With Special Reference to the First Colony Thereof, Called New-Plimouth* (Cambridge, 1669). Thomas Prince relied on Morton's *Memorial*, which was understood to be an abbreviated version of William Bradford's *of Plymouth Plantation*. In 1855, the Congregational Board of Publications republished Morton's *Memorial* and added relevant parts of Prince's *Chronological History* and Bradford's *Plymouth Plantation*. Warren's reference is to Prince under the year 1629, which is included in the 1855 edition at p. 320.]

laying taxes and imposing duties, payable by the people of this his majesty's most ancient colony—For settling and ascertaining the same to all future times, the house of burgesses of this present general assembly, have come to the several following resolutions:—

Resolved, That the first adventurers and settlers of this his majesty's colony and dominion of Virginia, brought with them, and transmitted to their posterity, and all others, his majesty's subjects since inhabiting in this his majesty's colony, all the privileges and immunities that have at any time been held, enjoyed, and possessed, by the people of Great Britain.

Resolved, That by the two royal charters granted by king James the first, the colonists aforesaid are declared entitled to all privileges of faithful, liege, and natural born subjects, to all intents and purposes, as if they had been abiding and born within the realm of England.

[406] *Resolved*, That his majesty's liege people of this his most ancient colony, have enjoyed the right of being thus governed by their own assembly, in the article of taxes and internal police; and that the same have never been forfeited, or any other way yielded up, but have been constantly recognized by the king and people of Great Britain.

Resolved therefore, That the general assembly of the colony, together with his majesty or his substitute, have in their representative capacity, the only exclusive right and power, to levy taxes and impositions upon the inhabitants of this colony; and that every attempt to vest such a power in any person or persons whatsoever, other than the general assembly aforesaid, is illegal, unconstitutional, and unjust, and has a manifest tendency to destroy British, as well as American freedom.

The following resolves were not passed, though drawn up by the committee. They are inserted as a specimen of the first and early energies of the *Old Dominion*, as Virginia is usually called.

Resolved, That his majesty's liege people, the inhabitants of this colony, are not bound to yield obedience to any law or ordinance whatsoever, designed to impose any taxation whatsoever upon them, other than the laws and ordinances of the general assembly aforesaid.

Resolved, That any person who shall, by speaking or writing, maintain that any person or persons, other than the general assembly of this colony, have any right or power, to impose or lay any taxation whatsoever on the people here, shall be deemed an enemy to this his majesty's colony.

——————— Note No. III. Page 19. ———————

On the twenty-first of October, the freeholders and other inhabitants of the town of Plymouth had a meeting, [407] and unanimously agreed on instructions to Thomas Foster, Esq., their representative in the general assembly of Massachusetts Bay. In which, after expressing the highest esteem for the British constitution, shewing how far the people of America have exerted themselves in support thereof, and detailing their grievances, they proceed as follows:

> You, sir, represent a people who are not only descended from the first settlers of this country, but inhabit the very spot they first possessed. Here was first laid the foundation of the British empire in this part of America; which from a very small beginning, has increased and spread in a manner very surprising, and almost incredible; especially when we consider, that all this has been effected without the aid or assistance of any power on earth; that we have *defended, protected,* and *secured* ourselves, against the invasions and cruelty of savages, and the subtlety and inhumanity of our inveterate and natural enemies the French: and all this without the appropriation of any tax by stamps, or stamp-acts laid upon our fellow-subjects in any part of the king's dominions, for defraying the expenses thereof. This place, sir, was at first the asylum of liberty, and we hope will ever be preserved sacred to it; though it was then no more than a forlorn wilderness, inhabited only by savage men and beasts. To this place our fathers, (whose memories be revered!) possessed of the principles of liberty in their purity, disdaining slavery, fled, to enjoy those privileges which they had an undoubted right to, but were deprived of by the hands of violence and oppression in their native country. We, sir, their posterity, the freeholders and other inhabitants of this town, legally assembled for that purpose, possessed of the same sentiments, and retaining the same ardor for liberty, think it our indispensable duty on this occasion, to express to you these our sentiments of the stamp-act, and its fatal consequences to this country, and to enjoin upon you, as you regard not only the welfare, [408] but the very being of this people, that you, (consistent with our allegiance to the king, and relation to the government of Great Britain,) disregarding all proposals for that purpose, exert all your power and influence in relation to the stamp-act, at least until we hear the success of our petitions for relief. We likewise, to avoid disgracing the memories of our ancestors, as well as the reproaches of our own consciences, and the curses of posterity, recommend it to you to obtain, if possible, in the honorable house of representatives of this province, a full and explicit assertion of our rights, and to have the same entered on their public records—that all generations yet to come may be convinced, that we have not only a just sense of our rights and liberties, but that we never (with submission to Divine Providence) will be slaves to any power on earth. And as we have at all times an abhorrence of tumults and disorders, we think ourselves happy in being at present under no apprehensions of any, and in having good and wholesome laws, sufficient to preserve the peace of the province in all future times, unless provoked by some imprudent measure; so we think it by no means adviseable, for you to interest yourself in the protection of stamp-papers or stamp-officers.
>
> The only thing we have further to recommend to you at this time is, to observe on all occasions, a suitable frugality and economy in the public expenses; and that you consent to no unnecessary or unusual grant at this time of distress, when the people are groaning under the burthen of heavy taxes; and that you use your endeavours to inquire into, and bear testimony against, any past, and to prevent any future, unconstitutional draughts on the public treasury.

———————— **Note No. IV. Page 20.** ————————

Names of the gentlemen delegated to meet at New York, in one thousand seven hundred and sixty-five, [409] on occasion of the stamp-act: with the resolves of this first American congress.

From the province of the Massachusetts Bay.
James Otis,
Oliver Partridge,   } Esquires.
Timothy Ruggles,

From the colony of Rhode Island and Providence Plantations.
Metcalf Bowler,   } Esquires.
Henry Ward,

From the colony of Connecticut.
Eliphalet Dyer,
David Rowland,   } Esquires.
William Samuel Johnson,

From the colony of New York.
Robert R. Livingston,
John Cruger,
Philip Livingston,   } Esquires.
William Bayard,
Leonard Lispenard,

From the colony of New Jersey.
Robert Ogden,
Hendrick Fisher,   } Esquires.
Joseph Borden,

From the province of Pennsylvania.
John Dickenson,
John Morton,   } Esquires.
George Bryan,

From the government of the counties of Newcastle, Kent, and Sussex, on Delaware.
Cesar Rodney,   } Esquires.
Thomas M'Kean,

From the province of Maryland.
William Murdock,
Edward Tilghman,   } Esquires.
Thomas Ringold,

[410] *From the province of South Carolina.*
Thomas Lynch,
Christopher Gadsden,   } Esquires.
John Rutledge,

Saturday, A.M. *October 19, 1765*

The congress met according to adjournment, and resumed, &c. as yesterday, and upon mature deliberation, agreed to the following declarations of the rights and grievances of the colonists in America, which were ordered to be inserted in their journals.

The members of this congress sincerely devoted with the warmest sentiments of affection and duty to his majesty's person and government, inviolably attached to the present happy establishment of the protestant succession, and with minds deeply impressed by a sense of the present and impending misfortunes of the British colonies on this continent; having considered as maturely as time will permit, the circumstances of the said colonies, esteem it our indispensable duty to make the following declarations of our humble opinion, respecting the most essential rights and liberties of the colonists, and of the grievances under which they labor, by reason of several late acts of parliament.

I. That his majesty's subjects in these colonies, owe the same allegiance to the crown of Great Britain, that is owing from his subjects born within the realm, and all due subordination to that august body, the parliament of Great Britain.

II. That his majesty's liege subjects in these colonies, are entitled to all the inherent rights and liberties of his natural born subjects within the kingdom of Great Britain.

III. That it is inseparably essential to the freedom of a people, and the undoubted right of Englishmen, that no taxes be imposed on them, but with their own consent, given personally, or by their representatives.

[411] IV. That the people of these colonies are not, and from their local circumstances cannot, be represented in the house of commons in Great Britain.

V. That the only representatives of the people of these colonies are people chosen by themselves, and that no taxes ever have been, or can be, constitutionally imposed on them, but by their respective legislatures.

VI. That all supplies to the crown being free gifts of the people, it is unreasonable and inconsistent with the principles and spirit of the British constitution, for the people of Great Britain to grant to his majesty the property of the colonists.

VII. That trial by jury is the inherent and invaluable right of every British subject in these colonies.

VIII. That the late act of parliament, entitled, "An act for granting and applying certain stamp-duties, and other duties, in the British colonies and plantations in America, &c." by imposing taxes on the inhabitants of these colonies, and the same act, and several other acts, by extending the jurisdiction of the courts of admiralty beyond its ancient limits, have a manifest tendency to subvert the rights and liberties of the colonists.

IX. That the duties imposed by several late acts of the British parliament, from the peculiar circumstances of these colonies, will be extremely burthensome and grievous; and from the scarcity of specie, the payment of them absolutely impracticable.

X. That as the profits of the trade of these colonies ultimately centre in Great Britain, to pay for the manufactures which they are obliged to take from thence, they eventually contribute very largely to all supplies granted there to the crown.

[412] XI. That the restrictions imposed by several late acts of parliament on the trade of these colonies, will render them unable to purchase the manufactures of Great Britain.

XII. That the increase, prosperity, and happiness of these colonies, depend on the full and free enjoyment of their rights and liberties, and an intercourse with Great Britain, mutually affectionate and advantageous.

XIII. That it is the right of the British subjects in the colonies to petition the king, or either house of parliament.

LASTLY. That it is the indispensable duty of these colonies, to the best of sovereigns, to the mother country, and to themselves, to endeavour by a loyal and dutiful address to his majesty, and humble applications to both houses of parliament, to procure the repeal of the act for granting and applying certain stamp-duties; of all clauses of any other acts of parliament, whereby the jurisdiction of the admiralty is extended as aforesaid; and of the other late acts for the restriction of American commerce.

After these resolves, they chose Thomas Lynch, James Otis, and Thomas McKean, Esquires, to prepare a petition to the house of commons. An address to the king and to the house of lords, was also prepared and forwarded.

--------------- Note No. V. Page 29. ---------------

Copy from Mr. Dickenson's original letter to Mr. Otis, accompanying the celebrated Farmer's Letters.

Philadelphia, Dec. 5, 1767

Dear Sir,

The liberties of our common country appear to me to be at this moment exposed to the most imminent [413] danger; and this apprehension has engaged me to lay my sentiments before the public in letters, of which I send you a copy.

Only one has been yet published; and what their effect may be cannot yet be known. But whenever the cause of American freedom is to be vindicated, I look towards the province of Massachusetts Bay. She must, as she has hitherto done, first kindle the sacred flame, that on such occasions must warm and illuminate this continent.

Words are wanting to express my sense of the vigilance, perseverance, spirit, prudence, resolution, and firmness, with which your colony has distinguished herself, in our unhappy times. May God ever grant her noble labors the same successful issue which was obtained by the repeal of the stamp-act.

In my gratitude to your province in general, I do not forget the obligations which all Americans are under to you in particular, for the indefatigable zeal and undaunted courage you have shewn in defending their rights. My opinion of your love for your country, induces me to commit to your hands the enclosed letters, to be disposed of as you think proper, not intending to give out any other copy. I have shewn them to three men of learning here, who are my friends. They think with me, that the most destructive consequences must follow, if these colonies do not instantly, vigorously, and unanimously unite themselves, in the same manner they did against the stamp-act. Perhaps they and I are mistaken: I therefore send the piece containing the reasons for this opinion, to you, who I know can determine its true worth; and if you can discover no other merit in it, permit me at least to claim the merit of having wrote it with the most ardent affection for the British colonies, the purest intentions to promote their welfare, an honest desire [414] to assert their rights, and with a deep sense of their impending misfortunes.

Our cause is a cause of the highest dignity: it is nothing less than to maintain the liberty with which Heaven itself 'hath made us free.' I hope it will not be disgraced in any colony by a single rash step. We have constitutional methods of seeking redress, and they are the best methods.

This subject leads me to inform you with pleasure, because I think it must give you pleasure, that the moderation of your conduct in composing the minds of your fellow-citizens, has done you the highest credit with us. You may be assured I feel a great satisfaction in hearing your praises; for every thing that advances your reputation or interest, will always afford sincere joy to, dear sir,

> Your most affectionate, and
> Most humble servant,
> JOHN DICKENSON

Hon. James Otis, jun. Esq. [John Dickinson to James Otis, Jr., December 5, 1767, in WAL, I: 3–4.]

———————— Note No. VI. Page 32. ————————

This measure had been contemplated by several gentlemen, a year or two before it took place; among others, by the learned and excellent doctor Jonathan Mayhew of Boston: see the annexed letter, written by him soon after the repeal of the stamp-act. The abilities, virtue, and patriotism of doctor Mayhew, were so distinguished, that the following fragment may be pleasing and particularly impressive, as it was the last letter he ever wrote to any one, and within three days after its date, this great and good man closed his eyes on the politics and vanities of human life.

[415]   *Lord's day morning, June 8, 1766*

HON. JAMES OTIS, JUN. ESQ.

Sir,

To a good man all time is holy enough, and none too holy to do good, or to think upon it.

Cultivating a good understanding and hearty friendship between these colonies and their several houses of assembly, appears to me to be so necessary a part of prudence and good policy, all things considered, that no favorable opportunity for that purpose ought to be omitted: I think such an one now presents. Would it not be very proper and decorous, for our assembly to *send* circular congratulatory letters to all the rest, without exception, on the *repeal,* and the present favorable aspect of things? Letters conceived at once in terms of warm friendship and regard to them, of loyalty to the king, of filial affection towards the mother country, and intimating a desire to cement and perpetuate union among ourselves, by all practicable and laudable methods? A good foundation is already laid for this latter, by the late congress, which in my poor opinion was a wise measure, and actually contributed not a little towards our obtaining a redress of grievances, however some may affect to disparage it. Pursuing this track, and never losing sight of it, may be of the utmost importance to the colonies, on some future occasions, perhaps the only means of perpetuating their liberties; for what may be hereafter we cannot tell, how favorable soever present appearances may be. It is not safe for the colonies to *sleep,* since they will probably always have some *wakeful* enemies in Britain; and if they should be such children as to do so, I hope there are at least some persons too much of men, and friends to them, to rock the cradle, or sing lullaby to them.

You have heard of the *communion* of *churches,* and I am very early to-morrow morning to set out for Rutland, [416] to assist at an ecclesiastical council. Not expecting to return this week, while I was thinking of this in my bed, with the dawn of day, the great use and importance of a *communion* of *colonies,* appeared to me in a very strong light, which determined me immediately to set down these hints, in order to transmit them to you. Not knowing but the house may be prorogued or dissolved before my return, or having an opportunity to speak to you, you will make such a use of them as you think proper, or none at all.

I have had a sight of the answer to the last very extraordinary *speech,** with which I was much pleased. It appears to me solid and judicious, and though spirited, not more so than the case absolutely required, unless we could be content to have an absolute and uncontrollable, instead of a limited, constitutional g————r. I cannot think the man will have one wise and good, much less one truly great man at home, to stand by him in so open and flagrant an attack upon our charter rights and privileges. But the less asperity in language the better, provided there is firmness in adhering to our rights, in opposition to all encroachments.

I am, sir,

Your most obedient,
Humble servant,
JONATHAN MAYHEW

———————————— Note No. VII. Page 32. ————————————

Copy of the circular letter which was sent from the house of representatives of the province of Massachusetts Bay, to the speakers of the respective houses of representatives and burgesses on the continent of North America.

* Speech of governor Bernard.

[417]   *Province of the Massachusetts Bay, Feb. 11, 1768*

Sir,

The house of representatives of this province have taken into their serious consideration, the great difficulties that must accrue to themselves and their constituents, by the operation of the several acts of parliament imposing duties and taxes on the American colonies.

As it is a subject in which every colony is deeply interested, they have no reason to doubt but your house is duly impressed with its importance, and that such constitutional measures will be come into as are proper. It seems to be necessary, that all possible care should be taken that the representations of the several assemblies, upon so delicate a point, should harmonize with each other: the house therefore hope that this letter will be candidly considered, in no other light than as expressing a disposition freely to communicate their mind to a sister colony, upon a common concern, in the same manner as they would be glad to receive the sentiments of your, or any other house, of assembly on the continent.

The house have humbly represented to the ministry their own sentiments; that his majesty's high court of parliament is the supreme legislative power over the whole empire; that in all free states the constitution is fixed; and as the supreme legislative derives its power and authority from the constitution, it cannot overleap the bounds of it, without destroying its foundation. That the constitution ascertains and limits both sovereignty and allegiance; and therefore his majesty's American subjects, who acknowledge themselves bound by the ties of allegiance, have an equitable claim to the full enjoyment of the fundamental rules of the British constitution. That it is an essential, unalterable right in nature, engrafted into the British constitution as a fundamental [418] law, and ever held sacred and irrevocable by the subjects within the realm, that what a man hath honestly acquired, is absolutely his own, which he may freely give, but cannot be taken from him without his consent. That the American subjects may therefore, exclusive of any consideration of charter rights, with a decent firmness, adapted to the character of freemen and subjects, assert this natural, constitutional right.

It is moreover their humble opinion, which they express with the greatest deference to the wisdom of the parliament, that the acts made there, imposing duties on the people of this province for the sole and express purpose of raising a revenue, are infringements of their natural and constitutional rights. Because as they are not represented in the British parliament, his majesty's commons in Britain, by those acts grant their property without their consent.

The house further are of opinion that their constituents, considering their local circumstances, cannot by any possibility be represented in the parliament; and that it will forever be impracticable that they should be equally represented there, and consequently not at all, being separated by an ocean of a thousand leagues. That his majesty's royal predecessors for this reason were graciously pleased to form a subordinate legislative here, that their subjects might enjoy the unalienable right of a representation. Also that considering the utter impracticability of their ever being fully and equally represented in parliament, and the great expense that must unavoidably attend even a partial representation there, this house think that a taxation of their constituents, even without their consent, grievous as it is, would be preferable to any representation that could be admitted for them there.

Upon these principles, and also considering that were the rights in the parliament ever so clear, yet for obvious [419] reasons it would be beyond the rule of equity, that their constituents should be taxed on the manufactures of Great Britain here, in addition to the duties they pay for them in England, and other advantages arising to Great Britain from the acts of trade; this house have preferred a humble, dutiful, and loyal petition to our most gracious sovereign, and made such representations to his majesty's ministers, as they apprehend would tend to obtain redress.

They have also submitted to consideration, whether any people can be said to enjoy any degree of freedom, if the crown in addition to its undoubted authority of constituting a governor, should appoint him such a stipend as it should judge proper, without the consent of the people, and at their expense: and whether while the judges of the land and other civil officers, hold not their commissions during good behaviour, their having salaries appointed for them by the crown, independent of the people, hath not a tendency to subvert the principles of equity, and endanger the happiness and security of the subject.

In addition to these measures, the house have wrote a letter to their agent, Mr. De Berdt, the sentiments of which he is directed to lay before the ministry; wherein they take notice of the hardship of the act for preventing mutiny and desertion, which requires the governor and council to provide enumerated articles for the king's marching troops, and the people to pay the expense; and also the commission of the gentlemen appointed commissioners of the customs, to reside in America, which authorizes them to make as many appointments as they think fit, and to pay the appointees what sums they please, for whose mal-conduct they are not accountable. From whence it may happen that officers of the crown may be multiplied to such a degree, as to become dangerous to the liberty of the people, by virtue of a commission which doth not appear to this house to derive any such advantages to trade as many have been led to expect.

[420] These are the sentiments and proceedings of this house; and as they have too much reason to believe that the enemies of the colonies have represented them to his majesty's ministers, and the parliament, as factious, disloyal, and having a disposition to make themselves independent of the mother country, they have taken occasion in the most humble terms, to assure his majesty and his ministers, that with regard to the people of this province, and as they doubt not of all the colonies, that the charge is unjust.

The house is fully satisfied that your assembly is too generous, and enlarged in sentiment, to believe that this letter proceeds from an ambition of taking the lead, or dictating to the other assemblies; they freely submit their opinion to the judgment of others, and shall take it kind in your house to point out to them any thing further that may be thought necessary.

This house cannot conclude without expressing their firm confidence in the king, our common head and father, that the united and dutiful supplications of his distressed American subjects will meet with his royal and favorable acceptance.

(Signed by the Speaker)

A copy of the above letter was also, by order of the house, sent to Dennis De Berdt, Esq. agent to the province in London, that he might make use of it, if necessary, to prevent any misrepresentations in England.

———————————— Note No. VIII. Page 55. ————————————

A few extracts from the letters of Mr. Hutchinson to Mr. Jackson, Bollan, and others, the year previous to the disturbance in March, one thousand seven hundred [421] and seventy, fully evince his sentiments of stationing and retaining troops in the capital of the Massachusetts.

Boston, January, 1769

Dear Sir,

I sent you under a blank cover, by way of Bristol and Glasgow, the account of proceedings in New York assembly, which you will find equal to those of the Massachusetts. Perhaps if they had no troops, the people too would have run riot as we did. Five or six men of war, and three or four regiments, disturb nobody but some of our grave people, who do not love assemblies and concerts, and cannot bear the noise of drums upon a Sunday. I know I have not slept in town any three months these two years, in so much tranquillity, as I have done the three months since the troops came.

Extract of a letter from Mr. Bollan to Mr. Hutchinson.

Henrietta Street, August 11, 1767

Mr. Paxton has several times told me, that you and some other of my friends were of opinion, that standing troops were necessary to support the authority of the government at Boston, and that he was authorized to inform me this was your and their opinion. I need not say that I hold in the greatest abomination such outrages that have taken place among you, and am sensible it is the duty of all charter, or other subordinate governments, to take due care, and punish such proceedings; and that all governments must be supported by force, when necessary; yet we must remember how often standing forces have introduced greater mischiefs than they retrieved, and I am apprehensive that your distant situation from the centre of all civil and military power, might in this case, sooner or later, subject you to peculiar difficulties.

[422] When Malcolm's bad behaviour made a stir here, a minister who seemed inclined to make use of standing forces, supposing this might not be agreeable to me, I avoided giving an opinion, which then appeared needless and improper, but afterwards, when it was confidently said, that preparations were making to send a considerable number of standing troops, in order to compel obedience, I endeavoured to prevent it.

Mr. Bollan goes on to observe, that "he had informed some influential gentlemen in England, that he had the highest reason to believe, that whoever should be instrumental in sending over standing troops in America, would be cursed to all posterity."

Extract from governor Hutchinson's letters to governor Pownal. It is uncertain on what occasion the following assertion was made, but it discovers the spirit and wishes of the writer.

Boston, June 22, 1772

The union of the colonies is pretty well broke; I hope I shall never see it renewed. Indeed our sons of liberty are hated and despised by their former brethren in New York and Pennsylvania, and it must be something very extraordinary ever to reconcile them.

——————————— Note No. IX. Page 64. ———————————

Extracts from Mr. Hutchinson's letters to Mr. Jackson, Pownal, and others.

Boston, August 27, 1772

But before America is settled in peace, it would be necessary to go to the bottom of all the disorder, which has been so long neglected already. The opinion that every colony has a legislature within itself, [423] the acts and doings of which are not to be controlled by parliament, and that no legislative power ought to be exercised over the colonies, except by their respective legislatures, gains ground every day, and it has an influence upon all the executive parts of government. Grand juries will not present; petit juries will not convict the highest offenders against acts of parliament: our newspapers publickly announce this independence every week; and, what is much more, there is scarce an assembly which has not done it at one time or another. The assembly of this province has done as much the last session by their public votes and resolves, and by an address which they have sent to doctor Franklin, to be presented to the king; so there is sufficient grounds for parliament to proceed, if there is a disposition. What, it will be said, can be done? A test as general as the oaths required instead of the oaths of allegiance and supremacy, would be most effectual; but this there is reason to fear would throw America into a general confusion, and I doubt the expediency. But can less be done than affixing penalties, and disqualifications or incapacities, upon all who by word or writing shall deny or call in question the supreme authority of parliament over all parts of the British dominions? Can it be made necessary for all judges to be under oath, to observe all acts of parliament in their judgments? And may not the oaths of all jurors, grand and petit, be so framed as to include acts of parliament as the rule of law, as well as law in general terms? And for assemblies or bodies of men, who shall deny the authority of parliament, may not all their subsequent proceedings be declared to be *ipso facto* null and void, and every member who shall continue to act in such assembly be subject to penalties and incapacities? I suggest these things for consideration. Every thing depends upon the settlement of this grand point. We owe much of our troubles to the countenance given by some in England to this doctrine of independence. If the people were convinced that the nation with one voice condemned the doctrine, or that parliament at all [424] events, was determined to maintain its supremacy, we should soon be quiet. The demagogues who generally have no property, would continue their endeavours to inflame the minds of the people for some time; but the people in general have real estates, which they would not run the hazard of forfeiting, by any treasonable measures. If nothing more can be done, there must be further provisions for carrying the act of trade into execution, which I am informed administration are very sensible of, and have measures in contemplation. Thus you have a few of my sudden thoughts, which I must pray you not to communicate as coming from me, lest I should be supposed here to have contributed to any future proceedings respecting America. I have only room to add that I am, with sincere respect and esteem,

Your's, &c.

Boston, December 8, 1772

To Mr. Jackson

[*Private*]

Dear Sir,

They succeed in their unwearied endeavours to propagate the doctrine of independence upon parliament, and the mischiefs of it every day increase. I believe I have repeatedly mentioned to you my opinion of the necessity of parliament's taking some measures to prevent the spread of this doctrine, as well as to guard against the mischiefs of it. It is more difficult now, than it was the last year, and it will become more and more so every year it is neglected, until it is utterly impracticable. If I consulted nothing but my own ease and quiet, I would propose neglect and contempt of every affront offered to parliament by the little American assemblies, but I should be false to the king, and betray the trust he has reposed in me.

*   *   *

You see no difference between the case of the colonies and that of Ireland. I care not in [425] how favorable a light you look upon the colonies, if it does not separate us from you. You will certainly find it more difficult to retain the colonies, than you do Ireland. Ireland is near and under your constant inspection. All officers are dependent, and removable at pleasure. The colonies are remote, and the officers generally more disposed to please the people than the king, or his representative. In the one, you have always the *ultima ratio;* in the other, you are either destitute of it, or you have no civil magistrate to direct the use of it. Indeed, to prevent a general revolt, the naval power may for a long course of years be sufficient, but to preserve the peace of the colonies, and to continue them beneficial to the mother country, this will be to little purpose; but I am writing to a gentleman who knows these things better than I do.

Boston, January, 1773

John Pownal, Esq.

My Dear Sir,

I have not answered your very kind and confidential letter of the 6th of October. Nothing could confirm me more in my own plan of measures for the colonies, than finding it to agree with your sentiments. You know I have been begging for measures to maintain the supremacy of parliament. Whilst it is suffered to be denied, all is confusion, and the opposition to government is continually gaining strength.

Boston, April 19, 1773

JOHN POWNAL, ESQ.

Dear Sir,

Our patriots say that the votes of the town of Boston, which they sent to Virginia, have produced the resolves of the assembly there, appointing a committee of correspondence; and I have no doubt it is their expectation, [426] that a committee for the same purpose will be appointed by most of the other assemblies on the continent. If any thing therefore be done by parliament respecting America, it now seems necessary that it should be general, and not confined to particular colonies, as the same spirit prevails every where, though not in the like degree.

Boston, October 18, 1773

JOHN POWNAL, ESQ.

[*Private.*]

Dear Sir,

The leaders of the party give out openly that they must have another convention of all the colonies; and the speaker has made it known to several of the members, that the agent in England recommends it as a measure necessary to be engaged in without delay, and proposes, in order to bring the dispute to a crisis, that the rights of the colonies should be there solemnly and fully asserted and declared; that there should be a firm engagement with each other, that they will never grant any aid to the crown, even in case of war, unless the king and the two houses of parliament first recognize those rights; and that the resolution should be immediately communicated to the crown; and assures them, that in this way they will finally obtain their end.

I am not fond of conveying this sort of intelligence; but as I have the fullest evidence of the fact, I do not see how I can be faithful to my trust and neglect it; therefore, though I consider this a private letter, yet I leave it to you to communicate this part of it, so far as his majesty's service may require, and as I have nothing but that in view, I wish it may go no further. The measure appears to me, of all others, the most likely to rekindle a general flame in the colonies.

The above extracts were taken from governor Hutchinson's letter book, found after he repaired to England, deposited [427] in a secret corner of his house at Milton. If the reader wishes a further gratification of his curiosity in regard to the subtil stratagems of Mr. Hutchinson, he is referred to the whole collection, as published in England.

Note No. X. Page 83.

Names of the members of the American congress, in one thousand seven hundred and seventy-four.

Peyton Randolph, *President*

NEW HAMPSHIRE, John Sullivan, Nathaniel Folsom.
MASSACHUSETTS BAY. Thomas Cushing, Samuel Adams, John Adams, Robert Treat Paine.
RHODE ISLAND. Stephen Hopkins, Samuel Ward.
CONNECTICUT. Eliphalet Dyer, Roger Sherman, Silas Deane.
NEW YORK. Isaac Low, John Alsop, John Jay, James Duane, William Floyd, Henry Weisner, Samuel Bocrum.
NEW JERSEY. James Kinsey, William Livingston, Stephen Crane, Richard Smith.
PENNSYLVANIA. Joseph Galloway, Charles Humphreys, John Dickenson, Thomas Mifflin, Edward Biddle, John Morton, George Ross.
NEWCASTLE, &c. Caesar Rodney, Thomas McKean, George Read.
MARYLAND. Matthew Tilghman, Thomas Johnson, William Paca, Samuel Chase.
VIRGINIA. Richard Henry Lee, George Washington, Patrick Henry, jun. Richard Bland, Benjamin Harrison, Edmund Pendleton.
NORTH CAROLINA. William Hooper, Joseph Hewes, R. Caswell.
SOUTH CAROLINA. Henry Middleton, Thomas Lynch, Christopher Gadsden, John Rutledge, Edward Rutledge.

Note No. XI. Page 99.

[428] Extract of a letter from governor Hutchinson to commodore Gambier.

Boston, June 30, 1772

Dear Sir,

*   *   *

Our last ships carried you the news of the burning the Gaspee schooner at Providence. I hope if there should be another like attempt, some concerned in it may be taken prisoners and carried directly to England. A few punished at Execution Dock, would be the only effectual preventive of any further attempts. . . .

On the same subject, to secretary Pownal.

Boston, August 29, 1772

Dear Sir,

I troubled you with a long letter the 21st of July. Give me leave now only to add one or two things which I then intended, but to avoid being too tedious, omitted. People in this province, both friends and enemies to government, are in great expectations from the late affair at Rhode Island of burning the king's schooner, and they consider the manner in which the news of it will be received in England, and the measures to be taken, as decisive. If it is passed over without a full inquiry and due resentment, our liberty people will think they may with impunity commit any acts of violence, be they ever so atrocious, and the friends to government will despond, and give up all hopes of being able to withstand the faction. The persons who were the immediate actors, are men of estate and property in the colony. A prosecution is impossible. If ever the government of that [429] colony is to be reformed, this seems to be the time, and it would have a happy effect in the colonies which adjoin to it. Several persons have been advised by letters from their friends, that as the ministry are united, and opposition at an end, there will certainly be an inquiry into the state of America, the next session of parliament. The denial of the supremacy of parliament, and the contempt with which its authority has been treated by the Lilliputian assemblies of America, can never be justified or excused by any one member of either house of parliament. . . .

Boston, September 2, 1772

SAMUEL HOOD, ESQ.

Dear Sir,

Captain Linzee can inform you of the state of Rhode Island colony better than I can. So daring an insult as burning the king's schooner, by people who are as well known as any who were concerned in the last rebellion, and yet cannot be prosecuted, will certainly rouse the British lion, which has been asleep these four or five years. Admiral Montague says, that lord Sandwich will never leave pursuing the colony, until it is disfranchised. If it is passed over, the other colonies will follow the example.

Note No. XII. Page 111.

The sufferings of the colony of Virginia, under lord Dunmore's administration, and the spirit and magnanimity of the inhabitants, might claim a larger detail in this narrative; but so distinguished have been many of their leading characters, through all the transactions of the great contest, from the introduction of the resolves by Patrick Henry, in the year one thousand seven hundred and sixty-five, to the [430] elevation of Mr. Jefferson to the presidential chair in one thousand eight hundred and one, as to be sufficient to furnish ample materials for a volume by itself. But every historical record of the American revolution and its consequence, must necessarily introduce the names of many illustrious characters that have adorned and dignified the state of Virginia.

Note No. XIII. Page 118.

Mr. Hancock retained his popularity to the end of his life. His death did not take place until the year one thousand seven hundred and ninety-three. He was chosen governor of the Massachusetts in one thousand seven hundred and eighty, and though a remarkable debilitation of body rendered him to appearance little able to discharge the duties of the first magistrate, yet the suffrages of the people kept him long in the chair, after he was reduced to such a state of weakness as to be lifted by his servants into his carriage, and thence into the state house, to deliver his public speeches. In this he acquitted himself with a degree of elocution, pleasing and popular, though his health did not admit of his writing them previously, and seldom had he strength to add his signature to the acts of the legislature. But his mental faculties were not much impaired by the infirmities of his bodily constitution; they were not indeed composed of those elementary sparks of genius that soon burn themselves out; nor were the energies of his mind blunted by industry and application.

He had been so long habituated to ideas of independence, that after they were thoroughly fixed in his mind, he uniformly retained his principles to the last. He was against the consolidation of the general government, and the monarchical views of many who had risen to power before he had finished his career of life. He supported his opinion of the sovereignty of the individual states, in a [431] manly manner, in one of his last transactions of a public nature; this was his conduct relative to the suability of the states. An experiment made by a process commenced against the Massachusetts, in favor of William Vassal, Esq., the governor of the state was summoned by a writ to answer to the prosecution. He declined the smallest concession that might lessen the independence and sovereignty of each state, and supported his opinion with firmness and dignity equally popular and honorable to himself. Litigations of this nature were soon after barred, by an amendment in the constitution of the United States.

An ample measure of gratitude was repaid to Mr. Hancock, both for public services and private benefits; a mantle of love was thrown over his foibles by his countrymen, and his memory was embalmed in the affections of his townsmen.

——————————— Note No. XIV. Page 124. ———————————

The state of Massachusetts continued this mode of legislation and government until the year one thousand seven hundred and eighty, when a convention was called for the purpose, and a more stable form adopted: by this, a governor, lieutenant governor, senate, and house of representatives were to be chosen by the free suffrages of the people; a council of nine were to be chosen by the legislative, either from the senate or the people at large.

————————— Note No. XV. Page 145. —————————

Copy of general Montgomery's last letter to general Carleton.

[432]   *Holland House, December 6, 1775*

Sir,

Notwithstanding the personal ill treatment I have received at your hands, notwith-standing the cruelty you have shewn to the unhappy prisoners you have taken, the feelings of humanity induce me to have recourse to this expedient, to save you from the destruction which hangs over your wretched garrison. Give me leave to inform you, that I am well acquainted with your situation; a great extent of works, in their nature incapable of defence, manned with a motley crew of sailors, most of them our friends and citizens, who wish to see us within their walls,—a few of the worst troops that call themselves soldiers,—the impossibility of relief, and the certain prospect of wanting every necessary of life, should your opponents confine their operations to a single blockade,—point out the absurdity of resistance; such is your situation.

I am at the head of troops accustomed to success, confident of the righteous cause they are engaged in, inured to danger and fatigue, and so highly incensed at your inhumanity, illiberal abuse, and the ungenerous means employed to prejudice them in the minds of the Canadians, that it is with difficulty I restrain them till my batteries are ready, from insulting your works, which would afford them the fair opportunity of ample vengeance and just retaliation. Firing upon a flag of truce, hitherto unprecedented, even among savages, prevents my following the ordinary mode of conveying my sentiments; however I will at any rate acquit my conscience: should you persist in an unwarrantable defence, the consequence be upon your own head. Beware of destroying stores of any sort, public or private, as you did at Montreal or in the river: if you do, by heavens, there will be no mercy shewn.

————————— Note No. XVI. Page 153. —————————

[433] The many protests of a number of the house of lords, which appeared from time to time against the high measures of a majority in parliament, epitomize the American grievances in a point of view that exhibited the opinion at the time, of a very considerable part of the most judicious and unprejudiced persons through the nation, both in and out of parliament. These protests may be found in a variety of British publications.

This general favorable disposition towards the Americans in the early part of the contest, was evinced by numberless circumstances; a crimination of the measures of administration against the colonies, existed on both sides of the Tweed, and indeed throughout the kingdom. Many letters, and other excellent writings on the subject of civil and religious liberty, were transmitted from England to America, from the year one thousand seven hundred and sixty-five, until the period when hostilities commenced. Among the numberless instances that might be adduced, of the spirit and disposition of the writers of those times, we will here only give the following extract of a letter from the earl of Buchan to Mr. Otis; this was accompanied by some very excellent essays on the subject of liberty, and by several portraits of his person, adorned at the foot with a cap of liberty in the centre of the annexed motto, "Ubi libertas, ibi patria."

London, January 26, 1768

Sir,

I take the liberty of transmitting to you the inclosed representations of a man, strongly attached to the principles of that invaluable liberty, without which no real happiness can subsist any where.

My family has often bled in the support of it; and descended as I am, from the English Henrys and Edwards, [434] I glory more in the banishment of my great-grandfather, lord Cardross, to Carolina, and the stand made by lord Halifax, my ancestor, than in all that title and descent can give me.

You may dispose of the other prints to the lovers of my principles; and I beg you will be so good as to transmit four of them to Messrs

* * *

as eminent defenders of those doctrines in the church, which are so intimately connected with liberty in the state.

* * *

Lord Chatham† has forsaken you, having loved this world; but his favorite, your humble servant, will not, I trust, ever follow his steps.

I am, sir, with great regard,
Your most obedient, humble servant,
BUCHAN

James Otis, Esq. Boston

——————— Note No. XVII. Page 169. ———————

In Congress, July 4, 1776

A DECLARATION BY THE REPRESENTATIVES OF THE UNITED STATES OF AMERICA IN GENERAL CONGRESS ASSEMBLED.

When in the course of human events, it becomes necessary for one people to dissolve the political bands which have connected them with another, and to

† Lord Chatham afterwards totally reprobated the conduct of administration towards the colonies.

assume among the powers of the earth, the separate and equal station to which the laws of nature and nature's God entitle them, a decent respect to the opinions of mankind requires, that they should declare the causes which impel them to the separation.

[435] We hold these truths to be self-evident: that all men are created equal; that they are endowed by their Creator with certain unalienable rights: that among these are life, liberty, and the pursuit of happiness: that to secure these rights, governments are instituted among men, deriving their just powers from the consent of the governed: and whenever any form of government becomes destructive of these ends, it is the right of the people to alter or abolish it, and to institute a new government, laying its foundation on such principles, and organizing its powers in such form, as to them shall seem most likely to effect their safety and happiness. Prudence indeed will dictate that governments long established, should not be changed for light and transient causes; and accordingly, all experience hath shewn, that mankind are more disposed to suffer, while evils are sufferable, than to right themselves by abolishing the forms to which they are accustomed: but when a long train of abuses and usurpations, pursuing invariably the same object, evinces a design to reduce them under absolute despotism, it is their right, it is their duty to throw off such government, and to provide new guards for their future security. Such has been the patient sufferance of these colonies, and such is now the necessity which constrains them to alter their former systems of government. The history of the present king of Great Britain, is a history of repeated injuries and usurpations; all having in direct object the establishment of an absolute tyranny over these states: to prove this, let facts be submitted to a candid world.

He has refused his assent to laws, the most wholesome and necessary for the public good.

He has forbidden his governors to pass laws of immediate and pressing importance, unless suspended in their operation till his assent should be obtained; and when so suspended, he has utterly neglected to attend to them.

He has refused to pass other laws, for the accommodation of large districts of people, unless those people would [436] relinquish the rights of representation in the legislature; a right inestimable to them, and formidable to tyrants only.

He has called together legislative bodies at places unusual, uncomfortable, and distant from the depository of their public records, for the sole purpose of fatiguing them into compliance with his measures.

He has dissolved representative houses repeatedly, for opposing, with manly firmness, his invasions on the rights of the people.

He has refused, for a long time after such dissolution, to cause others to be erected, whereby the legislative powers, incapable of annihilation, have returned to the people at large for their exercise,—the state remaining in the mean time, exposed to all the dangers of invasion from without, and convulsions within.

He has endeavoured to prevent the population of these states; for that purpose, obstructing the laws for naturalization of foreigners, refusing to pass others to encourage their migrations hither, and raising the conditions of new appropriations of lands.

He has obstructed the administration of justice, by refusing his assent to laws for establishing judiciary powers.

He has made judges dependent on his will alone, for the tenure of their offices, and the amount and payment of their salaries.

He has erected a multitude of new offices, and sent hither swarms of officers, to harass our people, and eat out their subsistence.

He has kept among us, in times of peace, standing armies, without the consent of our legislatures.

He has affected to render the military independent of, and superior to, the civil power.

[437] He has combined with others, to subject us to a jurisdiction foreign to our constitution, and unacknowledged by our laws, giving his assent to their pretended acts of legislation:

For quartering large bodies of armed troops among us:

For protecting them, by a mock trial, from punishment for any murders which they should commit on the inhabitants of these states:

For cutting off our trade with all parts of the world:

For imposing taxes on us without our consent:

For depriving us, in many cases, of the benefit of trial by jury:

For transporting us beyond seas, to be tried for pretended offences:

For abolishing the free system of English laws in a neighbouring province, establishing therein an arbitrary government, and enlarging its boundaries, so as to render it at once an example and fit instrument for introducing the same absolute rule into these colonies:

For taking away our charters, abolishing our most valuable laws, and altering fundamentally the forms of our governments:

For suspending our own legislatures, and declaring themselves invested with power to legislate for us in all cases whatsoever.

He has abdicated government here, by declaring us out of his protection, and waging war against us.

He has plundered our seas, ravaged our coasts, burnt our towns, and destroyed the lives of our people.

He is at this time transporting large armies of foreign mercenaries, to complete the works of death, desolation, and tyranny, already begun with circumstances of cruelty and perfidy, scarcely paralleled in the most barbarous ages, and totally unworthy the head of a civilized nation.

[438] He has constrained our fellow-citizens, taken captive on the high seas, to bear arms against their country, to become the executioners of their friends and brethren, or to fall themselves by their hands.

He has excited domestic insurrections amongst us, and has endeavoured to bring on the inhabitants of our frontiers the merciless Indian savages, whose known rule of warfare is, an undistinguished destruction of all ages, sexes, and conditions.

In every stage of these oppressions, we have petitioned for redress, in the most humble terms: our repeated petitions have been answered only by repeated injury. A prince, whose character is thus marked by every act which may define a tyrant, is unfit to be the ruler of a free people.

Nor have we been wanting in attention to our British brethren. We have warned them, from time to time, of attempts, by their legislature, to extend an unwarrantable jurisdiction over us; we have reminded them of the circumstances of our emigration and settlement here; we have appealed to their native justice and magnanimity; and we have conjured them, by the ties of our common kindred, to disavow these usurpations, which would inevitably interrupt our connexions and correspondence.

They too have been deaf to the voice of justice and consanguinity. We must therefore acquiesce in the necessity which denounces our separation, and hold them, as we hold the rest of mankind, enemies in war, in peace friends.

We therefore, the representatives of the United States of America, in general congress, assembled, appealing to the Supreme Judge of the world for the rectitude of our intentions, do, in the name, and by the authority of the good people of these colonies, solemnly publish and declare, that these united colonies are, and of right ought to be FREE AND INDEPENDENT STATES; and that they are absolved [439] from all allegiance to the British crown; and that all political connexion between them and the state of Great Britain, is and ought to be totally dissolved; and that, as free and independent states, they have full power to levy war, conclude peace, contract alliances, establish commerce, and to do all other acts and things which independent states may of right do. And for the support of this declaration, with a firm reliance on the protection of Divine Providence, we mutually pledge to each other our lives, our fortunes, and our sacred honor.

Signed by order and in behalf of the congress,
JOHN HANCOCK, President

Attest:—
CHARLES THOMPSON, Secretary

—————————— **Note No. XVIII. Page 194.** ——————————

Copy of a letter from general Lee to doctor B. Rush. See life and memoirs of general Lee.

Camp at Valley Forge, June 4, 1778

My Dear Rush,

Though I had no occasion for fresh assurances of your friendship, I cannot help being much pleased with the warmth which your letter, delivered to me by Mr. H***, breathes; and I hope, it is unnecessary to assure you, that my sentiments, with respect to you, are correspondent.

You will think it odd, that I should seem to be an apologist for general Howe: I know not how it happens; but when I have taken prejudices in favor, or against a man, I find it a difficulty in shaking them off. From my first acquaintance with Mr. Howe, I liked him: I thought him friendly, candid, good natured, brave, and rather sensible than the reverse: I believe still that he is naturally so: but a corrupt, or more properly, no education, [440] the fashion of the times, and the reigning idolatry amongst the English, (particularly the soldiery;) for every sceptred calf, wolf, or ass, have so totally perverted his understanding and heart, that private friendship has not force sufficient to keep a door open for the admittance of mercy towards political heretics. He was besides persuaded that I was doubly criminal, both as a traitor and deserter. In short, so totally was he inebriated with this idea, that I am convinced he would have thought himself both politically and morally damned, had he acted any other part than what he did. He is besides, the most indolent of mortals; never took further pains to examine the merits or demerits of the cause in which he was engaged, than merely to recollect, that Great Britain was said to be the mother country, George the third king of Great Britain, that the parliament was called the representatives of Great Britain, that the king and parliament formed the supreme power, that a supreme power is absolute and uncontrollable, that all resistance must consequently be rebellion; but above all, that he was a soldier, and bound to obey in all cases whatever.

These are his notions, and this his logic: but through these absurdities, I could distinguish, when he was left to himself, rays of friendship and good nature breaking out. It is true, he was seldom left to himself; for never poor mortal, thrust into high station, was surrounded by such fools and scoundrels. McKenzie, Balfour, Galloway, were his counsellors; they urged him to all his acts of harshness; they were his scribes; all the damned stuff which was issued to the astonished world was their's. I believe he scarcely ever read the letters he signed. You will scarcely believe it, but I can assure you as a fact, that he never read the curious proclamation, issued at the Head of Elk, till three days after it was published. You will say, that I am drawing my friend Howe in more ridiculous colors than he has yet been represented in; but this is his real character. He is naturally good [441] humored, complaisant, but illiterate and indolent to the last degree, unless as an executive soldier, in which capacity he is all fire and activity, brave and cool as Julius Caesar. His understanding is, as I observed before, rather good than otherwise, but was totally confounded and stupified by the immensity of the task imposed upon him. He shut his eyes, fought his battles, drank his bottle, had his little *****, advised with his counsellors, received his orders from North and Germaine, (one more absurd than the other,) took Galloway's opinion, shut his eyes, fought again, and is now, I suppose, to be called to account for acting according to instructions. But I believe his eyes are now opened; he sees he has been an instrument of wickedness and folly; indeed, when I observed it to him, he not only took patiently the observation, but indirectly assented to the truth of it. He made, at the same time, as far as his *mauvais honte* would permit, an apology for his treatment of me.

Thus far with regard to Mr. Howe. You are struck with the great events, changes, and new characters, which have appeared on the stage since I saw you last; but I am more struck with the admirable efficacy of blunders. It seemed to be a trial of skill, which party should outdo the other; and it is hard to say which played the deepest strokes; but it was a capital one of ours, which certainly gave the happy turn which affairs have taken. Upon my soul, it was time for fortune to interpose, or we were inevitably lost; but this we will talk over another time. I suppose we shall see one another at Philadelphia very soon, in attendance. God bless you!

Yours, affectionately,
CHARLES LEE

Note No. XIX. Page 197.

[442] The iniquitous conduct of speculators and swindlers, to secure to themselves the possession of most of the public securities, will leave a stain

on a large class of people, who by every art endeavoured to sink the faith of congress. Indeed their attempts to injure the credit of all public bodies, were attended with the most pernicious consequences to the honest and unsuspecting holders of public paper. By every insidious practice, they induced the ignorant and necessitous, to part with their securities for the most trifling considerations, to supply their immediate wants. Thus afterwards, when a new constitution of government was formed, and a funding system created, no discrimination was made in favor of the original holders, who had dispossessed themselves of the public securities. Those who had gained them by their artificial deception, were enriched beyond all calculation by subsequent circumstances: they afterwards received the nominal value in specie, while many of the former holders were reduced to extreme poverty.

It was pathetically observed, by one who felt these inconveniencies, that

the public securities, tired of their humble abodes, had soon fled to the splendid seats of wealth and greatness; and that while they remained with a class who had dearly earned them by their services, no interest was promised, no time, place, or person ascertained, to direct our application for payment. They fell into disgrace, which concurring with our necessities, as they could yield no present comfort or future hope, induced us to part with them for the most trifling considerations: but when they had chosen their elevated residence, their credit revived, and provision was made for the payment of interest upon them. We, in event, literally sold them for nothing, and are obliged to pay their present holders an annual sum for keeping them in possession; for many of us have, or must soon pay for the [443] interest of them, a sum nearly or quite equal to the money given to purchase them, and still be annually taxed to discharge the interest and principal of said securities.

This is an anticipation of what literally took place afterwards, though it is but justice to observe, that Mr. Madison of Virginia, a distinguished member of congress, and several others of that body, left no rational argument untried, to procure a discrimination, when the funding system was about to be introduced in one thousand seven hundred and eighty-eight, that would have made some equitable compensation to the original holders of public securities, and prevented a sudden accumulation of wealth to a class of men, who had, many of them, never earned by their own private industry, or their services to the public, sufficient for a competent support. They grew rich on the property of those who had suffered in the service of their country, who were left to complain, without a possibility of redress.

——————————— Note No. XX. Page 216. ———————————

Extracts of a short account of the treatment of major general Conway, late in the service of America, from general Lee's letters.

On Monday the 23d of November, 1778, the honorable major general Conway set out from Philadelphia, on his return to France. The history of the treatment this gentleman has received, is so singular, that it must make a figure in the anecdotes of mankind. He was born in Ireland, but at the age of six was carried into France; was bred up from his infancy to the profession of arms; and it is universally allowed, by the gentlemen of that nation, that he has, in their service, the reputation of being what is called un tres brave major d'infanterie, which is no small character; it implies, if I comprehend [444] the term aright, a man possessed of all the requisite qualities to fill the duties of a general officer in the secondary line, but by no means ranks him among those favored mortals, to whom it has pleased God to give so large a portion of the etherial spirit, as to render reading, theory, and practice unnecessary; but with the spectacle of this phenomena, Heaven entertains the earth but very seldom; Greece, as historians report, had but one; Rome none; England and France, only one each. As to this hemisphere, I shall be silent on the subject, lest I should be suspected of not being serious. But be this as it may, it is past doubt that general Conway is a man of excellent understanding, quick and penetrating,—that he has seen much service, has read a great deal, and digested well what he has read. It is not less certain, that he embarked with the warmest zeal for the great American cause, and it has never been insinuated, unless by those who have the talent of confounding causes, that his zeal has diminished. His recompense has been, what? He has lost his commission; he has been refused the common certificate, which every officer receives at the expiration of his services, unless his delinquencies have been very substantial indeed. And, for what crime? For none, by any law, or the most strained construction that can be put on any law. The reasons given are so far from being substantial, that they really ought to reflect honor on his character. It seems he has been accused of writing a letter to a confidential friend, communicating an opinion, that the commander in chief was not equal to the great task he was charged with. Is this a crime? The contrary. If it was really his opinion, it was decent, it was honest, it was laudable, it was his duty. Does it come under any article of war? I may venture to affirm that it does not. God help the community that should be absurd enough to frame a law which could be construed into such a sense; such a community could not long subsist. It ever has been, and ever ought to be, the custom in all armies, not absolutely barbarians, for the officers [445] of high rank minutely to canvass the measures of their commander in chief; and if his faults or mistakes appear to them many and great, to communicate their sentiments to each other; it can be attended with no one bad consequence; for if the criticisms are unjust and impertinent, they only recoil on the authors, and the great man who is the subject of them, shines with redoubled lustre. But if they are well founded, they tend to open the eyes of the prince or state, who, from blind prejudice, or some strange infatuation, may have reposed their affairs in hands ruinously incapable. Does any man of sense, who is the least acquainted with history, imagine that the greatest generals the world ever produced have escaped censure? Hannibal, Caesar, Turenne, Marlborough, have all been censured; and the only method they thought justifiable, of stopping the mouths of their censors, was by a fresh exertion of their talents, and a perpetual series of victories. Indeed it is observable, that in proportion to the capacity or incapacity of the commander in chief, he countenances or discountenances the whole tribe of tale-bearers, informers, and pickthanks, who ever have been, and ever will be, the bane of those courts and armies where they are encouraged or even suffered. Allowing general Washington to be possessed of all the virtues and military talents of Epaminondas, and this is certainly allowing a great deal; for whether from our modern education, or perhaps the modern state of human affairs, it is difficult to conceive that any mortal in these ages, should arrive at such perfection; but allowing it to be so, he would still remain mortal, and of course subject to the infirmities of human nature; sickness, or other casualties, might impair his understanding, his memory, or his courage; and in consequence of this failure, he might adopt measures apparently weak, ridiculous, and pernicious. Supposing this possible case, whether a law, the letter or spirit of which should absolutely seal up the lips, and restrain the pens of every witness of the defection, would it not in fact be denouncing vengeance [446] against those who alone have the means in their power of saving the public from the ruin impending, if they should dare to make use of these means for its salvation. If there were such a law, its absurdity would be so monstrously glaring, that we may hardly say, it would be more honored in the breach than in the observance. In the English and French armies, the freedom with which the conduct and measures of commanders in chief are canvassed, is notorious; nor does it appear that this freedom is attended with any bad consequences: it has never been once able to remove a real great officer from his command. Every action of the duke of Marlborough (every body who has read must know) was not only minutely criticised, but his whole conduct was dissected, in order to discover some crime, blunder, fault, or even trifling error; but all these impertinent pains and wicked industry were employed in vain; it was a court intrigue alone that subverted him.

General Wolfe, with whom to be compared it can be no degradation to any mortal living, was not merely criticised, but grossly calumniated by some officers of high rank under him; but that great man never thought of having recourse to the letter or construction of any law, in order to avenge himself; he was contented with informing his calumniators, that he was not ignorant of their practices, and that the only method he should take for their punishment, would be an active perseverance in the performance of his duty, which, with the assistance of God, he made no doubt would place him beyond the reach of their malice. As to what liberties they had taken with him personally, he should wait till he was reduced to the rank of a private gentleman, and then speak to them in that capacity.

Upon the whole, it appears that it never was understood to be the meaning of the English article of war, which enjoins respect towards the commander in chief; [447] and of course it ought not to be understood, that the meaning of that article of the American code, (which is a servile copy from the English,) is meant to prescribe the communication of our sentiments to one another, on the capacity or incapacity of the man on whom the misery or ruin of the state depends; its intention was, without doubt, in part complimentary, and partly to lay some decent restrictions on the license of conversation and writing, which otherwise might create a dissidence in the minds of the common soldiery, detrimental to the public service. But that it was meant to impose a dead, torpid silence, in all cases whatever, on men, who, from their rank, must be supposed to have eyes and understanding, nothing under the degree of an ideot, can persuade himself; but admitting, in opposition to common sense and all precedents, the proceeding to be criminal; admitting Mr. Conway guilty of it, to the extent represented, which he can demonstrate to be false; in the name of God, why inflict the highest, at least negative punishment, on a man untried, and unheard? The refusal of a certificate of having honestly served, is considered as the greatest of negative punishments; indeed in the military idea, it is a positive one.

And I sincerely hope, and do firmly believe, (such is my opinion of the justice of congress,) that when they have coolly reflected on the merits and fortunes of this gentleman, they will do him that justice, which nothing but the hasty misconstruction of a law hastily copied from another law, never defined nor understood, has hitherto prevented.

A P P E N D I X
T O   V O L U M E   S E C O N D

——————————— **Note No. I. Page 228.** ———————————

Note No. I. Page 228.

GENERAL BURGOYNE'S INSTRUCTIONS TO LIEUTENANT COLONEL BAUM

[389] The object of your expedition is—to try the affection of the country; to disconcert the councils of the enemy; to mount the Reidesel dragoons; to complete Petre's corps; and to obtain large supplies of cattle, horses, and carriages.

The several corps, of which the inclosed is a list, are to be under your command.

The troops must take no tents; and what little baggage is carried by the officers, must be on their own battalion horses.

You are to proceed from Batten Kill to Arlington, and take post there, till the detachment of the provincials, under the command of captain Sherwood, shall join you, from the southward.

You are then to proceed to Manchester, where you will again take post, so as to secure the pass of the mountains, on the road from Manchester to Rockingham: from thence you will detach the Indians and light troops [390] to the northward, toward Otter Creek. On their return, and receiving intelligence that no enemy is upon the Connecticut River, you will proceed by the road over the mountains to Rockingham, where you will take post. This will be the most distant part of the expedition, and must be proceeded upon with caution, as you will have the defiles of the mountains behind you, which might make a retreat difficult. You must therefore endeavour to be well informed of the force of the enemy's militia, in the neighbouring country; should you find it may with prudence be effected, ·you are to remain there, while the Indians and light troops are detached up the river; and you are afterwards to descend the river to Brattleborough; and from that place, by the quickest march, you are to return by the great road to Albany.

During your whole progress, your detachments are to have orders to bring in to you, all horses fit to mount the dragoons under your command, or to serve as battalion horses for the troops, together with as many saddles and bridles as can be found. The number of horses requisite, besides those necessary for mounting the regiment of dragoons, ought to be thirteen hundred; if you can bring more, for the use of the army, it will be so much the better. Your parties are likewise to bring in waggons and other convenient carriages, with as many draught oxen as will be necessary to draw them; and all cattle fit for slaughter, (milch cows excepted, which are to be left for the use of the inhabitants). Regular receipts in the form hereto subjoined, are to be given in all places, where any of the above articles are taken, to such persons as have remained in their habitations, and otherwise complied with the terms of general Burgoyne's manifesto; but no receipt to be given to such as are known to be acting in the service of the rebels. As you will have with you persons perfectly acquainted with the country, it may perhaps be advisable, to tax the several districts with the portions of the several articles, and limit the hours for the delivery; and should you find it [391] necessary to move before such delivery can be made, hostages of the most respectable people should be taken, to secure their following you the next day.

All possible means are to be used to prevent plundering. As it is probable that captain Sherwood, who is already detached to the southward, and will join you at Arlington, will drive a considerable quantity of cattle and horses to you, you will therefore send in these cattle to the army, with a proper detachment from Petre's corps, to cover them, in order to disencumber yourself; but you must always keep the regiment of dragoons compact. The dragoons themselves must ride, and take care of the horses of the regiment. Those horses that are destined for the use of the army, must be tied in strings of ten each, in order that one man may lead ten horses. You will give the unarmed men of Petre's corps to conduct them, and inhabitants whom you can trust.

You must always keep your camps in good position, but at the same time where there is pasture; and you must have a chain of centinels around your cattle when grazing.

Colonel Skeene will be with you as much as possible in order to distinguish the good subjects from the bad, to procure the best intelligence of the enemy, and choose those people who are to bring me the accounts of your progress and success.

When you find it necessary to halt a day or two, you must always intrench the camp of the regiment of dragoons, in order never to risque an attack or affront from the enemy.

As you will return with the regiment of dragoons mounted, you must always have a detachment of captain Frazer's or Petre's corps in front of the column, and the same in the rear, in order to prevent your falling into an ambuscade, when you march through the woods.

[392] You will use all possible means to make the country believe, that the troops under your command are the advanced corps of the army, and that it is intended to pass to Connecticut on the road to Boston: you will likewise insinuate, that the main army from Albany is to be joined at Springfield, by a corps of troops from Rhode Island.

It is highly probable, that the corps under Mr. Warner, now supposed to be at Manchester, will retreat before you; but should they, contrary to expectation, be able to collect in great force, and post themselves advantageously, it is left to your discretion to attack them or not; always bearing in mind, that your corps is too valuable to let any considerable loss be hazarded on this occasion.

Should any corps be moved from Mr. Arnold's main army, in order to interrupt your retreat, you are to take as strong a post as the country will afford, and send the quickest intelligence to me; and you may depend on my making such movements as shall put the enemy between two fires, or otherwise effectually sustain you.

It is imagined, the progress of the whole of this expedition may be effected in about a fortnight: but every movement of it must depend on your success in obtaining such supplies of provisions as will enable you to subsist for your return in this army, in case you can get no more. And should not the army be able to reach Albany, before your expedition should be completed, I will find means to send you notice of it, and give your route another direction.

All persons acting in committees, or any officers under the direction of the congress, either civil or military, to be made prisoners.

I heartily wish you success; and have the honor to be sir, your humble servant,

JOHN BURGOYNE, *Lieut. Gen.*

Head Quarters, August 9, 1777

―――――――― Note No. II. Page 230. ――――――――

[393] It was several years after the confederation of the thirteen American states, before Vermont was added to the union. The inhabitants kept up a long and severe altercation with the several governments, who claimed both territory and authority, until on the point of decision by the sword, both parties appealed to the general congress. This was a business that divided and embarrassed, and was not terminated until the agents of Britain interfered, and offered advantageous terms to the Vermontese, if they would withdraw from the confederated states, and become a province of Britain.

From their love of liberty, and their attachment to their country, these offers were rejected, though they complained heavily of the delays and evasions of congress. Rough as their native mountains, and strong and flinty as the rocks that surrounded them, they bid defiance to dangers; and equally despised the intrigues of Britain, the subterfuges of the claimants on their territory, and the suspension in which they were held for a time by congress. They resisted obstinately the interferences and the claims of the neighbouring governments: their alienation from them, and their hatred to the state of New York in particular, daily increased: and in spite of all opposition, they continued their claims and supported their rights to be considered a free, independent, and separate state, entitled to the same privileges as the thirteen old colonies.

Colonel Ethan Allen, one of their principal leaders; a man of courage and ferocity, of pride without dignity, a writer without learning, a man of consequence merely from a bold presumptive claim to a capacity for everything; without education, and possessed of little intrinsic merit; wrote to congress on this occasion, and observed, "that [394] Vermont has an indubitable right to agree to terms of a cessation of hostilities with Great Britain, provided the United States persist in a rejection of her application for a union with them. But not disposed to yield to the overtures of the British government," he added, "I am as resolutely determined to defend the independence of Vermont, as congress are that of the United States; and rather than fail, will retire with hardy Green Mountain Boys into the desolate caverns of the mountains, and wage war with human nature at large."

After long suspension and many impediments, congress thought proper, in order to prevent the effusion of blood among themselves, which this occasion threatened, to accede to the reasonable demands of these legitimate sons of freedom, who chose delegates for congress, maintained their independence, and were a strong link in the confederated chain, against the encroachments and the power of Britain.*

Note No. III. Page 237.

The afflictions of this extraordinary lady did not terminate in America. By the assiduity of the physicians, and the tender care of a most affectionate wife, major Ackland partially recovered from his wounds in a short time, and was permitted to repair to New York. It was not long before his health was sufficiently restored to embark for England: but his wounds incurable, and his mind depressed, he was led to habits of intemperance, that soon put a period to his life.

[395] The death of her husband, and the domestic afflictions of the family of lord Ilchester, the father of lady Ackland, all combined to overpower the heroism of a mind superior to most of her sex, and involved this unfortunate lady in a deep and irretrievable melancholy.

Note No. IV. Page 252.

Governor Penn was the last proprietary governor of the state of Pennsylvania. After the revolution, different modes were adopted. The patent granted by the crown to the celebrated PENN, the founder of that colony, included a vast territory; but the enormous claims of the family were extinguished by an act of the legislature of Pennsylvania. This was not in consequence of any political delinquency of the late governor, who had acquitted himself

---

* A further description of the settlement and progress of the Hampshire Grants, may be seen at large in a late accurate history of Vermont, written by doctor Samuel Williams. This work is replete with moral and philosophical observations, which are honorary to the very sensible writer, and at once entertain and improve the reader. [Samuel Williams, *The Natural and Civil History of Vermont* (Walpole, N.H., 1794), Chs. IX–XI.]

with ability and address, and retained his patriotism and attention to the interests of his country, to the end of the contest. The heirs of the family voluntarily relinquished their extensive claims, in consideration of a very handsome sum of money paid to the claimants by the legislature, in lieu of all quit-rents that might hereafter be demanded.

——————————— Note No. V. Page 288. ———————————

Articles of Confederation and Perpetual Union between the States of New Hampshire, Massachusetts Bay, Rhode Island and Providence Plantations, Connecticut, New York, New Jersey, Pennsylvania, Delaware, Maryland, Virginia, North Carolina, South Carolina, and *Georgia*.

ARTICLE I

The style of this CONFEDERACY shall be, "THE UNITED STATES OF AMERICA."

ARTICLE II

[396] Each state retains its sovereignty, freedom and independence, and every power, jurisdiction, and right, which is not by this confederation expressly delegated to the United States in congress assembled.

ARTICLE III

The said states hereby severally enter into a firm league of friendship with each other, for their common defence, the security of their liberties, and their mutual and general welfare; binding themselves to assist each other, against all force offered to, or attacks made upon them, or any of them, on account of religion, sovereignty, trade, or any other pretence whatever.

ARTICLE IV

The better to secure and perpetuate mutual friendship and intercourse among the people of the different states in this union, the free inhabitants of each of these states, (paupers, vagabonds, and fugitives from justice excepted) shall be entitled to all privileges and immunities of free citizens in the several states; and the people of each state shall have free ingress and regress to and from any other state; and shall enjoy therein all the privileges of trade and commerce, subject to the same duties, impositions, and restrictions, as the inhabitants thereof respectively; *provided*, that such restrictions shall not extend so far as to prevent the removal of property imported into any state, to any other state of which the owner is an inhabitant: *provided also*, that no imposition, duties, or restrictions, shall be laid by any state on the property of the United States, or either of them.

If any person guilty of, or charged with, treason, felony, or other high misdemeanors, in any state, shall flee from justice, and be found in any of the United States, he shall, upon demand of the governor or executive power of the state from which he fled, be delivered up, and removed to the state having jurisdiction of his offence.

[397] Full faith and credit shall be given in each of these states, to the records, acts, and judicial proceedings, of the courts and magistrates of every other state.

ARTICLE V

For the more convenient management of the general interests of the United States, delegates shall be annually appointed, in such manner as the legislature of each state shall direct, to meet in congress on the first Monday in November, in every year; with a power reserved to each state, to recal its delegates, or any of them, at any time within the year, and to send others in their stead for the remainder of the year.

No state shall be represented in congress by less than two, nor by more than seven members: and no person shall be capable of being a delegate for more than three years in any term of five years; nor shall any person, being a delegate, be capable of holding any office under the United States, for which he, or another for his benefit, receives any salary, fees, or emolument of any kind.

Each state shall maintain its own delegates in a meeting of the states, and while they act as members of the committee of the states.

In determining questions in the United States in congress assembled, each state shall have one vote.

Freedom of speech and debate in congress, shall not be impeached or questioned in any court or place out of congress: and the members of congress shall be protected in their persons from arrests and imprisonments, during the time of their going to and from, and attendance on, congress, except for treason, or breach of the peace.

ARTICLE VI

No state, without the consent of the United States in congress assembled, shall send any embassy to, or receive any embassy from, or enter into any conference, agreement, alliance, [398] or treaty with, any king, prince, or state: nor shall any person, holding any office of profit or trust under the United States, or any of them, accept of any present, emolument, office, or title, or any kind whatever, from any king, prince, or foreign state: nor shall the United States in congress assembled, or any of them, grant any title of nobility.

No two or more states shall enter into any treaty, confederation, or alliance, whatever between them, without the consent of the United States in congress assembled, specifying accurately the purposes for which the same is to be entered into, and how long it shall continue.

No state shall lay any imposts or duties, which may interfere with any stipulations in treaties entered into by the United States in congress assembled, with any king, prince, or state, in pursuance of any treaties already proposed by congress to the courts of France and Spain.

No vessels of war shall be kept up in time of peace by any state, except such numbers only as shall be deemed necessary by the United States in congress assembled, for the defence of such state or its trade: nor shall any body of forces be kept up by any state, in time of peace, except such number only as, in the judgment of the United States in congress assembled, shall be deemed requisite to garrison the forts necessary for the defence of such state; but every state shall always keep up a well regulated and disciplined militia, sufficiently armed and accoutred; and shall provide, and constantly have ready for use, in public stores, a due number of field pieces and tents, and a proper quantity of arms, ammunition, and camp equipage.

No state shall engage in any war, without the consent of the United States in congress assembled, unless such state be actually invaded by enemies, or shall have received certain advice of a resolution being formed by some nation of Indians to invade such state, and the danger is so imminent as not to admit of a delay, till the United States in congress [399] assembled can be consulted: nor shall any state grant commissions to any ships or vessels of war, nor letters of marque or reprisal, except it be after a declaration of war by the United States in congress assembled, and then only against the kingdom or state, and the subjects thereof, against which war has been so declared, and under such regulations as shall be established by the United States in congress assembled; unless such state shall be infested by pirates; in which case, vessels of war may be fitted out for that occasion, and kept so long as the danger shall continue, or until the United States in congress assembled shall determine otherways.

ARTICLE VII
When land forces are raised by any state for the common defence, all officers of, or under, the rank of colonel, shall be appointed by the legislature of each state respectively, by whom such forces shall be raised, or in such manner as such state shall direct; and all vacancies shall be filled up by the state which first made the appointment.

ARTICLE VIII
All charges of war, and all other expenses that shall be incurred for the common defence, or general welfare, and allowed by the United States in congress assembled, shall be defrayed out of a common treasury, which shall be supplied by the several states, in proportion to the value of all land within each state, granted to or surveyed for any person, as such land and the buildings and improvements thereon shall be estimated, according to such mode as the United States in congress assembled shall, from time to time, direct and appoint. The taxes for paying that proportion, shall be laid and levied by the authority and direction of the legislatures of the several states, within the time agreed upon by the United States in congress assembled.

ARTICLE IX
The United States in congress assembled, shall have the sole and exclusive right and power of determining on peace and war, except in the cases mentioned in the Sixth Article; [400] or sending and receiving ambassadors; entering into treaties and alliances; (*provided*, that no treaty of commerce shall be made, whereby the legislative powers of the respective states, shall be restrained from imposing such imposts and duties on foreigners, as their own people are subjected to or from prohibiting the exportation or importation of any species of goods or commodities whatsoever;) of establishing rules for deciding in all cases, what captures on land or water shall be legal, and in what manner prizes taken by land or naval forces in the service of the United States, shall be divided or appropriated; of granting letters of marque or reprisal in times of peace; appointing courts for the trial of piracies and felonies committed on the high seas, and establishing courts for receiving and determining finally, appeals in all cases of captures; (*provided*, that no member of congress shall be appointed a judge of any of the said courts).

The United States in congress assembled, shall also be the last resort on appeal, in all disputes and differences now subsisting, or that hereafter may arise, between two or more states, concerning boundary, jurisdiction, or any other cause whatever; which authority shall always be exercised in the manner following:—Whenever the legislative or executive authority, or lawful agent, of any state in controversy with another, shall present a petition to congress, stating the matter in question, and praying for a hearing, notice thereof shall be given by order of congress to the legislative or executive authority of the other state in controversy, and a day assigned for the appearance of the parties by their lawful agents, who shall then be directed to appoint by joint consent, commissioners or judges to constitute a court for hearing and determining the matter in question: but if they cannot agree, congress shall name three persons out of each of the United States; from the list of such persons each party shall alternately strike out one, the petitioners beginning, until the number shall be reduced to thirteen; and from that number not less than seven nor more than nine names, as congress shall direct, shall in the presence of congress be drawn out by lot; and the persons whose names [401] shall be so drawn, or any five of them, shall be commissioners or judges, to hear and finally determine the controversy, so always as a major part of the judges who shall hear the cause shall agree in the determination; and if either party shall neglect to attend at the day appointed, without shewing reasons, which Congress shall judge sufficient, or being present shall refuse to strike, the Congress shall proceed to nominate three persons out of each state, and the secretary of Congress shall strike in behalf of such party absent or refusing; and the judgment and sentence of the court to be appointed, in the manner before prescribed, shall be final and conclusive; and if any of the parties shall refuse to submit to the authority of such court, or to appear or defend their claim or cause, the court shall nevertheless proceed to pronounce sentence, or judgment, which shall in like manner be final and decisive, the judgment or sentence and other proceedings being in either case transmitted to Congress, and lodged among the acts of Congress for the security of the parties concerned; provided that every commissioner, before he sits in judgment, shall take an oath to be administered by one of the judges of the supreme or superior court of the state, where the cause shall be tried, "well and truly to hear and determine the matter in question, according to the best of his judgment, without favour, affection, or hope of reward:"—provided also that no state shall be deprived of territory, for the benefit of the United States.

All controversies concerning the private right of soil claimed under different grants of two or more states, whose jurisdictions as they may respect such lands, and the states which passed such grants are adjusted, the paid grants or either of them being at the same time claimed to have originated antecedent to such settlement of jurisdiction, shall on the petition of either party to the Congress of the United States be finally determined as near as may be in the same manner as is before prescribed for deciding [402] disputes respecting territorial jurisdiction between different states.

The United States in Congress assembled shall also have the sole and exclusive right and power of regulating the alloy and value of coin struck by their own authority, or by that of the respective states—fixing the standard of weights and measures throughout the United States—regulating the trade and managing all affairs with the Indians, not members of any of the states, provided that the legislative right of any state within its own limits be not infringed or violated—establishing and regulating post offices from one state to another, throughout all the United States, and exacting such postage on the papers passing through the same as may be requisite to defray the expenses of the said office—appointing all officers of the land forces, in the service of the United States, excepting regimental officers—appointing all the officers of the naval forces, and commissioning all officers whatever in the service of the United States—making rules for the government and regulation of the said land and naval forces, and directing their operations.

The United States in Congress assembled shall have authority to appoint a committee, to sit in the recess of Congress, to be denominated "*A Committee of the States*" and to consist of one delegate from each State; and to appoint such other Committees and civil officers as may be necessary for managing the general affairs of the United States under their direction—to appoint one of their number to preside, provided that no person be allowed to serve in the office of President more than one year in any term of three years;—to ascertain the necessary sums of money to be raised for the service of the United States, and to appropriate and apply the same for defraying the public expenses—to borrow money, or emit bills on the credit of the United States, transmitting every half year to the respective states an account of the sums of money so [403] borrowed or emitted—to build and equip a navy—to agree upon the number of land forces, and to make requisitions from each state for its quota, in proportion to the number of white inhabitants in such state; which requisition shall be binding, and thereupon the legislature of each state shall appoint the regimental officers, raise the men, and clothe, arm, and equip them in a soldier-like manner, at the expense of the United States; and the officers and men so clothed, armed and equipped, shall march to the place appointed, and within the time agreed on by the United States in Congress assembled:—But if the United States, in Congress assembled shall, on consideration of circumstances, judge proper that any state should not raise men, or should raise a smaller number than its quota, and that any other state should raise a greater number of men than the quota thereof, such extra number shall be raised, officered, clothed, armed, and equipped, in the same manner as the quota of such state, unless the legislature of such state shall judge that such extra number cannot be safely spared out of the same, in which case they shall raise, officer, clothe, arm, and equip as many of such extra number as they judge can be safely spared. And the officers and men so clothed, armed, and equipped, shall march to the place appointed, and within the time agreed on by the United States in Congress assembled.

The United States in Congress assembled shall never engage in a war, nor grant letters of marque and reprisal, in time of peace, nor enter into any treaties or alliances, nor coin money, nor regulate the value thereof, nor ascertain the sums and expenses necessary for the defence and welfare of the United States, or any of them; nor emit bills, nor borrow money on the credit of the United States; nor appropriate money, nor agree upon the number of vessels of war, to be built or purchased, or the number of land or sea forces to be raised, nor appoint a commander in chief of the army or navy, unless nine states assent to the same; nor shall a question on any other point, except for adjourning from day to day, be determined, unless by the votes of a majority of the United States in Congress assembled.

[404] The Congress of the United States shall have power to adjourn to any time within the year, and to any place within the United States, so that no period of adjournment be for a longer duration than the space of six months, and shall publish the journal of their proceedings monthly, except such parts thereof relating to treaties, alliances, or military operations, as in their judgment require secrecy; and the yeas

and nays of the delegates of each state on any question shall be entered on the journal, when it is desired by any delegate; and the delegates of a state, or any of them, at his or their request, shall be furnished with a transcript of the said journal, except such parts as are above excepted, to lay before the legislatures of the several states.

A R T I C L E   X
The committee of the states or any nine of them, shall be authorized to execute, in the recess of Congress, such of the powers of Congress as the United States in Congress assembled, by the consent of nine states, shall from time to time think expedient to vest them with; provided that no power be delegated to the said committee, for the exercise of which, by the articles of confederation, the voice of nine states in the Congress of the United States assembled is requisite.

A R T I C L E   X I
Canada acceding to this confederation, and joining in the measures of the United States, shall be admitted into, and entitled to all the advantages of this Union; but no other colony shall be admitted into the same, unless such admission be agreed to by nine states.

A R T I C L E   X I I
All bills of credit emitted, monies borrowed, and debts contracted by, or under the authority of Congress, before the assembling of the United States, in pursuance of the present confederation, shall be deemed and considered as a charge against the United States, for payment and satisfaction whereof the said United States, and the public faith are hereby solemnly pledged.

A R T I C L E   X I I I
[405] Every state shall abide by the determinations of the United States in Congress assembled, on all questions which by this confederation are submitted to them. And the articles of this confederation shall be inviolably observed by every state, and the union shall be perpetual; nor shall any alteration at any time hereafter be made in any of them; unless such alteration be agreed to in a Congress of the United States, and be afterwards confirmed by the legislatures of every state.

These articles shall be proposed to the Legislatures of all the United States, to be considered, and if approved of by them, they are advised to authorize their delegates to ratify the same in the Congress of the United States; which being done, the same shall become conclusive.

By order of Congress,
HENRY LAURENS, *President*

Note No. VI. Page 292.

The name of THOMAS PAINE has become so generally known both in Europe and America, that a few strictures on his character may not be uninteresting.

Mr. Paine was a native of England, but he had resided in America some time before the American Revolution took place. He warmly advocated the cause of the Colonies, and wrote in the spirit of the times with much applause. Several of his bold publications displayed a considerable share of wit and ingenuity, though his arguments were not always conclusive. His *Crisis*, his *Common Sense*, and some other writings were well adapted to animate the people, and to invigorate their resolutions in opposition to the measures of the British administration.

[406] Though not generally considered a profound politician, yet as it was then thought he wrote on principles honorable to the human character, his celebrity was extensive in America, and was afterwards disseminated in England; and his merit as a writer for a time appreciated by a work entitled the *Rights of Man*, which was replete with just and dignified sentiments on a subject so interesting to society.

His celebrity might have been longer maintained, and his name have been handed down with applause, had he not afterwards have left the line of politics, and presumed to touch on theological subjects of which he was grossly ignorant, as well as totally indifferent to every religious observance as an individual, and in some instances his morals were censured.

Persecuted in England he repaired to France, some time before *monarchy* was subverted in that nation. There, after listening to the indigested rant of infidels of antecedent date, and learning by rote the jargon of the modern French *literati*, who zealously laboured in the field of *scepticism*, he attempted to undermine the sublime doctrines of the gospel, and annihilate the Christian system.* Here he betrayed his weakness and want of principle, in blasphemous scurrilities and impious raillery, that at once sunk his character, and disgusted every rational and sober mind.

It is no apology that this was done at a period, when all principle seemed to lie prostrate beneath the confusions and despotism of the *Robespierrian reign*. It is true, this insignificant theologian, who affected to hold in contempt all religion, or any expectations of a future state, was at this time trembling under the terrors of the *guillotine*; and while imprisoned, he endeavoured to ingratiate himself [407] into the favor of the ruling faction of France, by levelling his sarcastic pen against opinions that had been for ages held sacred among mankind.

The effusions of *infidelity*, entitled the *Age of Reason*, would not have been thought worthy of a serious refutation, had not much industry been employed, to disseminate this worthless pamphlet among the common classes of mankind.

* The infidel has shot his bolts away,
   Till his exhausted quiver yielding none,
   He gleans the blunted shafts that have recoiled,
   And aims them at the shield of truth again.
                                                                    COWPER

The young, the ignorant, the superficial and licentious, pleased with the attempt to let loose the wild passions of men by removing so efficient a guard as is contained in the sacred scriptures, this pernicious work was by them fought for, and read with avidity. This consideration drew out the pens of men of character and ability, to antidote the poison of licentious wit.

No one had more merit in the effort than the learned, pious, and excellent Dr. Richard Watson, bishop of Landass. His works have always been read with pleasure and applause, by every man of genius, virtue, and taste, in whatever branch of literature he drew his pen. His observations on the writings of Paine, his letters to Mr. Gibbon, with a concluding address to young gentlemen, will be read with delight and improvement by every person who adores the benignity of divine government, long after the writings of infidels of talent and ingenuity are sunk into oblivion.

Men of discernment are ever better pleased with truth, in its most simple garb, than with the sophisticated, though elegant style of wit and raillery, decorated for deception; and the name of Voltaire, with other wits and philosophers of the same description will be forgotten, and even the celebrated Gibbon will cease to be admired by the real friends of the Christian dispensation, while its defenders will be held in veneration to the latest ages.

The lovers of liberty on reasonable and just principles, were exceedingly hurt, that a man so capable as was Mr. [408] Paine, of exhibiting political truth in a pleasing garb, and defending the rights of man with eloquence and precision, should prostitute his talents to ridicule divine revelation, and destroy the brightest hopes of a rational and immortal agent.

Mr. Paine out-lived the storms of revolution both in America and in France, and he may yet add one instance more of the versatility of human events, by out-living his own false opinions and foolish attempts to break down the barriers of religion, and we wish he may by his own pen, endeavour to antidote some part of the poisons he has spread.

——————————— Note No. VII. Page 316. ———————————

The count Kosciusko was a gentleman of family without the advantages of high fortune. His education, person, and talents, recommended him to the king of Poland, by whom he was patronized and employed in a military line.

Early in life he became attached to a lady of great beauty, belonging to one of the first families in the kingdom. The inequality of fortune prevented his obtaining consent from her parents to a union, though the affections of the lady were equally strong with his own. The lovers agreed on an elopement, and made an attempt to retire to France; pursued and overtaken by the father of the lady, a fierce rencounter ensued. When Kosciusko found he must either surrender the object of his affection, or take the life of her parent, humanity prevailed over his passion, he returned the sword to its scabbard, and generously relinquished the beautiful daughter to her distressed father, rather than become the murderer of the person who gave being to so much elegance and beauty, now plunged in terror and despair from the tumult of contending passions of the most soft and amiable nature.

[409] This unfortunate termination of his hopes was one means of lending this celebrated hero to the assistance of America. Wounded by the disappointment, and his delicacy hurt by becoming the topic of general conversation on an affair of gallantry, he obtained leave from his sovereign to retire from Poland. He soon after repaired to America, and offered himself a volunteer to general Washington, was honorably appointed, and by his bravery and humanity rendered essential services to the United States. After the peace took place between Great Britain and America, he returned to his own distressed country.*

His sufferings and his bravery in his struggles to rescue his native country from the usurpations of neighbouring tyrants, until the ruin of the kingdom of Poland and the surrender of Warsaw, are amply detailed in European history. Wounded, imprisoned, and cruelly used, his distresses were in some degree ameliorated by the compassion of a Russian lady, the wife of general Chra-cozazow, who had been a prisoner and set at liberty by the count. This lady could not prevent his being sent to Petersburgh, were he was confined in a fortress near the city; but he surmounted imprisonment, sickness, misery, and poverty, and afterwards revisited America, where he was relieved and rewarded, as justice, honor, and gratitude required.

———————— Note No. VIII. Page 333. ————————

The cruel oppressions long suffered by the kingdom of Ireland from the haughty superiority of British power, induced the wretched inhabitants to avail themselves of this invitation, and to resort by thousands to America after the [410] peace took place between Great Britain and the United States. After this, the confusions and distractions in Ireland arose to such a height as rendered a residence there too insupportable for description. The miserable inhabitants who escaped the sword, the burnings, and the massacre of the

---

* It was a question in a literary society afterwards in London, which was the greatest character, lord Chatham, general Washington, or count Kosciusko. *Analytical Review*. [*Analytical Review; or, History of Literature, Domestic and Foreign* (London, 1788–1798).]

English, had flattered themselves, that if they could retreat from their native country, they should receive a welcome reception to an asylum to which they had formerly been invited, by the congressional body who directed the affairs of America. There they justly thought their industry might have been cherished, their lives and properties be secure, and their residence rendered quiet; but a check was put to emigration for a time, by an alien law enacted by Congress in the year one thousand seven hundred and ninety-eight.

This was very contrary to the policy and to the principles expressed by governor Trumbull of Connecticut to Baron R. J. Van der Capellen, "Seigneur du Pol, Membre des Nobles de la Provence D'Overyssel, & c." dated Lebanon, August 31, 1779.

He observes, that

the climate, the soil, and the productions of a continent extending from the thirtieth to the forty-fifth degree of latitude, and in longitude an unknown width, are various beyond description, and the objects of trade consequently unbounded. There is scarce a manufacture, whether in the useful or ornamental part of life, of which you will not here find the materials, collected, as it were, in an immense magazine. In every requisite for naval armaments we abound, our forests yielding prodigious quantities of timber and spars; our mountains, vast mines of iron, copper, and lead; and our fields producing ample crops of flax and hemp. Provisions of all kinds are raised in much greater quantities than are necessary for our own consumption; and our wheat, our rye, our cattle, and our pork, yield to none in the world for quality.

[411] The price of cultivated lands is by no means extravagant; and of uncultivated, trifling; twelve thousand acres, situated most advantageously for future business, selling for three hundred guineas English, that is, little more than six pence sterling the acre. Our interests and our laws teach us to receive strangers from every quarter of the globe, with open arms. The poor, the unfortunate, the oppressed from every country, will here find a ready asylum; and by uniting their interests with ours, enjoy, in common with us, all the blessings of liberty and plenty. Neither difference of nation, of language, of manners, or of religion, will lessen the cordiality of their reception, among a people whose religion teaches them to regard all mankind as their brethren.